How Management
Wins Union
Organizing Campaigns

How Management Wins Union Organizing Campaigns

ALFRED T. DEMARIA

Executive Enterprises Publications Co., Inc.
New York

ALFRED T. DEMARIA is a partner with the labor law firm of Clifton, Budd, Burke and DeMaria in New York City and has many years of practical experience in successfully meeting union challenges. He specializes in combatting union organizational campaigns and in developing programs to keep companies operating in a union-free environment. He handles labor matters and develops union prevention programs for numerous industries.

Edited by Robert Freiberg

ISBN 0-917386-32-9

Printed in the United States of America

Dedication

This book is dedicated to the author's clients over the years; we have learned much from each other. My thanks also go to my wife, Lynne, and daughters, Lisa and Laura, for letting me take so many hours away from them to write this book.

A. T. D.

Table of Contents

Chapter 6
Preparing the Campaign

Chapter 7
Structuring the Campaign

Chapter 8
Free Speech Rights 131

Chapter 9
Training Supervisors to Be a Campaign Force 192

Chapter 10
The Fine Art of Rebuttal 212

Chapter 11
Anatomy of an Election Reversal 233

xiv

Preface

Too often, employer losses in NLRB campaigns are attributed to the "inevitability" of unions. In reality, the election loss is more properly attributable to management mistakes, inability to communicate in crises, and basic unfamiliarity with the art of running successful election campaigns.

Unionism is certainly *not* a panacea for all employees, nor is it the relentless wave of the future. This is evidenced by the fact that the proportion of the unionized work force has been on a downward trend for the last fifteen years. Despite intensive union organizational activity, and hundreds of millions of dollars spent by the unions in attempts to organize the unorganized, today approximately three-quarters of the total work force remains union-free. In recent times, unions, for the first time in history, have lost more than half of the elections conducted by the NLRB each year. The pervasive appearance of nonunion shops in previously solid union areas in the construction and mining industries, and the recent decertification phenomenon, are further evidence denying the proposition that unionization is inevitable.

This book contains the tactics and strategy necessary to avoid a successful union campaign attempt. It is a partisan approach written for the managers and attorneys vested with responsibility to conduct successful campaigns. Without unions, many modern companies are providing their employees with a better workplace and an improved work environment—physicallly, socially, economically, and psychologically—than that portion of the work force covered by collective bargaining agreements. This book is primarily devoted to those employers who wish to maintain union-free status.

Years ago, a book such as this might have been considered antisocial. Today, however, labor's overreaching efforts in many areas, such as the treatment of its own members, handling of pension funds, restrictive work practices, unjustified strikes, and championship of mediocrity in the workplace, have brought about a reaction to the union. Big labor's losses in Congress on such important issues as repeal of the right-to-work laws and situs amendments, and the lack of success in rectifying their own organizational inadequacies and defeats through the approach of "labor reform," are strong examples of the public's disenchantment with labor organizations today.

Conducting a thorough and hard-hitting campaign is harder work for management than most company endeavors. The effort is also complicated by prevailing myths, inadequate information, misdirected efforts by well-meaning corporate officials without a background of campaigning, and improper advice. The information in this book provides managers with the fundamentals of campaigning, and it embellishes those fundamentals with advice, information, and ideas to enable them to defeat the organizing attempts by competent, hardworking, aggressive union adversaries.

In the table of organization of many employers there will be labor relations experts who already know much of what this book teaches. There will also be those who are inexperienced, such as the presidents, vicepresidents, personnel directors, and plant managers who are unaware of the fundamentals. This book is addressed to both groups. Although attorneys and labor consultants may have mastered the details of a campaign, on occasion they must step back to obtain a basic view of strategy and to incorporate others' insights into their own knowledge and modus operandi.

The principles outlined in this book offer a constructive campaigning approach applicable alike to manufacturing operations, clerical and professional units, service employees—indeed, to any private sector employer. One caution, however: Every plant of office is a unique community with its own roots, history, and tradition. There are wide variances in attitudes and practices between industries, regions, and even between plants owned by the same employer. Accordingly, the approach to problems discussed in this book may have varying applicability. Each campaign, like the snowflake, is different; each has its own issues and nuances.

This is particularly true regarding the statement of legal principles and cited NLRB cases. The NLRB itself has differed from time to time as to the law, given identical facts. Members of the Borad disagree with each other, and they often disagree as to what the law is when reviewing decisions of NLRB administrative law judges. NLRB members differ with the opinion of their Regional Directors in the same cases, and the same is true when courts reverse the NLRB and establish the law as something other than the Board perceives it. Citations to precedents may be dangerous in the hands of laymen: The law can change, nuances may develop, and shifts in emphasis may occur. So the emphasis in this book is on the strategy and tactics necessary to defeat a union. Where citations are necessary or useful, they have been provided. Moreover there has been an attempt to avoid "filler"; instead, there are appendices designed to assist the reader and to refer him to more specific information and NLRB precedents.

It is no secret to those involved in the art of management communications that the soft underbelly of modern American management is its inability to converse freely with its employees on matters dealing with company affairs and employee matters. Management's particular genius is focused on the scientific and productive processes involved in making a profit; communication with their employees is less effective. Accordingly, a lengthy chapter has been devoted to communications in crisis.

Because of the strict limitations by the NLRB on employer statements during campaigns, many of those in management believe that unions have the advantage in communicating messages to the employees. Yet, the reverse is true. The employer has the decided advantage in this contest. Long ago, Judge Learned Hand observed that employer communication has a dual aspect. He stated:

> [O]n the one hand, it is an expression of his own beliefs and an attempt to persuade his employees to accept them; on the other, it is an indication of his feelings which his hearers may believe will take a form inimical to those of them whom he does not succeed in convincing. *NLRB v. American Tube Bending Co.*, 134 F.2d 993, 994 (2d Cir.), *cert. denied*, 320 U.S. 768 (1943).

The employer's greater opportunity to communicate with its employees, the virtually complete access to the minds of the voters during working hours, and the control management can exert over employees give the employer a considerable advantage over his union counterparts. This advantage can legally be utilized to produce a winning vote on election day. The entire emphasis in this book has been to apprise the employer of what to do during the crisis period when the allegiance of the voters and management's credibility are the prime concerns. Avoidance of unfair labor practives is stressed. Legal campaigning and the lawful conduct of one's business will enable the employer to win most campaigns. Violations of the law are an expensive way of doing business and totally unnecessary.

Unions do lose elections. They lose them because of informed, intelligent management campaigning based upon sound employer practices in conducting labor relations. The ultimate choice is the employees'. Their decision is normally based on the sum total of all the messages they have received from both union and management, as well as upon existing predispositions. The notion that employee voting is largely predetermined is contrary to the experience of virtually all practitioners in the field whose professional careers have been devoted to changing employee opinion and producing a management victory on election day.

A. T. D.

Introduction

The law applicable to union campaigning is baffling to both the small business man and the large corporation. NLRB rules and decisions are complex, often unclear, and frequently unsettling or confusing. The philosophic base of many decisions in the free-speech area also lends uncertainty to the process of ascertaining employers' rights.

Who has the need to become acquainted with both the fundamentals and the nuances of campaigning? Two groups: business people who do not have the assistance of trained labor relations experts, and corporate managers trained in labor relations. This book provides winning techniques to those who are inexperienced, and will improve the skills and performance of those already familiar with the topic.

The author is a well-known New York-based labor lawyer who has great experience in the art of handling NLRB campaigns. His nationwide seminar, "Winning NLRB Campaigns," which is sponsored by Executive Enterprises, Inc., has enabled attendees to profit by a combination of practical experience and an academic approach to the subject.

Most companies confronted with a campaign have available to them either extremely complicated reference books or skimpy booklets and pamphlets that do not fully explicate *tactics and strategy*.

This text provides a middle ground whereby a manager, confronted with a union organizational campaign and responsible for running a successful campaign for his company, can find the practical and tactical advice in language that the uninitiated will understand and the professional will appreciate. This is not a treatise on labor law. The objective is to provide a nontechnical text, one that gives the reader a concise, well-organized, and practical handbook on **winning an NLRB campaign**. The book is not a substitute for a lawyer. But professionals will find the book a comprehensive review of the fundamentals, and they may find the author's experience and suggestions helpful in their own approach to winning campaigns.

This book is devoted to maintaining a union-free atmosphere through intelligent and lawful campaigning, and to those readers who wish to remain among the thousands of U.S. employers who provide a union-free work environment and a better working experience for their employees.

Chapter 1

The Union Organizer

The professional organizer is the indispensable element in the union's drive to organize an employer. He is responsible for selling an intangible product—unionism—to a majority of the employees. For an employer to combat the professional union organizer, he must know the enemy and be thoroughly familiar with his characteristics, techniques, methods, tactics, and mode of operation.

General Profile of the Union Organizer

The successful union organizer, in addition to being a super salesman, is thoroughly professional and competent. He is a good organizer, a skilled politician, a counselor, lawyer, teacher, missionary, and anything else he needs to be in order to win the employees' votes.

He would probably be a success as a salesman in any other field because he maintains a good appearance, is able to inspire confidence in others, speaks well, is a leader, displays a good personality, is sincere and patient with the employees with whom he deals, and exercises judgment, initiative, and imagination in his job. He not only is a good talker, but a good listener as well.

This composite picture of today's organizer is at odds with the stereotyped image of organizers of fifteen years ago. He often holds a college degree and has worked in a particular industry as a rank-and-file employee. He understands the nature of your business or has had sufficient exposure to it to be able to understand its problems.

The organizer is carefully trained by the union. He has often attended labor-relations and training schools operated by the union, combining academic training with field training as an apprentice to skilled organizers. He has probably handled dozens, if not hundreds, of organizational campaigns; he is aware of every nuance, tactic, and strategy you will employ, and he may well be a veteran of the

1

negotiating table, having negotiated hundreds of contracts with employers in various industries after successful organizing campaigns.

The organizer also has the ability to adapt himself to the type of work force he is dealing with. He is friendly with your employees and their families. He can speak "up" to employees with higher intelligence and "down" to employees with little education. His intent will be to blend with the scene and to become one of the gang. He will frequent places where the employees hang out, buying drinks—hard or soft—for them. Thus it is easy to see that a common management error is to underrate a professional organizer because of his style of dressing or his seeming lack of sophistication.

The organizer can make a potential card signer feel as though he is dealing with a friend who is interested in his welfare. If the organizer detects a reluctance to go union, he will not press for an immediate signature. He will be patient and await the right opportunity, often working through a friend, relative, or colleague of the target employee. He is never at a loss, because he is imaginative and resourceful in inventing new techniques and arguments to meet any employee objections to union affiliation.

The professional union organizer is also a capable actor. He can inflate management mistakes out of proportion and make sound policies look unfair. He portrays unionism very appealingly: If an employer pays low wages, the union will obtain high wages; if the employer already pays high wages, the union will get even higher ones. He will exploit favoritism, poor supervision, inadequate job security, and every other vulnerable area, including insufficient parking space, poor physical facilities, industrial accidents, and similar matters.

The organizer will be interested in every gripe related to him by your employees. In each case, his remedy will be unionism. He will cite examples of how similar problems at "another company" the union represents were solved by a union contract. For instance, he may relate how the union induced that company to fire a poor supervisor.

But the organizer will studiously avoid mentioning union dues or initiation fees. If a question is asked about them, he will say that no one pays dues until the contract is actually approved by the employees, and the higher wages obtained will more than offset their cost. More than likely, the organizer will represent himself as not being interested in money by waiving the initiation fee for all present employees.

Perhaps the organizer's outstanding characteristic is that he is extremely dedicated to the concept of collective bargaining and the principles of trade unionism. His views may at times be radical, but he fully believes in the trade union movement and can transmit this enthusiasm to employees who previously never dreamed of joining a union. He will be facile with facts and figures—including the salaries of corporate officers, bonus arrangements, profits, stock prices, owner-ship interests, and other items.

In sum, the union organizer is a highly effective adversary. He will know more—and probably be more effective—than any business adversary or competitor you have dealt with.

The remainder of this book will deal with the techniques, strategies, and tactics necessary to neutralize, counterbalance, and counteract this initial disadvantage in competitive skills.

Chapter 2

The Organizer's Methods

Basically, organizing is selling a product to the majority of the employees in a particular target group. The good organizer follows the rules of good selling. He—or she—has done the homework and is well informed about the company and its industry. Although the organizer suits his methods to the situations he finds, most campaigns have elements in common—planning, undercover work, maintaining grievance files and other informational data, establishing and organizing committees, visiting homes, distributing literature, and holding meetings.

Most unionization attempts originate with one or two disgruntled individuals communicating with the union. But even when the union approaches a company cold, steps will be taken to establish personal contact with employees.

The union will tell of the many improvements "won" at other companies, taking credit for all gains over a long period of time and creating the appearance that, but for the union, no benefits would have been won. Once some individuals are persuaded of the benefits of unionization, the organizer will ask them to gather a small core of people who would also be likely to support the union. In most cases, these are dissatisfied employees. This process may go on for months without the employer or the supervisors knowing that the process is taking place.

In the beginning, the organizer is interested in "quality" employees—those with leadership ability and those who can carry out the job of organizing on a day-to-day basis. He concentrates on contacting key employees and potential leaders, those with credibility among their co-employees. He cultivates their friendship and often makes direct promises of such benefits as shop stewardships, positions on the union's negotiating committee, local officerships, and, in some cases, paid jobs within the union's own organization.

Many company managers believe that if they win an election, it will make them immune from organization in the future. On the contrary, an employer who has won a successful campaign may find himself under *increasing* attack by the union. This is so because the organizer will find a ready-made hard core of employees who voted for the union in the last election and who are ready, willing, and able to take advantage of their past mistakes and solicit more effectively the second time around. Another campaign is particularly likely when the employer's original campaign was built on promises that were not kept or only partially fulfilled.

An organizer who has lost an election will often maintain his contacts in the plant and will test the waters from time to time. He will often await an employer mistake so that he can use it to justify his return to the plant or office with an "I told you so" approach. The support generated by employer mistakes may make the second unionization attempt more successful than the first.

Compiling Data

Prior to making a final decision on whether to proceed with an organizing campaign, the union organizer will compile an amazing amount of data on the target company: the location of the plant; its physical structure and entrances; the locations of employee gathering points; the number of the floors in the building occupied by the company; the starting and quitting time; the company's product, sales, profits, and return on investment; the nature of its ownership; its distribution methods; the services rendered or goods manufactured; transportation facilities near the plant, including the names of trucking companies used to deliver all materials to the plant and to transport finished products out (including whether the transport companies are unionized and, if so, which union); the company's labor history; its major competitors; eating and drinking establishments close to the plant; whether the plant is locally owned or part of a larger company; the profits of the parent company and whether it has labor contracts at other locations or in other divisions; the number of employees in the unit to be organized; information about executive and administrative personnel; salaries of corporate officers; the company's newsletters, employee manuals, and handbooks; whether the business is seasonal in nature; a recent history of layoffs; the location of branch sales and distributor centers; previous organizing efforts by other unions; all paternalistic practices such as bowling teams and picnics; and any other information deemed relevant to the organizer, such as recent discharges, safety complaints, OSHA investigations, treatment of minority employees, and discrimination charges filed against the company. Armed with this data, the union organizer plans his attack. As much information as possible will be garnered before the unionization attempt is begun.

The organizer then learns as much as possible about the company's work force. The number of people over 50 years of age is often of importance, as well as the number of people under 30, the ratio of male to female employees, and the distribution of employees in the local community as compared to those who come from outside the community. Information on the racial and ethnic composition of the plant's work force is often a crucial area of inquiry, for all the information gathered will be used in planning the appeal that will be most effective for the particular target group. The union may hire translators and interpreters or employ staff members of the same national origin and race as the employees at the target company.

Employee Lists

A bonanza for the union organizer would be to acquire a list of company employees and their addresses. This would enable the organizer to make a general mailing to each employee and to plan home visitations. Access to such a list would make the union's attempt to organize considerably easier, particularly in the beginning stages of the campaign. Such lists might be obtained in a variety of ways: from employer records or time cards, through assiduous use of local telephone books, by recording the license numbers of cars in the company parking lot, and through the union's card-signing campaign itself.

Undercover Work

Companies that do not learn that a union organizing drive has taken place until they receive a communication from the NLRB enclosing the union's petition for an election or a "demand letter" from the union demanding recognition on the basis of a claim of majority status lose much more frequently than employers who find out about the campaign early. Unions attempt to organize in secret because they know that once the employer learns of the union's efforts, it will begin to counteract the activity. Thus a secret campaign is preferred by all organizers.

The Cell Technique

Often, the union business agent convinces the small group of employees doing the organizing that the effort must be kept secret or else their jobs will be jeopardized by employer discrimination against union activists. In this connection, the "cell" technique is often used. The organizer keeps the names of the prime movers secret; he does not even tell the prime movers the names of their counterparts in other departments. Each department has a "cell." At or about the time of petition filing, the authorization cards from all the employer's departments will be collated and used to support the petition—and only then is the identity of union adherents made known.

In small companies, organization cannot always be undertaken in secret. Supervisors should be made aware of the typical early warning signs of union activity and should be instructed to report all signs of disgruntlement or of suspected union activity to the company official with prime responsibility for maintaining a union-free atmosphere in the plant or office.

Organizing Committees

Although most of the day-to-day work of organizing is done by employees, the organizer will orchestrate the campaign. Early in the attempt, he will establish a plant organizing committee composed, where possible, of a representative sampling of all employees in the plant. He will try to get representation from each department, from all major job classifications, from minority groups and females. Thus, the committee will be able to obtain maximum penetration into every corner of the plant and into every social or ethnic group.

The committee will contact the remaining employees in an attempt to sell the union to them. When they run into difficulty with certain groups or individuals, the issue will be referred to the organizer, who will then attempt to make a direct pitch via a home visitation, a letter, or a meeting at a local restaurant or pub.

The organizer will attempt to remain in the background as much as possible, because employees are more likely to listen to their co-employees and to decide for themselves whether representation is necessary, rather than to take the word of an outside stranger. However, the organizer will always be available to feed the committee members with facts, figures, information, ideas, and arguments as to how to sell any particular individual on the concept of unionism.

Visiting Homes

Home calls enable the organizer to establish personal contact with employees, to meet their families, and to sell employees who might not be persuaded to join the union on the basis of a leaflet or a pamphlet. The home calls are directed at winning over uncommitted employees.

The organizer will often be accompanied to the home by a pro-union employee. He will make an appointment in advance, at a convenient hour. He will present a facade of friendliness and will attempt to woo members of the potential member's family, including the children. He will work the family into the discussion, talk about increased purchasing power, and stress pensions, health coverage insurance, time off, and other benefits that tend to appeal to the worker, the spouse, and the family.

The home visit is one of the most strategic and effective weapons employed by the organizer. It is a common mistake for employers to underestimate the impact of such visitations, especially if only a small minority of employees have been visited. The employer may assume that because 85 percent of the employees have not been visited, those employees support the company. In reality, the 15 percent visited may have been only those who were on the fence, and the home visit by the union organizer may have been the final attempt to sell the uncommitted group on unionism. In larger plants, the organizer may not make all the personal visits himself; he will designate members of the plant committee to act in his place to transmit the union message.

Complaint Collection

No organizer will succeed unless he pictures the employer as an organization that cannot respond to employee complaints. He must plan his campaign around the job problems and gripes he has heard from his prime movers. The organizer will maintain a record of complaints and will classify them in terms of whether they are individual, department-wide, or plant-wide complaints. The organizer will be extremely interested in the employer's methods of handling seniority, wage rates and ranges, employee complaints, hours of work, vacations, paid holidays, premium pay, benefit programs, physical conditions in the plant, safety complaints, layoff policy, recent discharges, and a host of other conditions.

Excellent company benefits are overlooked; weak company benefits are emphasized. Company conditions are compared unfavorably with other local plants or other plants with which the union has a contract. Great emphasis is placed on gripes and complaints that the organizer has heard repeatedly from employees in the target group.

The organizer will pay extreme care and attention to an employee's individual grievance and create the impression that, if a union had been in existence in the plant, the grievance either never would have come about or would have been rectified promptly by the union. He will contact other people with similar complaints and explain that those complaints can be rectified if they will each sign an authorization card.

A prime target will be unpopular supervisors. The organizer will ask about unreasonable actions and favoritism. It will not be long before the organizer will have a long list of real or imagined injustices suffered by employees at the hands of front-line supervisors. The campaign is then geared accordingly.

Union Meetings

Employers are often encouraged by the absence of union meetings, believing that this means a lack of interest in the union. This is a mistake. It is also a mistake to assume that lack of heavy early turnout by employees at meetings called by the union is evidence of lack of overall union support.

Many union organizers will not call meetings until the campaign comes out into the open. Moreover, many of the initial meetings are held primarily among the small cadre of prime movers. Many pro-union people will be afraid to attend such meetings for fear that the information will leak back to the employer.

When meetings are held, the union is interested not only in signing up new members, but also in obtaining names and lists of new prospects, including home phone numbers and addresses. Usually, the meeting is called by the plant organizing committee rather than the union, to create the impression that the movement is a spontaneous feeling among well-informed employees. The atmosphere is social, and refreshments are available to the participants.

The organizer may make a speech referring to himself as one of the workers, discuss shop problems in order to create the impression that he is familiar with everything that has happened, and imply that he is knowledgeable and able to deal with the boss.

Being extremely adept at sensing the spirit of his audience, the organizer can adjust the tenor of his remarks to the feelings of the group. If employees seem reluctant to go union, he will adopt an extremely low profile and deemphasize the adversary nature of the union effort. But he will be armed with examples of employee complaints and employer mistakes. He will point out where employees attempted to change particular items only to be ignored or given broken promises. He will claim that self-respect and dignity can be obtained only through a union that represents employees as a group. He will paint a picture of a union fighting for improvements from a management reluctant to make them.

The organizer will also be open to questions about dues, how the union functions, how committees are formed, and how shop stewards are elected. He will emphasize the fact that union affiliation is protected by federal law and that the NLRB will bring effective and quick remedies to bear upon the employer who retaliates for a union activity.

Meetings may be staged, with questions planted so that the answers are effective. Union supporters are placed in the front rows to create the feeling that most employees are in favor of the union. The meeting will often be in a room too small to accommodate the expected number of attendees to create the impression that there is great interest among the plant employees. Also, the employees will hear speeches by employees of other local companies and by shop stewards at other plants the union represents; they will point out the great improvements won by the union over the years.

The frequency of meetings depends on a number of factors. Lack of meetings should not be assumed to be the result of lack of interest. In most cases, frequency of meetings will increase during the period immediately preceding the actual election date. The meetings will be used to generate emotionalism, to discuss the procedures involved in elections, to predict the employer's moves, and to maintain the unity of the group. During such meetings, the organizer tries to generate support and induce enthusiasm, to mock management and its practices, and to create a feeling that pro-union employees are "in" and that it is only a matter of time before the employer will be forced to sit down and negotiate with the union.

Written Material

In addition to heavy verbal contact, the organizer employs pamphlets or leaflets to arouse employee interest in what the union has to offer.

The leaflets also preserve the tempo of the campaign and reinforce the attitude of those who have signed up with the union. Such handouts are especially useful in larger plants because they can reach more employees than union meetings or personal contact. The leaflet campaign may open with a barrage of circulars handed out at the entrances to the workplace or put into nonwork areas by union adherents, or placed in eating and drinking establishments near the plant; sometimes they are mailed to the employees.

Lack of open leaflet distribution does not indicate lack of strength. Campaigns often are run with very little literature; most of the work is done in the homes, or in coffee shops, bars, rest rooms, and parking lots. The number of leaflets distributed usually increases as the election draws closer.

The leaflets are of two types. Some are canned, published by, for example, the AFL-CIO. These materials deal with unionism in general; they stress unity of purpose, the strength of collective action, and the dignity of the union employee. Department of Labor publications and famous persons will be quoted to create the feeling that being nonunion is atypical and that much more can be obtained by simply joining the union. Such materials are usually excellent propaganda pieces and are used during the early stages of the campaign. As the campaign proceeds, the other type of leaflet is handed out. The organizer tailors these leaflets to the particular employer and to the issues that have been raised at the target company. The materials will often rebut company letters, tactics, and speeches, and they may list unionized companies giving supposedly better benefits. Much of the literature will also be humorous; often, satirizing company officials is used to great advantage.

In general, most union leaflets and handouts have a high degree of eye appeal. They are brief and to the point, and they are well structured, concluding with an appeal to the employee to take some kind of action, such as signing a card or voting yes. In many cases, the employee will sign the authorization card attached to the leaflet without thinking twice about its meaning. (Employers would do well to take note of the style of union literature and to pattern their own written material on the fundamental communication principles observed by the unions.)

The employer should carefully evaluate the written material distributed by the union. Pay particular attention when the union switches from standardized material (issued by either the international union or the AFL-CIO) to leaflets geared to specific situations at your plant. This is a sign that the union's campaign is gaining ground.

After determining the union's overall approach and the type of information it is giving, decide whether the union's message should be rebutted on the spot or left alone until some more appropriate point in the campaign. A direct piece-by-piece rebuttal is neither necessary nor desirable.

Do not make the mistake of evaluating union propaganda from the standpoint of its impact on a manager's mind; it must be judged by its impact on the employees. Analyzing from the proper viewpoint will prevent the common mistake of either overrating or underrating union propaganda. Often, union literature that management discounts as untruthful or unpersuasive will have a high degree of credibility among the rank-and-file employees—and such communications must be answered. On the other hand, some written material that appears extremely potent to management will be discounted by the average employee. Answering these communications may, in many cases, lend unnecessary credence to the union point of view.

Management's campaign should be an offensive one, an integrated campaign with a plan of attack and arguments made at the most effective moments. Simply rebutting each piece of union literature is entirely too defensive. More important, it creates in the minds of employees the feeling that management is doing nothing but simply *replying* to union arguments. During the course of such a campaign, employees will have been conditioned to look for the employer's response within hours after each union pamphlet is received. Management may feel that it is doing a tremendously effective job and pat itself on the back for rebutting union material almost as quickly as it is issued. On the contrary, employees are not so impressed by such a campaign tactic.

The volume of union literature varies in each case, depending on the effort the union is putting into the campaign, the effectiveness of its other communication devices, and the company's approach. The more effective a union campaign is, the less need it has for written communication. The employer should not be lulled into believing that the absence of union literature implies a lack of determination on the union's part or the absence of interest on the part of employees.

The employer's campaign should be planned on grounds that are independent of the union's literature. It should *embody* the arguments and data contained in the union's pamphlets, but should not constitute a rebuttal. No campaign has ever been won on rebuttals. Successful employer campaigns are based on overall campaign methods and strategies designed to cover all the issues and to generate employee interest in the many affirmative points that the employer can make.

Telephone Campaigning

Particularly since the advent of the "Excelsior" list, telephone campaigning has become more and more common. Moreover, since elections are being conducted more efficiently by the NLRB, time pressures force the union to supplement its home visits and other communications methods with telephone campaigns.

Calls are made either by the organizer himself or by employees who volunteer. The numbers are obtained from local telephone directories after the employer has supplied the union with a list of the names and addresses of all voters. (See the "Excelsior List" requirement, p. 000.) The telephoners ask the employees to join the union and to sign cards. Any objections voiced by the employees are recorded by the telephoner, who either discusses those objections during that call or makes an appointment to discuss them later.

Although employers are not permitted to visit the homes of employees to discuss the union campaign, there is no prohibition against telephone calling. In certain cases, particularly with strategic employees, it might behoove employers to take a page from the union handbook and utilize home telephoning. Normally, however, employers have access to employees during the workday, and the use of telephone campaigns to any large extent is not necessary.

Where such techniques are used, the employer-telephoner should be aware of the dangers of indiscreet interrogations, veiled threats, and implied promises. He does not want to commit any unfair labor practices that would result in setting aside the election or more serious NLRB remedies.

The Substance of Union Statements

Unions characteristically couch their messages in language and concepts pertinent to the employees. They will often discuss monthly dues and explain exactly where the dues money is spent. But very little will be said about dues supporting the union organizers' salaries, expense accounts, and life style. Rather, they will indicate that the money is spent in negotiations, settling grievances, legal expenses to represent members before government agencies, research to help employees bargain, company newspapers, defense funds, strike funds, lobbying by the international union, and other noble purposes. Other communications will advertise the benefits of union life. Sometimes letters from members of the union working at other plants will be distributed. These testimonials will outline how terrible conditions were before the union came in and compare them with the benefits now.

Many communications will simply report news of the campaign as it develops. One of the key points a union will try to make is that the union should be formed immediately so that the rewards can be received right away. The organizer implies that improvements always follow automatically as soon as the union is voted in, that the company can change working conditions at will, that a union will contractualize benefits so that management cannot rescind them. He takes great pains to stress that the union is not interested in conducting strikes—that strikes are a "last resort." He implies that the union has no affirmative, aggressive role in the strike-making decision but leaves the issue completely up to the employees; he leads the employees to believe that a strike will not occur unless they will it.

Such arguments are made by an organizer who knows what points are most effective with which type of employee. He appears vitally interested in the welfare of the individual he is speaking to, always ready to help him with his problems or refer a union lawyer to him—even for personal legal matters. He makes the employee feel important.

Plant Leaders

During an organizing campaign, the union organizer has the ability to seek potential plant leaders. This is probably the greatest test for being a successful organizer. Having found a potential leader, he looks for a personal grievance. He enlarges on that grievance, encourages the prospect to talk about his own problems and those of others, magnifies the complaint, then sells the idea that, individually, employees are too weak to correct their own conditions and that the obvious answer is collective bargaining. Once he accepts that idea, the leader will sell that cause to his coemployees.

Management must compete for the loyalty of these same natural leaders. You must attempt to spot key individuals, those who have influence over a number of coemployees because of their natural ability to attract people and inspire confidence. If they are identified prior to a campaign, it will be much easier to channel communications through them to achieve your communication objectives *during* a campaign.

Most company managers with successful records in union elections recognize that a statement from a co-worker, espousing a pro-company point of view, is more convincing to other employees than the same statement coming from the "boss" or higher management authority.

Threats to Disclose Names of Card-Signers

Some organizers will tell employees during a campaign that if the union loses the election, they will disclose the names of employees who signed authorization cards to the employer. This creates fear in the minds of the employees that their card-signing activities will come to the attention of management. Afraid that the company will engage in retaliation, they vote for the union so that their union sympathies will never be disclosed.

Such statements, made by union representatives or employee organizers, form the basis for setting aside an election if the employer loses. The best move for the employer if such statements come to its attention after a petition is filed is to communicate to its employees that the law prohibits it from firing employees for supporting a union and that, in any event, the employer will not retaliate against any employee.

In-House Plants

An effective technique utilized frequently in recent years is sending a union associate to the target company to apply for employment, which in large organizations will not be difficult to obtain. The "plant" may be a skilled union organizer, a member of the union staff in training, a local union officer or shop steward on leave from another plant, or a laid-off union member who is articulate and able to drum up support for a union. Once on the payroll, this employee is protected under federal law from discharge or retaliation because of his pro-union activities, or even though he may also be on the union's payroll, paid for his organizing activities. His job will be to obtain information about company conditions, generate gripes and complaints from co-workers, and contact the natural leaders within the plant to win them over to his side. He will obtain the names of employees who are uncommitted, supply counterintelligence, and otherwise provide the outside organizer with information. A clever union agent can also be on the lookout for unfair labor practices. He takes notes of everything said by management and questions co-employees as to what was said to them by management during conversations. Thus, a running tally of the employer's statements is garnered by the agents and used by the union as a basis for filing unfair labor practice charges, which can be extremely damaging to the company.

As soon as the organizing drive gains headway, the agent often quits and goes on to some other targeted employer to perform his undercover work there. In most cases, the employer never becomes aware of the union's undercover connection.

Here is what happened to one employer. An individual who was paid $200 a week and given an automobile and expense account by the union, obtained employment with a company under express instructions from the union to organize the company. While employed at the company, the "plant" had continued to receive full salary and expenses from the union and he turned over the paychecks received from the employer to the union. It was also clear that the employee was under the control of the Local's president and that he would have terminated his employment at the company and taken an assignment elsewhere if the union had instructed him to do so. When he was laid off by the company, it was claimed that he had been discriminated against because of his union solicitations. The employer argued that the individual was not a bona fide employee of the company. Nevertheless, the Board held that such an organizer has the full protection afforded to any other employee under the Act, that he was a bona fide employee, and could not be discriminated against because of his union affiliation. Where such a violation is found, the Board will order back pay and reinstatement. *Anthony Forest Products, Co.*, 231 NLRB 976 (1977).

Existing Employee Committees

Companies often establish committees on various plant matters— safety, improved production, complaints, and other matters. A clever organizer is often able to convert these neutral committees into committees willing to go union. Sometimes the union organizer will work through a committee and encourage it to make demands that sound reasonable but that the organizer knows the company cannot meet. Once the company turns down the demands, the union organizer is easily able to convince the committee that it is helpless and that the answer to the problem is a strong outside union. Since the other employees have often been trained by the employer to follow the lead of the committee, once the organizer convinces the half-dozen people on a committee that collective bargaining is the only way to improve their conditions, it is an easy matter for the committee to swing the rest of the plant into line.

Many employers who have aided in the establishment of an independent "company union" have found to their dismay that they have provided the vehicle for official union organization. While many employers view such company unions as a buffer to full scale AFL-CIO unionization, in practice, such company unions are often a temporary step and a precursor to full scale organization. By assisting and dealing with such company unions, the employer demonstrates that there are benefits to collective action, and accustoms his employees to acting through a spokesman or small group. In so doing, employees tend to become acutely aware of the greater strength inherent in collective action. As time goes by, the tendency is for such groups to become more militant and aggressive. An astute organizer will often acquire the names of the persons on the committee and will socialize with them or invite them to dinner at which the benefits of formal unionization, including the financial strength of the parent organization, professional negotiators, legal resources and other virtues of unionization will be explained. The committee members become soft touches for the union's argument and will often convince the committee to persuade a majority of plant employees that formal union organization, AFL-CIO style, is in their best interests. The legal principles and pitfalls applicable to such in plant committees are discussed more fully in Chapter 3.

The House Party

If the organizer finds it difficult to get employees out en masse, a number of small meetings are held in the homes of employees who are union sympathizers.

Often, both mass meetings and small house-party meetings are held. The employer, aware only of the mass meeting, is lulled into a false sense of security. He may believe that union meetings are drawing only minor attendance, whereas the organizing campaign is steaming ahead via the small house-party meetings. Small meetings are more intimate and are held in a congenial atmosphere that lends itself better to persuasion. The organizer has time to work on individuals who have not signed. This one-on-one approach may be more effective than speaking from a podium at a mass meeting; the organizer can appear more friendly and can personally discuss the employee's fears and reluctance.

The organizer pays for the refreshments, and in an atmosphere of food and drink an employee may sign up, either because he feels indebted or because he has been treated royally at the home of a co-worker.

Oral Promises

The main weapon in the organizer's arsenal is the oral promise. To persuade employees to join the union, he must condition them into believing that unions and higher wages and benefits automatically go together. Employees are always willing to hear about getting higher wages, better benefits, or improved physical facilities. Often the organizer will draw up a sample set of demands that he will make to the company, implying that even if the company does not agree to all of them, it certainly will to some, and the employee will be better off.

During the course of the campaign, as issues arise the union organizer will have a cure ready. If an employee has an article of clothing stolen, the union will promise safe, secure lockers. If there is a minor accident on the job, the union will promise safe working conditions.

Employers should not make promises during a campaign. First of all, it is illegal; secondly—and as a very practical matter—the organizer will often take credit for the results, thereby making unionism a more attractive possibility. The employer's promises during a campaign serve only as visible, tangible evidence that the union *can* accomplish results.

Written Promises

In some campaigns, unions may put their promises in writing in a "contract" containing all the demands the organizer has been promoting. The "phantom" contracts are distributed to the employees, who are then led to believe that the union promises will be incorporated into a collective bargaining agreement. Armed with these contracts, pro-union employees will also try to enlist the sympathies of nonjoiners, arguing that even if only half the demands are granted, the employees will have gained a big advantage.

Often, unions will issue written guarantees in the form of documents that look official (they are strikingly similar to stock certificates). They list the benefits that will "automatically" accrue to employees when the union wins the election. They usually contain language guaranteeing the right to vote on a strike, and similar benefits. But there is no legal or practical way of holding the union to its representations.

To counter this tactic, the employer may challenge the union to sign a bond stating that it will make good on its promises. Its language can be couched in such a way that, if the union organizer dares to sign it, it is a legally enforceable document. Union organizers will never sign such a document, and the employer can then communicate the union's failure to sign as proof of the union's misleading and often fraudulent promises. (See Chapter 7.)

Prepayment of Fees

One of the latest techniques is for the union organizer to require a majority of the employees of the target unit to prepay a reduced initiation fee and a month's dues before the union will even file a petition for an election with the NLRB. If a majority prepay the fee and the petition is filed, but the union loses the subsequent election, all funds advanced by the workers are forfeited to the union to defray the campaign expenses. If the union wins the election, the advanced monies paid are credited to the employees' accounts.

Such an organizing policy is quite effective, since employees who have paid the fee naturally feel that, regardless of how their sentiments may have changed during the course of the election campaign, they must vote for the union or risk forfeiting their payments.

Rumors

Many union organizers start damaging rumors. They thrive on the frictions, doubts, and uncertainties such rumors create. Once the employees believe the rumor, the union organizer will step in and promise the employees protection against the unfavorable consequences.

Whether to rebut such a rumor is a judgment that must be made at the time it comes to management's attention. Efforts to refute the rumor may be construed by employees as proof that it has some substance. In other cases, however, the rumor must be squelched quickly. The best way is by offering some type of proof through memos, bulletin boards, or plantwide or departmental talks. Outline the false nature of the rumor and the reason it was initiated, and end with a request that employees come to the company for their information and to verify any dubious information passing around the plant by word of mouth.

False Statements

Departures from the truth are common techniques. The union organizer must spread confusion and discontent to clear the way for the union's entry onto the scene. Half-truths, exaggerations, distortions, and important information left unstated serve to arouse employees and encourage them to view the union as a savior. Thus, unions exaggerate benefits and wage scales obtained at other unionized plants, create suspicions concerning layoffs and discharges made in the normal course of business, and accuse management of discriminatory policies and favoritism with respect to routine plant decisions.

Peer Pressure

Pressure is often applied on an individual through his peers. The employee told that most of his co-workers have signed and that he is one of the few holdouts may find the pressure too great to resist. Most employees will find it easier to sign a card and join a union rather than become the object of scorn and name-calling by fellow workers.

Debate Entrapment

Seasoned organizers like to trap employers into public debates on plant or union premises. Many employers accept such debates for fear of appearing afraid of the union. They fear that declining to debate will make employees think that the union arguments are correct.

No matter how tempting the offer may appear, accepting the union's challenge is a mistake. The employer can communicate with his own employees forty hours a week, under conditions where the employer can control *what* is said, *when* it is said, and *how* it is said, *without rebuttal*. Once the employer gives up this control and offers to debate the union organizer, that initial advantage is lost.

Moreover, the union organizer is extremely skilled and trained at the infighting of such debates. He knows the union arguments and counterarguments and can rebut almost any employer advocate because of his long experience and training. Even an employer representative who is a good debater cannot keep pace with a trained union organizer.

If the employer's representative is an aggressive opponent, the employees are exposed during the debate to the union arguments. Thus, ironically, it is the employer accepting the challenge who provides the union organizer with a forum. It gives the union organizer an opportunity to make bold statements unsupported by the facts, to toss out accusations, and to make crowd-winning appeals. He often comes prepared with embarrassing information, such as company profits, company managers' salaries, and other things that employers find difficult to rebut in front of an employee group. The challenger appears to the employees as the underdog and may enlist a great deal of sympathy.

The employer will usually find that the debate is not an opportunity for him to rebut the union, but an opportunity for the union organizer to inflame emotions. Such a challenge is a mismatch under the best conditions.

The best way to counteract the challenge of a debate is to issue a statement, posted on the bulletin board, indicating that the union has had ample opportunity to speak to employees during the initial stages of its campaign—after work, in the homes and at union meetings, etc.—so there is no need for a debate. Such a communication normally will end the matter. However, company supervisors should be thoroughly briefed on the reasons the employer has not taken up the union challenge so they will be prepared to answer questions, often planted by the union organizer, as to why the company did not debate the union.

Public Advertising

Over the last decade, the public image of unionism has changed considerably for the better. Radio and television programs are often sponsored by a union. News broadcasts, interviews, and other radio and TV shows feature union leaders. Often, a union will sponsor a five-minute news program with one or two advertisements publicizing the union, recent contract settlements, and the pay and benefits won recently. The pitch will end with a request for every interested party to send the union a postcard with his name, address, and company name specified. Unions offer scholarships to students and contribute to telethons and other charitable causes in a way that will attract the highest regard. Awards are given to outstanding union leaders by local clubs and organizations. Politicians (often those with a campaign looming) are asked to give striking employees speeches that down-grade the employer and favor the union. Highly persuasive and emotional motion pictures depicting the history of the labor movement and its role in American life are shown to private groups, schools, and other organizations. With the increasing acceptance of unionism by teachers and others in the educational field, textbooks more and more frequently are casting unions in the role of champions of the people.

Vote Buying

Payment of money to an employee for signing a card or voting for the union constitutes an unfair labor practice on the part of the union. However, a union's offer to waive initiation fees for the entire voting unit is a permissible tactic. But an offer to waive union fees only for those who sign cards prior to the election is viewed as impermissible by the Board and the courts. Unions have used considerable imagination in providing *indirect* financial inducements to employees to join a union. But economic inducements to influence an employee's choice have been held objectionable by federal courts on the theory that they constitute indirect bribes.

Membership Rewards

An extremely effective technique is a reward to each union member who "organizes the unorganized." Under this system, a substantial fee is offered to the existing member for each employee who becomes a union member and is included in a collective bargaining agreement. This induces the member to search out nonunion shops and attempt to organize them; this strategy is particularly useful where union members have been laid off and now seek employment in nonunion shops. Under the strong inducement of a reward, the employee becomes an active and highly motivated organizer. Here is an actual example of such a bounty offer:

REWARD

Dear Brothers and Sisters:

The Officers and Executive Board of this Local Union did recently take under consideration the "Organization of the Unorganized".

We are, therefore, proposing a program that will not only

strengthen this Local Union, but also to involve the membership in a significant phase of the operation of your Union.

Any member obtaining designation cards in an unorganized Air Freight Forwarder, Airline, Custom House Broker, Air Freight Trucker, or any other Airline related Employer shall receive a FIFTY DOLLAR ($50.00) finder's fee for each unorganized employee who becomes a member of this Union through the conclusion of a Collective Bargaining Agreement with that unorganized Employer.

For Example—If an unorganized/Non-Union Employer employs four hundred (400) employees and through you, as a member in good standing, those employees sign Union designation cards and a successful contract is concluded between the Union and that Employer, you would receive, upon signing of that contract, $50.00 X 400, or $20,000.00 from your Union.

If you have any questions, or need any materials, feel free to contact the undersigned.

Looking forward to many successful organizational campaigns and hope many of you can receive additional compensation through this new organizational program.

Very truly yours,

Government Assistance

Union organizers will utilize every opportunity to persuade the employees that the federal government and the union are behind the organization drive. They often try to create the impression that the NLRB is in favor of the employees joining the union—that the NLRB and the union are aligned against the employer. In fact, the Board's role is to insure that a fair election takes place. The federal government does not take sides in election campaigns.

Yet clever union organizers will inform employees that the union has "brought the government in" to conduct an election and will imply that the federal government is present on the scene to prevent any unfair tactics by the employer. When unfair labor practice charges are filed, the organizer will use the government's investigation of such charges as an example of how the government is behind the workers' drive to establish a union in a plant. He will report every unfavorable decision by the NLRB and will try to take political advantage of simple NLRB procedures, such as the routine issuance of notices of hearings and other administrative matters.

Where the union uses this tactic, the employer must dispel the notion that the government and the union are on the same side of the fence and point out that (1) the NLRB is *neutral*, and (2) the law supports the employee's right *not* to join a union. Pertinent sections of the Taft-Hartley Act can be quoted. An excellent tactic is to reproduce relevant portions of the NLRB's publication, "Layman's Guide," which contains the statement that employees have the right not to choose unionism. Prompt reporting and explaining of NLRB actions tends to dispel any notion that government and the union are partners.

Would it be a successful strategy to advise employees during the course of a Board investigation into alleged employer unfair labor practices that they may obtain an attorney's advice before talking to the Board agent? In one case the company, after it had won an election, and during the pendency of a Board investigation into unfair labor practice charges, distributed the following letter to its employees:

> If a National Labor Relations Board agent should drop in on you, you may ask for an opportunity to obtain legal counsel before you talk to him. If you should want some legal assistance, or just help in handling any of the situations described above, all you need to do is let your supervisor know. He will put you in touch with someone who can help you.

The NLRB found, in view of all of the circumstances of that case including a previously demonstrated pattern of unlawful conduct, that the letter was a patent attempt to obstruct the investigation of the Board by discouraging employees from supplying information to Board agents. It found that the letter was distributed by the company for the purpose of obstructing Board investigations.

However, a federal Court of Appeals, on review of the case, found that the letter neither said nor suggested that employees *should* inform their supervisor to obtain his assistance. Rather, the court found the letter offered employees the assistance of the company in securing legal counsel *if* the employee should want and ask for such help. The letter offered assistance to all employees, regardless of their union disposition and regardless of the position they had taken with respect to talking to the Board agent. The court held that there was nothing on the face of the letter that required or compelled the employees to do anything, therefore, there was no coercion, threat of reprisal, or force in the letter, or any words of restraint or interference with the exercise of rights that are guaranteed to employees under the Act. It refused to approve of the Board's finding. *Florida Steel Corp. v. NLRB,* 587 F.2d 735 (5th Cir. 1979) *enforcing* 233 NLRB No. 74 (1977).

The Cumulative Effect

The organizer's literature, arguments, letters, home visits, and other inducements may add up to a successful union campaign. The organizer knows the views of various employees. His arguments are increasingly directed at reluctant or uncommitted voters, and as election day nears, he brings more and more pressure to bear on them. Unless the employer's countercampaign is powerful and credible, the organizer will succeed.

Chapter 3

Employer Unfair Labor Practices

Most, if not all, campaigns can be won without committing unfair labor practices, but history shows that employers often respond to the union's presence by using methods and means that overstep the law. Some of these unfair practices have been intentional; the majority, however, were probably unintentional—i.e., actions taken without thorough knowledge of the legal complexities involved.

Employers must avoid committing unfair labor practices. Quite aside from the fact that elections can be won legally, an employer's unfair labor practices may affect his campaign. Board findings that the employer has violated the law lend great credibility to the union's effort to discredit the employer. And if an employer is required to reinstate laid-off individuals, the union appears as a powerful force able to effectuate the changes it has been promising.

The NLRB's variety of remedial orders can seriously affect a business enterprise. An employer who has won a union election may find that the Board has ordered a second election on the basis of unfair labor practices committed during the campaign. The most drastic Board remedy is the "card-based bargaining order," discussed in Chapter 4, in which the Board requires an employer to bargain with a union despite an election *victory* by the employer. The theory behind this is that the employer's serious unfair labor practices have made it impossible for a second election to be fair. The union returns to the status quo it enjoyed prior to the commission of the unfair labor practices. If the union had a majority of cards signed when the campaign began, the cards take precedence over the secret ballots.

Most employers seek to deny the union the psychological advantage obtained by NLRB support of union charges.

Some employer unfair labor practices are briefly outlined in this chapter and will be discussed in more detail in subsequent ones. The practices are intended not as an encyclopedic listing, but as a general guide. Before any action is taken during the campaign, it should be evaluated by the company's labor attorney.

Interference With Employee Rights

Section 8(a)(1) of the Labor-Management Relations Act makes it an unfair labor practice for an employer to interfere with, restrain, or coerce employees in the exercise of their right to form, join, or assist any labor organization. Violations of this section are the most common form of employer unfair practice, and frequently involve threats that the employee will be subject to retaliatory action if he or she votes for the union. Another unfair practice is for the employer to promise, directly or indirectly, some specific course of conduct that will benefit the employee if he or she rejects the union.

Thus, granting wage increases, promising promotions, or providing new benefits (even minor ones) in order to block the union's organizational efforts are prohibited by law, since this unfairly persuades employees that their goals can be achieved without the union. Conversely, taking away benefits to show employees that they will lose by supporting the union is also a violation, even when the change is as minor as disallowing the existing privilege of playing radios during working hours.

The theory underlying the campaign rules against promises and threats was summarized by the Supreme Court in *NLRB v. Exchange Parts Co.*, 375 U.S. 405 (1964), in now famous language:

> We have no doubt that [the Act] prohibits not only intrusive threats and promises but also conduct immediately favorable to employees which is undertaken with the express purpose of impinging upon their freedom of choice for or against unionization. . . . [T]he danger inherent in well-timed increases in benefits is the suggestion of a fist inside the velvet glove. Employees are not likely to miss the inference that the source of benefits now conferred is also the source from which future benefits must flow and which may dry up if it is not obliged.

Here is a typical example of how employers have used the disapproved "fist inside the velvet glove" approach: The employer spoke to his employees about job descriptions and responsibilities, pay raises, and benefits policies; however, he also told employees that he did not need the plant being organized in order to continue operations. The Board found that the statement was a clear and un-ambiguous threat to close. In effect, the employer conveyed his underlying message that enjoyment of the benefits he referred to was conditioned on the continuation of a nonunion plant. *American Spring Wire Corp.*, 237 NLRB No. 185 (1978).

Changes that have been planned before the union appears are privileged under the law. However, the employer will have the heavy burden of proving to a suspicious NLRB that the changes would have taken place even without the union activity.

Interrogation is another form of interference with employee rights. Even though an employee is not actually intimidated by employer questions, it is a violation. The employer should assume that even the most "innocent" question geared to obtaining information about union activity or interest on the part of the employees is an unfair labor practice.

Care should be taken in this area since many violations are inadvertent. For example, questioning employees even indirectly about the attitude of others toward the union or the extent of union membership, politely asking an employee if he or she is involved in union business, asking about union membership on job applications, asking whether or not there has been any pro-union sympathy in the plant, and similar conduct, even if asked casually or sympathetically—and even if asked of an employee who opposes the union—are all illegal.

Surveillance of union activities is also prohibited. In fact, even creating the impression that employee union activities are being scrutinized is impermissible. Recording license numbers of cars parked outside of union meeting places, efforts to discover who has attended union meetings, driving past the site of the union meeting while it is in progress or shortly before or after the meeting takes place, informing employees that the employer is aware of who the union activists are, and taking note of which employees accept union leaflets are unfair labor practices.

Interfering with employee rights to show support for a union and to persuade their co-employees to join is also illegal. An employer may not prohibit employees from soliciting on their break times or lunch hours. And an employer cannot prohibit employees from wearing union buttons or other insignia or from pasting union insignia and posters on personal property, even though the employer may believe that such insignia will create dissension in the plant.

Exercise caution in making promises. Promising to take care of those who vote against the union and to deal with and correct employee complaints is impermissible. Veiled promises such as that the employer is certain "things will get better" without the union are impermissible. Likewise, be careful in making predictions. Predictions that the appearance of the union on the scene would lead to a loss of privileges, that the employees would have to work harder, or that the employer might decide to change the location of the plant as a result of a union victory have all been held to be impermissible.

Assisting employees in withdrawing from union activity is prohibited in most cases. The employer may not suggest such withdrawals, take an active role in them, or solicit key employees to circulate petitions rejecting the union.

It is not possible to cover the infinite variety of unfair labor practices. What is important is to realize that conduct may be illegal even if it affects only one or two employees, and even if a seemingly minor matter is involved, such as withdrawal of free coffee. Virtually any action affecting terms and conditions of employment may be illegal. Furthermore, the Board has also pinned responsibility on companies for not repudiating the remarks or acts of non-employees, such as local businessmen or a town's mayor.

Drawing the line between permissible and impermissible conduct is often difficult. However, the standard is that an employer is free to communicate to employees its general views about unionism or its specific views on a particular union as long as the communication does not contain a threat of reprisal or force or a promise of benefit. An employer is allowed to make a prediction as to the precise effects he believes unionization will have on the company. These predictions must be carefully phrased on the basis of *objective fact*. If there is any implication that an employer may take action for reasons unrelated to economic necessities and known only to him, the statements are no longer reasonable predictions based on fact but are a threat to retaliate.

Stating that if the union is voted in the easy relationship between the employer and employee will no longer exist constitutes a threat, as does a statement that a union can cause employees to lose pay by reducing management's flexibility to shift people from one department to another.

Other examples of employer interference include: reprimands designed to harass pro-union supporters; interrogation concerning information employees have given NLRB agents investigating charges; assigning pro-union employees to undesirable shifts; offering employees an in-plant grievance committee as an alternative to union representation, etc.

Under limited circumstances, an employer may repudiate an unfair labor practice after it has been committed. One employer discovered that a supervisor drove through a motel parking lot looking for cars with company parking stickers when a union meeting was being held there. On a different occasion, he stopped for a drink at a different motel when employees were holding a meeting there. The employer posted a notice in its plant disclaiming the supervisor's actions and assuring employees of their right to join or not to join the union. This voluntary posting was sufficient to expunge the ill effects of unlawful surveillance.

The Board will hold the employer attempting to repudiate an unfair labor practice to a high standard. The repudiation must be absolutely unequivocal, timely, and not motivated by knowledge that an unfair labor practice complaint is imminent. The disavowal must be communicated to the employees exposed to the unlawful conduct, and all employees must be adequately informed of the retraction. The commission of the unfair labor practice should be admitted and employees should be assured that such interference with their rights will not occur in the future. *Kawasaki Motors Corp.*, 231 NLRB 1151 (1977).

Dominating or Assisting a Labor Organization

Section 8(a)(2) makes it unlawful for an employer to dominate or interfere with the formation or administration of, or to contribute financial or other support to any labor organization. This situation may arise during an organizing campaign if a competing organization, such as a shop committee, is already established within the plant. Shop committees, and other antiunion groups, are considered to be labor organizations.

The law respecting employee committees can probably be summarized thus: The NLRB (with court approval in most cases) has struck down virtually all forms of employee committees except where they have functioned independently and have demonstrated all the typical characteristics of a labor union, including arm's-length bargaining with the employer.

The Board has held that a suggestion committee was a labor organization; the good faith of an employer in setting up the committee and/or assisting it is not a defense. The Board has even gone as far as to comment that the mere presentation to management of employee views by employee committees is sufficient to make the committee a "labor organization." Such activity, in the Board's view, constitutes dealing with management. Therefore management may not assist, interfere with, or dominate such committees. Employee councils that are financed and administered by employers are illegal. Even allowing such procompany groups to meet on company time and property, or allowing them to obtain the benefit of vending machine profits, has been held by the NLRB to violate the Act. Supplying the organization with office facilities to type antiunion propaganda is considered an unfair labor practice.

It is extremely difficult for the employer to avoid an unfair labor practice finding when organizations of this kind spring into existence, because the Board is extremely suspicious of such relationships. Even the suggestion by management that such a committee be formed has been held to be unfair labor practice; and when such a committee is established spontaneously, without the support of the employer, the Board may order its disestablishment if it does not exist independently of the employer.

Here is a typical impermissible scenario:

During a campaign in which the employer clearly expresses its opposition to a union, a small group of employees approaches a management official over problems in the plant. The leader may ask if there is any way in which the employees can communicate with management other than through supervisors who are disliked. The management official, seeing an opportunity to avoid the union, promises to support any effort on the part of the employees to set up a "form of communication" between management and the production employees.

The Board would find that the company violated the law by suggesting "communication" with the employees without a union, by broaching the possibility of establishing a committee in lieu of the union, and by promising employees help and support in establishing an employee committee for the purpose of dealing with management. See *Cerro CATV Devices, Inc.*, 237 NLRB No. 179 (1978).

Discrimination Against Employees Engaged in Union Activity

Section 8(a)(3) of the Act prohibits an employer from discouraging membership in a labor organization by means of discriminating against the employee with respect to conditions of employment. The prohibition is much broader than merely covering firing employees for such activities.

Where an employer reduces an employee's hours in order to reduce his earnings as a reprisal for union activity, it is a violation; so, too, is a refusal to hire an applicant for employment if union predilection is suspected. Many discriminatory charges center around the layoff of union supporters. Even where the economic justification for a layoff does in fact exist, many layoffs have not withstood Board scrutiny. Often, the Board may concede the economic justification for a layoff but will challenge the manner of selecting employees for layoff. Out-of-seniority layoffs are suspect and may be held to be discriminatory even when there is valid economic justification. A critical inquiry in cases like this is whether or not the layoff hits heavily on those who have signed union authorization cards. The same reasoning holds true if both union adherents and pro-company employees are laid off, but the number of union adherents is out of proportion to the number of pro-company employees.

Where seniority has been followed by the company in the past, but there is a sudden deviation that adversely affects union supporters, the union may be able to prove a violation. The employer should avoid giving conflicting reasons for the layoffs or discharges, or reasons that are not readily believable as justification for the discharge. Extreme care should be taken to ensure that supervisors do not pass offhand remarks immediately before or after the discharge that may serve as evidence that part of the reason for an otherwise valid discharge was the employee's union affiliation.

Demotion of employees because of union activity also violates the law. Discriminatory transfers from one job classification to a less satisfactory job classification, or transfers of union adherents to the night shift, are examples of such discrimination. Changes in working conditions, such as denial of overtime work to departments where heavy union activity is suspected, and changes in methods of operations that adversely affect the earnings of union supporters are all discriminatory and in violation of the law. In order to prove a violation of Section 8(a)(3), however, the Board must prove that the motive of the employer was to discourage union activity.

The Board also follows the doctrine of "constructive discharge." If the employer, with a motive of discouraging union activity, makes working conditions difficult for a prounion employee and the employee quits his job because of such conditions or employer harassment, the Board may find a violation of Section 8(a)(3) on the basis of a constructive discharge.

However, the Board has also held that aggressive prounion behavior that creates dissension on the plant floor, altercations on company premises, and work slowdowns are not protected and may appropriately be the subject of employer discipline. Moreover, if an employee is disciplined for breaching the company's valid no-solicitation or no-distribution rule, no violation will be found. (No-solicitation and no-distribution rules will be discussed later.)

If the employer can show that the employee violated existing plant rules or commonly accepted codes of conduct—or was guilty of excessive tardiness or absenteeism, leaving work without permission, clocking out other employees, or violating safety rules—a defense may be spelled out by the employer. However, merely asserting the defense, even assuming that the conduct has occurred, will not necessarily free the employer from an adverse finding. All the evidence will be scrutinized carefully by the Board to determine the *real* reason for the discharge. Thus, even though employees are guilty of insubordination, disrupting production, drinking in the plant, and other forms of unacceptable conduct, a violation may be found by the Board if the conclusion is that the conduct was merely a pretext for the discharge.

In determining whether or not the employer's defense is a pretext, the Board will carefully look at the employer's antiunion attitude. Evidence that company representatives have made hostile statements to the union or that supervisors have made statements indicating their disposition to punish or harass union supporters will detract from the validity of the defense.

Other areas of Board inquiry include failure to warn employees that their work or conduct is unsatisfactory, failure to investigate carefully the charges against the employee, failure to consider an employee's excellent work record as a mitigating factor in the discipline, and the timing of the discharge (i.e., whether it is closely connected in time with either the signing of a union authorization card or union organizational activity). Also damaging to the employer's defense are situations in which similar prior conduct by the employee was not disciplined by the employer, and cases in which conflicting reasons are given for the discipline or in which there is no credible explanation for a precipitate action. Particularly damaging is a departure from the employer's normal standards or policies. Delay in the discharge after knowledge of the offense, failure to tell the employee the reason for the discharge at the time of termination, and similar insufficiencies can destroy what might appear to the employer to be lawful conduct at the time.

The typical remedy in Section 8(a)(3) cases is back pay for time lost and reinstatement to the job. In addition, the Board will require that the employer post notices throughout the plant publishing the fact that a violation has occurred and that the employee was the object of employer discrimination.

The Board, in addition to its usual remedies, has been quite imaginative in using its powers. It has required employers to mail notices publicizing the unfair labor practices to employees at other plants, has required a company official or NLRB agent to read the notice to employees, has ordered the employer to furnish the union with employee names and addresses, and has granted the union access to plant bulletin boards for specified periods of time. Pervasive and flagrant violations can also support a card-based bargaining order.

Discrimination Against Employees Who Testify or Participate in Board's Proceedings

Discrimination against an employee because he has filed charges with the NLRB or has given testimony in a Board proceeding is prohibited by Section 8(a)(4) of the Act.

It is a violation for an employer to discharge employees who give sworn written statements to NLRB agents in support of unfair labor practice charges filed by the union. It is not necessary that the discharged employees file the charges themselves or testify formally at a Board proceeding. A violation has also been found when employees were discharged because the employer merely *suspected* that they had filed or were about to file a charge against the employer.

If an employee is subpoenaed by the union or the NLRB, the employer must not interfere with his right and obligation to attend the scheduled hearings by advising employees that they need not appear. *American Service Corp.*, 227 NLRB 13 (1976). No reprisals may be undertaken because he was subpoenaed by the adverse party. This concept holds even though the employee involved failed to follow established company protocol regarding authorized absence from the plant. The employer's claim that absence of particular employees or even a large group of employees will interfere with the production process is not a defense: The employer must permit employees to testify. The right to appear at a hearing involves taking sufficient time off for the employee to travel to the hearing, and employer disciplinary measures for such absenteeism are unlawful. This does not imply that employees may voluntarily absent themselves from work at any time to attend a Board hearing without clocking out, in violation of company rules. See *E. H. Limited*, 227 NLRB 1107 (1977), *enforcement denied*, *Service Employees Local 250 v. NLRB*, F.2d (D.C. Cir. 1979), 101 LRRM 2004, for a discussion of the applicable principles.

An employer who maintains the wages of employees appearing on his behalf at a hearing may refuse to pay employees testifying contra, or may pay the former more than the latter.

Certain factual circumstances may make discrimination permissible. For example, if an employee *intentionally* files false charges with the Board or gives false testimony, he may be discharged.

Refusal to Bargain

Section 8(a)(5) makes it unlawful for an employer to refuse to bargain collectively with a union that has been certified or recognized. A great deal of law has evolved in connection with this crucial section which requires an employer to bargain in good faith once a bargaining relationship has been established. Therefore, the principles applicable to refusal-to-bargain charges assume that the union has been certified as an exclusive representative of the employees. Accordingly, they will be discussed in subsequent chapters.

Chapter 4

Procedures
Leading to Elections
and Card-Based Recognition

One of the initial questions that must be resolved is whether the employer is under the jurisdiction of the National Labor Relations Act. If not, then a state labor board may have jurisdiction over the employer, and state agency rules will govern both the substantive and procedural issues of the campaign. If the employer is covered by the federal jurisdiction, all proceedings will be conducted according to NLRB rules.

Most businesses, even small ones, are covered by federal jurisdiction. In general, if the business affects interstate commerce by the selling or purchasing of goods or rendering or receiving services outside the state, the employer will be covered by federal law. The interstate sales or purchases need not be direct; an employer's business may affect interstate commerce if sales and purchases are channeled through other companies within the state whose transactions cross state lines.

If the business qualifies as interstate, the Board has dollar-volume jurisdictional standards that must be met. For example, jurisdiction as to nonretail businesses will be asserted if there is a yearly outflow or inflow, direct or indirect, of $50,000 or more. Jurisdiction will be asserted over retail and service firms if annual gross volume is $500,000. The Board's rules with respect to the employer's type of operation should be checked by competent counsel.

Union Authorization Cards

Use to Support Union's Showing of Interest

The union must petition the Board for an election to be held. But the Board has a policy that discourages unions from filing petitions when there is no reasonable assurance that a real desire for union representation exists. This policy requires that a union petition be supported by at least 30 percent of the employees in the group that the union claims is an appropriate voting unit.

Despite the 30 percent rule, most unions do not file a representation petition until at least 50 *percent* of the employees in the union's version of the appropriate unit have signed authorization cards, because the employer's counter-campaign will detract from the union's support. A union with cards signed by 60 or 70 percent of the group may find that 20 percent of its support is eroded once the employer begins a hard-hitting, aggressive campaign.

It is therefore unwise for the employer to assume that a union has only one-third of the employees signed at the time a petition is filed. Much time and energy is wasted attempting to fight the union's "showing of interest" (number of authorization cards); this detracts from the energy that should be expended in planning an appropriate campaign. Unions often lull employers into a false sense of security by understating their estimate of the total number of employees in the unit when filing their petition, making employers believe the union is weaker than it actually is.

An authorization card states that the employee signing it designates the named union as the exclusive collective bargaining representative for the purpose of negotiating wages, hours, and other terms and conditions of employment.

The employer should be extremely attentive to what the union says during the card-signing process. If the union's statements and tactics are recorded, they may serve the employer well if the necessity to file objections to the election arises. Even if collected after the election, this information can support objections to the election. The union's activity in soliciting cards is crucial to its success, and the card-signing process is not merely a mechanical one, but one that deserves the employer's careful scrutiny.

But the circumstances under which these cards are obtained by union organizers are often highly suspect. Coercion, misrepresentations, wild promises—and even forgery—have led both the Board and the courts to view these cards as extremely unreliable. One court even commented that cards are frequently obtained under circumstances that are "an abomination."

It is therefore important for the employer and its supervisors to understand that many cards are signed without firm conviction. For example, some cards are obtained through the representation that everyone else in the department has signed. Other employees are told, "Sign now, and make up your minds when you vote." Some are told that the purpose of the card is only to obtain an election. Others are told that they will not be able to attend union meetings and will not obtain the benefits of a union contract unless the card is signed immediately. Some are even told that if they do not sign they will not obtain raises, or that they will be discharged if the union wins the election.

The Board alone decides whether or not the union has met the 30 percent requirement. Any attempts by the employer to see the cards are destined to fail. The Board's determination is final, and it will not hear argument on such issues as supervisors' participation in obtaining signatures, or union agents' misrepresentations.

Proof of Fraud

In extremely unusual circumstances, where there is solid and substantial evidence that the cards are tainted with fraud, the Board has from time to time conducted a special investigation into the validity of the cards. These attacks on the showing of interest must be formidable to induce the Board to investigate the authenticity of the signed cards. For example, the Board dismissed the union's petition when an employer introduced an affidavit signed by more than 70 percent of the employees in the unit alleging that at no time had these employees signed any card intending to support the union. The Board concluded that reasonable cause existed for believing that the union's showing of interest may have been tainted by fraud. In cases where there is not an adequate showing of interest, or where the evidence reveals that the appropriate unit finally agreed to is larger than the union's requested unit, the union petition may also be dismissed—but subject to the union's right to produce a new, valid showing of interest.

Union instructions to their organizers state that the cards should always be signed and dated by the employees. Unsigned or undated cards are invalid. Organizers are also cautioned to sign up the employees personally, whenever possible, and to initial each card so that they can testify to the signing at a later date if necessary. On request of the employee, organizers may fill in the blanks and date the card themselves. Union office employees are cautioned to staple the postmarked envelopes to the cards and to initial each card upon receipt. In-plant agents are also instructed to date and initial each card they have observed being signed.

Stale Cards

The timeliness of cards is frequently an issue. While there are no hard-and-fast rules, the Board will ordinarily count a card if it is less than one year old. The general rule is that cards will be counted, regardless of age, if they are part of a continuing campaign. Cards obtained in a prior campaign are deemed to be stale. If stale cards have been reaffirmed by employees, the chances are greatly increased that the NLRB will accept such cards despite the passage of time. Each case must be treated individually according to its own facts.

When the employer suspects that there is an issue of timeliness involved, prompt steps should be taken to challenge the showing of interest on that basis. The cards of those who are no longer employees will not be counted by the NLRB. However, cards of employees who are on leave of absence or on military or maternity leave are counted in judging the union's showing of interest.

Use to Support Union's Request for Recognition

Where the union files a refusal-to-bargain charge based on a majority of signed cards in an appropriate unit, the validity of the cards is very much in issue and may be litigated by the employer. In such a case, the employer may question the signer of each card to determine its validity. The administrative law judge then will rule on whether the cards may be counted as a part of the union's claimed majority.

Both the Supreme Court and the NLRB have ruled that if an authorization card is unambiguous—that is, the card states on its face that the employee authorizes the union to represent the employee for collective bargaining purposes and *not* merely to seek an election—that card will be counted, even if the employee believes that the card was signed only for the purpose of obtaining a union meeting. If the organizer tells an employee that the "principal purpose" of the cards is to obtain an election, the Board will count that card as valid. Unambiguous cards are considered valid even if the employees are falsely told that the union organizer needs only ten more cards in order to file a petition for an election.

Language added to the card by the signer, if it is not inconsistent with the language on the card or does not otherwise restrict the authorization, does not invalidate the card.

Misrepresentations

If an employer attempts to set aside the cards on the basis of a material misrepresentation, the proof must be strong. Evidence that card-signers were told that the cards would be used to petition for an election, or to show interest in the union and get a union agent to visit the employees to discuss the union, has been held insufficient to invalidate these cards.

Even if the employee is told that signing is to obtain an election, the card will not be deemed invalid as long as there is proof that the employee read the unambiguous card prior to signing it and that the solicitor did not expressly contradict the statement of purpose contained on the card itself.

However, if the employer can prove that the authorization cards were represented as being for the sole purpose of obtaining an election, the cards will not be valid for purposes of determining the union's majority status, although they will be valid for purposes of the 30 percent rule. The Board has invalidated cards of employees who were told that the sole purpose was to enable the union to keep in touch with the employees and that the card did not mean that the employees desired a union to represent them. In such cases, the employer was able to prove that the employees signed the cards without reading them and in express reliance upon the misrepresentation. In other cases involving misrepresentations where it was stated that the purpose of the card was to indicate who was interested in having a union or to allow the union representative to speak to the employees' president, the Board refused to invalidate the cards.

Initiation Fee Waiver

The union will often attempt to buy endorsements by offering to waive the initiation fees for employees who sign authorization cards prior to a Board election. If the union organizer offers to waive initiation fees, but does not condition this waiver upon support for the union during the election campaign, if the waiver is available to all eligible voters, not just the card-signers, and if it is available to them both before and after the election, then the authorization cards obtained in such a manner are valid. However, representation that the initiation fee would be waived for all *present* employees who make application for charter membership is considered by the Board subject to ambiguous interpretation and the card is held to be invalid. The Board has found that a union interfered with the election because of its statement that there would be no initiation fee for anyone joining "now, during this campaign." The promise was interpreted as being conditioned on the employees' making the commitment to the union *prior* to the election. But union statements that the union "usually" did not charge an initiation fee until employees had a period of time to join the union after a Board election do not invalidate the cards. The union has the burden of clarifying any ambiguities in its offer to waive initiation fees, and cards will not be counted when it is not clear whether the solicitors offered to waive fees.

Supervisory Solicitation and Involvement

It is a common misconception that supervisory involvement in obtaining signed cards is automatically a basis for invalidating those cards. While serious interference or direct solicitation by supervisors of signed cards does invalidate these cards, the Board will evaluate the total circumstances surrounding the supervisors' participation.

For example, it is not considered sufficient to invalidate the cards when a supervisor merely signed a card on his own behalf and also attended union meetings. Moreover, cards signed in the presence of an individual the signers believed to be a rank-and-file employee but who in fact was a supervisor were not invalidated by supervisory interference. But supervisors' soliciting cards, distributing union literature to employees, attending union meetings, and otherwise assisting the union in its campaign will invalidate the cards. Those cards are also invalidated where supervisors help to arrange the initial union meeting and also solicit card-signers. Yet, the *mere presence* of a management official when cards are being signed is not sufficient to invalidate the cards. Also, where a supervisor requests the employees who are signing cards to keep his attendance a secret, such cards may be valid, since the supervisor's conduct conveyed to the card signers that management was opposed to the union.

The following case will illustrate the employer's difficulties in attempting to nullify cards that have been signed by employees. An employee signed a card, stating that she was opposed to the union but was persuaded to sign by a persistent co-employee on the ground that signing would help the co-employee obtain reinstatement. The administrative law judge ruled the card to be valid and

> "reject[ed] any rule that requires a probe of an employee's subjective motivations" and held that "employees should be bound by the clear language of what they sign unless that language is deliberately and clearly canceled by a union adherent with words calculated to direct the signer to disregard and forget the language above his signature." (395 U.S. at 607, 608.) The employee's resistance itself proves that she very well understood what she was doing. There is no doubt that cards are signed and ballots cast for a union contrary

to the personal wishes of employees and only to placate insistent spouses, sweethearts, and friends; as long as the signer or voter understands the import of his act, the designation is valid. Pinter Bros. 233 NLRB No. 83 (1977).

Handling the Demand for Recognition

A union with signed authorization cards from a majority of the employees will often demand recognition without an election. Such demands sometimes are made even without a majority. This bluff is made in the hope that the employer will resign itself to the fact that unionization is inevitable and will recognize the union as collective-bargaining agent without an election. The demand may be transmitted by letter, telegram, personal visit, or a phone call to a company official. Occasionally the approach is made to a small company by an employee who claims to represent the union and to speak for a majority of the card-signing employees.

Unions use this tactic to avoid the delay that an election may involve. They often hope that an unsuspecting employer will either recognize the union or commit some act that may preclude the holding of an election, because, more often than not, the steps the employer undertakes constitute unfair labor practices. Unions realize that the delay of an election might mean that some employees who have signed cards will change their minds after the employer has mounted a campaign informing employees of the disadvantages of unionization.

If such a demand is received, no action should be taken until you have consulted competent, full-time labor counsel on how to react to the demand. The advice will be to reject the request; the issue will be the best possible form for doing it. A response will be drafted in coordination with the company's attorney's advice.

It is a mistake for the employer to ask to look at the authorization cards and then refuse to recognize the union as collective bargaining agent. Even if it is suspected that the union is bluffing, it is rarely worth the risk involved. It should be recognized that the initial demand is more often than not an attempt by the union to obtain a powerful propaganda weapon—to impress employees with the feeling that the union presence in the plant is a *fait accompli* and that it is only a matter of time before the union begins to bargain with the employer.

If the demand for recognition contains copies of the signed authorization cards, a safe route is not to count or examine the cards. Otherwise, in any subsequent charge alleging discrimination against employees for union activities, the NLRB may find that the employer's knowledge of individual employee's union activities is present by virtue of the retention of authorization cards. If a secretary or mailroom employee has innocently opened the letter and examined the cards, he or she should be instructed not to discuss the identity of the individuals who signed the cards or the number of the cards with company officials. The envelope should be sealed in the presence of a witness, and a memorandum should be made recording the date, time, place, and circumstances of receipt of the demand with enclosures.

If the union organizer appears in the office of a company official demanding recognition, the best course is not to discuss the question of recognition or any other issue. The organizer should be asked to put his demand in writing and to forward it to a named company official. If the organizer declines to do so, the company official should refuse to discuss the matter with the organizer and indicate that the subject will be given to the company's attorneys. If the organizer offers to prove the union's claim of majority by demonstrating the signed organization cards, refuse the offer.

If, as a ploy, the organizer leaves the cards (or copies of the cards) in the office, they should be sealed in an envelope with appropriate documentation and witnesses. The witnesses should testify that the cards were in fact enclosed in an envelope without examination.

While an employer has an initial right to insist upon a Board election, voluntary recognition of the union, and/or other dealings amounting to tacit or implied recognition, may preclude the employer from ever asserting its right to an election. As an example of how an employer can unwittingly lose his right to a Board election, consider the following situation. After having garnered a majority of the employees' pledge cards, two representatives of the union arranged a meeting with the company president and requested that he recognize the union as the bargaining agent for the company's production and maintenance employees. They presented a majority of authorization cards to the president who, after examining the cards, admitted that the union did represent a majority and agreed to meet with the union to begin contract talks. Subsequently, the company president obtained legal counsel who informed the union that he was cancelling the bargaining session and that the employer doubted the union's majority status, as well as the appropriateness of the unit, and refused the recognize the union unless it won a Board-conducted election.

The National Labor Relations Board decided that the oral recognition was binding upon the employer. The error in this case, was the original voluntary commitment of the employer to bargain upon some demonstrated showing of majority representation by the union. Where such a showing is made and a company official concedes the majority status and agrees to begin bargaining, the union has been recognized and all opportunity for an NLRB election is lost. *Jerr-Dan Corp.*, 237 NLRB No. 49 (1978); *Brown & Connolly, Inc.*, 237 NLRB No. 48 (1978). Conceding that the employer was "the victim of an orchestrated encounter," and may have been unaware of his right to require an election, a federal court upheld the oral recognition. *NLRB v. Brown & Connolly*, 593 F.2d 1373 (1st Cir. 1979).

If the union demand comes from an employee professing to act as a spokesman for his co-workers, company officials should refuse to deal with the employee as a spokesman for the group. The official should indicate that he will not deal with the employee as a *spokesman* for other groups, but will deal with his own complaints and will discuss that employee's situation individually and privately.

The statements of a union representative regarding the demand for recognition should be reduced to memorandum form for future reference.

A frequently used gimmick is for the union representative to offer to prove the majority status by comparing the signatures on the authorization cards with official employee signatures in the company's possession. Often, in an attempt to appear fair and impartial and to lend a degree of plausibility to the union's request, the union may suggest that some independent third party compare the signatures and "certify" the union as a majority representative. Under no circumstances should such an offer be accepted. Acceptance binds the employer to recognition of the union once the signatures have been certified as valid by the independent third party. This rule applies even if the unknowing employer did not understand the significance of the procedure when it was agreed to. But the union is *not bound* by such an offer. If the independent third party concludes that the union does not have a majority of employees signed, it is free to obtain the requisite cards and to make a subsequent demand or file a petition for an election with the NLRB.

Under no circumstances should the employer undertake to question employees as to whether or not they have signed union cards. Although it is possible under certain circumstances to conduct such a poll, such polling is generally held to be unlawful. Polls should be undertaken only under the strictest legal supervision. If the employer polls its employees and finds that the union does in fact represent a majority, it may be tantamount to *de facto* recognition of the union, and it will be difficult for the employer to deny independent knowledge of the union's majority.

The denial of recognition should be prompt and unconditional. The employer should also be certain that the demand is for recognition within a unit which is appropriate. If the unit in which a recognition is sought is not appropriate, this, by itself, would justify denial of recognition.

Employers are justified in rejecting a recognition demand based on authorization cards. As noted above, these cards have been proven to be notoriously unreliable as indicators of employee sentiment.

Once it is decided to reject the demand for recognition, the union should be so advised. The employer should express doubt that the union represents a majority of the employees. The union's offer to prove its majority status by means of an independent third-party check of the signatures should be specifically rejected, on the grounds that such a signature check would not reveal whether any misrepresentations were made by union organizers regarding the purpose of the card. The rejection should also include a suggestion that the union file a petition with the NLRB and that its claim of majority status should be tested in a secret-ballot election.

It is important to display a copy of the rejection letter to unit employees, usually on plant bulletin boards. Don't let the union obtain the advantage of initial reporting of developments in its organizing campaign. The employer should promptly and candidly report all material events, including the fact that the union's claim of majority status has been denied. Such communication serves several purposes. It publicly contests the union's claim and creates a doubt in the employee's mind as to whether the union actually does represent a majority. It avoids giving the union an opportunity to tell employees that the employer's silence in the face of the demand is tacit admission that the union does in fact represent a majority. It can also prevent a "bandwagon" effect of other employees signing cards on behalf of the union.

Employers nervous about acknowledging the union's campaign by means of such a letter can easily switch the emphasis from writing to the union to writing to the employees, explaining why the company has declined to recognize the union and why a mechanical count of the cards would not be a fair way of testing the union's true standing. The employees will readily understand the reason for the denial, will not misconstrue the employer's silence as a sign of weakness, and will recognize and understand that the employer is ready to stand up to the union, to challenge its claim, and to meet the union head on at a secret-ballot election requested by the employer.

Choosing the Type of Election

Once the union has invoked NLRB jurisdiction by filing a petition for an election, the employer can either consent to an election or request that a hearing be held and that an election be directed by the regional director.

A consent election involves agreeing with the union as to the appropriate unit for the election, the election date and time, and the job classification included within the voting unit. A directed election means that the regional director will conduct a hearing, determine the issues, and direct an election.

Consent Agreement

The employer can choose from two types of consent agreement. In the first, a *consent election* agreement, the regional director is granted authority to rule on all matters involving the election, including its conduct, the mechanics of balloting, the campaigning of the parties, etc.

The second type of consent agreement is a *stipulation*. Here, the parties agree that the NLRB in Washington, as opposed to the regional director, shall have the final authority to rule on all questions involving the election.

The choice between the two can involve the difference between victory or defeat for the employer. Therefore, the choice should be evaluated thoroughly by the employer and its counsel. If the employer has confidence in the director of the region where the petition is pending, and if it is possible with a fair degree of assurance to predict the general trend of regional rulings in election cases, it may be advantageous to sign a consent agreement. On the other hand, the stipulation gives the employer the opportunity to seek review of an adverse regional director's report and recommendation. The stipulated consent agreement also usually means a greater lapse of time between the election and the outcome of any disputed issues.

Most company lawyers prefer the stipulated agreement because of the opportunity afforded to appeal, a valued right in almost every instance. In view of the Board's recent shifts in opinion (they are now willing to monitor misrepresentations), there may be other shifts in Board opinion regarding questions of free speech during union campaigns. A regional director will be limited to making determinations based on *existing* NLRB rulings. Thus, if a more liberal trend toward free speech in elections is anticipated, it is probably wiser for the employer not to waive its right to appeal, but to avail itself of any possible shift in Board opinion.

It should be noted that neither the consent election agreement nor the stipulated consent necessarily resolves all questions concerning the eligibility of voters. Ordinarily, all employees who are to vote will be included in the employer's list; if a desirable list has been accepted by the union during the negotiations for a consent agreement, it would be wise for the employer to stipulate to the eligibility of all voters contained in the list. This is called a Norris Thermador agreement; it is binding on the parties and will eliminate most litigation concerning eligibility and related matters. The employer should be aware that without a Norris Thermador agreement, the union is not bound by the list (neither is the employer), and the parties are free to challenge votes, regardless of prior understandings concerning the eligibility of voters. The Norris Thermador agreement essentially eliminates the opportunity for the parties to renege on previous understandings concerning eligibility.

However, even the Norris Thermador agreement cannot resolve an issue of eligibility where the issue is determined to be in contravention of the Act or is repugnant to established Board policy. For example, a union could still challenge a professional employee or a supervisor even though he or she was included on the Norris Thermador list. Such a challenge is allowable because the inclusion would contravene policies underlying the Act. On the other hand, if the union and company agree to omit or include an employee from the list on the basis of his community of interest with other employees (or lack of it), a challenge in contravention of the agreement will not be upheld because the applicability of a statutory exclusion is not involved. *Pilgrim Foods., Inc.*, 234 NLRB No. 23 (1978).

Probably the most important consideration involved in determining whether or not to consent to an election, as opposed to requesting a hearing, is the factor of *time*. In almost all cases, the passage of time works in favor of the employer. It is recognized by virtually all lawyers in the field, and by the unions themselves, that the longer the time between the filing of the petition and the election, the more difficult it is for the union to maintain its suasion among the bargaining unit, and the more difficult it is for them to produce a victory on election day. This is one of the prime considerations behind labor's recent attempts to amend the National Labor Relations Act to obtain more speedy elections.

The employer should not agree to a consent election unless all or most of the factors are in the employer's favor. If the employer is completely satisfied with the appropriate unit, the date on which the election is to be held, and the employees eligible to vote, then a consent election may be entered into. But in all cases, the employer should strive for the maximum amount of time within which to campaign. Some employers want to shorten the election campaign period on the theory that the union will have less time to campaign among the employees. It assumes that the union can campaign better than the employer, and that the shorter the period of campaigning, the better it is for the employer; this is a fallacy. This philosophy is self-defeating. It is almost always best to obtain the latest possible date. In most cases, the union will have been organizing for a number of weeks and will have established a high degree of penetration. During this time, the employer has probably been unaware of the organizing activity and has done little or nothing to counteract the weeks of undercover work performed by the union. Moreover, the employer may underestimate the union's strength and may be unnecessarily overconfident. Few employers know the exact degree of penetration accomplished by the union, and few are such excellent campaigners that they can safely agree to a quick election. Of course, there are always exceptions to general rules, but it is rare that the employer will gain from a quick election.

Under Board rules, the earliest an election can take place is ten days from the date that the agreement is signed. This is so because under a Supreme Court ruling (in the *Excelsior* case) the union must have in their possession for ten full days the names and addresses of all employees scheduled to vote in the election. Neither the union nor the employer can waive this requirement.

The employer should not feel bashful at requesting the maximum amount of time permitted. The Board agent involved in handling the case will ordinarily be cooperative in establishing the employer's preferred date, since he is usually anxious to avoid the added time and expense of conducting a hearing. The employer, at this stage, has great leverage with both the union and the Board, and it is usually possible to obtain the time needed to campaign. The Board can be told point blank that you wish this additional time; no excuse or justification has to be asserted in support of your chosen election date.

The employer ordinarily can also have its choice as to the exact day of the week for the election. In most cases, the employer will want a full turnout on election day, because the union will see to it that all *its* supporters are present in the plant on election day. In contrast, those who are absent from the factory or office on election day are those who are either undecided or who have no particular interest in voting. In effect, those who do not vote leave the choice up to the union supporters. If enough such voters remain away from the polls, the election will be controlled by union supporters, and the union will win.

Accordingly, the employer should insist on scheduling the election on a payday. Mondays should be avoided, if possible, to avoid giving the union an opportunity to visit employees in their homes or to reach them by phone over the weekend. Moreover, the time of day during which the polls are open for balloting should be carefully controlled by the employer to make sure that its final speech, which must be given at least twenty-four hours prior to the balloting, can be conducted on the day before the election. A weekend should not intervene between the employer's last appeal and the balloting.

An additional consideration is the time of day in which the election is to be held. If the election hours are set at starting time on any particular day, the employer will find that he has in effect foreclosed himself from speaking to his employees on the full day prior to the election. Therefore, care must be taken in setting the actual election hours. Night-shift hours must also be taken into consideration so the employer's "twenty-four-hour speech" can be directed to the night-shift employees without the lapse of a day between the speech and the balloting.

Another question is whether to have bilingual election notices where there are a substantial number of non-English-speaking employees. The different languages spoken in the plant must be ascertained, and where advantageous to the employer, a request for a multilingual ballot should be made. This is important, since it is usually incumbent upon the employer to make certain that employees are absolutely aware of what they are voting for and that they are able to read the ballot. If no such request is made, the union may have grounds for setting aside the election.

The count of the number of non-English-speaking employees will also be helpful in another area once the campaign gets under way. It may be important for the employer to prepare the campaign materials in several languages so that its communications may be readily understood by all. In this connection, a survey may be made of the employees' wishes. The employer should not assume that any particular individual would desire his or her communications in the mother tongue. The choice should be left up to the employee so that no resentment is created.

Directed Election

Unless all these factors fall into place, the employer should not consent, but rather should request a directed election. In most cases, this will give the employer a longer period of time to campaign. It is especially important to follow a directed election route when a greater-than-normal time is needed to combat the union's organizational efforts. This route would involve raising various issues, such as the appropriate unit and the eligibility of voters. The Board will set a hearing date, take testimony from both the union and the employer as to the issues, and, after an appropriate time for briefs to be filed, issue a decision and direction of election. Approximately 25 days after the directed election, the election will take place.

The adroit employer, together with legal counsel, can usually raise a sufficient number of issues to provide the basis for a hearing. In exceptional cases, a hearing can be obtained by the employer even where there are no issues. However, the employer then may gain more time via the consent route than a "no issue" hearing.

An exploration of Board rulings on appropriate units and voting eligibility is best left to the expertise of counsel and is outside the scope of this work. However, for the purpose of issue-raising during representation elections, a part of the employer's basic strategy will be to ferret out issues that are inherent in the election and raise them during Board hearings. Bargaining unit issues often involve employees located off the premises of the main unit, employees in "grey collar" categories, supervisors, independent contractors, driver-salesmen, owner-operators, persons related to the corporate officers, semi-retired employees, seasonal employees, casual employees, part-time employees, employees on layoffs, dual-function employees, technical employees, confidential employees, managerial employees, guards, professionals, craft and/or departmental units, multilocation units, and the unit placement and community of interest of a host of other types of persons employed by the employer—even illegal aliens.

The decisions involving a consent versus a directed election are *critical*. In evaluating these choices, the employer must compile accurate information on the depth and degree of the union's campaign, its popularity among the employees, the attitudes of the employees who have not yet signed cards, its likelihood of success, and a number of other factors. This reconnaissance must be conducted by the employer in a legal fashion without polls, interrogation of employees, or other violations of the Act.

Suppose on the day that a hearing is scheduled before the NLRB, several employees are subpoenaed by the union or the NLRB in order to testify at the hearing. You too, have your own employee witnesses. Is there any obligation to pay the employees called by the union for the time lost while attending the hearing? No. More pertinently, may an employer reimburse its own witnesses for wages lost while attending the hearing while failing to pay union witnesses? The Board has held that with regard to reimbursement of witnesses' wages, an employer is not obliged to finance litigation against himself and the failure to pay wages to employees testifying against the employer is not *per se* discriminatory. If the employer decides to compensate its witnesses, and the union does not, the employer is not held liable for the difference in treatment created by the union. However, the employer may not discriminate against employees who do not testify in its behalf with respect to conditions of employment, other than reimbursement for attendance at hearings, such as denial of a perfect attendance award where the denial is based upon absence due to Board hearings. *General Electric Company*, 230 NLRB 683 (1977).

Employer Action After an Election Date is Scheduled

Once an election date has been scheduled, the employer's first step should be to advise employees of the date, time, and place of the election. This is an important step, for employees should be conditioned to look to the employer, rather·than to the union, as the source of prompt, factual data.

Notices to employees that an election has been scheduled should be posted on the bulletin boards before employees clock out. The notice should stress the employer's efforts at agreeing to a time, date, and place. Employees should be told that the election will be held on the employer's premises, and reassured that the vote will be secret. They should be advised at the outset of the secrecy of the ballot since many of them will feel intimidated by pro-union campaigners and may feel that somehow the union will find out how they voted. Moreover, if some employees have signed union authorization cards, they may feel somewhat committed to voting for the union. The initial and subsequent notice should tell employees that having signed an authorization card for the union does not mean an obligation to vote for it in the election.

The employees should also be told that, in the near future, *the company* will provide additional information concerning the election, and that it will frequently be speaking and writing to the employees before election day on why union representation is not in the best interests of either the employees or the employer.

How Unions May Obtain Bargaining Rights Without an Election

Card-Based Bargaining Orders

The duty of an employer to recognize and bargain with a union does not always depend on the union's winning an election. The duty to bargain may be established independently of the NLRB election procedures.

The United States Supreme Court, in a decision of extreme importance to all employers, adopted the authorization-card approach to establishing a bargaining obligation. The now-famous *Gissel* case held that a bargaining obligation may be created without an election. The key is the *commission of serious, unfair labor practices* that interfere with the election process and tend to preclude a fair election. The NLRB—an agency that is not the employer's best friend—may exercise its discretion in determining whether the impact of the unfair labor practices is serious. The Supreme Court command is for the Board to determine the extensiveness of the employer's unfair labor practices in terms of their effect on election conditions and the likelihood of their recurrence.

Although authorization cards are often accompanied by misrepresentations and coercion and are often signed by employees without conviction and under pressure from their peers, the Court found authorization cards a reliable indicator of employee sentiment. While critical of the reliability of these cards in the normal context, the Court held that when the employer has impeded the election process by committing serious unfair labor practices the cards may be relied on as the only remaining way of assuring a fair employee choice.

Unless the employer has acquired independent knowledge that the union has a majority (by means of inspecting the cards, verifying their signatures, or other means), it *may decline* the union's demand for recognition based on cards signed by a majority of the employees and insist on an election. An employer may request that the union file for an election or file a petition itself. However, if the employer commits independent and substantial unfair labor practices disruptive of election conditions, the Board may, instead of an election, issue a bargaining order as a remedy for the various violations. The unfair labor practices outlined in Chapter 3 may serve as a basis for a card-based bargaining order.

Under normal circumstances, the NLRB will not consider employer conduct occurring before the date the petition is filed with the Regional Director (not the date the petition is received by the employer) as a basis upon which to set aside an election. In order for the Board to nullify an election and to schedule a rerun, the conduct or statements found to have been unlawful must occur between the date the petition is filed and the date of the election. This rule has been misinterpreted by many to mean that an employer is free to commit unfair labor practices prior to the petition being filed without having to suffer any of the normal consequences of unfair labor practice violations. This concept is completely in error. The Board's normal remedies, reinstatement, back pay, notice posting, etc., do apply to pre-petition violations. Most importantly, the Board may find when it examines an employer's pre-petition conduct that the unfair labor practices committed before the petition was filed add "meaning and dimension" to related post-petition conduct occurring before the election. Thus, an employer's post-petition statements and conduct may be found to be unlawful based upon unfair labor practices committed *prior* to the petition being filed. A single violation occurring during the pre-election period may be viewed as an *extension* of an employer's consistent pattern of anti-union conduct! Moreover, the Board may find that statements made prior to a petition being filed can reasonably be expected to be repeated and discussed by employees during the election campaign. *Dresser Industries*, 242 NLRB No. 14 (1979). The conclusion to be drawn by the successful campaigner is that the careful avoidance of unfair labor practices should be fostered *at any time* during the attempt by a union to organize the employer's enterprise.

Employers should be aware of one extremely important aspect of this rule lest they be lulled into a false sense of security: When a union that has a card majority does *not* make a bargaining demand, it may still obtain a card-based bargaining order. The absence of a demand by the union throughout the entire election process does not insulate the employer from a subsequent finding that the union did in fact have a majority (but made no demand) and that the commission of serious unfair labor practices warrants the issuance of a card-based bargaining order.

When an election has been held, however, it will be deemed valid in the absence of meritorious objections to the election. Thus, if the five-working-day period following the election elapses without the union having filed objections, or if objections are filed and they are dismissed, there is no way (under present law) that the union can obtain a card-based bargaining order. Moreover, the Board has never issued a bargaining order unless a majority of cards were signed. Appendix 1 lists types of unfair labor practices found serious enough to justify a bargaining order, as well as those not requiring an order.

Independent Knowledge of the Union's Majority Status

An employer that has declined to recognize a union on the basis of its asserted card majority is not required to bargain without an election but this is true only if the employer does not agree to some other means of establishing a majority. If the employer agrees to verify the cards personally, or agrees to a card check by an independent third party, it cannot reject the finding that the union does in fact have a majority of the cards; the employer is bound by its choice. It cannot request an election and can be ordered by the NLRB to bargain with the union on the basis of the alternative system used. The bargaining obligation may also be established if the employer engages in a pattern of interrogating or polling employees to verify majority support. If the results reveal a union majority, the company cannot disavow the results.

An employer faced with a demand for card-based recognition has a number of general defenses available. *Lack of majority status* is always a defense to a bargaining obligation. The *nature of the cards* may be contested at a Board hearing on the basis of possible misrepresentations, coercion, and related interference in the signing of the cards, the nature of the card itself, i.e., whether the wording on it is ambiguous or clear, or serious supervisory participation in the union's acquisition of the cards. The numerous grounds upon which the Board has invalidated authorization cards and applicable case citations appear in Appendix 2.

Chapter 5

Critical Early Reactions

Once union activity has been detected, the employer must take a number of strategic steps. This chapter is concerned with the employer's actions prior to and immediately after a petition is filed.

Discouraging Card Signing

The first issue confronting the employer is the decision to take a position with respect to employee card-signing activity. If the union's campaign is an ineffective one, or if there is no real interest on the part of the employees in the union's solicitation efforts, there may be no reason for initiating any activity in this area. However, if it is known that the union is passing out authorization cards, and if it is suspected that some employees are signing them, the employer's first reaction should be to explain to the employees the effects of authorization cards. It should then take active steps to discourage card-signing activity.

Typical signs that an anticard campaign should be undertaken are meetings called by the union at local establishments, distribution of handbills and leaflets, the presence of pro-union talk among employees, and similar activities.

Many employers balk at the prospect of launching such a communications program at the onset of union card solicitation for fear that the program might backfire and actually foster additional card signing. Other employers are also reluctant to admit that the union is soliciting at their plant or office; they hope to avoid "panic," or they hope the union will simply disappear without the issue ever having to be faced. These tendencies should be resisted. Because of the great likelihood of employees' misunderstanding the nature of the cards and the possibility of outright fraud in the cards' solicitation, it is imperative to advise employees at the outset about the nature of the cards and ask them not to sign them because a union is not needed in the plant or office.

If this initial employer campaign is successful, the union may never obtain the 30 percent needed to file a petition with the NLRB for an election. Since many unions adopt a policy of not filing a petition for an election until at least 50 percent of the employees have signed authorization cards, a union with only 40 percent may decide not to file. Most significantly, though, with the advent of "card-based bargaining orders" it is important for the employer to prevent the union from obtaining a majority of signed cards in the appropriate unit. The NLRB has never issued a card-based bargaining order where the union has obtained less than a simple majority of the signed cards.

In most cases, the employees have not been made aware of the employer's position on unions or on card signing. Some union literature leads employees to believe that the employer at least would not be opposed to unionization. Some employees are not aware that the employer vigorously opposes the entry of a union into the plant or office.

Therefore, the employer must react quickly to a card-signing campaign. It must frankly and unequivocally state its opposition to a union and ask the employees to come forth with any questions they may have in connection with the signing of the cards. A timely explanation of the meaning of the authorization cards may be enough to cause the union organizer to turn elsewhere for more fertile ground.

The employer should advise its employees to be wary of misrepresentations, and it must counter any inaccurate statements made by the union. At the very least, this may persuade an employee to hear the employer's side of the story before signing the card.

Lawful Communications

An effective strategy is to obtain a copy of the card being passed out, reproduce it, and underline, circle, or otherwise emphasize the various portions of the card that may contain pitfalls for the employee. A handout can be distributed on the day card-signing commences, advising employees not to "sign a blank check," to avoid being bothered by phone calls and home visits, to avoid representation by strangers, and to avoid union dues, charges, strikes, and other disadvantages of unionization. When they see it graphically depicted in this manner, many employees will understand that signing a union card is a serious matter.

The form of communication must be determined according to the facts and circumstances of each case. Many employers call a plant- or office-wide meeting to announce opposition to the union and urge employees not to sign. Others transmit the same message through supervisors or a written communication. No matter what the form of communication, employees should be told:

(1) Signing can commit them to union membership without their knowing the full ramifications of such membership.

(2) Signing can commit them to dues, initiation fees, and assessments.

(3) Cards can be used as a basis for calling a recognition strike.

(4) Cards are *legal documents* that authorize the union to represent the employee for collective bargaining purposes, and they are often accompanied by false statements and other misrepresentations.

The communication should end with an affirmative statement about the company, a brief, positive statement of opposition, and conclude by urging the employees not to sign. Employees should not be commanded or directed not to sign, but it is permissible for the employer to *suggest* or strongly *advise* employees not to participate in this form of union activity.

The Board has approved some surprisingly strong employer statements. For example, one employer said the employee should not swallow exaggerated union claims or lies. It implored the employee not to listen to the union if he did not care to. Especially, said the employer, "Don't sign any cards; they can be fatal to a business." Another employer urged employees to avoid unnecessary turmoil by not signing. These communications were approved by the Board on the ground that in the context in which they were uttered they contained no promise of benefits or threat of harm.

In another case, the employer admonished employees in the following manner:

> Stay away from union meetings. They always put pressure on you. One of your friends might persuade you to sign a [union authorization] card or do something else you don't want to do. You don't have to go, so just stay away.

The Board found that there was no implied threat of retaliation in that statement.

In other cases, paycheck "stuffers" were distributed outlining the company's opposition to the union, advising them not to join, expressing the seriousness of unionization to the employee and his family, and stating that if the union were voted in it would work not to their benefit but to their serious harm. Cases illustrating the Board's

point of view on such communications are: *Airporter Inn Hotel*, 215
NLRB 824 (1974) and *North American Philips Corp.*, 217 NLRB 435
(1975).

Cards' Lack of Confidentiality

Another important concept that may also be communicated is the idea
that union cards are not necessarily kept confidential by the union. Indeed, they are often executed *for presentation* to the employer. Once
employees are informed that the cards may not be kept confidential, a
number may refuse to sign or become extremely reluctant to do so.

Often, the union offers to display them to the employer to support
a demand for majority recognition. A union seeking a card-based bargaining order must prove its majority status by producing the employees who signed cards as witnesses at an NLRB hearing. In such cases,
the nature, circumstances, and background of the card-signing, including any possible misrepresentations that may have been made by
the union at the time of signing, may be the subject of cross-
examination by the employer's attorney.

The exact manner in which the possible lack of confidentiality is
communicated should be carefully explored with counsel before any
statement is made. The Board has held (with some federal courts dis-
agreeing) that such statements violate Section 8(a)(1) of the Act in
that their only purpose is to create the impression that the employer
is interested in knowing who has signed cards solely for the purpose
of reprisal. Accordingly, in most cases, the employer should not make
the point-blank statement that the cards will not be kept confidential.
The safest course would be for the employer, with counsel's guidance,
to tell its employees about the significance of signing union authorization cards and the various ways the union could disclose the cards to
achieve recognition.

Here is how *not* to communicate to employees on the issue of
confidentiality:

> "Don't be fooled into signing misleading union cards. The Team-
> sters claim that these cards are secret. This is not the truth. In many
> instances, the signed card is disclosed to the company by the union,
> the NLRB, or both of them. Be careful about what you sign—don't
> sign anything unless you know what you're signing and what it
> might mean to you, your family, or your fellow employees."

While some federal courts disagree, the Board found that the sen-

tence cautioning employees to be careful about what they sign was coercive since it clearly suggested the possibility that harm will come to
employees as a result of disclosure to the employer of the names of
employees who sign union authorization cards. The Board found such
a statement to be an implicit threat to engage in reprisals against employees who sign cards. *Fisher Cheese Co.*, 238 NLRB No. 91 (1978).

Withdrawing Authorization Cards

It tends to demoralize union supporters in the plant when employees
seek revocation of previously executed authorization cards. Cards revoked prior to a demand for recognition or before the union files a
petition do not count toward the union's majority status if a refusal-
to-bargain charge is filed based upon a card-based bargaining order.
Thus, employer information on the *procedure for revocation* can have a
significant impact on the potential success of the employer. Imparting
accurate information is also essential. For example, if employees seek
to revoke their cards by notifying the NLRB, rather than the union,
the revocation is ineffective—revocation is invalid unless the union is
notified.

   If an employee asks management how to recover a card he has already signed, management may respond by suggesting that the employee ask the person who solicited his signature to return the card. A
letter to the union requesting the return of the card may also be suggested and management can supply the name and address of the
union. In any case, the employee should be advised that he is not
bound by having signed a card, and that the best way to negate his signature is to vote against the union if an election is eventually scheduled.

   The employer should note, though, that under NLRB rules it may
not encourage or solicit employees to revoke their authorization
cards. The distinction between "soliciting" employees to revoke cards
that they have signed and explaining their legal rights to them is a
complicated one.

   The Board allows an employer to disseminate unsolicited "advice"
to employees with regard to the mechanics of withdrawing their authorization cards, but management should steer clear of any attempt
to find out whether employees avail themselves of this advice. The
Board has also held that an employee may revoke a card by telling the
co-employee who solicited the signature that she "really did not want
to sign the authorization card" and that it should be destroyed. *Production Plating Co.*, 233 NLRB No. 25 (1977).

As long as an employee initiates a request for assistance to withdraw an authorization card, the Board will allow an employer to render limited assistance, such as the preparation of withdrawal letters or help in phrasing the petition. *See, Poly Ultra Plastices, Inc.*, 231 NLRB 787 (1977). If lawful assistance is given, the employee should not be asked to send the employer copies of letters of revocation. This could be a fatal error. Moreover, such employer communications should be made, if possible, by letter to all members of the unit, rather than by pursuing individuals. A sample of a letter which may be sent to employees in response to legitimate employee inquiries regarding withdrawals is:

> Dear Employee,
> It has come to my attention that certain employees would like to know if they can withdraw a pledge card they have already signed.
> Our attorneys have informed us that you can withdraw any card you may have signed by sending a letter to the union telling it that you are resigning your membership. Your resignation would then become effective immediately. This is a voluntary matter and the Company takes no position on your right to withdraw. If you have changed your mind and want to leave the union, you have every right in this democratic society of ours to withdraw your card right now.
> The best way is for you to vote NO in the election to keep our plant going without the problems that can be brought by outsiders coming in.
>
> _____

A shorter form of the same type of communication may be used:

> The regulations of the National Labor Relations Board forbid the Company from giving assistance to employees in getting signed pledge cards back from the union.
> However, if you want your card withdrawn, you should write a letter directly to Local _____, at _____ _____, requesting that it be returned. (Keep a copy of your letter for your own records.)
>
> _____

Management has also successfully assisted employees in their efforts to withdraw by leaving copies of resignation letters available in rest areas, cafeterias, and other places around the plant or office so that employees who desire to withdraw their authorization cards may avail themselves of the convenience of pre-typed letters with envelopes pre-addressed to the union attached.

A sample withdrawal letter is:

> Gentlemen:
>   I am an employee of (name of employer) (address)
>   I do not desire to have your Union represent me and effective
> immediately withdraw any authorization I may have signed.
>   Yours truly,
>   _____

Management should not furnish stamps, mail letters for the employees, identify who chooses to sign cards, or ask employees to sign letters of withdrawal. As long as the employer furnishes only minimal assistance to employees who have independently decided to withdraw their support and approach the employer for help, the Board will tend to find that there has been no intrusion upon the rights of employees. See *Payless Drug Store*, 210 **NLRB** 134 (1974).

Alerting Supervisory Personnel

Supervisors can play an important role in the employer's campaign against the union. (See Chapter 9 for a thorough discussion of supervisors, their role, and how to select and train them to be a campaign force.) Call a meeting of supervisors at the first sign or rumor of union activity. The purpose of the meeting is to obtain information on what each supervisor knows about the extent of union activity. Supervisors often have had some inkling that union activity has been going on but have not bothered to inform management of it. The supervisors' information, after evaluation by management, can be helpful in determining whether immediate action is necessary. If union activity is scant, the employer's reaction may be to await further developments before taking any steps. On the other hand, if the campaign is serious, a speech to employees pointing out the disadvantages of having a union may be necessary.

Supervisors can be especially helpful in counteracting the union's card-signing campaign. During the initial stages, management should thoroughly inform them about the nature of these cards, what they may or may not say to employees about the cards, and how to discuss card-signing with the employees. They should be told that they can advise employees not to sign cards: If asked by an employee whether or not to sign a card, they may—and should—urge the employee not to sign. Supervisors should also know how to answer employees who desire to rescind already signed cards.

On the whole, supervisors should be fully informed about the employer's benefits, practices, and policies. They should be acquainted with the "do's" and "don'ts" of campaigning. Union leaflets should be reviewed with the supervisors: The fallacies of union statements should be pointed out, and the company's rebuttal to such statements should be explained so that they can communicate these concepts to employees at appropriate points in the ensuing campaign.

Gathering Information About the Union

Knowledge of the enemy is indispensible in any organizing campaign. The union may have been investigating the company at great depth to determine its policies, practices, financial standing, and other information useful for the campaign. The employer is often at an informational disadvantage when organizational activity first surfaces. Therefore, the employer should immediately take steps to determine the official name of the organizing union, including any subdivisions under which it operates and the name of any parent organization or district council of unions. Check the officers' background, including the possibility of convictions, arrests, and indictments for state and federal crimes and violations of the federal labor laws.

Financial Status

The employer should gather as much data as possible about the union's finances—assets, organizational expenses, officer's salaries, strike funds, amounts collected in fines and assessments, the amount of dues charged, initiation fees, and other relevant information. This may be obtained from the Disclosure Bureau, United States Department of Labor, Labor Management Services Administration, 200 Constitution Ave., N.W., Washington, D.C. 20216. The information should be acquired immediately, since there is often a lag of two to five weeks between the request and the delivery.

Bylaws and Constitution

The union's bylaws and constitution should also be obtained from the United States Department of Labor. These documents will invariably provide helpful information about union policies that can be used by the employer during the initial stages of the campaign. A close examination of the bylaws and constitution by a labor lawyer will often reveal union methods of increasing dues, special assessments, procedures by which charges are filed against union members, and the mechanics of union trials, including whether or not the right to counsel is afforded to the employee. A variety of other useful information about the union, its structure, and the legal obligation of its members is revealed by these public documents. One international constitution, for example, authorizes the doubling of dues during the four months preceding negotiations for a renewal contract. Other constitutions contain provisions on union philosophy regarding overtime and merit or incentive systems. The astute employer will be able to isolate the provisions that will have the most antiunion impact on employees and utilize this information to the maximum advantage. Copies of the relevant sections of the constitution and bylaws can be enlarged and displayed on bulletin boards or used as attachments to letters and other campaign material. The salaries of the international presidents and of local officials may often be instructive, along with expense accounts and other union expenditures.

History of Strikes

The union's strike history should be ascertained. In this connection, the employer is not limited to the strikes conducted by the particular union, but may refer to strikes conducted by the parent in any part of the country. Strike compilations are available through the Bureau of National Affairs and other sources at modest expense.

Where to Obtain Information

Clipping Bureaus and Libraries. Clipping bureaus are available in major cities and are an extremely helpful source of information. Local libraries will also provide information, in their magazine and newspaper sections, concerning a particular union, past strikes, violence, criminal activities and accusations, Communist affiliations, and other relevant information.

Union Publications. If possible, obtain back copies of the union's own international newspaper or magazine so that the union's activities can be minutely inspected for information helpful to the employer. These publications will often contain stories of lengthy strikes, negotiation of wage freezes or *reductions*, plant closings and removals, letters to the editor criticizing incumbent union officials, and other relevant data.

Industry Associations. Many large industries have employer associations that provide the employer with a great deal of information about the particular union. Some organizations offer actual campaign material, cartoons, etc. The United States Chamber of Commerce, the National Association of Manufacturers, and similar nationwide or regional organizations can provide an immense amount of information about the organizing union.

U.S. Department of Labor, Bureau of Labor Statistics. Both federal and state departments of labor often compile useful information on wage levels, strikes, wage settlements, negotiations, and other helpful information. A piece of information gleaned from such sources can often be made into a major issue in any campaign.

The NLRB. The NLRB itself can provide helpful information to employers. Its summary of election results is public information; it is categorized by name of the union, the company involved and its location, the industry, and the results of elections conducted by the NLRB. From these charts, the employer can find out what companies the union has been organizing and call them to obtain information about the union—its background, campaign techniques, settlements, copies of contracts, etc. Discussions with companies that have opposed the particular organizing union will provide a great deal of insight into how to combat the union effectively.

Conventions. Newspaper and magazine reports concerning union conventions often provide excellent information on internal difficulties, increases in dues, and similar items. Statements made by union officials at such conventions, expressing philosophies on such issues as layoffs, overtime, plant removals, and other issues, can often be used by the employer in support of its position during the campaign.

Pension and Welfare Funds. Jointly trusteed union-management benefit plans must be filed on Forms D-1 and D-2 with the Bureau of Labor Management Services in Washington. The employer should request copies of all plans filed by funds that are administered by the organizing union. The employee will then have helpful information concerning the exact nature of the benefits offered by the union under its welfare and pension plans or any other plan that it jointly trustees. In a number of cases, the employer will be surprised to find that its own health coverage plans exceed those offered by the union, or that its pension plan is more liberal than the union's. This information can be used to counteract union propaganda that joining the union will bring improved health and pension benefits. In many cases, the employer can show that becoming a member of the union's pension and welfare plans would actually amount to a *loss* of existing benefits.

Union Contracts. The local union's labor agreements, particularly with nearby or competing employers, may be obtained from those employers, possibly from the Bureau of National Affairs in Washington, and often from large industry associations such as the National Industry Conference Board. State departments of labor also carry copies of negotiated agreements, which are available to the public.

In summary, a wealth of information is available to the employer. Equipped with this information—strike authorization procedures, selection of shop stewards, election of union officers, levying of assessments, fines for not attending meetings, union officers' automobile and expense allowances, union disbursements for strike benefits, union income from receipt of fines and assessments—the employer will be well equipped to conduct a vigorous and affirmative campaign, will be able to avoid being put on the defensive, and will be in the position to impart a great deal of information to employees that will enable them to make the proper choice on election day.

Posting NLRB Notices

When a petition is filed, the Board immediately sends the company an announcement intended to alert workers as to their rights under the Act and to warn them about conduct that may impede a fair election. Since the examples the Board uses apply in major part to improper employer conduct, they imply that the NLRB is in favor of union organization and against the employer. Such an announcement should not be posted, notwithstanding the fact that the literature accompanying it implies that the posting is mandatory. In sharp contrast, the notice of the actual date, time, and place of the election sent to the employer must be posted within 72 hours of the election. Failure to post this will constitute valid grounds for setting aside an election.

The Union's Showing of Interest

A typical reaction of most employers is to ask counsel to question the validity of the union's 30 percent showing of interest. In most cases, this tendency should be resisted. Information that the employer attempts to garner concerning the legitimacy of the union's showing of interest often leads to unlawful questioning and interrogation, which violates the Act. More important, even if the company gathers information that taints the union's showing of interest (next to impossible under Board rules), the union may simply continue its organizing campaign and obtain new cards. The decision to question the union's showing of interest should be carefully reviewed with counsel.

The best approach for an employer is to recognize that the union is present and that it may be conducting a competent campaign. All efforts should be directed toward gathering information about the union, planning management's strategy and tactics, and utilizing the employer's free-speech rights to defeat the union.

The Appropriate Unit

As soon as organizing activity starts, the employer should analyze its work force to determine which groups or individuals are likely to be included in a voting unit. In many cases, the unit in which the election is held may determine the result of the election. The employer should strive to obtain the unit best suited to its own advantage and should line up its facts at the onset of organizational activity so that, if a hearing is held, the best possible case in favor of the employer's unit will be presented to the NLRB.

Smaller employers should note that under existing NLRB rules a limited amount of "stacking" the payroll is permitted. It comes as a surprise to many employers that it is possible to add employees to the payroll even after the union files a petition. Bona fide employees who are on the payroll as of the ending of the payroll period immediately preceding the agreement to a consent election or as of the ending of the payroll period immediately prior to the direction of an election are eligible to vote, provided that they are also on the payroll and working on the date of the election. Employees are "bona fide" if they have not been hired in order to "flood" or "pack" the voting unit. Examples of employees *not* considered to be bona fide are a company official's sister hired one day before the mass termination of union supporters, a warehouseman suddenly turned into a "salesman" during the preelection period, and a social security annuitant hired precipitously under circumstances indicating a scheme to flood the payroll with employees hired to vote against the union.

Careful planning by the employer and attention to the composition of the voting unit in the early stages may mean the difference between victory and defeat. The job duties and unit placement of all *potential* voters should be scrutinized carefully. Often, employees perform dual functions. By that, it is meant that they perform work both inside the proposed bargaining unit and outside of it. If such dual-function employees present the possibility of favorable votes for the employer, their inclusion should be considered. The Board will give substantial weight to the amount of time spent by the employee in performing voting unit work compared to the employee's total work time, and the mere fact that the employee spends less than 50 percent of his or her time performing voting unit work does not necessarily disqualify the employee as an eligible voter. The facts of each potential voter should be examined carefully and, where appropriate, the employee included on the eligibility list.

Likewise, careful attention should be paid to part-time employees. Where the opinion of the campaign manager and supervisors is that part-time employees are favorably disposed toward the employer, the regularity of their work history should be examined. The Board's rule varies according to industry.

However, non-full-time employees who, because of regularity of employment or otherwise, have a substantial community of interest with the unit full-time employees in wages, hours, and conditions of employment generally are regarded as regular part-time employees and are includable in the voting unit. For example, an employee who works every Saturday and does the same kind of work as a full-time employee in the voting unit will normally be included. Some of the factors to be considered are regularity of work, quantum of work, nature of work, and similarity of pay scale.

Of course, if the part-time employees generally do not favor the employer, their exclusion should be vigorously pursued. Even if such employees qualify under the Board's normal rules, it is often possible to agree with the union to exclude regular part-timers from the voting unit.

Another often-overlooked group is seasonal employees, or employees who have unstructured schedules. Where the employer retains one or more employees who have no established work schedule but are called in to perform jobs as the need arises, they may be eligible to vote even though they work infrequently. If such employees have a reasonable expectation of future employment, the Board may take an extremely broad view and allow them to vote in order to prevent them from being disenfranchised. Any employees in this category should be scrutinized carefully for their voting propensity. If favorable, the employer can press for their inclusion. Also, there is a measure of control which the employer may assert in these situations since it can restrict or enlarge assignments to particular individuals during the pre-election planning stages. Such assignments would tend to enhance or detract from their voting eligibility in accordance with the employer's ultimate goal.

In dealing with any fringe group or job classification outside the union's petitioned-for unit, the employer should be bold in seeking inclusions where favorable and exclusions where appropriate. In its haste to avoid delays in scheduling elections, the Board will often put informal pressure on the union to agree to the employer's conception of the unit. Thus, the employer may frequently "bargain" a unit almost wholly acceptable to it, maximizing its chances for a winning vote. Where possible, "Norris-Thermidor" agreements should be executed in such situations.

Norris-Thermidor Agreements

In the interest of the expeditious handling of representation cases, and in order to avoid hearings, the Board will honor concessions made by the parties on voter eligibility. Accordingly, the parties to a consent agreement may resolve between themselves any eligibility issue prior to the election, provided the agreement is in writing. Such a writing is called a "Norris-Thermidor" agreement, after the case in which the Board first announced its ruling. Under the ruling of that case, where the employer and the union enter into a written, signed agreement which expressly provides that issues of eligibility resolved in that agreement are final and binding upon the parties, the Board will consider such an agreement a final determination of the eligibility issues decided therein, *unless*, in part or in whole, the issue is decided contrary to the principles of the Act or in violation of established Board policy.

Care should be taken to avoid telling employees—even those not on the official eligibility list—that they are not eligible to vote. In one case, *Kansas City Bifocal Co*, 236 NLRB No. 219 (1978), a voter telephoned a manager's secretary and told her that he had been informed that he was eligible to vote. The secretary advised him that his name was not on the eligibility list and that he did not qualify to vote. The employee never appeared at the polls.

The NLRB determined that the issue of whether or not the employee was on sick leave and eligible to vote was an issue to be determined by the NLRB only if the voter had been challenged by one of the parties when he appeared at the polls. It was concluded that the employer had usurped the Board's authority to make such determinations and had interfered with the Board's orderly election process. One vote separated the parties, and the election was set aside.

Legal Advice

Employers who fail to engage a thoroughly competent attorney who specializes in labor law are virtually doomed to failure during a campaign. Almost every idea that occurs "naturally" to the employer constitutes an unfair labor practice.

General practitioners or local attorneys who work "in coordination" with labor lawyers may be highly respected, but they should not be relied on during a campaign. Changes in the state of the law occur frequently, and many decisions depend on extremely fine concepts that call for the judgment of a specialist. Every attempt should be made not to violate the National Labor Relations Act.

Every campaign that can be won can be won legally. A firm, aggressive campaign by the employer, availing itself of its broad free-speech rights and taking advantage of the letter and the spirit of decided NLRB cases and opinions, will result in a winning campaign effort.

No-Solicitation Rules

Employees who favor the union have the right to contact other employees *on company property* to discuss the advantages of joining a union and to solicit their support. Therefore, it is important that the employer develop a consistent framework of rules dealing with solicitation.

Solicitation involves distribution of written materials on the employer's property, and discussions with employees. Solicitation includes inducing co-employees to sign union authorization cards.

Employers often exceed permissible bounds in promulgating no-solicitation rules. A blanket prohibition of all solicitation and distribution on company property at all times is not permitted. A company may not forbid solicitation during *nonworking time*, even in work areas. However, solicitation may be forbidden in work areas and on company time (with lunch, coffee breaks, and clean-up time considered to be the employee's time even if the employer pays for it). Solicitation may not be prohibited at any time employees are officially not required to be working. However, solicitation cannot interfere with employees who *are* required to be working.

A no-solicitation prohibition should be clearly posted and made known to employees. A sample rule would be:

> Solicitation by an employee for any cause or organization is prohibited during his or her working time and during the working time of the employee being solicited. Distribution of literature on company property by employees is prohibited during their working time and at any time in working areas of the plant. Non-employees are not permitted to solicit or distribute literature anywhere on company property.

Should the employer receive reports from supervisors that the pro-union in-plant cadre is soliciting for the union or distributing literature during working time, the employer may post a notice warning against these practices, just as if a no-smoking rule were being violated. The notice could read:

> As you know, we are involved in a union organizing campaign. We hope that employees will not see fit to bring a third party into the plant, for reasons we have already stated. We will be talking about this from time to time, because we want to give employees the facts that will enable them to make a reasonable choice. In the meantime, as everyone can understand, working time is for working. We have long had a rule prohibiting solicitation of any kind during working time. This rule is on page ____ of our Employee Handbook; a copy is attached below. We want to call this rule to your attention again and remind you that violation of company rules will result in discharge.
>
> Some no-solicitation rules—including ours—cover the person engaging in the solicitation as well as the person being solicited. The reason behind such rules is that many employees feel threatened or pressured by union organizers and sign cards in order to "get the organizer off my back." Because the rule applies to both solicitor and solicitee, the latter can refrain from signing the card in a graceful manner, referring to the employer's rule prohibiting solicitation or distribution of literature or material during the working time of the employee who is doing the soliciting or being solicited.

It is obvious, then, that having a valid no-solicitation, no-distribution rule in the Employee Handbook enables the employer to invoke it when union activity begins, a most vital initial defense to an organizing drive. Additional sample rules appear in Appendix 3, Part A. (Legal counsel should be obtained if there has been no rule and the employer seeks to promulgate one only after the advent of union activity.)

The rule, and its application, may not discriminate against pro-union solicitation. If the employer permits solicitation during working time for charitable contributions, gifts for special occasions, pools, raffles, etc., the Board will remedy employer attempts to discipline for no-solicitation rule violations. The terms "working time" or "work time," not "working *hours*," should be used in drafting the no-solicitation rule, because "working hours" may be interpreted by employees as applying from nine to five, including break periods. Also, a generally worded rule to the effect that there can be no working-time solicitation without advance approval of management for any purpose except where allowable under federal law is not permissible. The term "working area" includes the lobby of a business office building, the space around a time clock located in a work area, and only those portions of a plant or office where work is actually performed. *See, The Times Publishing Co.*, 240 NLRB No. 157 (1979). Sample no-solicitation, no-distribution, and no-access rules appear in Appendix 3A.

If employees violate the rule they may be discharged or otherwise disciplined if the employer has witnesses to the solicitation. Over-zealous implementation of discipline pursuant to no-solicitation rules can be hazardous. In one case, an employee went a few steps from his work station and spent less than a minute to give an authorization card to a co-employee; no words were spoken, and the production of both employees was not curtailed. The Board ruled that the employee did not violate the no-solicitation rule that had been posted.

Disparate treatment of pro-union and anti-union employees should be avoided. For example, if an avowedly antiunion employee approaches a pro-union employee at his work place and loudly berates him for his union activities in clear view of supervisors, who do nothing but stand idly by declining to enforce the company rule, while, by contrast, the employer stands ready to discipline any pro-union activity by employees, this inaction may constitute a violation of the Act. The fact that the company takes no formal action against the antiunion employee, together with supervisors' silence during the altercation, would be viewed by the NLRB as creating the impression that the employer welcomed and encouraged employee efforts to defeat the union. In general, all discipline during a campaign should be discussed with counsel prior to implementation.

Of course, non-employees, may be barred from entering the employer's property at any time (except in the highly unlikely situation where there is absolutely no other way for the union to contact the employees). Implementation of the no-solitication rule is important because it will keep on-premises union activity at a minimum and will force non-employee organizers to make themselves known.

Care should be taken not to allow any group or individual to violate the rules. Even such groups as the United Fund, the Red Cross, or other community organizations should have the rule applied to them. If the no-solicitation rule is invoked only against union activities but not against these other groups or individuals, the entire no-solicitation effort may fail.

If it is company policy to permit solicitation for the United Fund, for U.S. Savings Bonds, or for other causes, you can continue to do so without imperiling your no-solicitation rule. As long as the activity is sponsored by the company, you can solicit employees during working time or any time you want to. It is better to have the solicitation done by employees than by outsiders, but in any event, conducting a company-sponsored activity will not invalidate the no-solicitation rule. Since the Board views company-sponsored exceptions with suspicion, any rule—as well as a careful analysis of how the rule will work in practice—should be reviewed with counsel prior to publication. Exceptions for solicitations by employees in case of death, illness, hardship, etc., have been upheld as long as the exceptions are not extensive, frequent, or pervasive. For example, in a case where union soliciting was causing interference with production, the Board allowed occasional instances of solicitations that did not result in any interference with production. The Board has shown some tolerance for collections that alleviate the misfortunes or bereavements of employees. *Uniflite, Inc.* 233 NLRB No. 159 (1977) (raffle and donations to family of a deceased worker were the only two exceptions); *Lutheran Hospital of Milwaukee*, 224 NLRB 176 (1976) (United Fund and Women's Auxiliary exceptions).

Distribution of Literature

Distribution of literature may be prohibited in order to keep the premises clean and/or to prevent interference with production. Employees have the right to pass out leaflets and other printed matter during nonworking time, but it is permissible to forbid distribution in work areas. Employees cannot be prevented from distributing literature during nonworking time in nonwork areas, such as employee parking lots and at plant gates, except under the most unusual circumstances.

Enforcing no-solicitation rules often involves difficult legal judgments. Employees often become involved in political causes involving unionism which are not necessarily related to an ongoing union campaign. Thus, where employees distribute on plant premises informational material declaring their union's views on right-to-work laws, federal minimum wages, or attempts by the AFL-CIO to reform the labor laws, such distribution is privileged under the law. Thus, in implementing the no-solicitation rule, an employer may not bar in-plant distribution of literature that is "political" in nature or not directly related to the employee's relationship with the employer.

A closely related problem is that of limiting mass speeches and demonstrations by pro-union sympathizers on the employees' free time in nonwork areas (usually in cafeterias, etc.). An employer may not lawfully require an employee to secure permission to engage in protected activities, but the employer may place *reasonable* limitation on union activities by adopting a rule (preferably before union activity commences) precluding speech making or demonstrating in a company cafeteria. Solicitation itself may not be prohibited, and there must be some alternative opportunity for employees to engage in speech-making functions, for example, a hallway or other nonwork area. *AMC-Air Conditioning Co.*, 232 NLRB 283 (1977); *Farah Mfg. Co.*, 202 NLRB 666 (1973).

Employers often ask, "If I promulgate a valid no-solicitation and no-distribution rule, do I violate the Act if my own supervisors distribute pro-company literature and talk to employees during working hours about the election?" It is generally acknowledged that when the employer himself engages in antiunion solicitation or distribution that, if engaged in by employees, would constitute a violation of the company rule, the enforcement by the employer of an otherwise valid no-solicitation or no-distribution rule against the employees is not an unfair labor practice. See *Head Ski Division, AMF, Inc.*, 593 F.2d 972 (10th Cir. 1979).

No-Access Rules

Union organizers will attempt to get as close as possible to the employer's plant to distribute leaflets or talk with employees as they enter or leave the plant, or when they take their breaks or lunch times. Where organizers who are not company employees appear on any property owned or leased by the employer, the employer has the right to prevent such access. State trespass laws may be invoked, and the police may be called to evict the trespassers and to require them to operate only on public grounds *outside* plant gates. The employer should be prepared to spot the union organizers and to alert police so that they may be barred from entering the premises before they hand out any leaflets.

Employers often enlist the assistance of police in advance, requesting local police jurisdictions to patrol the premises at the start and near the end of work shifts. The premises should be posted with "no trespassing" signs, or words allowing only authorized employees to enter company property. Such signs make enforcement of the trespass laws easier for the police to administer.

Also important is the ability of the employer to be able to deny access to the plant to employees who are not on duty. Limit access to the interior of the plant and other working areas solely to on-duty workers. It should be applied to all off-duty employees seeking access to the plant for any purpose, but it cannot deny off-duty employees entry to outside nonworking areas, such as parking lots and gates. The no-access rule *must* avoid mentioning employee solicitation or distribution of literature. Like the no-solicitation and no-distribution rules, the no-access rule may be critically important, since a great deal of union organizational activity takes place when employees who are finished working linger on the premises to solicit co-employees on the same shift or the next shift.

The Board's approval of rules denying off-duty employees access to the employer's premises is valid only if the rule: (a) imposes limitations on access that apply only to the interior of the employer's plant and other working areas; (b) is clearly published and known to all employees; and (c) applies to off-duty employees seeking access to the plant for *any* purpose and not just to employees soliciting on behalf of the union. Accordingly, a no-access rule would be invalid if it denied permission to off-duty employees to solicit and/or distribute union leaflets in a company parking lot. Also invalid would be a rule prohibiting all loitering on the premises by off-duty employees; the illegality arises because the rule is ambiguous and potentially unlimited in application. Moreover, it would be unlawful to prohibit solicitation by employees on company premises where such employees have completed their shift but are still lawfully and properly on company property pursuant to the work relationship.

If an employer enforces the "off-duty" rule against employee solicitation for the union, but allows other off-duty employees to wait for co-employees to finish work, or to pick up their paychecks on days off, or to return to the premises to eat with co-workers, the rule will be declared invalid. The rule will also be nullified if the employer enforces it against former employees returning to the premises but allows other non-employees, such as food and news vendors, to enter a parking lot for nonunion purposes.

Where an employer is partially organized at a particular facility, it is most important for management to deny union officials access to non-bargaining-unit personnel. The Board has even approved employer rules restricting access of union business agents to production areas—and only when their presence was absolutely required. Business agents may be told to meet with employees in the lunch room during lunch hour or break times but not in production areas. When invoking such rules, however, the employer should be careful to avoid inhibiting the union's ability to investigate grievances.

Employers who are not aggressive in asserting their rights to control work time and to protect their premises give an advantage to the union which need not be given. Each of the protective rules discussed herein should be studied and applied under the law; preferably, all measures should be taken *prior* to the advent of any union organization. A selection of legal principles and precedents applicable to no-solicitation rules appears in Appendix 3, Part B.

Chapter 6

Preparing the Campaign

An employer has a vital stake in the outcome of the election, and the law recognizes that an employer has the legal right to express itself during any organizing attempt by a union. Within the limits of avoiding any unfair labor practices (as outlined in Chapter 3), and within the parameters of the free speech concepts discussed in Chapter 8, an employer must organize a campaign to persuade its employees to reject unionism.

Unions have a formidable plan of attack, and the employer must match or exceed the union's effort. An employer's strategies and techniques are very important, and its campaign must be properly planned and timely conducted. If properly done, even the most "hopeless" of cases can be overcome. In many cases—even where the union has obtained more than 90 percent of the cards in an appropriate unit—employers have been able to "correct the record" and persuade employees overwhelmingly to reject the union on election day. Conversely, a poor campaign may drive employees into the union.

There is no typical campaign and no impeccable way to run a campaign. However, there are principles of general applicability. The particular tactics and strategies may differ, but the fundamental principles of campaigning remain the same. Follow the guides outlined on the following pages.

A Positive Approach

In expressing the company's philosophy against unionization, many employers overlook the fact that unionization is not necessarily good for the employees. Millions of employees—in fact, a large majority of employees in the United States—work in union-free atmospheres, are relatively happy, and do not want the blandishments of a union organizational campaign. Thus, a campaign can be run primarily on the premise that a union is not necessarily advantageous for the employees.

A positive approach should be used. Under today's conditions, where many employers maintain generous levels of benefits and uphold prevailing local wages, many employers' operations compete most favorably with any union contract. Therefore, make constant and telling comparisons between benefits and conditions enjoyed in a nonunion atmosphere versus conditions the union has been able to obtain elsewhere. Most nonunion employers automatically assume that union contracts provide more benefits than they already have. Surprisingly, in many cases, the employer will learn that its own benefits are comparable to, if not better than, union conditions. Labor agreements negotiated at other companies often reveal some conditions not as favorable as those enjoyed by nonunion employees.

Timing

Many employers wait to start campaigning until an election date has been established. The campaign is then confined to the period of time following agreement to a consent election or the scheduling of an election by the Regional Director.

Such an approach is unsound. It gives the union an unnecessary advantage and a monopoly over the communications process during the time preceding the scheduling of an election. In many cases, the union already has had several weeks to campaign with employees, sometimes without the knowledge of the employer; it therefore has a head start in the organization process. In addition, during the time that cards are being signed, many employees are uncertain as to what they should do, and an employer's silence during this critical period creates confusion in their minds. Under pressure from their peers, they may decide to sign cards thinking that the employer either is inattentive to their needs or has no interest in the outcome. They may get the impression that unionization is inevitable.

By initiating the campaign at the first sign of significant union activity, the employer unequivocally informs employees that a union is not wanted and not needed. This approach often slows down the card-signing process and moderates the union's attempt to solicit further support.

A most important consideration is that the NLRB will not consider unfair labor practices prior to the filing of the petition as a basis for setting the election aside. This is not to say that employer conduct cannot amount to an unfair labor practice before the filing of the petition; it can, and it may be adjudicated as such by the NLRB. However, an election may not be *set aside* on this basis. Thus the employer has greater leeway before the petition is filed—an advantage that should not be lost by postponing the start of the campaign until a formal petition has been filed.

As soon as the election date has been set, the employer should be the first to inform the voters of this fact and to disseminate information pertaining to the election and its consequences. An appropriate notice is:

TO ALL ELIGIBLE VOTERS

Information About the NLRB Election.

_____[Date]_____, has been established as election day to decide whether or not the Union will come into our company, take over and represent you. There have been a lot of questions raised about how an NLRB election works, so we've put together some information about the election process so that you can understand how very important the vote on __[Date]_____ will be.

1.   *How the Election Procedure Works.*

There will be two choices on the ballot—the_____ Union and "No Union." To win, the union must get a majority of all the votes cast. It is extremely important that each of you turn out to vote and let your voice be heard. The union will certainly pressure all its supporters to vote, and not voting can therefore hurt you.

The election will be by secret ballot, and no one will ever know how you vote. No employee is bound to vote any particular way because he or she signed a card with the union, attended union meetings, paid the union some money, or promised a pro-union supporter to vote for the union. People who have taken positions in public often change their minds in the secrecy of a polling booth. Therefore, you can vote the way you wish without fear that anyone will ever know how you cast your ballot.

2. *What Happens if the Union Wins?*

If the union wins, it becomes the exclusive bargaining representative for all employees in the voting unit and all those in that unit *in the future*. The union's control will extend to everyone, regardless of whether they are union members, whether they voted for the union, or whether they agree with the union on any particular point. If the union won it would be unlawful for the Company or any management or supervisory personnel to deal favorably with individual employees on any condition of employment or merit increase or raise, or to make different or special arrangements for any individual.

This union always seeks a "union shop agreement"—that is, one *forcing* all employees to join the union. If such an agreement were made, all employees in the unit would have to pay monthly dues. If you did not want to join you would be legally discharged with no

way of challenging it. The union would also want dues to be automatically deducted from your paychecks, just like withholding tax.
In return for these provisions favoring the union, the company
would gain concessions on other issues important to us.

If the union is selected, it has the right to bargain with the Company. There is no automatic raise. No specific contract will come
into being just because the union wins. Regardless of whatever campaign pledges a union has made to our employees, it can deliver
only those employment terms and conditions which the Company
agrees to give. If the Company and the union cannot agree, the
union has the right to go on strike to try and enforce its demands. If
the union goes on strike, it can direct its members to stay away
from work and slap substantial fines on those who do not. Employees are not paid while on strike, and the Company can permanently
replace them so that its work can be carried on.

3. *Can the Union Be Voted Out After a Year?*

Once a union is elected as a bargaining representative, it remains
the designated representative of the unit. It is extremely difficult to
get a union out once it is voted in. There is no such thing as trying a
union out for a year. Once it is in, you can expect it to stay forever.
Employees can even be expelled for trying to oust the union.

We hope that this gives you some idea of how the election will
work and, in a very general way, some of the serious consequences
of union representation. We want to stress to you that when the
question of whether or not you want the union to come in and act
for you comes down to a vote, we would like you to go into that secret voting booth and vote against union representation because we
firmly believe that bringing a union in here would not be in your
best interest. We would like the vote to come out "No Union," and
we believe you will keep it out and place a vote of confidence in
your management.

Essentials of Employer's Communication

It is not unusual for management, at the inception of known
organizational activity, to give a plant-wide speech to employees. Explain the pitfalls of card-signing, express the company's solid opposition to unionization, and outline the reasons unionization is not
needed. Some communication, quite possibly a letter to the home,
should be made at this early stage of organizational activity.

The initial communication, whether written or oral, should stress
the following matters:

- Point out that unionization is of serious concern to the
  employee: If the union enters the plant, it could seriously
  harm the employee's interests.

- Stress that it is not necessary for *anyone* employed by the company to belong to a union in order to obtain the company's benefits.
- Point out the financial obligations of becoming a union member.
- Express the company's intention to oppose unionization in every legal way possible.
- Ask employees not to sign authorization cards.
- Request those employees who are bothered by union organizers or co-employees to notify the employer so that appropriate legal action can be taken to avoid the harassment.
- If a valid no-solicitation/no-distribution rule has already been promulgated, remind the employees that no one will be allowed to carry on union organizing activities during working time and that anyone doing so may be subject to discharge.
- Encourage employees to bring their questions to frontline supervision or top management. (Care should be taken, however, to avoid the *solicitation of grievances*, which is considered to be an unfair labor practice.)

Ascertaining the Causes of Union Interest

It is almost axiomatic that union organizational attempts come about because of mistakes made by management—in particular, by frontline supervision. There is usually an immediate precipitating incident that propels an individual or a small group of employees to seek out a union organizer, and more often than not there are general feelings of dissatisfaction preceding the precipitating event. Employees seek out a union because they believe (often erroneously) that a union will correct or eliminate the reasons for their complaints. To determine the issues in a campaign, the employer must discover not only the directly precipitating events underlying the unionization attempt, but also the more general causes.

In typical cases, the causes involve discrimination, favoritism, and unfair treatment by frontline supervision. Much of the union's initial campaign material follows the recurring theme that supervisors are unfair in the treatment of their workers, and that the only way to neutralize the supervisors' discrimination or favoritism is by the introduction of a third party into the relationship, since top management will almost always support the supervisor in his decisions.

Another factor creating dissatisfaction is company conduct that creates feelings of job insecurity, such as layoffs and actions that disregard seniority. Employees often believe that unions can magically protect against layoffs and other reductions in staff due to poor business conditions. It is up to the employer in such cases to stress that unions cannot prevent layoffs and to convey the message that unions are often associated with job losses rather than job gains. For example, U.S. Department of Labor studies show that heavy industrialized states have lost more jobs, despite the presence of unions, than have rural right-to-work states, where unions are less prevalent. The non-unionized states have experienced job *gains* rather than losses. The employer may find that general dissatisfaction is also based on such conditions as lack of workable grievance procedures, low wages, and insufficient or poorly administered fringe benefits.

At the same time that the employer looks behind any specific incident to ascertain the general causes of dissatisfaction, he must also take care to avoid illegal solicitation of grievances. Questioning employees about the causes of their dissatisfaction and coupling such conduct with implied promises of correction may constitute serious unfair labor practices. It is not unlawful to ask employees during an election campaign about grievances they may have or to ask about suggestions for improving conditions. However, a statement that something will be done to correct the complaint or implement the suggestion is illegal. Stating that the employer will look into the problems or is "ready to deal directly with employees" should be avoided since these statements may carry with them an inference of an implicit promise to correct injustices discovered as a result of the inquiries.

The employer should stay within the bounds of established grievance solicitation systems. If there are any major changes in the employer's procedures for resolving employee complaints (such as holding such meetings at a different location under formal circumstances, or the appearance of higher-level corporate officers at such meetings) this may signal the NLRB that the established complaint resolution procedure was strengthened after the petition had been filed—and may therefore constitute an unfair labor practice. Employees must be told that the employer can make no promises regarding the grievances raised.

The employer should take care not to make statements at these meetings that are inconsistent with its disavowal of any promise. If the employer makes such statements not wholly in accord with its "no promises" position, the Board may find that repetition of the no-promise phrase was mere formality, serving only as an all-too-transparent gloss on what was otherwise a clearly implied promise of benefit.

In one case, the employer, for the first time, held three employee meetings preceding a representation election. At each meeting, it described the procedures involved in the election, explained its existing wage policies and fringe benefits in detail, and announced that it could make no promises or commitments because the law precluded it. Management representatives then invited questions from employees. In responding to these, the employer reiterated that it could make no promise with respect to the matters being raised. The Board found that the structure of such preelection meetings provided a compelling inference that the employer was impliedly promising that grievances which were raised would be corrected. The Board found that the employees' reason for voicing their complaints was the hope that they would be remedied; the employer's continued interest in entertaining the grievances demonstrated that its disavowals were not offered in good faith and were not taken at face value by the employees.

At these meetings, the employer also announced an "open door" policy which had not been previously publicized. The announcement of this expanded avenue of access constituted not only a promise of an additional benefit but also a change in conditions. *Raley's, Inc*, 236 NLRB No. 97 (1978).

In another case, an employer with an established open door policy who had occasionally solicited complaints from individual employees was nevertheless found to have improperly solicited employee grievances by acting in a manner that had not been customarily followed. The employer's mistake consisted of replacing an old suggestion box with a new one in a more convenient location; failing to limit employee questions (at meetings initiated by the employer) to subjects other than employee grievances; distributing pencils and paper to employees at these group meetings and asking them to submit questions; posting employee suggestions together with employer responses such as "checking into," "finished," "done," or "forthcoming"; and indicating that certain grievances would be corrected. The solicitation of employee grievances was found not to have been justified by legitimate business reasons. Moreover, the method of solicitation was significantly altered, leading to setting aside the election for impermissible solicitation. *Carbonneau Industries, Inc.*, 228 NLRB 597 (1977). The Board said, in connection with the issue of whether a past policy and practice may justify solicitation of employee grievances during the campaign period:

It is well established that an employer who has had a past policy and practice of soliciting employee grievances may continue such a policy and practice during an organizational campaign. Lasco Industries, Inc. 217 NLRB 527 (1975); Reliance Electric Company, Madison Plant Mechanical Drivers Division, 191 NLRB 44, 46 (1971). In this case, the Employer had a past practice of maintaining an "open door" policy and soliciting complaints on occasion from individuals. However, this past practice is not an adequate justification for the manner and methods by which Carbonneau solicited employee grievances during the organization and preelection periods. . . .

The Board has ruled in the following situations that an employer cannot rely on past practice to justify solicitation of employee grievances where the employer significantly alters its past manner and methods of solicitation: soliciting grievances more frequently than regularly done in the past, Grede Foundries, Inc. (Milwaukee), 205 NLRB 39 (1973); searching out grievances more carefully than before, Rotek, Incorporated, 194 NLRB 453 (1971); initiating group discussions of employee grievances where the employer had merely discussed grievances on an individual basis previously, Flight Safety, Inc., 197 NLRB 223 (1972); and the installation of a suggestion box where one had not previously been located, H. L. Meyer Company, Inc., 177 NLRB 565 (1969). The Employer's conduct of initiating a systematic series of meetings among groups of its employees, wherein it asked for questions at each meeting and failed to limit the questions to subjects other than employee grievances, and the Employer's actions in replacing an old suggestion box and installing the new one in a more convenient location constitute a significant alteration of the Employer's past practice.

The Board is entitled to conclude, and in most circumstances will, that an employer's willingness to consider employee requests at a time that coincides with the first union organizational attempt might indicate to the average employee that better conditions would be automatically forthcoming as a result of the survey. The Board could also find that the questions were asked in a way that would leave the employees with the impression that the company was promising to remedy the employees' grievances if they would forget the union. NLRB v. Tom Wood Pontiac, Inc., 447 F.2d 383 (7th Cir. 1971), enforcing 179 NLRB 581 (1969).

Each case involving solicitation of employee grievances is considered against a background of the particular facts involved. Consider what happened in the following instance.

The employer prepared and distributed to employees a questionnaire consisting of 18 questions ranging from "Will you be at the company picnic?" to whether the employees understood various benefit plans, how management could reduce absenteeism and turnover, and how production, quality, earnings, and working conditions could be improved. It also asked: "What would you choose as the next benefit to add to our fringe benefit program?" Questionnaires of a similar nature had been distributed by the employer from time to time over a period of years.

In referring to the questionnaire, management spoke about past problems and stated that when a problem arose they were able to achieve a solution by working together. Management indicated that it could learn things from the questionnaire that might otherwise take months to learn and that the company and front line supervisors would be studying the comments, which would get "the attention they deserve." Management further stated that while it could not hope to solve all of the problems at once, employees deserved to have their individual ideas considered. Management stated its determination to get completely involved in working with employees to bring about as quickly as possible the goals that both management and employees desired.

The NLRB argued that the solicitation of grievances carried with it the implied promise to rectify some of the complaints and that the questionnaire indicated what the employer could do to satisfy employee grievances. On the other hand, the employer argued that the questionnaire was circulated in accord with a long-established policy of obtaining employee consensus on matters of company policy. It denied that the questionnaire was distributed for any ulterior motive or for the purpose of soliciting and resolving employee grievances. *In light of the fact that in the past the employer had circulated such questionnaires*, which included questions similar to the one involved, the Board held there was no violation of the Act. It also found that the statements did not amount to a promise to redress employee grievances but merely indicated that management would follow its previous policies. *Mt. Ida Footwear Co.*, 217 NLRB 1011 (1975).

While it might appear strange to an employer that expression of concern for employee welfare may be impermissible, if the timing of such expressions coincides with an imminent representation election, if the manner of convening the work force is not in accordance with prior regularly scheduled sessions of the same type, if the meetings are called by management and not by the employees, and if the characteristic method of dealing with employee complaints is on an individual and informal basis as opposed to convocation of the entire work force, then the Board will find that the sessions were timed to nip the union effort in the bud. *Rich's of Plymouth, Inc.*, 232 NLRB

No. 98 (1977), enforced 578 F.2d 880 (1st Cir. 1978).

Since solicitation of employee grievances is a natural response by employers faced with organization, avoiding unfair labor practices based upon solicitation of grievances merits the employer's careful attention because solicitation violations, *by themselves*, may support a card-based bargaining order.

Campaign Discipline

Management does not lose the right to discipline during a union campaign. In many respects, discipline *must* be invoked, not only for business reasons but also because a lack of discipline during the campaign may create the feeling that management is indeed afraid of the union.

On the other hand, overly strong punitive measures should be avoided. Harsh punishment may create sympathy for the employee involved and allow the union to use that as an example of management's obliviousness to employee needs. The campaign may then focus on a minor disciplinary incident rather than on the basic issues. If it is necessary to invoke serious discipline during the campaign, it will usually serve the employer's interest to post the fact and give the reasons for it. If any discipline is motivated in part by an employee's union activity, it is illegal, despite the existence of sufficient cause for discipline on other grounds. Discipline can be viewed by the NLRB as discriminatory, if in the past, the employer has *not* disciplined employees for similar conduct.

In the heat of union organizing campaigns, threats are often made by a pro-union sympathizer against fellow employees. When such threats are revealed, the tendency for management is to discipline immediately. In most cases the Board will not find the threat alone sufficient to constitute the basis for a discharge, but will require, in addition, some form of menacing action.

When the employer believes that grounds exist for a valid discharge, it should take care that a reasonable investigation is made before the discharge, that both sides are given an opportunity to submit facts, and that the basis for the discharge is a reasonable concern that future violence might occur. In this connection, management may post or distribute a notice stating:

> We have been informed by one of our employees that the union is threatening and pressuring employees who do not sign authorization cards, or who do not wish to vote for the union or support it. You have the right not to support the union, which is guaranteed to

you by law, and also the right to be free from any form of union
pressure and threats. If you are threatened by any union organizer,
or by any of your co-employees, report it to your supervisor immediately. The company will see to it that the National Labor Relations Board will protect your rights and keep you free from intimidation and coercion caused by the union and its sympathizers.

As can be seen, disciplining known union adherents, for statements
or conduct connected with their solicitation efforts on behalf of the
union, is dangerous. Nevertheless, it can be done. While the Board
will not uphold discipline based upon an isolated threatening remark,
particularly where that remark is made in a casual conversation with
other employees (and where the listener does not take the remark seriously) and while the Board will not view a statement which falls
short of a threat of physical harm as warranting discharge, it will validate *appropriate* employer discipline. So where the union solicitors'
words are accompanied by conduct such as producing dangerous
weapons, or are a constant and repetitive part of the employee's behavior, the discharge or discipline may be valid. Simply discharging a
union prime mover for threatening that he would "fix" co-employees,
or for similar terminology, would not be sufficient to justify employer
discipline.

Reporting Union Pressure

If management asks employees to report any pressure upon them to
support a union, this request will be viewed by the NLRB as an attempt to persuade employees to inform management of the identity
of union adherents. The result would be the same if the employer: (a)
asks an employee who is threatened or constantly badgered to join a
union to report this to management; (b) asks an employee to bring a
union authorization card to management without signing it; (c) tells an
employee to let supervision know about anyone attempting to get
them to sign a union card. Each of these is a violation on the ground
that management is asking employees to inform it as to the nature of
union activity and the identity of union prime movers.

However, it *would be* permissible for the employer to state:

We have been told by one of our employees that the union is
threatening and pressuring our employees to make false statements
against the company. You have the right not to sign any statement
and to be free from any union threats. If you are threatened, report

it to me immediately and I will see to it that the NLRB will protect your rights.

To illustrate the Board's "tough" point of view on employer statements of the type under discussion, consider this case. The following notice was posted:

> To all employees:
> A number of employees have reported that they are being pressured to sign union cards. Some are told that they will have to join the union if they want to continue to work here.
> You should know that no one will have to join a union as a condition of employment. You don't have to put up with pestering or pressure to join.
> Please let me know if you are bothered. I will do my best to see that the law is observed.

The Board found that the letter was a clear invitation to employees to report the names of union organizers to management. The letter did not distinguish between organizing activities that are statutorily protected and conduct that is illegal. It would have been reasonable for an employee who received the letter to draw the inference that any organizational activity on behalf of the union would be reported to management and that the identified participants in the organizational campaign would be punished. The Board concluded, notwithstanding testimony by the employer that the letter was sent in response to the request of complaining employees, that the purpose of the communication was to intimidate potential participants in the organizational campaign rather than to protect the rights of the employees, and it therefore constituted an unfair labor practice *Lutheran Hospital v. NLRB*, 564 F.2d 208 (7th Cir. 1977).

Asking Employees to Solicit Co-Employees

Does an employer violate the Act by asking its employees to campaign against the union, by soliciting them to vote no, and by requesting that they solicit other employees to vote no? If these requests and solicitations are made to all employees through the indirect and rather impersonal medium of a form letter, rather than directly to selected employees by their supervisors, the Board will view these statements as customary campaign statements that do not reasonably tend to coerce employees.

For example, an employer's communication may ask employees to do what they can to get everyone to vote "no" or to do their best to see that co-employees keep the union out.

An employer may also approach loyal or trusted employees to solicit their assistance during the campaign and to ask them to explain to co-employees that a union is not needed in the plant. But if the employer goes further and impliedly conditions wage adjustments, promotions, or other advantages on their assisting the company in its anit-union campaign, the Board will view this conduct as prohibited solicitation.

Changes in Pay and Working Conditions

As noted in Chapter 3, any change made by the employer that either improves or detracts from existing working conditions during the campaign period—even the smallest change, undertaken for the purest of reasons—may result in unfair labor practice findings. Even minor changes in operating procedures may constitute a violation of the Act if motivated by the presence of the union. For example, installing better lighting, obtaining new equipment, providing protective clothing, or installing a heater in the receiving area may be an unfair labor practice. This is so even though the employer claims that maintenance of equipment was a continuing practice and that even prior to the union's organizing campaign improvements had been made as a result of business growth and suggestions and complaints by employees and management officials.

Where the improvements are done in a manner that departs radically from past methods, the Board will find an unfair labor practice. *Sears Roebuck & Co.,* 182 NLRB 491 (1970), enforcement denied, 450 F.2d 56 (6th Cir. 1971). Therefore, any changes contemplated should be evaluated carefully by the employer. In most cases, unless there is a specific advantage that outweighs the possibility of an eventual unfair labor practice finding, the change should not be made.

Perhaps the most perplexing issue facing the employer is wage increases during a campaign. In many cases, wage increases constitute an effective strategy in defeating the union. In other situations, granting wage increases can create a backlash. Even if the employer withholds a wage increase, there are political as well as legal considerations to take into account.

If an employer introduces a legal wage increase, the union will often take credit for it. The organizer will contend that the increase did not result from the employer's desire to be fair, but from its desire to avoid unionization. He will ridicule the employer's newly found generosity and make the clinching argument that a union need merely be on the scene for employees to receive added benefits. The organizer will then hint that when the union actually puts pressure on the employer during bargaining, there will be many more improvements.

Often, the union will also file unfair labor practice charges contesting such increases, claiming they are a ploy to get rid of the union. The union has little to lose by filing these charges because the NLRB has never ordered such increases to be rescinded. In fact, the union may gain, if the result is that notices have to be posted throughout the company stating that the employer attempted to buy off employees with wage increases.

The area of wage increases is rife with other potential traps. A typical union tactic is to have a sympathizer inform the employer that by giving him and a few other selected pro-union employees a small pay increase, the employer can buy immunity from further union penetration. If the employer agrees to the suggestion, the union supporters will point out to their co-employees that the employer can be maneuvered into a wage increase and that joining the union is obviously a means of getting raises themselves.

Since, during an election campaign, wage increases involve sensitive areas, the opinion of counsel should always be obtained—even when the increase is for a single employee. In general, it is not an unfair labor practice to give an increase if the decision to do so is made before the employer learns of the union organizing efforts, or if the company has a well-defined policy of granting wage increases or other benefits at a particular time of the year or on employee anniversary dates, and the employees are aware of this policy.

But the increases should not be unreasonably larger than they have been in the past. When they are announced, no mention should be made of the pending election. During subsequent campaign speeches and in written materials, the employer would be wise to avoid mention of the wage increases. Any references may enable the NLRB to find an illegal motivation.

In postponing expected wage increases, the employer may make clear in its campaign statements that its only reason for doing so was to avoid the appearance of bribing employees. The Board has approved such statements as long as they are not made in the context of antiunion propaganda and as long as the Board is convinced that the withholding was not intended to affect the election.

It is a violation for the employer to inform its employees that an automatic wage increase will not be implemented if the union wins the election. The fact that a union has been certified does not justify an employer's withholding of a wage increase that would have been granted in the absence of the certification. An employer who withholds a promised wage increase because in the interval between the promise and the effective date of the wage increase, the employees selected a union to represent them and the employer anticipated that wages would be part of any package in a collective bargaining agreement violates the Act. *Montgomery Ward & Co.*, 225 NLRB 112 (1976).

Where preplanned merit raises or scheduled increases are granted during a campaign, many employers take the added precaution of giving the employee a letter explaining the increase:

> Dear _____,
> When you were promoted to_____ at the beginning of June, I told you that you would receive a salary increase in three to six months. The attached check includes an increase in your salary effective _____, to reflect the increase you were promised in June.
> Because a union has petitioned to represent our staff and an election is pending, our attorneys advised us that we can be charged with an unfair labor practice whenever we change an employee's salary. If we fail to give promised or scheduled increases, we can be charged with attempting to retaliate against employees for having shown interest in a union; if we give an increase, we can be charged with trying to buy votes. We have also been advised by our attorneys that the company is entitled to continue to operate normally (indeed, the law requires us to do so). That is what we are doing. This note is simply to make sure you understand that the increase included in this check is the one I promised you upon your promotion in June. It would have been given to you as of _____, whether a union had petitioned to represent our staff or not, and has nothing to do with the upcoming union election.
> We want to make it clear to you that the company would like you to vote in accordance with the way you personally feel. Please do not let this normal and previously promised increase influence your vote one way or the other.

To understand the NLRB's approach to wage changes during the critical preelection period, it is necessary to distinguish between two basic situations:

1. Granting or withholding wage increases in deviation from a clearly apparent established practice; and
2. Granting or withholding wage increases where there is no established practice.

When the policy with respect to wage increases is *clearly apparent* and it can be said with assurance that the denial of a wage increase constitutes a *change* from the practice, the employer, in such a case, inevitably conveys the message that it, not the union, controls the purse strings. There need be no specific finding that the employer was prompted by antiunion motivations since the Board assumes that employees will believe that the union is somehow responsible for their failure to receive expected raises. Under these conditions, the denial of an increase will result in setting aside the election. Likewise, the giving of an unexpected raise will invariably be understood as an attempt by the employer to demonstrate that unionization is unneeded or as an attempt to buy the votes of the employees so benefited. Giving such messages interferes with employee free choice, regardless of the employer's intent.

For there to be interference with an election, there must be an established practice with regard to wage increases which was clearly apparent to an objectively reasonable employer at the time the increases were given or withheld. When it is not clear whether a wage increase would conform to the policy or depart from it, no inference automatically attaches in the mind of the employee to the giving or not giving of wage increases. In this situation, it must be affirmatively shown that the employer's conduct was motivated by anti-union sentiments.

A complicated issue often arises when a group excluded from the voting unit, such as a clerical department, is given a raise during the time an election is pending in the main unit. If the employer indicates to the voters that "his hands are tied" and adds that the voters should "trust the company and give it some time to prove itself," such a statement or appeal would be readily considered by the Board to carry the plain implication that voters would enjoy wage parity with the outside group as soon as the union issue is removed.

The employer is not necessarily free to do completely as it pleases with respect to employees excluded from the voting unit. Giving increases to excluded groups, particularly where there is no precedent for such increases, may cause the Board to conclude that the denial of the increase to voters implemented a divisive and discriminatory stratagem leading to the prejudice of voters solely because they were the immediate object of the union's effort to become the exclusive statutory representative. Certainly, where the employer capitalizes upon such raises to excluded groups, blames the union for the failure to grant the increase to the voters, initiates commentaries on the withholding of the raises, repeats the withholding in formal campaign documents and other messages, this strategy may be held violative of the Act. See *Hanover House Industries, Inc.*, 233 NLRB 164 (1977).

However, if an increase in wages or benefits is implemented throughout the corporation in a normal business fashion, the change will receive NLRB approval. *Northern Telecom, Inc.*, 233 NLRB 1104 (1977).

The employer must also be extremely careful in the area of making other improvements. Even where the decision to make an improvement was made before the initiation of union activity, the NLRB has found a violation when management *accelerated* the action. However, where a benefit has previously been decided upon, the employer does not have to conceal its intention to implement the benefit in answering a direct question by an employee.

An employer that validly implements a benefit—for example, a pension plan—prior to the onset of union activity can gain the maximum advantage by explaining the benefits of the new program to employees, either individually or in groups, during the election campaign. Of course, it is safest during such informational meetings to make no reference to the impending election.

Even if the employer exercises the greatest amount of care, unfair labor practice charges will inevitably be filed by the union. When such charges are filed, it is usually best for management to notify the employees and to give a brief explanation of the charges to lessen the possibility that the union will spread erroneous information about the nature of the allegations and their disposition. (Often, the union will try to imply that the charges have been upheld simply because an NLRB agent is in the plant interviewing employees and acquiring the facts of the case.) In some cases, particularly when the charge has every prospect of being upheld, the best management action may be silence. Thus, before acting, each case must be treated individually, on the basis of such factors as the closeness of election day, the relative merit of the charge, and the persons affected.

Management may wish to consider not allowing the Board agent to interview witnesses at the plant or in full view of other employees since the union can imply that the mere presence of the agent is proof of company wrongdoing and is evidence that the federal government favors the union in its organizing efforts. (If the union erroneously states that the employer has been found guilty by the NLRB of having committed unfair labor practices, when, in fact, only a hearing has been scheduled or a complaint has been settled with a clause not admitting guilt, the employer may file valid objections to the election.)

To summarize the principles governing the legality of increases during an election campaign, the following criteria have been established. If the timing of the improved benefit is consistent with past practice, the chances are that the increase will be permissible. Increases provably decided upon prior to the onset of union activity will also be upheld. The amount of the increase will be closely scrutinized by the Board. If the amount coincides with previously granted wage or salary increases and are in line with company policy, cost of living, and other historical factors, the NLRB will be less likely to find fault with the increase. Moreover, the employer must be able to show substantial business justification for granting the increase. For example; (a) a length of time has elapsed without employees having received wage increases; (b) there is a demonstrated inability to meet competitors' working conditions; (c) difficulty in attracting or retaining employees on the staff and similar business reasons. It is also important that employer announcements in connection with the increase avoid references to the union or to the pending representation proceeding. Even where the employer conducts itself carefully in light of the foregoing principles, the existence of independent unfair labor practices, such as unlawful interrogation, threats, promises of benefits by supervisors and similar conduct may be sufficient to lead the NLRB to conclude that the improvements were nevertheless calculated to impinge upon the employees' freedom of choice in the upcoming election. The principles governing the legality of increases during a campaign have been set out by the NLRB in *Marine World USA*, 236 NLRB No. 10 (1978). Sample communications to employees on the issue of wage increases during an election are given in Appendix 5.

The Hobson's choice faced by an employer in deciding to grant increases or to withhold scheduled increases during a campaign has been duly acknowledged by the courts and presents the employer with one of the most frustrating aspects of electioneering. The United States Court of Appeals in *NLRB v. Planters Peanuts*, 574 F.2d 400 (8th Cir. 1978), stated the dilemma perfectly. The court said:

> An employer who has been contemplating or planning a wage increase, and subsequently learns of a union petition for an election among his employees, is placed between the proverbial 'devil and the deep blue sea.' He can grant a wage increase and face the risk of unfair labor practice charges and/or objections for trying to buy off his employees, or he can withhold the increase and face similar charges and/or objections for trying to influence the vote of his employees in the election.

This area deserves the employer's most considered attention. One safe defense to the Board's often inconsistent decisions was suggested by a federal court:

> We are not unsympathetic with an employer who, having decided to increase his employees' wages, finds himself trying to navigate a

'perilous' course between the Scylla of a violation of the Act for
granting a wage increase to employees when a representation election is pending and the Charybdis of a violation of the Act for
withholding such an increase when such an election is pending. His
uncertain compass is the board's rule to act 'as he would if a union
were not in the picture.' On the other hand, the board's suggestion
that 'there was nothing to prevent the Company from announcing
. . . that the wage increase would be put into effect immediately
after the election, regardless of the outcome, with the Union's
consent [if it won the election],' although somewhat inconsistent
with the board's rule to act as if the Union were not in the picture,
constitutes one approach that would have been both an effective response and a neutral response. *Sun Chemical Corp. v. NLRB*, 560
F.2d 470 (1st. Cir. 1977).

The Campaign Spokesman

It is imperative for the company to select one person as the campaign
manager to coordinate all efforts during the union campaign. A common mistake made by employers is to adopt a committee approach to
managing the campaign. Internal political processes interfere with a
unified voice for the company. And a committee approach is not suited
to the quick decisions necessary during a campaign to counteract
union tactics, while a campaign manager has the authority to make in-
stant decisions according to campaign developments.

The campaign manager should have a sound working knowledge of
personnel and industrial relations. He need not be a lawyer, but he
should know labor laws because he will be in constant communication
with qualified labor specialists. It would be ideal for the campaign
manager to have been through an organizational campaign and to have
had prior exposure to the collective bargaining process as a party to
negotiations. The campaign manager's normal duties should be reas-
signed for the duration of the campaign; any trips or other business
matters should be postponed to leave the manager free to supervise
the campaign on a daily basis.

The campaign manager should be fairly well known to the employees who will be voting in the election. He must also be high enough
in the managerial chain of command to hold the respect of the employees. A prime function of this manager is to provide an authoritative source of answers to employees during the campaign; he must
have sufficient credibility so that his answers are not only believed by
the employees, but also perceived by them to be the company's position on the issue. The appointment of such a management spokesman

to coordinate strategy and to serve as the nucleus of the campaign is one of the most important requirements of a successful campaign.

The campaign manager is responsible for coordinating company strategy, recommending tactics, and obtaining legal advice. He oversees all campaign literature and speeches and reviews union tactics as they develop. Thus, all communications should be sent directly to the campaign manager as soon as they are received. The normal chain of command should be suspended to assure flexibility and speed during the campaign.

It is also the campaign manager's duty to hold periodic meetings with supervisors to obtain information on the progress of the campaign from their point of view. It is his duty to brief top management on the latest events. He is responsible for getting the necessary information to combat the union's campaign, such as contacting other companies when it is appropriate to obtain facts about the organizing union. His responsibilities also include insuring the preparation of graphic displays, posters, newspaper clippings, and other materials well in advance of intended distribution; the printing of literature; the preaddressing of envelopes; etc. He establishes and enforces the machinery for getting the message to the employees.

Establishing A War Room

The nerve center of the employer's campaign should be a war room in which those involved in the campaign effort collect and evaluate all information relevant to the union organizational campaign and plan management's strategy. This command post is the center of activity for the employer during the campaign. An excellent suggestion for keeping track of the shift in sentiment among employees is to post a wall chart listing the names of all employees by department with the designation "Union," "company," and "?" The chart should be updated periodically, more frequently in the early stages of the campaign. Keeping such a master index of information, in addition to any individualized data received from supervisors, will enable management to determine its strengths and weaknesses, and will also enable it to determine shifts in opinion. The chart will also indicate which employees will need to be contacted more frequently by supervision. The information is collated by management spokesmen as it is received by supervisors. The supervisors' knowledge, in turn, is based upon educated guesses about the people they supervise, their attitudes, and discussions the supervisors may have had with voters on the union issue. All information should be reported to the war room daily, including information that may appear insignificant to the average supervisor. The information will enable management to determine strategy and to decide upon effective counterattacking techniques.

The Employer's Statement to the Supervisors

Management must enlist the full support of front-line supervisors and others who will be involved in the effort to thwart the union's attempt to organize the company. Management should not assume that front-line supervision is automatically opposed to the entry of a union in the plant or office, or will necessarily be aware of the reasons for the company's opposition. Supervisors may believe that the union does in fact protect employees and that the only purpose the company has in opposing the union is to save money. They rarely see the broad picture and are seldom in a position to understand why the company opposes the union. Because of this, management must make its supervisors familiar with the spirit of the company's opposition and state formally the reasons for the company's campaign and why it would not be in the employees' best interest to vote for the union (See Chapter 9 for a full discussion of the supervisor's role in the campaign.)

At the very outset of the campaign, even before an election date has been scheduled, the company should outline its position in writing so supervisors will have an opportunity to read as well as hear the company's position. The policy statement should be prepared by the campaign manager and his legal adviser, and after it is distributed, it should be immediately followed up by a verbal session outlining the same points.

The employer's position statement should have three essential components. The first is an expression of company policy containing a clear and unequivocal statement that the company does not want a union and that the employees do not need one. Along with that, the employer's policy of paying fair wages and providing fringe benefits should be stated; when possible, reference can be made to local examples of unionized companies that pay less. The company's policy of improving wage and benefit levels over the years without a union and without the cost to employees of union dues should also be pointed out. In addition, it should be pointed out that management is convinced that employees are far better off without a union and the company is far better off without the prospect of crippling work stoppages. The goal of this part of the policy statement is to convince the supervisors that *the company's record justifies their support.* It is much better to make this kind of logical appeal based on facts than to threaten supervisors with loss of jobs or other reprisals if the union is successful in its drive. A clear, sharp, and factual presentation of the company's record and the reasons for employer opposition will motivate supervisors to act on behalf of the company.

The second component of the position statement should be an explanation of the supervisors' role in the campaign. They should be advised that employees look to them for leadership and for answers to questions concerning unionization. They should be told that their acts bind the company and that they must not discriminate against employees who may be in favor of the union; they must treat all employees under their jurisdiction with respect and dignity, whether or not they have union sympathies. Supervisors should be told that management expects them to take an active part in convincing employees of the pitfalls of unionization, and that management will assist them in every way possible to be informed about what these pitfalls are. They should be told that if a union does gain entry into the plant, much of the adverse impact will be on the supervisors' ability to fulfill their daily obligations.

The third essential component of the employer's position statement is informing the supervisors of their free-speech rights under the Act. The statement should contain a summary of the "do's and don'ts" for supervisors. As the campaign progresses, the campaign manager and the legal adviser will brief the supervisors more thoroughly and elaborate on what supervisors may and may not do and say.

If management has obtained adverse information about the organizing union, that information should be explicitly and specifically set out in the position statement and attached exhibits. For example, if the organizing union has a contract with another local company whose benefit programs are not as good as yours, excerpts (or the contract itself) can be provided to the supervisors. Comparisons should be made and explained to the supervisors so they can discuss the facts with the employers in their charge.

The position statement can also contain a list of strikes recently engaged in by the organizing union and a report of the amount charged by the union in dues and initiation fees. If the organizing union is alien to the employer's locale or industry, this should be pointed out.

Especially when the union is stressing job security, the position statement should point out to supervisors that unions do not bring job security to any plant. The company's layoff and seniority system should be explained and compared with the layoff policy in union contracts. Where possible, supervisors can be given newspaper clippings reporting those union factories that have either closed down or moved out of the area, leaving union members without jobs and without remedies.

In general, supervisors should be alerted to the many opportunities they have to influence their employees against the union by relating facts about the union and its limitations and about the company and its programs. An outline of all company benefits should be provided to the supervisors; they should be told to become familiar not only with the general benefits enjoyed by the employees, but also with the details of the more complicated benefits, such as the pension program and medical/hospitalization coverage.

The employer will find that this written statement of its position will reinforce what the supervisors have heard and will constitute a ready reference guide for them throughout the campaign.

Estimating the Extent of Union Organization

The campaign manager will collate all sources of information and determine how much of an inroad the union has made in its organizing efforts. It would be wise to learn the campaigning style and the tactics and strategy of the organizing union from companies that have been involved with the union in other campaigns. Find out the types of campaign literature used by the union, whether they campaign heavily throughout the election or wait until the last week, and whether their style relies heavily on literature or involves more verbal contact, with many face-to-face meetings and home visitations.

Of extreme value in determining the union's progress are polls designed to elicit information from the supervisors about the pro-union sympathies of those under their jurisdiction. Supervisors can be asked to estimate the depth of the union's penetration by predicting how each individual employee would vote if the election were conducted on the day of the poll. When doing this, take care to exclude employees who may not be viewed as supervisors by the NLRB; soliciting their opinion as to the pro-union sympathies of their co-workers will constitute an unfair labor practice.

If any supervisor is suspected of being less than loyal to management, he may be excluded from these meetings, and the company will have to decide whether to terminate his or her employment. Discharge of a supervisor for not campaigning on the employer's behalf is permissible. (However, discharging a supervisor for refusal to perform illegal campaign activities would violate the Act.)

To take a supervisory poll, give each supervisor a list of his employees and ask him to classify the individuals into three groups: (a) pro-union, (b) pro-company, (c) undetermined. Supervisors should be asked to make a "conservative" estimate, resolving any doubts *against* the company. For example, if a supervisor believes an employee may be a union sympathizer but is not sure, that employee should be listed in the pro-union column. This will ensure a more accurate estimate and will serve as a check against supervisory reluctance to classify those in their own departments as pro-union. Requiring supervisors to classify individuals in these categories also forces them to think early in the campaign about the individuals under their jurisdiction and how to persuade them to vote for the company.

To guard against undue supervisory optimism, it would also be wise after the poll to ask each supervisor to give his estimate of what the final vote will be—for example, 60 percent for the company, 40 percent for the union. The plant-wide estimates given by the supervisors will invariably be less optimistic than their predictions in the individual polls. To guard against overoptimism, some employers even double the number of employees classified as pro-union by the supervisors.

Supervisors should be urged to give honest estimates; they should be told that there will be no reprisals taken against them if they report a heavy incidence of union activity in their own departments. But even if such a poll is inaccurate, it will serve the campaign manager well, because when subsequent polls are taken, he will be in a position to determine any *shift of opinion*. Usually, opinion will shift in favor of the company as the campaign progresses. If there is a strong pro-company shift in opinion, the campaign manager may consider conducting a more temperate campaign. If the trend moves in the direction of the union, the employer's campaign must be accelerated and its campaign efforts doubled.

Some sophisticated employers ask supervisors to classify their employees on a sliding scale of one to five—one for those who are ardently pro-union and five for strong pro-company supporters. The numerical designations are then averaged. If the company gets an average of, for example, 3.2, it would indicate a pro-company stance among employees as a whole, since 3 would be neutral. Many companies believe that this type of classification system will register more sensitive changes in employee sentiment—e.g., a later poll of 3.5 on the scale will indicate a shift toward the company.

To assess the extent of union penetration, the campaign manager should require that all key incidents relating to the union, as well as all employee statements or inquiries on union issues, be reported. These statements can be evaluated and diagnosed by the campaign manager so that developing patterns can be ascertained.

Information from employees loyal to the company's cause can also yield a great deal of information about the union activity. Management need not simply sit back and await such information. By telling employees that the company appreciates the support of pro-company individuals, management may find that much information will be volunteered. There is no prohibition against management discussing the union with pro-company employees, but because they are non-supervisory employees, what is said must be carefully screened by the company's legal adviser. When calling such nonsupervisory groups together, it would be wise to preface the meeting by stating that the employees are present because they have expressed an interest in giving their views on unionization to their co-employees. Since they have expressed an interest in ascertaining what can be said to co-workers and the best way of saying it, the meeting has been called for the purpose of providing this information. Employees cannot be told to campaign affirmatively for the employer or to encourage co-employees to reject the union. Such conduct is an unfair labor practice. But they may be told that they have a right to express their opinion on the union's organizational campaign and that the company therefore is telling them what can be said and the best way to say it.

Some employees make it a practice to report on union activities, union meetings, the number of attendees at union functions, and the location of heavy pro-union sentiment within the plant. They will turn over union leaflets and other informational material and will report on union house calls and phone solicitations by the outside organizers. A careful review of this information can reveal a great deal about the union campaign. In accepting such information, it is not permissible for an employer to ask employees to report on union activities or to request that they continue to make regular reports.

Credible nonsupervisory, nonvoting employees who have some knowledge of the employees in the voting group, may also be utilized in the same manner or may be drafted to campaign for the employer as agents. These individuals should be thoroughly prepared on permissible campaigning.

Counting the number of employees who wear pro-union buttons, T-shirts, or insignia, or who display pro-union bumper stickers can assist in estimating the degree of penetration and can help in identifying the issues so management can campaign on the issues that are scoring campaign points for the union. In such cases, management may wish to make an immediate explanation of a particularly troublesome issue.

Some employers utilize other sources of information—for example, the history of layoffs, seniority spreads, promotional opportunities, placement within pay ranges, and so forth. When all this information is collated by the campaign manager, it will be possible for the company to isolate trends, predict sympathies, and accurately forecast the union's strength.

When supervisors communicate early with the employees in their departments, the flow of information is increased. One effective tactic is to have supervisors write personal letters to the employees in their charge at the beginning of the campaign. These letters can emphasize the relationship between the supervisor and the employee, point to favorable aspects of company employment, volunteer to supply information to employees during the course of the campaign, and urge employees to ask any questions they wish on the union issues.

If the supervisor is not considered to be the right person to write such a letter, another appropriate company official can do so instead. This letter should start conditioning employees to look to the front-line supervisor for information and actively encourage them to ask questions of management, rather than relying on the union as a source of information on campaign issues and happenings. Information gleaned in this manner will help the company to determine where corrective action is needed and will quickly expose company weak spots. Of course, no corrective action should be undertaken before it is thoroughly evaluated with counsel, because correcting employee complaints during the course of a campaign, where designed to discourage union activity, is considered to be an unfair labor practice.

Information obtained from loyal employees by the supervisors should be appreciated, but the appreciation should not be made obvious to the voters during the course of the campaign for fear of subjecting pro-company employees to pressure from union sympathizers and other peer groups.

Other signs can be used by the employer in continually assessing the union's strength so that management's campaign can be shaped to suit the relative effectiveness of the union's campaign. For example, the union's continued solicitation of authorization cards, even after the election has been scheduled, may reveal that the union is unsure of its position. (It is true, however, that many unions have a policy of continuing to solicit cards even when they have made great inroads.)

Attendance at meetings is another indication. Even though management may not ask employees to spy on union meetings or ask employees what went on at them, it may happen to learn of the number of persons attending such meetings from an employee who volunteers the information to his supervisor. Many companies assume that the union has approximately twice as many hard-core adherents as appear at any given meeting.

A close examination of the union's campaign material will also provide management with clues to the union's strength. If the campaign is on the silent side or is temperate, it may be a sign that the union has great strength. On the other hand, if the campaign is characterized by name-calling, wild accusations, and criticisms of company personnel and policies, the union may be less certain of its standing at the polls.

If a great many employees publicly avow their sympathies with the union and make these sympathies known in a blatant manner, it is a negative sign for the company.

When company officials make speeches during the course of the campaign, someone other than the speechmaker should study employee attitudes during the speech, particularly at the conclusion. If the group's reaction is quiet, it should cause some management concern.

The questions asked and the standing of the questioner should be evaluated and analyzed. They can provide strong hints about employee attitudes; for example, questions like "What will happen if the union loses?" often reveal that employees sense a union loss. Management should encourage employees to ask questions. Where necessary, management can have a supervisor or other individual ask certain questions at the meeting in order to prompt active participation and to make sure that a particularly good management point is communicated.

The frequency of union home phone calls and visits may also provide clues. Visits to employees viewed as pro-company usually indicate a lack of union support. When there are a great many house calls, the union may believe that it is running behind in the campaign. It is extremely dangerous to generalize in this area, however; the union's strategy away from the plant depends on a variety of factors and must be carefully evaluated.

In the last analysis, though, supervisors' opinions about the attitude of their employees is the best barometer of employee feeling. If management is concerned about the accuracy of the supervisors' opinion, it may prefer to solicit their unsigned estimates of the number of votes in their departments. The tallies can be added by a supervisor other than a management official so that supervisors will not be revealed by the number of employees in their departments. Moreover, supervisory estimates may be checked with the opinion of higher-level managers who are familiar with the employees, such as assistant superintendents and plant managers.

Management should utilize all these devices for determining the extent of union penetration, and use good judgment and the experience of a professional adviser to evaluate the results. This will enable management to change its emphasis in a campaign, to react intelligently to developments, and to structure its campaign accordingly.

Avoiding Dealings With Employee Groups

Occasionally, during the course of an organizing campaign, a group of employees will ask the employer whether it is permissible to establish their own union or committee, reject the outside organizing union, and deal directly with the employer.

This presents a pitfall for most companies. Although there is no requirement under the National Labor Relations Act that the union be an official AFL-CIO union, so-called independent unions are rarely independent. If the employer is found assisting in the establishment of the organization, or contributing financial support to it, or if it is found that the relationship between the in-plant group and the employer is something other than an arm's-length one, the Board will find that the employer's dealing with the union constituted an unfair labor practice and will either set aside the election or, possibly, order the employer to bargain with the organizing union.

An employer runs the same risk where in-plant groups form for the purpose of campaigning against the union. Indirect employer support, such as allowing the organization to use company facilities, company time, or food and drink concessions, have aroused the NLRB's suspicion. If the employer allows the inside union special privileges, such as use of the company bulletin boards, meeting rooms, duplicating equipment, typing facilities, profits from vending machines, etc., the organizing union is sure to file charges that may well result in a finding that the employer has interfered with the employees' right to organize.

Thus any dealings with such independent groups must be reviewed and scrutinized carefully by counsel. Moreover, statements by pro-company independent groups must be monitored by the employer. If they make statements that would be unfair labor practices if uttered by the employer, it might be wise to disavow the statements and to correct the record to avoid having the election set aside.

Another pitfall involved in dealing with the formation of such employee committees is that their dealings with the employer may be ineffective. Militant elements rise to the top of the organization, and if the employer does not meet its demands the militants may seek affiliation with an AFL-CIO union. This can be accomplished by majority vote of the independent union's members—without an NLRB-supervised election! Management would then be obligated to deal with the new union. This conversion from independent to AFL-CIO affiliate has occurred frequently enough in the past that management should be forewarned before encouraging such committees or dealing with them.

The best posture for management when confronted with these situations is to continue to deal with the employees on an individual basis and to make a firm, strong pitch for maintaining direct dealings between employer and employees rather than adopting a collective approach.

The Excelsior List

When the consent election agreement is signed, or when the Board orders an election pursuant to a hearing, the employer is required to furnish the NLRB with a list of the names and addresses of all eligible voters in the agreed-upon unit. The list is known as the "Excelsior" list after the name of the Supreme Court case establishing the requirement that the list be provided by the employer. The names and addresses are due in the Regional Director's office within seven days of the date of the direction of, or agreement to, an election. The Board, in turn, will transmit the list to the union. The names and addresses can be listed alphabetically, by clock number, department, or other logical system. The list must be supplied even if the union already has the information at its disposal. Failure to submit a list, or submission of an incomplete or inaccurate list will cause the election to be set aside. Therefore great care must be exercised in fulfilling the Board's requirement.

Although the Board has said that it does not apply the rule in an absolutely rigid fashion, exceptions have been allowed only for minor, inadvertent errors. It is inexcusable for the employer to fail to comply with this rule and thus give the union a second chance solely because of a technical error or a delay in compiling the list. The Excelsior list will be used as the voting list on the date of the election and should be kept current.

Many employers include on the list only the first initial of the employee's first name rather than the entire first name. This makes the union address letters to the home using the first initial only, which is much less personal than the use of the full first name.

Chapter 7

Structuring the Campaign

To assist the campaign manager in the actual work of running the campaign, the employer must establish a task force. The task force is responsible to the campaign manager for obtaining information, planning and coordinating the campaign effort, and advising the campaign manager on matters within its dominion.

Under the guidance of the campaign manager, the task force will establish a timetable for the campaign, mapping out the day-to-day anticipated strategy for the three-to-four-week duration of the campaign. It will outline the issues that management will emphasize and determine when those issues should be developed. It will decide when letters to the home will be mailed and the subject of each letter, what handouts, leaflets, clippings, posters, and other communications should be used and how they should be distributed. It will determine the major issues and the basic themes on which the company will base its campaign. It will be responsible for training the front-line supervisors, obtaining feedback from the staff, evaluating the content of union communications, and generally coordinating the campaign effort. Each member of the task force should be an effective communicator.

Campaign Psychology

In determining the company's basic approach, it should be remembered that the NLRB ballots are structured in a way that employees may vote either *for* or *against* the union. There is no way to vote in favor of the *company*. Accordingly, the language of company communications should be designed to induce a "vote no" response—i.e., the message should emphasize *vote against the union* rather than *for the company*.

The company's communications should also do most of the following:

- Tell employees why a union would be harmful to their interests. Advise them to maintain control of their own affairs without the interference of outside union strangers.

- Explain the company's existing benefits, which may not be obvious. List the whole program, from the most important down to such less-significant benefits as company picnics, bowling leagues, and Christmas parties.

- Refer to adverse past experiences the company may have had with unions or unfavorable past experiences other local companies, known to the employees, have had with the organizing union or some other union. Explain the consequences of strikes and the financial loss involved when a strike takes place. Urge employees to evaluate the financial motive of the union; explain the nature of a union as a business institution, motivated by the financial incentive.

- Inform employees that management has the right to discipline and to lay off under a union contract and that a union contract does not protect employees from either discharge or layoff.

- Refer to the unpleasant social situations that can result from a union's entering the plant and dividing the employees between those who favor the union and those who oppose it. Point to the demonstrable divisions the union has already caused. Refer to the common practice in non-right-to-work states where employees are forced to join the union against their will. Compare existing benefits to the lesser benefits enjoyed by other specific companies with union contracts (almost always, relevant analogies will be found).

- State that the company is the true source of job security and that unions do not create jobs. Point to the number of the organizing union's members who are not employed (if true) as a specific fact to bolster the general concept.

- Emphasize union dues, initiation fees, fines, and other assessments. Point out the union's right to increase dues.

- Inform employees that benefits do not automatically occur simply because a union is voted into the plant—the union only obtains the right to discuss and negotiate the demands that it places on the table.

- Explain why the company does not want a union, referring to the loss of flexibility and operational control and the great deal of time necessary to deal with unions in the plant.

Management must study where to concentrate its attack. Evaluate the company's and the union's strengths and weaknesses. Then concentrate on the union's weaknesses and emphasize the company's strengths. Invariably, a main issue will crop up on either side of the fence. However, management should not feel irrevocably attached to those issues. The tenor of a campaign often changes; new issues may arise to alter its character. Thus, management's campaign may be legitimately diverted from its original purpose into other areas.

In this connection, management should heed the following caveat: *Never run a canned campaign.* There is a tendency to repeat campaign material from previous campaigns or to borrow campaign material used by other employers. In a multilocation corporation, local management may be tempted to use the canned materials offered by main-office corporate industrial relations advisers. The danger in utilizing these canned materials, from whatever source, is that they encourage the campaign manager to force the campaign in the direction of the prefabricated materials rather than letting the issues control what is said.

Moreover, reliance on previously successful arguments in the present situation may be entirely misplaced. Overkilling a weak organizing attempt may actually play into union hands and create unnecessary sympathy for the union. The use of successful arguments and campaign materials against the Bakery Workers may simply not work in a case against the Chemical Workers because of differences in the types of companies involved, the personalities of the union organizers, the experience of the employees with past organizing drives, and the quality of the union campaign. Management must isolate the issues and facts that the voters in the election are concerned with. This can rarely be done from the outside; it takes diligence and expertise that can be provided only by those on the scene.

Generally, an employer has a choice between appealing to employees' loyalty and their *fears* over unionization. The best campaign appeals to the employees' loyalty to the company. This is possible when the company has engaged in excellent prevention programs, when its communications systems are working well, when wages meet or are better than competitive wages, and when the company maintains a generous program of fringe benefits. In such cases, the major appeal will be to the company's record and the employees' loyalty to the company, based on what the company has done for them in the past. Where the company's credibility is high, the appeal to employee loyalty is effective.

However, when the company has not done its homework in terms of preventive medicine, when wages or benefits lag, when no effective communications systems or feedback methods have been developed, and particularly when supervisors have not developed the rapport necessary to win a campaign, the company's theme must center upon the dangers of embracing unionism. In this type of campaign, the undesirable consequences of unionism, the possibilities of strikes, plant closures, and union violence, and other negative facts about unionism must be skillfully portrayed—at all times keeping within the employer's free-speech rights and avoiding crossing the line into the area of impermissible campaign statements. (*What* may be said in a union campaign is treated extensively in Chapter 8.)

Determining the timing of what is said and the exact methods by which the messages will be communicated requires expertise and a thorough knowledge of the issues. In some campaigns, it may be decided that two to three letters will be sent to the home and only one "captive audience" speech will be made, in addition to other routine communications. Other elections may require as many as four plant-wide speeches (one each week during the campaign), and a great variety of leaflets, posters, and other campaign materials.

Basically, the timing and method of communication will be determined by management's assessment of how well it is doing in the campaign. If supervisory polls and other information lead the company to believe that it is not gaining as much ground as it should, management must zero in on the issues affecting the employees and accelerate the flow of communications. When the voting group is large, a greater reliance on the written word may be necessary.

The *union's* campaign is another determinant of the timing and method of communication. Generally, if the union campaigns heavily, management will also. If management's information leads it to believe that the union is engaging in a strong campaign of home visits and telephone solicitation and using very little literature, this may be a danger signal. The absence of literature may mean that a union is making great headway in its oral and personal solicitations, thereby decreasing the need for literature. Smart unions often avoid literature campaigns to keep management in the dark as to the true issues. When this union strategy is suspected, and when there is an inordinate number of home visits and telephone calls, it may be time for management to accelerate its campaign.

Every campaign is different, but some rules always apply. The basic rule is: *Management's campaign should not be defensive!* The saying that the best defense is a good offense applies. Management has more options than to simply answer union charges; in fact, some union charges are best handled by silence. Undue concern with each and every union pamphlet, leaflet, or statement may detour management from its campaign plan.

To avoid an excessively defensive campaign, management should emphasize the company's strong points and constantly repeat its views on those areas in which management believes the union is the weakest. A good sign that the company's campaign is an offensive one is union preoccupation with defending *itself* against the company's campaign. When that occurs, the union has been distracted from the issues and spends an inordinate amount of time defending itself against charges rather than converting undecided employees into the union camp. Newspaper clippings, listings of strikes the union has engaged in, and other articles and information reflecting on the union's character are among the weapons in the employer's arsenal.

Developing Employee Feedback

Employees are reticent to speak up or speak out on issues, particularly at the start of a campaign, and equally hesitant to ask questions about the election or the campaign. To induce employee questions and increase communication, it may be advisable for the company to make available a suggestion box for employee questions concerning the election. A system that does not indicate that the employer intends to use it to solicit and adjust grievances is proper. Here is a suggested notice for advertising the system.

**DO YOU HAVE ANY QUESTIONS ABOUT
THE UNION ELECTION?**

IF SO, HERE'S WHAT YOU CAN DO:

TO KEEP YOU INFORMED SO YOU CAN HAVE ALL THE FACTS BEFORE YOU VOTE, WE ARE ESTABLISHING AN ANSWERING SERVICE FOR ANY QUESTION YOU MAY HAVE.

IF YOU WANT TO ASK ANY QUESTION ABOUT WHAT IS GOING ON DURING THE UNION CAMPAIGN, WRITE IT OUT ON A SLIP OF PAPER AND DROP THE QUESTION IN THE BOX WE HAVE SET UP FOR THIS PURPOSE NEAR THE TIMECLOCK.

BETWEEN NOW AND AUGUST 3, WE WILL ANSWER, PUB-

LICLY AND IN WRITING, ALL QUESTIONS ASKED BY
ANYONE VOTING IN THE ELECTION.

DON'T SIGN IT BECAUSE WE ARE NOT INTERESTED IN
YOUR IDENTITY; WE ARE ONLY CONCERNED WITH
MAKING ALL THE FACTS CONCERNING THIS VERY IM-
PORTANT VOTE KNOWN TO ALL. WE'LL CHECK THE BOX
FOR QUESTIONS EACH MORNING AND GIVE YOU OUR
ANSWERS IN WRITING, ON THE BULLETIN BOARD
WITHIN 48 HOURS.

DON'T BE BASHFUL! IF YOU HAVE A QUESTION . . .
ASK IT.

Announced in this manner, the suggestion box is merely a vehicle
for campaign propaganda and perfectly permissible. *Aircraft Hydro-
Forming, Inc.*, 221 NLRB 581 (1975).

May an employer, upon learning of union organizational activity,
conduct an employee opinion poll concerning working conditions?
This depends on the exact factual setting in which the poll takes place
and the nature of the questions asked. If the poll is taken prior to the
"critical period" (the union's filing for an election) the employer can
be confident that even if the Board subsequently considers the polling
to be improper interrogation, the election will not be set aside. Only
conduct occurring between filing and the date of the election will be
considered in deciding whether to set aside the election. The Board
may conclude that the survey constitutes improper interrogation, an
unfair labor practice, and issue a cease and desist order, but not nullify
the election.

What determines whether a survey is legal or illegal? There is no violation of the Act if the survey is not accompanied by an implied
promise of benefits and does not inquire into the employees' opinions
of unions in general or the particular union attempting to organize the
employer. The Board has held that an opinion survey of employees
administered *during an organizational campaign* did not imply any
promise of benefits. *I.T.T. Telecommunications*, 183 NLRB 1129
(1970). In that case the employer inquired about employees' opinions
on numerous areas, such as:

I know where I stand with my supervisor.

My supervisor fails to give credit for work well done.

Merit pay increases are handled fairly.

I'm really doing something worthwhile in my job.

I'm proud to work for this company.

Many company employees I know would like to see the
union get in.

The company pays fairly for the kind of work I do.

During the past six months I have seriously considered leaving the company for another job.

Employees in my group feel they must hide their mistakes.

I would recommend employment with this company to my friends.

My supervisor takes time to discuss my job performance with me.

My pay has little influence on my attitudes about my job.

Favoritism is a problem in my area.

I am satisfied with the food available where I work.

Most people I know in my community have a good opinion of the company.

It is hard to find out what jobs are open here in the company.

I can usually find my supervisor when I need him.

Most employees are in jobs that make good use of their abilities.

I feel lost in a company this size.

I've gone as far as I can ever go in the company.

My job seems to be leading to the kind of future I want.

The efforts of my group are appreciated.

The amount of effort a person puts into his job is appreciated here with the company.

I feel that there is someone in authority in this plant, either the Plant Manager or some other member of management, that I can go to with any problem I may have about my work and who will help me and take a personal interest in my problem.

I think the company is fair in trying to provide things within reason for its employees.

The crucial item was, "Many company employees I know would like to see the union get in." The Board found the question innocuous in the context of that case. However, to minimize the possibility that the Board will find such a question an improper attempt to learn of the employees' attitude toward unionism, avoid inquiring into the employee's union sympathy or the attitude of his co-employees.

Thus, absent a promise, surveying attitudes is not illegal particularly if the stated purpose of the survey is to achieve greater motivation toward efficient and productive work. The questionnaire form returned by the employee should not reveal the employee's department or supervisor or contain any other information that might identify the questionee.* Care should be taken to compose the letter announcing

---

* Sample questionnaires are contained in Appendix 4.

and accompanying the survey so that there is nothing in the communication that may imply a promise of remedying grievances solicited in the survey. Nor should the letter specify that improved working conditions may come about as a direct result of the survey.

As noted in the discussion of ascertaining the causes of union interest (Chapter 6), absent a statement indicating that the employer will not remedy grievances which surface as a result of the questionnaire, the Board may read into the fact situation an implied promise to remedy a grievance. Consequently, I suggest that a paragraph be inserted in the accompanying letter which contains "no promises" language. Such a clause might read: "This opinion survey is only for the purpose of achieving greater motivation toward efficient and productive work. Since NLRB rules prohibit changes in working conditions during election campaigns, the company cannot promise that any problem which becomes evident through the survey will be remedied or corrected."

However, the question of whether the "no promises" language will rebut the inference of solicitation and promises of benefits is still an open one.

If the employer prefers to institute a less risky and more informal method of prompting employees to communicate their views on working conditions, letters such as the following have received approval of the Board:[1]

> To Our Employees and Their Families:
>
> We watched with interest while the "strangers at the gates" handed out propaganda on their respective unions proclaiming your rights and their promises. There is something we should tell you about those cards which were attached.
>
> The cards, when signed by you, directly authorize these strangers to represent you during negotiations with the company. There will be *no* election. That's right. NO election. NO chance for you to express your opinion. NO opportunity for you to vote whether you want a union or not. That card is as good as a ballot, and when the National Labor Relations Board is convinced that the union has enough cards (that's right; the NLRB decides, not you), you will have a union whether you wanted one or not.[2] Read it carefully. It says that I *your name* authorize *union name* to represent me in collective bargaining. What could be clearer?
>
> Yes, it is frightening, but you *can do* something about it whether you have sent in a card or not. Here is what you can do:

---

[1]*Aircraft Hydro-Forming, Inc.*, 221 NLRB 581 (1975).

[2] While such a statement is an oversimplification of the law, it was not viewed by the Board as violative of the Act.

A.   If you have sent in a card, you can send a certified letter (return receipt requested) to the union requesting that they return your card. They *must* do this. You have that right.

B.   If you are still undecided, don't send in your card. Make these strangers give you your right to vote.

Either union would like to avoid an election. Not only do these cards insure them immediate recognition as the *sole* bargaining agent for you, but the cards save them from spending *other union members' dues* on a long, costly campaign that may not succeed. No one is going to spend a lot of money on anything that doesn't have a profitable return.

Again, *we invite your comments and questions concerning this new, very complex problem.* Don't let your rights be negated by a few clever individuals.

Sincerely yours,

_____

To Our Employees and Their Families:

During the past few days, several of your fellow employees have indicated an interest in having a union represent them. Your company does not feel that a union is in the best interest of you, our employee.

The company prefers to continue to deal directly and openly with its employees rather than through some outside organization. We are not in favor of a third party, who is neither employer nor employee, speaking about problems that concern you and not them. We have worked together in a friendly, cooperative manner in the past, and we do not believe that it is in your best interest to bring in outsiders, *pay your money* to them, and at the same time run the risk of *strikes* and other associated problems.

We will continue our open door policy of listening to your problems, and *we invite your comments concerning this serious matter.*

Sincerely yours,

_____

Therefore, before attempting any type of attitude survey or method of inviting employee comments during an ongoing campaign, the Board's latest precedents must be consulted with great care to avoid any possibility of the election being set aside or a card-based bargaining order being issued on the basis of pervasive questioning during the campaign.

An excellent technique designed to develop feedback as to employee sentiments, complaints, and questions during the campaign is to attach to any letter to the home a separate sheet with an appropriate legend requesting employees to write their comments, questions and complaints and return them to management in a pre-stamped, self-addressed envelope without the identity of the writer being known. The return address could be marked to the direct attention of a popular person in a top-management position. As long as the letter contains no implication that complaints will be rectified, such a device may be useful in developing the issues and preparing campaign materials.

Another excellent technique involves using questionnaires to test employee understanding of the employer's campaign argument. This is explained in chapter 8 (Contests and Prizes).

Reporting the Facts

Employees should be conditioned to *look to the employer* for the facts. The employer should constantly put itself in the position of "writing the record," centering its campaign around a constant repetition of facts that are important to the company's theme and a constant exposure of the union's exaggerated promises, innuendoes, and half-truths. When this is done in a calm, temperate manner, without bitterness, company credibility increases. Do not fall prey to the temptation of matching the union's violent statements and extreme accusations against the company.

Management should constantly be in the position of pointing out the union's falsehoods and exaggerations.

Some managements gather together a number of union misstatements and expose them at the appropriate time, either in a letter sent to the homes or in a speech to all employees. When exposing union falsehoods, management should try, where possible, to rely on outside documentary evidence of the truth—facts, statistics, U.S. government reports, newspaper clippings, and other source material—to improve management's credibility and maintain employee respect. Management's posture should be that it is the union that makes wild claims, but it is the company that provides the facts on which the individual employee can make his decision on whether to vote for or against the union.

Anticipating the Union's Reaction

Before issuing any campaign material, the employer must carefully evaluate what the union reaction will be to a particular piece of information. Communications should be designed to avoid effective rebuttals by the union. For example, if the company decides to publicize the high salaries and expense accounts of the union organizers involved in the campaign, it must first assess whether the salaries of high company officials are a matter of public knowledge. Often, the employer, anxious to embarrass the union and to expose its financial motives, will find that it is embarrassed itself when the union obtains from public sources the fact that the company's president's salary is double or triple the salaries of the union organizers.

Making Supervisors a Part of the Team

Supervisors should not be overlooked in the process of communicating. They should not receive campaign literature or home mailings at the same time the employees do. Handouts, leaflets, and letters should be given personally to the supervisors before they are given to the voters. This will let supervisors know that they are truly a part of management's team and will sponsor a greater spirit of cooperation and campaign morale. Supervisors should be kept constantly aware of developments in the campaign, and frequent meetings should be held to explain the company's position in response to union leaflets, arguments, or issues.

Supervisors should be told to be extremely cautious in dealing with known pro-union supervisors. In the first place, there is very little to be said to them; no amount of persuasion will affect the way they vote. Second, there is the danger that any discussion between supervisor and a known union sympathizer might be misquoted and used as a basis for an unfair labor practice charge against the company.

In its zeal to mail letters home and to publish and distribute effective leaflets, posters, bulletins, rumor sheets, and other campaign items, management should never lose sight of the fact that the most effective overall campaign technique is the "eyeball-to-eyeball" talk between supervisors (or other company officials) and individual employees. (Methods of training supervisors for campaign activity are treated extensively in Chapter 9.)

Bulletin Boards

The bulletin board is an effective method of reiterating points that have already been made verbally. Most verbal discussions should be reinforced. Clippings and other material can be posted from time to time to keep the campaign fresh and alive. The material should be constantly changed so that the bulletin board will remain a center of employee attention.

Union organizers' manuals often stress that campaign material should be brief. Management is well advised to steal a page from the union book in this respect. Company messages should be to the point. Preferably, each piece of posted written literature should address one topic and be no longer than a page, with a liberal use of headlines, simple words, short sentences, and short paragraphs. Exclamation points, captions, and upper-case emphasis should be liberally sprinkled throughout the communication. Photographs, graphic factual support of the main message contained in the letter, cartoons, clippings, and excerpts create and hold attention and are remembered.

A management communication should not make any untrue statements. Any figures used by management should be verifiable instantly upon demand. The campaign material should be read by each member of the task force, and if possible by several supervisors, to look for any information that may not be well received by the employees. Care should also be taken that the union does not pick out a management statement and convert it to its own use during the campaign. Once the literature has been thus reviewed and analyzed, it is ready for distribution in the most eye-catching manner possible.

Each bulletin board should be in a locked glass case; this permits management to control the postings. If the company has a practice of allowing employees to post their own notices on company bulletin boards, there may be an obligation to allow their use for union literature.

An employer may uniformly enforce a rule prohibiting the use of its bulletin boards by employees for all purposes. However, implementing a rule by prohibiting the posting of material relating to employee concerted activity, *while having previously allowed* the posting of other miscellaneous matters by the employees, is a discriminatory denial of access to an employer's bulletin board. *Vincent's Steak House*, 216 NLRB 647 (1975). So, where an employer has a practice of permitting employees to post on its bulletin boards notice of various types unrelated to their employment, but removes only notices of union meetings and other topics on the subject of unionism which the employer finds distasteful or unsuitable to its campaign posture, a violation of the Act occurs. *Nugent Service Inc.*, 207 NLRB 158 (1973). Accordingly, bulletin boards should be reserved strictly for messages *from management*. Guidelines concerning the use of the bulletin board should be either published in the employee handbook or posted on the bulletin board.

Letters Home

Management should address the letters to the home not only to the employee but to the spouse as well. This is particularly true of communications outlining the possibility of strikes, since they will often cause the spouse to influence the voter in favor of the company. The timing of the letters depends on circumstances, but certainly one letter should reach employees on the weekend before the election. The letters should be personally signed and, if possible, reproduced in a manner that makes each letter look like an original. This tends to create a feeling on the part of the recipient that the letter is directed to him or her as an individual, and is not part of a mass campaign. Each letter should be *short* and should emphasize only one or two issues. Simple language should be used, "employee" language, not "executive jargon." The letters should be *clear* and *personal* and should never create the feeling that they have been written by outsiders.

When the electorate is small, it will be worth management's time to individualize the letter, making certain points in one letter and different points in another, depending on the individual being communicated with. These personally tailored letters are a most effective technique and should be encouraged whenever the size of the electorate does not make them impracticable.

Mid-Campaign Speeches

Other than the "captive-audience speech" given 24 hours before the election, management will often find it necessary to give at least one or two other general speeches to employees. The speeches should not make employees feel that they are being brainwashed, and they should not create a feeling of boredom when it becomes known that the employer is about to make "another speech." Thus, mid-election speeches should be shorter than the captive-audience speech—probably no longer than fifteen minutes. The speech should be tailored to one or two particular issues and may often be geared to rebutting a union claim in a more extensive manner than would be possible by way of written campaign literature. Questions from the floor should be encouraged so management can evaluate the issues and determine what is on the minds of the employees. This will enable it to strengthen its subsequent campaigning. A tape of the speech should be made for future reference in the event that unfair labor practices are filed or objections are made to the conduct of the election.

The Union's Request for Equal Time

Frequently, the union will send management a letter or telegram demanding an equal opportunity to reply to management discussions with employees. The employer is under no obligation to respond to such requests. However, good campaign strategy dictates that a reply to the union be made so that management does not appear to be unreasonable or afraid of the union. A sample hard-hitting response is:

> The union's latest pitch is to ask for a chance to debate me in the plant.
> We reject this attempt by *outsiders* to get *inside* our plant. We won't let them in! They were out there attempting to get your dues long before we knew it. They have their own meetings *and we have ours*.
> So, SORRY MR. UNION PROFESSIONAL DUES COLLECTOR, you can't come into our plant to try to seduce our employees to share their paychecks with you.

A less argumentative approach would be:

> In today's leaflet, the union has complained that we would not give them an "equal" opportunity to debate with me in the plant.
> We think this is a strange request.
> For many, many weeks now, the union has had daily opportunities to meet with you, hand out leaflets, and try to organize you.
> The union has had many meetings and it has the opportunity to talk to you after work. They can even visit you in your homes—we can't. They were approaching you long before we knew about it, and they have many opportunities to speak to you.
> The union never gave me equal time with them; therefore, it is only fair that we should not give them equal time with us.
> They're outsiders, and we hope you will keep them that way!

Another form of response could read as follows:

> Dear _____:
> We have received your communication requesting permission to address our employees on company time within the plant during working hours. We would be happy to debate you. However, the NLRB allows unions to make any promise or statement whatsoever about what the union will obtain for employees whether or not the union actually does obtain these benefits. The same rule is not true for management. The federal government prohibits any company official from making statements about what conditions will be like if the union is voted out. No matter what a union official said, there would be no violation of law. However, almost anything manage-

ment said about future policies beneficial to employees would be illegal.

Therefore, we will agree to debate you only if you send us a registered letter stating that no matter what we say, you will not file any unfair labor practice charge against us and you will not file any objection to the election based upon any statement made at this meeting.

Yours truly,

_____

The 24-Hour Speech

This speech, given as close to the 24-hour period prior to the election as possible, should be the most carefully planned effort of the campaign. The task force should outline the issues and assign them priorities in terms of which issue has the greatest impact on the employees. Any lingering union arguments that have not been effectively rebutted and that may incline employees toward the union should be destroyed in this last speech.

The talk should also contain an explanation of the ballot and the election procedure. Employees should be reminded that the ballot is secret, and they should be urged to vote. The consequences of *not* voting should be fully explained. The speech should end with a strong emotional appeal, and since it is usually the employer's last word in a campaign, it should end with strong emphasis on the positive, a reiteration of what the company has done for the employees without a union, and reminders of the benefits they have received without union dues. The employees should be assured that the company's record is a fair one and that the company intends to continue its record of paying competitive wages, building on the existing level of fringe benefits, treating employees fairly, and encouraging them to continue their present, pleasant work situation without the interference of outside strangers who charge dues for their services.

The Board administers its 24-hour rule in a strict, technical fashion. Therefore, it is vital to ensure that the speech ends no later than 24 hours before the election, so that it does not extend into the 24-hour prohibited period.

The Board's 24-hour rule does not prevent speeches at which attendance by employees is *voluntary* and *on their own time*. This is true whether the speech takes place on or off company property. When employers believe that they are behind in the election campaign, the day of the election may be used for campaign purposes *as long as at-*

tendance is voluntary. However, any such campaigning addressed to mass assemblies of employees within the 24-hour period should be carefully checked with counsel.

The rule does not prohibit *individual discussions* with employees within the 24-hour period, or discussions with small groups of employees.

The groups, however, must not be too large. For example, if election day speeches are made by management officials to groups of from three to ten employees in a planned and systematic manner, the Board would find a violation and would consider the *Peerless Plywood* rule to have been violated. The rule against speeches to "massed assemblies" may embrace groups as small as three employees where, as noted above, all or most unit employees are reached by such a series of small group meetings. In close cases it is recommended that one or several management officials campaign within the 24-hour period with individual employees separately on an informal, personal basis without calling employees away from their work stations or addressing them as a group. Such brief comments do not constitute a formal speech, nor do they create the "mass psychology" on which an employer's unfair advantage can be grounded. The Board has held that the repetitious nature, reach, location, and timing of individual conversations do not singly or in combination transform the comments into a collective speech that violates the 24-hour moratorium on election speeches to massed assemblies of employees. *Associated Milk Producers*, 237 NLRB No. 120 (1978); *Electro-Wire Prods., Inc.*, 242 NLRB No. 144 (1979). Since the rule does not apply to written materials, literature may be distributed within the 24-hour period.

An important practical point: The speech should be made without advance notice to employees whenever possible. This will minimize the opportunity for the union to "plant" questions among employees or to circulate a list of suggested questions to be asked by employees during the speeches.

An aggressive union may induce employees to heckle the company's speaker during the speech by persistently asking questions. This can be in part avoided by stating prior to commencement of the speech that because of the NLRB rules on deadlines, questions cannot be answered during the speech. If employees insist on harassing the speaker during the speech, and if the employer can prove that the employees engaged in planned conduct calculated to disrupt the company's meeting and to dilute its legitimate purpose, hecklers may be discharged or otherwise disciplined for such interruptions. However, if the interruptions are spontaneous, spur-of-the-moment reactions not part of a planned effort, discipline would probably not be upheld by the Board, particularly if there is no showing of violent conduct, improper motive, or bad faith on the part of the employees.

Companies may also invite their employees to a dinner or other affair where refreshments are served, at a local restaurant, other establishment, or on company premises within the 24-hour period (usually the night before the election) *if attendance is voluntary*.

Picture Illustrations

The more graphic the campaign, the more effective the communication. Perfectly permissible are the use of photographs or illustrations depicting union strike headquarters, picketing by unions at other locations, empty plants closed down, and similar items.

Some companies raffle off a market basket full of grocery items; the market basket is on constant visual display throughout the campaign. The cost of the items in the market basket approximates the yearly dues charged by the union. This is a constant visual reminder of the cost of union dues and is much more effective than simply stating the monthly amount of dues in employer literature.

Movies and Films

The use of professionally scripted and acted motion pictures in Board elections is a tactical device of enormous potential and influence. The motion picture is a much more powerful instrument than the printed or spoken word in arousing emotions and influencing attitudes. Not only is its initial impact greater, but it also has a more lasting effect. Skilled direction and the expert use of characters, dialogue, and situations can create powerful messages.

Two of the films most commonly shown to employees during the course of campaigns are "And Women Must Weep" and "Springfield Gun."

The NLRB previously ruled that these films created such an emotional impact that their exhibition during a campaign constituted a proper basis for objecting to the election. The Board noted that the film told the story of property destruction, violence and the near murder of a child allegedly committed by a union during the course of a strike ostensibly called for no justifiable reason. The Board viewed the picture as portraying a labor dispute as something in which Americanism, religion, family, motherhood, and innocent children are arrayed on one side, and goons, brutes, and murderers on the union side. It ruled that the use of the motion picture painted a fearsome picture of what could happen to employees if they voted for union representation, and that the film unjustifiably aroused emotions and influenced an antiunion attitude.

However, the federal courts consistently disagreed with the Board. As a result, the NLRB reversed its own decisions and has held that both films may be legally exhibited.* Another film, "A Question of Law and Order," is often shown and is permissible.

A more recent production (1978), "Stranger In My House,"** involving a combination of slides and sound, is also suitable for most levels of employees. It depicts modern abuse of union power and illustrates the lack of need for unions today.

Management must screen these films carefully and decide whether the material contained in these presentations (often unreal and in many respects outdated) will have the intended favorable impact upon the employees. The opinions of supervisors and of one or two loyal employees should be solicited before the films are shown to the electorate.

Company produced slide presentations can also be an effective method of presenting information to groups of employees. For example, company benefits can be shown on slides and explained orally. Other slides may show strike violence and headlines, clippings, or cartoons ridiculing the union movement. The recent headlines and articles depicting abuses of union pension funds may also be effective in dissuading employees from placing their future in the hands of union officials who administer the trust funds that support pension payments.

A more recent technique is to develop an in-company film showing the history and progress of the company from its inception to the present, and the company's history of fair dealing and improvement in wages and benefits. The tempo of the movie changes sharply, however, once the union is depicted on the scene. Their techniques, exaggerated promises, and misrepresentations are revealed. The picture concludes with an emotional depiction of the disadvantages of unionization, the undesirable consequences of having a union in a plant, and the prospect of strikes. It reiterates that a union is not needed in a plant. The value of such movies is that they related to the *particular*

---

* The films may be obtained from the National Right-to-Work Committee, Washington, D.C., on a sale or rental basis. In the author's opinion, since the films stress the right-to-work aspect, they should be purchased so that they can be edited prior to use.

** This film, which has not been the subject of legal review by the NLRB, is available through Modern-Mass Media, Inc., New York, New York.

unionizing effort and are tailored to the individual company. An offsetting disadvantage is the expense involved in producing the film. But when the number of employees involved justifies the expense, a well-produced motion picture of this type may be one of management's most dramatic techniques.

Pro-Company Insignia

The NLRB has upheld the use of "Vote No" buttons and bumper stickers, "happy face" buttons, and pro-company statements on T-shirts and other items. However, management must take great care to insure that no employee is pressured into wearing such insignia and that employees are not asked, in effect, to declare themselves by choosing to wear or not to wear the insignia. Management may make such items *available* to employees, but may not specifically ask an individual to take one or require that they be worn. Company representatives and supervisors should also refrain from *passing out* buttons or similar insignia and observing who accepts or rejects them.

Thus, if an employer's supervisor places a button on the work station of each employee or passes a box containing the buttons to eligible voters, this would constitute improper pressure. The reasoning is that when employees are approached by a supervisor and offered buttons, they have only two alternatives: accept the buttons and thereby acknowledge opposition to the union; or reject them, and thereby indicate their support of the union. In either case, the fact that the employees must make an observable choice is really a form of interrogation. Furthermore, if employees feel compelled to choose a button passed around in this manner, and the button contains a message opposite to their views, that constitutes coercion and it likewise interferes with the election. *Pillowtex Corp.*, 234 NLRB No. 89 (1978).

Two contrasting examples will reveal the fine line between lawful distribution of buttons and improper pressuring of employees.

In one case, the employer, on three occasions during the month preceding the election, placed pro-employer and anti-union buttons in a central location (the employees' cafeteria). Also, in the area was a large red paper arrow pointing toward the buttons. Before the buttons were made available, the employer instructed its supervisors not to discuss the pending distribution with employees. A substantial number of employees wore the buttons during the campaign as did some of the supervisors. However, the supervisors did not participate in the distribution of the buttons.

In another case, the employer announced to assembled groups of employees that buttons were available and supervisors, following instructions, gave buttons to employees who requested them.

In the first example, the Board ruled that merely making buttons available during the campaign does not warrant setting aside the election where supervisors are completely absent from the distribution process, and where management does not pressure employees to make an open choice between the company and the union. *Black Dot, Inc.*, 239 NLRB No. 136 (1978). As an additional safeguard, the employer might also consider announcing, contemporaneously with the distribution of the items, that wearing or not wearing the button is strictly personal and is a voluntary act which in no way will favorably or adversely affect any employee.

The Dues Theme

Management often is able to convey the impact of union dues by issuing two paychecks for a month or a year, one for the net amount and one for the union dues. The checks are distributed in two envelopes, with an explanation to make employees aware of what would happen in the event the union were voted in and a checkoff clause were negotiated by the company. "Play" money and other representations of U.S. currency in the amount of union dues, whether computed on a monthly or an annual basis, are also viewed as permissible by the NLRB. This device is more effective than a simple statement of the amount charged by the union in monthly dues. The use of such graphic devices is encouraged. No matter how many times employees are informed about the high cost of unionism, the real amount of lost income is often not appreciated until after the union wins and deductions hit the paycheck. The cost of a union must be *vividly* demonstrated before the vote.

Plant Posters

Many companies underplay the use of posters. They can be an extremely effective method, since the messages on the posters are usually short and highly visible because they are posted around the plant, in cafeterias and other nonwork areas. The subject matter of the posters should be limited to one or two of the company's prime points; too many issues on the posters diffuses the impact.

Questions and Answers

During the course of a campaign, there may be occasional lulls in campaigning by either side. These lulls present an excellent opportunity for management to post questions and answers on the bulletin boards on issues that management deems relevant. The style should not be argumentative; the questions should be answered factually and positively, leaving employees to their own conclusions.

There are two kinds of questions and answers. First, some questions are applicable in all campaigns and may be used in any context. They pertain to the company's obligation to bargain if a union is chosen, the use of the strike weapon, compulsory unionism, the negotiability of present benefits, and mechanical questions concerning procedures, voting, and other matters germane to all campaigns. (Samples of such questions and answers appear in the Appendix.)

The other type of questions and answers are in response to particular issues that have arisen in the plant, such as recent discharges, layoffs, or other matters. In such cases, management's questions and answers will be tailored to developing events at the plant.

Questions and answers can also be used effectively during the time when the company and union are engaged in a hearing before the NLRB on eligibility or appropriate-unit issues. During the several weeks that it will take to decide the issues, management is often wise to keep a low profile to avoid "peaking" too early. In such cases, the question-and-answer technique is an excellent method of conveying management views and at the same time keeping the most effective arguments for use later in the campaign when they will be more telling. Moreover, this approach prevents the union from learning what management's campaign will be about and what issues the employer will be using as a prime focus. The handling of questions and answers is treated comprehensively in Chapter 9.

Rumor Sheets

Closely related to questions and answers are rumor sheets: The rumor promulgated by the union is stated on the left-hand side of the page and the facts are indicated on the right. This is often an effective way to rebut minor falsehoods by the union and to correct the record.

Management need not await the development of a rumor; it can state perceived rumors and questions. Thus, provisions of the union's bylaws and constitutions that are particularly distasteful to employees can be set up and answered by the employer. When there is a particularly telling point to be made, management may choose not to post the rumor sheet on the bulletin board, but have supervisors distribute it and explain it to each employee personally.

One danger of rumor sheets is that the employer's communication itself may unintentionally advertise the very points that the union wants to make. Thus judgment must be carefully exercised when rumor sheets are used.

Fortune Cookies

An effective device often used in white-collar elections is the distribution of fortune cookies with messages relating to the union campaign substituted for the usual messages contained in the cookies. Sample statements include:

> Union dues put rice in someone else's bowl. VOTE NO!

> One who does not find time to vote may find time to pay union dues. VOTE NO!

> One who uses another's voice loses own ability to speak. VOTE NO!

> Union dues like some tolls; you pay—one way!! VOTE NO!

> So sorry! No fortune with union. VOTE NO!

> One who gives vote to union gives away $120. VOTE NO!

> Union dues ships bread to someone else's table. VOTE NO!

> Union strikes mean minus in paycheck. VOTE NO!

> NO Union = NO Dues = NO Fines = NO Assessments = NO Strikes. Vote NO!

> Remember unions strike. VOTE NO!

> Beware of dragon in organizer's magic lamp. VOTE NO!

> Benefits paid for by dues, fines, assessments, and strikes are no benefits at all. VOTE NO!

> One who gives YES vote to stranger gives away own voice. VOTE NO!

Outside Assistance

It is often helpful to the employer to bring in an outsider to express his or her views on the union campaign. Unions have been known to bring in labor leaders, community leaders, clergymen, and others to assist them in their campaigns; management can adopt this tactic as well. A community leader, a former employee, or a well-liked manager who has been transferred to another facility may be brought in on an occasion to communicate his or her views on maintaining nonunion status.

Statements made by these outsiders should be carefully screened, and the same rules that management applies to itself in the campaign should be applied to the outsider's statements. The NLRB has tended to view outsiders' statements, if coercive, as suffcient to set aside the election, whether or not the statements were authorized by the employer.

Leaks

Management sometimes attempts to leak information that it cannot state openly for fear of incurring unfair labor practice charges. Position papers and other documents have often been "pilfered" by employees, and the information, usually threatening in nature, becomes known to the electorate.

This kind of campaigning is basically unhealthy; management should control its own campaign and articulate its views in a lawful manner. Having to leak information is a sign that the employer's campaign is not being conducted properly. More importantly, the NLRB has set aside elections when such leaks have occurred, even when the leaks could in no way be attributed to management—the NLRB is concerned with the information itself and not its source.

Pro-Company Employee Committees

From time to time, a pro-company committee will form for the purpose of aiding management in the campaign against the union. Unfortunately, most of these committees present more in the way of problems than aid. Management must avoid coordinating its efforts with the union committee or assisting it, since this is considered by the NLRB to be an unfair labor practice. From the practical side, company assistance to the pro-company group may also place the antiunion committee members in the position of being management pawns, thus undercutting the committee's credibility to a considerable extent.

Management's dealings with any antiunion committee should be carefully reviewed by counsel. The legal problems should be communicated to the group, and the committee members should be informed that it may not be in their best interests to be seen with management representatives. In addition, the statements made by committee members should be carefully reviewed, since it may be necessary for the company at some point in the campaign to disavow the statements made by committee members.

When *individuals* act on their own, and not as members of a committee, it is a different matter. Unless an agency relationship between the employee and the company can be proven by the union, the statements of the antiunion employee, acting as an individual and not as part of a group or committee, normally will not be attributed to the employer.

The Locus of Authority

Management campaigning is best conducted in areas of the plant other than supervisory or managerial offices. Although the NLRB's views have softened with respect to the prohibition against bringing employees into a supervisor's office to discuss unionization with them, the safest course is still to avoid campaigning in such areas. Home visitations by management are also prohibited, as is campaigning in the area immediately surrounding the voting booths on the day of the election.

Timing Communications

In employing all these communication techniques, management should be careful not to speak so often that its employees tune out. The timing of campaign communications is important. Most of the heavy campaigning should be concentrated within the last week or two, particularly within the last two or three days before the vote. Management can initiate its campaign early in the game, shortly after being advised of the union's petition, but the tempo of the campaign should pick up from that date and reach its peak on election day.

Election Eve Parties

Many employers who do not understand the application of the 24-hour "captive audience" prohibition do not recognize that an election eve party among eligible voters and members of management, where the employer's position opposing the union is stated, is a legitimate campaign device. Furnishing employees with a free meal and beverages at such functions is also permissible. Before scheduling such a party, each aspect must be carefully planned in advance. A useful checklist, once the propriety of the party has been agreed to, is:

1. Attendance should be voluntary. No one should be excused from work or otherwise paid for any portion of the time spent at the affair.
2. The nature of the establishment or restaurant should be suitable for the people who are invited.
3. Decide between a sit-down dinner, buffet, picnic, etc.
4. A day or two before, evaluate whether to make formalized campaign remarks or simply have the party without campaigning.
5. Decide who should attend from top level management or home office personnel.
6. How the party is announced should also be considered, i.e., oral invitation only, notice posted on the bulletin board, handwritten or typed invitation, or any combination of the above. The exact date of notification should also be planned. Notice should be far enough in advance to be appropriate, but not so far as to give the union an opportunity to schedule a counter-party of its own.
7. Whether spouses are invited is also an issue, the answer to which depends upon the personalities involved, the nature of the occasion, past practice, and other local factors.

An example of a brief informal notice to white-collar employees is:

TO ALL EMPLOYEES

_____ will host an informal cocktail party tomorrow, Tuesday, March 19, 4:00 P.M. to 6:00 P.M. for all employees at the _____. We hope to see each of you there.

Very truly yours,

_____

A more lengthy, conversational white-collar notice can be drafted with the following tone:

NOTICE TO ALL EMPLOYEES

The Company wishes to extend to you an invitation to an after-hours party at 8 P.M., on Wednesday, June 17. The party will begin after work Wednesday afternoon. The idea is to eat, drink, and be merry.

Attendance is entirely voluntary. You can come or not as you choose. The point is to unwind and have fun, and no one's feelings will be hurt if you decide not to come.

We hope you all can make it. It will give us a good chance to loosen up and see each other in a more relaxed setting. That, and the good food and music should do us all some good.

Cordially yours,

_____

But if an employer informs employees that it will hold a Christmas dinner dance, or institutes a practice of giving its employees a free turkey for Thanksgiving, such changes, if made when an election is pending, can constitute a symbolic and tangible economic reminder of the employer's commitment to a happy, satisfied work force. In the context of the employer's overall campaign, the Board could easily conclude that the announcements of the changes were calculated to influence employees with respect to the election.

Chapter 8

Free Speech Rights

The critical provision of the Labor-Management Act is Section 8(c), the free speech provision, which provides that management may express any view, argument, or opinion. The expression of such views is not an unfair labor practice as long as the statement contains no threat of reprisal or promise of benefit.

This section is the foundation stone for the employer's campaign. The law does not require employers to remain aloof from the union's organizational drive while allowing the union the advantage of fierce campaigning. Most employers have strong opinions on the subject of unionization in their enterprises; most honestly believe they can run their businesses better without the intervention of outsiders. If management leaves the choice of unionization up to its employees and takes a neutral stand on the issue, a loss on election day is a foregone conclusion.

Most employees will be told the advantages of unionization by persuasive union organizers. Unless the employer presents its arguments in a forceful and graphic manner, and unless all the facts are marshaled and the disadvantages of unionization plainly made known, the union can anticipate a victory on election day.

Threats

An employer's communication is coercive and illegal if it contains a threat or a promise. A statement can be virulently antiunion, but if it is devoid of threats or promises, it will be considered legal. For example, a statement in a letter sent to the employees' homes indicating that forming and selecting a union would not be in the employee's best interest and, in fact, could hamper the employee's personal relations with the company was found not to be a threat. A stronger statement, to the effect that the employee's job might be affected by having a union in the plant and that the employee's family was dependent on his paycheck was also found unobjectionable by the Board.

The distinction between a legal statement or expression of opinion and an illegal threat or promise, or between a threat and a "prediction," is a complex question. NLRB members often split on the issue. Typical coercive expressions are statements that the employer will never sign a union contract or that it will close the plant if the union wins the election. Threats often involve statements made to individual employees to the effect that voting for the union might result in adverse consequences: discharges, present benefits withdrawn, layoffs for those who associate with the union, poor business conditions because of the union, and injury or prejudice to working conditions. These statements all involve conduct sufficient to set aside the election.

A threat also results when the statement, reasonably construed, would lead an employee to believe that working conditions would be adversely affected by a union victory. For example, the statement that the employer would not bargain with the union if it won the election constitutes a clear threat. However, the less direct but equally unlawful implication that the employer will not change its wage and benefits policies, "union or no union," creates the impression in the minds of the employees that it is futile to support the union. When such an impression is created, the election will be set aside.

In order to constitute an unfair labor practice, the statement need not necessarily be made by a management official or a supervisor. A rank-and-file employee may bind management if an agency relationship is established. Even with no agency relationship, a rank-and-file employee's unauthorized statement, if it becomes well publicized and is not disavowed or neutralized by management, may result in setting aside an election. The same is true of supervisors working outside of their authority or of third parties, such as local politicians or businessmen, who act on their own.

Interference in the election can also be spelled out by *conduct*, even in the absence of statements. For example, an employer's conduct in parading job applicants through the plant was held to constitute a threat to employees that they would lose their jobs if they had the temerity to strike. Where the employer posted "Help Wanted" signs throughout the neighborhood, had job applicants fill out applications in full view of employees at work, and escorted the applicants openly throughout the plant, the manner of the advertisement in recruiting the potential employees was considered to have exceeded the reasonable requirements of the employer. The purpose, the Board held, was to intimidate employees.

Threats do not necessarily have to be specific. The NLRB has found impermissible threats grounded in vague language. For example, if the employer indicates that a number of unfavorable things "might happen if the union wins the election," or that the entry of a union in the plant will result in a loss of "existing conditions," the statements are threats, even without a specific reference.

Furthermore, threats do not have to be made to the employee group as a whole. There are cases on record where elections were set aside because of a statement that was made to only one employee.

It is not considered a threat for an employer to emphasize the fact that he is willing to spend large sums of money in order to oppose unionization. For example, it is permissible for an employer to underscore his opposition to the union's organizing campaign by stating he is willing to spend $20,000 to keep the union out. An employer is free to spend as much as he wishes in an attempt to remain nonunion and may emphasize this determination by stating his opinion.

Discussions in Company Offices

The Board had long held that the calling of employees individually or in small groups into a private area removed from the employees' workplace and urging them to reject the union interfered with the employees' free choice. This was true *whether or not* the conversation itself was coercive. Thus, a perfectly legal statement has been held impermissible simply because of the *location* of the conversation.

This automatic approach, however, has been revised by the Board. It now considers the following factors in determining whether the employer's conduct warrants setting the election aside:
   (1) The location of the interview;
   (2) The position of the interviewer in the employer's table of organization;
   (3) The size of the groups interviewed;
   (4) The tenor of the speaker's remarks.

It is still advisable, notwithstanding the Board's most recent views, to avoid union discussions in areas of high management authority—for example, a company president's or other high official's office, a conference room regularly used by management, and similar places.

Promises

Promises may be just as illegal as threats. Employers' statements that benefits or wages will be increased if the union is voted out are typical illegal specific promises. Unacceptable also are general promises indicating that employees will receive more favorable treatment for opposing the union, or saying that those voting "no" will be "taken care of" or "appreciated." Promises that all employee complaints will be investigated and remedied, or that a grievance procedure will be instituted, or that the company has certain improvements in mind, constitute illegal promises of benefit.

As long as the employer only predicts what the union *might* do if it wins the election, the statement most likely will be permitted by the Board. However, stating that an employer would *definitely* undertake a course of conduct detrimental to employees if the union wins is considered to be a threat. The difficulty in drawing a line of distinction between prohibited threats and privileged predictions is quite apparent.

Predictions are carefully scrutinized by the board. Management is safest in relying on an accurate factual basis for its statements or predictions. The absence of other unfair labor practices is extremely helpful and may serve to tip the scales in favor of management. When a company explains its difficult economic position in a temperate, moderate, and noninflammatory way, and when its overall campaign is free of unfair labor practices or implied threats or promises, the Board is more likely to allow adverse predictions. This underscores the importance of maintaining an atmosphere free of unfair labor practices during the critical period between the filing of the election petition and the date of the election. Chapter 3 should be carefully reviewed for guidelines to the avoidance of unfair labor practices.

Another safe practice is for management to condition its statements on what *might* occur if the plant or office is unionized. In this connection, the factual setting of the case, which is almost always unique will affect the Board's holding. Extreme care should be undertaken in this area. Every campaign statement, particularly "predictions," should be scrutinized carefully by the company's counsel.

Predicting the Adverse Consequences of Unionization

With the help of expert advice, there is a great deal that a company may say concerning the adverse consequences of unionization. For example, an employer may state that it does not have any "particular desire" to move the plant to some foreign location, but that, if the union were voted in, it would have to consider the move because of increased costs of operation, thousands of hours spent dealing with the union, and other expenses. When such statements have been combined with assurances that the employer was not threatening to move the plant simply because the union wins the election, they have been viewed as legal.

An employer may also say that it could not state with "certainty," but it would predict that if the union wins the election and the employer has to operate under a union contract that adds considerably (not minimally) to costs, then, "as a good businessman" it would have to carefully consider the necessity of moving operations out of the country, so that costs would be reduced and the product could be sold at a profit.

In addition, the employer may state that it is under no obligation to continue to accept losses. In this connection, the employer's statement is strongest when it can point to unreasonable demands made by the union in its campaign literature. The employer can state that if the union were able to get the increase it has promised, costs would have to go up so much that the company's competitive position would be impaired and as a result it might have to close. In a specific case, a cartoon of a company with a "Closed" sign on its gate was considered legal. The important factor to the decision was that the employer had also informed its employees that it hoped to use the facility to the fullest extent regardless of the outcome of the election.

The Board has approved an employer's statement in which it said that it did not want the union, with its "crazy demands," to be the "straw that broke the camel's back." The point is that if the union attains increases that the company is not able to meet, it could force the company to abandon its business operation as unprofitable, thus affecting or eliminating employee jobs. Since it is possible that a bargaining relationship may lead to closing down a plant, the Board does not preclude an employer from saying so in a fair way.

The employer may refer to other companies that have moved because of the high cost of doing business. Any such statements should be coupled with an assurance that the employer will not close or move the plant merely because there is a union, but would move strictly as the result of economic conditions.

If an employer refers to other facilities owned by the company which have closed as a result of unreasonable union demands and explains that it is free to move once its lease expires, the Board may view such campaigning to be a coercive overstatement designed to make employees fearful of the consequences of unionization. If the comment is uttered for no reason other than to imply that if the organizing union were to become the employee's bargaining representative, the same consequences would ensue, i.e., the union would make unreasonable demands which would eventually require the employer to close and result in unit employees losing their jobs, the election may be overturned. Similarly, if the employer, particularly in the context of other impermissible remarks, states that the union at a closed-down facility would have to assume a large share of the responsibility for having made it impossible for the company to continue doing business, such a statement would be impermissible. The heart of the threat is the *unconditional* statement that a facility had been closed directly as a result of the unreasonable demands. Such statements, if not absolutely accurate and documented, are outside the protection of the free speech provisions of the Act because the employer can avoid such conscious overstatements which he knows will mislead his employees. Careful attention must be paid to the exact wording used to convey plant closings at other facilities and at other companies. Workers must not be led to believe that the references to other plant closings were directed toward their decision to join the union. Both the Board and the courts will hold the employer to a harsh standard. It is the burden of the employer to choose his words carefully to avoid the likelihood of being misunderstood. In all such cases, the employer should add qualifying statements or disclaimers to the effect that the facility being organized will not close simply because of a union victory, but only if the union's demands make continuation of the business impracticable. Caution must be exercised, however, since rote disclaimers and expressions to abide by the law or to bargain in good faith do not automatically insulate an employer's campaign statements.

References to increased prices leading to a shutdown of the plant are also fraught with difficulties. If an employer declares that if a union were successful in organizing the employees and in securing improvements in their wages, hours, and working conditions, he would *undoubtedly* have to raise his prices and this would make him noncompetitive and force him to lay-off employees and possibly close the plant, the statement would be improper *unless* the company adduced objective evidence to support the predictions. The employer must be prepared to prove, in order to validate the statement, that one of the only remaining recourses would be to raise prices, and that this would adversely affect his ability to compete. Care should be taken to give a candid picture of the company's economic situation and a true comparison of its wages with that of its competitors, as well as the reasons increases in costs could not be offset by more economical and efficient operations or other production improvements.

The lesson is clear: the burden is on an employer to see to it that his employees do not reasonably infer from his statements and conduct during an organizational campaign a threat of reprisal or promise of benefit. In these cases the employer acts at his peril. He cannot walk between the rain drops. He cannot proclaim his right to free speech while garnering at the same time the benefit of his employees' induced concern that disaster would befall them and their families if they voted for the union.

While an outright statement *or implication* that the plant will close if the union is voted in is illegal, an employer may imply that it would close the plant if it sets forth a proper basis for the prediction. If campaign material indicates that the union causes or has caused friction between employees and notes that as a result of such a condition production has declined, the employer may warn that if production continued in that trend, while costs remained up, the plant would close *for that reason.* Since these statements indicate that the employer would close the plant only if production declined while costs remained high, the statements fall short of an implied threat to close the plant because the employees select a union to represent them. *Leggett and Platt, Inc.*, 230 NLRB 463 (1977).

The employer may also state that the "chief worry" facing the company and the employees is job security. Increased labor costs could make it more difficult for the company to bid competitively for new work. Increased costs and/or strikes might cause customers to switch to competitors' products, resulting in layoffs.

The employer has great leeway in criticizing any union policy, practice, rule, or program. Where any company benefits—for example, the provisions of a pension plan—are more generous than the provisions of a union plan, the company has full freedom to inform employees that if the union bargains with the company and insists on the union's plan, this would definitely result in a loss of benefits.

Overall, in depicting the adverse consequences of unionization, the following principles should be followed:

- The employer's financial losses should be emphasized.
- The adverse impact of *union demands* (not a union victory) should be related.
- The employees should be told that they are free to vote as they please.
- The company should disclaim any intention to close down simply because of a union victory.
- The statements should be made in the context of responses to union statements and leaflets.
- Added cost factors that may lead to closing or moving should be emphasized.
- The company should indicate that a closing, if it occurs,

would be a decision forced upon it by the financial facts of
life beyond the ability of the company to control.

The plant closing theme is as treacherous as it is beneficial. If the
employer's oral and written communications—taken singly or as a
whole—impliedly threaten plant closing if the union wins, the election
may be set aside or a bargaining order directed. If the company repeatedly emphasizes unemployment, plant closings, the inability of
the union to prevent such plant closings, its own ability to move on
short notice, and other unionized businesses that have moved from
the area, the Board may find that such a campaign conveys the unmistakable message that selection of the union will result in a termination
of operations. The Board is particularly likely to find that the employer has transgressed the bounds of free speech if no cost comparisons or other data are used by the employer to support its position, or
if the employer makes repeated vague references to "economic conditions" or "financial reasons" that might force it to close. Helpful citations and examples of both permissible and unlawful statements are
found in Appendix 5.

In one case, the employer stated what it anticipated in the future
with respect to sales and new products. He indicated that the selection of the union as bargaining representative *would* jeopardize the re-
call of certain employees and prejudice the economic recovery of the
company. The employer made no effort to explain exactly why representation by the union would thwart the economic recovery. Rather,
he simply asked the employees to accept the proposition that a union
victory in the election and prejudice to the employer's economic recovery went hand in hand. This was construed by the Board as a
threat rather than as a prediction because of the employer's failure to
demonstrate that it was based upon objective considerations. It also
failed to establish that the adverse economic effects it predicted would
result from circumstances beyond the employer's control. The lesson
is clear: Whenever explicating the adverse effects of unionism, be as
specific as possible in detailing the facts upon which the prediction is
based. Management should *condition* its predictions with words such
as *might* or *may*, as opposed to flat statements of what *will necessarily
occur* if the union is voted in. Where an employer stated his belief that
the employees' opportunity for advancement and the employer's possibilities for expansion would be hampered by the presence of a
union, the statement was upheld as permissible since the employer explained that the basis for its belief was the "strife and tension" the employer thought likely to be introduced by the union. The employer
had taken pains to elaborate the reasons for his opinion, citing examples of such strife and tension. Presented in this way, the employer's

statement of belief did not amount to a threat of possible retaliation against the employees involved for their continued support of the union. *Honeywell, Inc.*, 225 NLRB 617 (1976).

Here is what the employer said in another case:

> If you decide in favor of a union, we would have to dock you for being late, which we are not now doing. Our friendly relationship with you would not be the same in the future. It would be strictly by the book, that is, strictly by the contract which would be negotiated.

This type of statement reflects a fairly typical attitude on the part of many companies, and an attitude which most employers, untrained in the complexities of the labor laws, would believe to be legal. Nevertheless, the Board held such a statement to be improper. In what way did the campaigner go wrong? The statement constitutes a warning that unionization would *definitely* bring a loss of present benefits and the imposition of stricter working conditions. The problem with the statement is that the prediction of probable adverse contractual terms and working conditions was not based on objective facts from which the employer could convey a reasonable belief as to the demonstrably probable consequences of unionization. The employer ran afoul of the law by implicitly and *automatically* equating such adversities with a union election victory. *Jamaica Towing, Inc.*, 236 NLRB No. 223 (1978).

In any event, the employer must lose no opportunity to depict the unionization's adverse consequences that are not of the employer's own volition. For example, where a group about to vote on unionization have worked side by side with another group of unionized employees, it would be entirely permissible for the employer to outline what union membership would have cost the first group. A typical communication depicting this cost is shown on the following page.

Placing the Union in an Unfavorable Light

The employer's initial investigation will have uncovered a great deal of information unfavorable to the union; that information may be fully communicated to the employees. When the union's finances are precarious, or when there has been a decrease in membership (a common occurrence recently), the union may be portrayed as weak and ineffective. When the union's weakness is contrasted with the power of the employer, employees may have doubts about the union making

IF YOU HAD
BEEN IN THE UNION FOR THE
PAST YEAR . . .
HOW MUCH MONEY WOULD MEMBERSHIP HAVE
COST YOU?

1. Dues   _____
2. Personal and weather days
   (You were paid, but *under the union contract,*
   your co-employees were not.)   _____
3. Wildcat Strike(s)   _____

TOTAL DOLLARS LOST

THIS IS THE
REAL COST OF A UNION IN
<u>DOLLARS</u> ($$$) AND <u>CENTS!</u>

---

good on its promises. Learning the salaries and expense accounts of union organizers often disturbs employees, who begin viewing the union not as crusaders, but rather as salesmen. When the employer's investigation uncovers convictions, indictments or arrests for violations of state and federal laws (not necessarily limited to labor laws), these facts will often serve to dissuade employees from association with the union organizers.

If the union has taken a public political position on some relevant national or local issue that the employer believes is incompatible with the beliefs of its employees, this, too, may be communicated.

Dues

Dues is an issue that is often underestimated by management. Company officials often view the $10 or $12 a month in dues as inconsequential, but rank-and-file employees rarely feel the same way. The amount of dues and/or initiation fees should be stated in as graphic and effective a way as possible, referring to the amounts charged on either an annual or two-year basis. If there has been a prior campaign—for example, five years previously—the union dues that *would have been paid* can be calculated, interest added, and the total sum communicated to the employees. A simple initial way of communicating the costs of a union is:

TWELVE WAY$ A UNION CAN GET INTO YOUR POCKET$

1. Due$.

2. Fine$.

3. A$$e$$ment$.

4. Political contribution$.

5. Initiation Fee$.

6. Donation$ for $trike benefit$ to aid member$ of union$ on $trike el$ewhere.

7. Contribution$ for union new$paper$.

8. Contribution$ for union periodical$.

9. Gift$ for organizer$.

10. Money Lo$t due to $trike$ called.

11. $pecial A$$e$$ment$.

12. Rein$tatement Fee$.

VOTE **NO** AND KEEP YOUR MONEY. **ONLY TIME CAN TELL** HOW MUCH IT WILL CO$T YOU. THEY **PROMI$E** YOU EVERYTHING, **BUT** PROMIE ARE WORTH WHAT THEY CO$T—**NOTHING.** BUT IT I$ YOU WHO DOE$ THE **PAYING.**

Unions start with "U." "U" do the paying. "U" do the striking. "U" do the suffering. "U" do the union's work. "U" do the picketing. It's "U" "U" "U"! but, "U" don't have to do the above to keep what "U" have now.

UnionS end with "S." "S" means strike. "S" means suffering. "S" means sadness. "S" means scalawag. "S" means scandalous. "S" means sabotage. "S" means sacrifice. "S" means Scuffle. "S" means Secret—Yes this is the end to uNiOnS.

VOTE NO to uNiOnism. —— **VOTE NO to uNiOnism.**

Vote No and Save Your Dough!

Other ways of dramatizing the high cost of unionism are explained later in this chapter.

Union Benefits

If the union's contracts with other employers and its benefit plans (filed with the federal government) are examined, the employer will invariably find that in a number of respects the benefits negotiated by the union do not equal some of the benefits the employees already enjoy. The employer's attack should focus on these weak spots, since this will break down the union myth that union wages and benefits are automatically better than nonunion benefits.

Union Failures

NLRB election reports can be checked for instances in which the parent union has been decertified. Since the number of decertification elections has been increasing remarkably over the past several years, this area presents more and more of an opportunity for employers. The question may then be legitimately posed to the employees: if the union is so good, why have the employees at X, Y, and Z locations decertified them? Also, the employer should disclose cases, gleaned from NLRB reports, where the union has been rejected by the employees. The employer need not limit itself to instances in which the particular local has lost an election; election losses by the parent union can also be cited.

Union Constitution and Bylaws

An effective technique is to reproduce and editorialize on adverse provisions contained in union constitutions and bylaws. Provisions authorizing fines, trials of union members, strike authorization procedures, control by the parent organization, the conditions under which the strike benefits are paid, and such onerous membership obligations as compulsory attendance at meetings and fines for nonattendance should all be pointed out, and their implications stressed.

One case involved a strike in which union members were instructed to honor the picket line and to refuse to perform any work. Several union members crossed the picket line and worked during the strike, although this was a violation of the union's constitution and bylaws. The union brought the strikebreakers before a union board and fined them for their conduct. When the employees refused to pay, the union brought suit against them in a state court; the employer was not allowed to intervene. The court decided that the union's constitution and bylaws were binding between the union and its members and that the fines could be legally enforced. The decision of the court in this case, and its exact language, *Steelworkers v. Bailey,* 329 N.E.2d 867, 90 LRRM 2188 (Ill. App. Ct. 1975), may be reproduced and quoted by the employer and distributed to employees as a real example of the disadvantages of unionization.

Other Relevant Information

Any fact that can be uncovered about the union is fair game. Union unfair labor practices, illegal strikes, secondary boycotts, lawsuits charging the union with discrimination against minorities, and any other fact about the union or its officials may be communicated during the election campaign. Often, union policies discriminate against part-time employees. Since such groups are becoming a larger part of the work force, it is important for the employer who utilizes regular part-timers to investigate union practices such as elimination of part-time staff from certain fringe benefits, denial of union membership, discriminatory dues, or exclusion from the bargaining unit. An inspection of the union's contracts with other employers may reveal such discrepancies or may uncover other evidence of union bias against part-time personnel. If this is the case, let your part-timers know how unionization can affect them to their detriment, and pay careful attention to what the union may be saying [or not saying] to this sector of the electorate.

An employer may also utilize the union movement's historical reluctance to accord minority factions, including blacks and women, their rightful place in the union's institutional hierarchy. Numerous articles in newspapers and magazines depict unions as flagrant violators of our discrimination laws.

Almost fifteen years after the passage of the Civil Rights Act, the AFL-CIO itself has a record of blatant sex discrimination in its upper echelons. There was not one woman on its 35-member policy-making Executive Council. Dozens of vacancies had been filled exclusively by males despite the fact that the AFL-CIO has declared itself in favor of the Equal Rights Amendment. The Federation's sexist behavior has been so notorious that it has not even covered its activities with the gloss of tokenism. In the late seventies, with one exception, there were no women on the Resolutions Committee at the national convention. Important international unions with large female constituencies have been represented by all-male delegations. The AFL-CIO's dismal performance in this area is a legitimate fact employers can rightfully bring to the attention of female voters. The same is true of wholesale instances of union recalcitrance in integrating its membership rolls and the concomitant publicity which has attended union reluctance in this area.

Closely related to this issue is the frequent discrimination by an organizing union against certain minority groups in a plant or office. Union organizers often look for organizing opportunities where minority group employees constitute a majority of the voters, and imply that the union will favor them if they vote for the union. Where signs of such union discrimination appear, the employer should be keenly aware of the impact of communicating this information to other voters who might be alienated by the union's catering to particular groups. Where the union engages in this kind of conduct, the employer must not waste the opportunity to point out this discrimination to the electorate. This is a particularly telling argument where the union has previously put out campaign information lauding its democratic processes, its fair treatment of all employees, and the fact that the union will put an end to employer discrimination and favoritism. When the union itself can be validly accused of discriminating, many voters will be impressed and will hesitate to endorse the union with their vote.

An employer may explain to employees its belief that unions often bring strife and tension to a plant or office. Even if an employer couples that statement with its belief that employees' opportunity for advancement and the company's possibilities for expansion would be hampered by the presence of a union, such a tandem statement would be viewed by the Board as permissible campaign propaganda. In making such statements, the employer should detail as much as possible the basis for its asserted belief. Thus, if the employer is a party to a collective bargaining agreement at one location, it may tell its voters at another location that a union victory would involve strict enforcements of work rules if that is the practice at the unionized location.

The employer may also refer to the more rigid work relationships that *might* come about if the union were elected. Threatening employees with the institution of conditions of employment that are more onerous in order to discourage support of a union is illegal. *Fidelity Telephone Co.*, 236 NLRB No. 26 (1978). The employer should refer to specific union contract provisions and avoid implying that the more rigid conditions are what *will* occur if the union is voted in rather than what *might* prevail under union conditions.

Other ways of emphasizing how employees may lose existing cordial relations is through the use of reminders and flyers such as these: (See next two pages.)

YOU HAVE SOMETHING TO LOSE BY VOTING FOR A UNION

YOU CAN LOSE GOOD FELLOWSHIP AMONG EMPLOYEES

This Is What Happens In Almost Every Plant Where They Have A Union. One Employee or Group of Employees Is Set Against Another. All Employees Are Set Against The Management. Everyone Soon Becomes Suspicious of Everyone Else and Good fellowship Soon Disappears

IT HAS HAPPENED ELSEWHERE ..DON'T LET IT HAPPEN TO US!

Stay Ahead Of Our Competition!

YOU HAVE SOMETHING TO LOSE BY VOTING FOR A UNION

YOU CAN LOSE FRIENDLY RELATIONS BETWEEN EMPLOYEES and MANAGEMENT

It Is The Practice of Many Union Professionals To "Keep The Pot Boiling" By Creating Mistrust and Suspicion Between Employees and Betwee Employees and Management...Stirring Up Grievances..Spreading Misinformation ...Keeping Everyone In A Turmoil... Because It Is Much Easier To Sell Dissatisfied and Unhappy Employees On The Idea That They Need A Union, And To Collect The Regular Monthly Union Dues

IT HAS HAPPENED ELSEWHERE ..DON'T LET IT HAPPEN TO US !

Stay Ahead Of Our Competition !

When explaining the disadvantages and obligations of union membership, an employer may inform its employees that the union can require them to picket if the union has a dispute with the company, even during the life of the contract and *even when the employees themselves are not on strike.* While the employer might believe at first glance that a union cannot order employees to picket during the life of a contract which contains a no-strike, no-slowdown clause, the NLRB has held that such picketing, even when in apparent violation of the contract, may be protected activity and thus permissible. Thus, where there is no clear and unmistakable waiver by the union of its right to picket during the life of the contract, a union may discipline any employee who refuses to picket the company's premises. *John Hancock Mutual Life Ins. Co.*, 236 NLRB No. 50 (1978).

The employer may also cite other "horror stories"—for example, the permissible fining in the amount of twenty thousand dollars of a member who worked during a one-day strike! While such a fine might appear excessive to the unsophisticated employer, the Board's view is that where a fine is imposed to implement a legitimate union rule, the government will not interfere by evaluating either the amount of the fine or the fairness of the discipline meted out. *Printing Pressman's Union*, 190 NLRB 268 (1971).

Indeed, attempted fines in excess of three thousand dollars for employees who cross a union picket line, or who defy the union by working during a strike, are commonplace. See *Sperry Rand Corp.*, 235 NLRB No. 20 (1978).

Unions have even threatened their members with disciplinary action for not supporting the union's attempt to organize a new plant or office! 1977 LRA 296.

Exposing Financial Support for Pro-Union Employees

It will often come to the attention of management that certain union prime movers are being compensated for soliciting on behalf of the union. Typical union tactics involve paying prime movers a lump sum upon a successful election, or a stipend for each valid signed card obtained by the employee. Where the employer suspects that this condition prevails in the plant or office, it may capitalize upon it by advertising this belief. The employer need not have to prove the facts, but may merely make the assertion. Normally, if employees are paid by the union to solicit, this inspires resentment among co-employees and serves to chill support for the union. The utmost marketing advantage should be taken if this condition is suspected. Even if the facts of the case ultimately demonstrate that no payments were made, the Board would not upset the election on the basis of this employer statement.

The Disadvantages of Union Membership

Once the adverse facts about the union's organization, structure, and character have been communicated, the employer can proceed to harder-hitting arguments about the burdens of union membership.

For example, the fact that in all likelihood the union will seek a union-security provision *forcing* membership often displeases employees. Copies of the union's contracts with other employers (with the recognition, union-security, and checkoff provisions enlarged) are most effective in this regard.

If the union campaigns on a local or national level and donates money for political candidates, the fact that such money is being used for political causes that employees may not favor can also be communicated.

Seniority

The argument may also be made that seniority clauses may be extremely restrictive and may keep younger and/or more capable employees from advancing within the company. This argument must be handled with care, however, because most employees regard seniority rather highly. The employer must treat the seniority issue in accordance with traditions at the plant and the past history concerning layoffs.

Union Restrictions

Information about production quotas that may be legally established by the unions, union opposition to such desirable company practices as merit-pay programs, company incentive systems, and other matters may persuade employees that the presence of a union may "rock the boat." Excerpts from Board decisions that approve such restrictive union practices are effective communications.

Why the Company Opposes the Union

Early in the campaign, employees and the union are likely to ask why the employer is opposing the union so strenuously. The implication is that it must be because the union is good for the employees. Therefore the employer must make the reasons for its opposition perfectly clear.

The company can point out that the employees' strong feelings of company loyalty will be disrupted by a union, and that this will interfere with the existing congenial, flexible, and sensible working relationship. Such disruption may reduce the effectiveness of the company and hurt the profitability on which everyone's security depends.

Possible strikes, burdensome work rules, increased tension between workers and supervisors, constant grievances and arbitrations, union politics, visits by union representatives to the plant or office to stir up issues, loss of individual recognition, and other reasons can also be cited.

Furthermore, if the union were certified, employees would be assigned job classifications, making it difficult—if not impossible—to shift employees from job to job. Or the scope of job classifications would become narrower and narrower, making it more difficult for the company to operate. Some employers have gone further and stated that if union policies on job classifications were to result in the loss of operational flexibility, employees might have to be sent home when there was no work for a particular classification.

In making this argument, the employer should be as factual as possible. Ideally, the statement should refer to specific union practices, contract provisions, and the custom and contracts of the organizing union. It is permissible for the company to express opposition to inefficient and restrictive union work rules.

The risk of costly production interruptions each time a contract is renegotiated may be cited. If the company already has one union at the location, it can express its opposition to negotiating with another union and being subjected to the doubled risk of failure of reaching an agreement.

It is also permissible to make statements about the desirability of keeping the policy of shifting personnel from one area to another when slackness develops in certain areas of the plant; the value of maintaining the merit system; the importance of avoiding artificial work-time rules that may interfere with delivery schedules to customers; and, in general, all the advantages of maintaining flexibility of operations without having them impaired by union discussions, arguments, negotiations, unfair labor practice charges, and litigation over what may or may not be done by the employer.

The Appeal to Company Loyalty

The relationship between management and its employees must be constantly emphasized if it is a good one. The company's programs and policies should be marketed to the fullest extent. Employee benefits and personnel department programs are legitimate topics of communication. The more generous the benefits, the more effective the communication. Obviously, where management lacks credibility or where relationships have deteriorated, little emphasis can be placed on this aspect, and the company's campaign will have to shift into other areas. Equating union activity with disloyalty should be avoided.

The company's successful experiences in dealing with employee grievances should be explored. Even if there is no formal grievance procedure, management may find that there have been quite a number of successful examples of employee complaints that were handled expeditiously, fairly, and to the employee's satisfaction. These examples can be publicized as illustrative of a company's ability to deal individually with its employees without the necessity for outside intervention.

It is true that unionization leads to a depersonalization of the relationship, since the shop steward takes the place of the supervisor in dealing with the company. Union practices, customs, and traditions usually supplant employee desire for individuality. Group psychology replaces individual adjustment. Yet, in referring to company-employee relationships, care should be taken to avoid predictions that the advent of a union will mean a loss of individuality. This concept is a tricky one and must be handled carefully.

There are ways in which this deterioration of the personal relationship between company and employee can be communicated. For example, an employer may be able to say that throughout the years his door has always been open to employees for their problems, whether business or personal. He can maintain (if true) that he has always listened to their problems and tried to help in any possible way—and that he does not think the union would act in such a manner. Stated this way, the statement amounts to nothing more than a review of the past relationship and a supportable appraisal of the effect on that relationship that would necessarily come about by union entry into the shop.

However, the depersonalization theme cannot be carried too far. The employer may not state that the personal relationship between the supervisors (or other company managers) and the employees *would cease* if the union came in. Stating that employees would lose the right to present their problems to management if the union gained entry into the plant or office is not an accurate statement of law. Under Section 9(a) of the Act, any individual employee has the right to present grievances to the employer. Likewise, an employer may not state that if the union wins the election, employees would not be able to talk to management, and management would not be able to talk to employees, except through the union. Such statements have been interpreted as a threat that employees, by electing union representation, forfeit their right to individual presentation of grievances, which is guaranteed in the Act. Where an employer stated that under a union contract, personal privileges could probably not be granted and that "the human things that we are now doing as a matter of course would no longer be possible," the Board found that this statement was calculated to instill the fear of the lost privileges strictly as a result of employees' adherence to the union. It is a much better approach for the employer to stress that the new relationship with the union in the plant will not be as close as the prior nonunion relationship, that the employer's door has always been open to employee problems and that the employer has always listened to those problems and attempted to help in any possible manner. If the employer recalls the past relationship, ventures the opinion that the union could not maintain that relationship, and argues that the prior relationship will necessarily be altered by the advent of a union, this constitutes a supportable appraisal of what might happen under union conditions rather than the threat that employees inevitably will lose the right to deal with management directly.

In order to pass muster with the Board, the employer should refer to any probable loss of individuality and increasing rigidity of treatment only in the context of *actual union practices* or known conditions under existing collective bargaining agreements, rather than mere speculation as to probable consequences. While the Board's view is fairly strict, the federal courts sometimes disagree and adopt a more liberal approach in favor of the employer's exercise of its free speech rights. *NLRB v. Golub Corp.*, 388 F.2d 921 (2d Cir. 1967).

Two examples of such statements appear on the following two pages.

Explaining the Company's Record

As the beginning stages of the campaign fade away and the employer launches into the meatier issues, the company's record of providing decent working conditions for employees becomes more and more of a theme that bears constant repetition. Having revealed the unfavorable facts about unionism and the disadvantages of unions, the employer's campaign takes on greater substance, and management's record, where appropriate, must be stressed. In referring to what management has done for the employees in the past, managers should preface their remarks by stating that the NLRB does not permit man-

YOU HAVE SOMETHING TO LOSE BY VOTING FOR A UNION

YOU CAN LOSE YOUR RIGHT TO THINK .. WORK .. ACT TO LIVE YOUR LIFE AS AN INDIVIDUAL

Once They Are Voted In, Many Unions Find Plenty of Ways To Make It Disagreeable For The Employee Who Does Not Conform To The Selfish Ideas of The Union Leaders. Threats, for Example, And Intimidation..Ridicule..Misrepresentation..Name-Calling..Insults.. Brow-Beating... Etc.

IT HAS HAPPENED ELSEWHERE ..DON'T LET IT HAPPEN TO US !

Stay Ahead Of Our Competition !

YOU HAVE SOMETHING TO LOSE BY VOTING FOR A UNION

YOU CAN LOSE YOUR FREEDOM TO HANDLE YOUR OWN PROBLEMS INDIVIDUALLY and DIRECTLY WITH THE MANAGEMENT

Many Unions Take Away Your Rights of Individual Action. At The Same Time Through Union "Pressure Tactics" of Intimidation, Coercion and Discrimination They Make Employees Afraid To Be Seen Talking With Any Representative Of Management

IT HAS HAPPENED ELSEWHERE ...DON'T LET IT HAPPEN TO US!

Stay Ahead Of Our Competition!

agement to make promises during a campaign.

Management should distribute listings of all employee benefits, together with explanations of the various portions of the more complex benefit programs. Here is a checklist of common benefits:

Hospitalization insurance program
Life insurance program
Equal employment opportunity
Jury duty
Company picnics, bowling & other sports
Surgical reimbursement program
Scheduled periodic increases
Scheduled periodic evaluations
Suggestion system awards
Social security coverage
Paid holidays
Vacation policy
Tuition reimbursement program
Military leave
Maternity leave
Free coffee
Major medical coverage
Disability coverage
Pension program
Merit reviews
Seniority preferences
Credit union
Accident insurance
Leave of absence
Pay for weather emergencies
Wash-up time
Clean working environment
Profit-sharing
Job security systems, no-layoff policies, etc.
Parking privileges
Flex time

Prescription reimbursement program
Sick leave
Less than 40-hour week
Premium pay for overtime
Grievance procedure, gripe sessions
Modern kitchen facilities
X-ray & laboratory expense reimbursement
Workmen's compensation
Dental program
Employee interviews & meetings
Unemployment insurance
Dinners, dances
Funeral leave
Morning and afternoon breaks
Christmas party
Employee savings program
Training programs
Personal time off
Premium time for Sundays & holidays
Severance pay
Bonuses
Promotion policy
Fair discipline
Shift differential
Call-in pay
Safety program
Vending machines
Scholarships

Constant emphasis should be placed on the fact that the company has *voluntarily* provided these benefits without outside interference. A great impact can be made by listing all company benefits on one graphic display, but it may be better psychology to "feed" employees benefit information at intervals. An important follow-up is to show employees the trend of improvements over the past several years.

Employees should be shown, in graphic form, where possible, each of the increases in formal benefit programs and informal advantages. The employer may then state that it intends to continue its policy of improving on the existing level of benefits. To combat the impression that only unions can protect employees against inflation, it is permissible to chart the cost of living over a relevant time period and compare it to the wage increases over the same period of time. In demonstrating the company's record, management should constantly repeat that these benefits have been improved over the years and wages have been increased without one day's pay being lost due to striking and without one penny having been paid in dues for the privilege of enjoying the benefits.

Where practical, written communications outlining benefit programs and improvements in wages over the years should be reinforced by having supervisors speak individually with those in their department. When such discussions take place, the supervisors should be prepared with factual documentation, such as the employee's wage history, in order to lend as much credibility as possible to the company's claims. Where the bargaining units are not exceptionally large, management may tailor each written communication to the individual by publishing and mailing a "personal wage [or salary] progress guide" containing the name of the employee, the date the company hired the employee, the starting wage rate, the current wage rate, and the amount of increase expressed in weekly terms in both dollars and percentages. Where the company's record has been a good one, employees are often surprised to see how well they have done during the relevant time period. In one case, the company president's statement that company policy was to watch trends in the industry and maintain a competitive position was viewed by the NLRB as a permissible statement.

Any explication of past company policy, benefits, and wage increases should conclude with statements that the company's policy has always been generous benefits and fair wages consistent with the company's economic situation.

Paternalistic Propaganda

In many instances the employer may make promises of a seemingly general nature and yet the Board does not set the election aside. This is because these promises are termed "paternalistic propaganda." As an example, the employer may say that in the past the company has not relied on the union to make decisions concerning improved benefits or the payment of steady and ever-increasing wages. The employer may continue by stating that the outlook for the future *continues to be optimistic* and that the employer looks to the same ingredients that provided past increases in benefits to take the company even further. The company may pledge itself to maintain progressive and enlightened wages and benefits policies.

In one case, the employer stated:

> As I have said, I can't make promises to get your vote. The law prohibits this. All I can ask you is to look at my record. Not only do you have job security, but you have benefitted from increases in wages, insurance, holidays—all without a union. What makes some of you believe I will change or that you will need outsiders to watch over me? That is what I frankly don't understand and probably never will. I have kept my word with you, and that is why I firmly believe a majority will reject this union.

In another case, the employer, in discussing a profit-sharing plan, pointed out that he had attended a seminar on such plans a few months before the union appeared on the scene. He then stated that to promise any improvement in the profit-sharing plan might, during a campaign, be misconstrued as an unfair labor practice, and concluded his remarks by saying that he hoped that the coming election would be conducted fairly and with no unfair labor practices.

The Board viewed such statements as paternalistic campaign propaganda to the effect that the employer would take better care of them in the future *generally*. No specific improvement of any substantial nature was mentioned even as a distinct probability. The Board believed that employees could have evaluated those election tactics for themselves.

Expressions of Legal Opinion

Closely related to predictions are statements of legal opinion as to a course of action the employer intends to take. An example was a statement by the employer that it believed the Board's appropriate-unit determination was wrong, and that the only way the employer could litigate the question if the union won was by refusing to bargain with the unit. In conveying this message, care should be taken to avoid creating the impression that a union victory will lead to futility at the bargaining table. Statements that if the union won the employer was obligated to negotiate but was not obligated to sign a contract have also been viewed as permissible.

Wherever statements relating to a legal course of action are used, caution and expert advice are indicated. Employers have also been successful when distributing copies of their attorney's legal opinion on certain matters. Statements that the employer intended to appeal certain decisions of the NLRB (which would have the effect of postponing bargaining indefinitely), statements about the company's right to hire permanent replacements for economic strikers, and other legal opinions from counsel to the effect that no concessions are required under the law and that a union is not entitled to automatic benefits as a result of winning an election have all been successfully and effectively utilized as permissible campaign tools. An example of such materials, often distributed in poster form, is shown on the following page.

The employer should take extreme care to insure the absolute legal accuracy of such statements of legal opinion and to avoid overgeneralization. Utilization of the Board's own publication, "A Guide to Basic Law and Procedures Under the National Labor Relations Act," will provide the employer with a number of useful and authoritative representations of the law.

Negating Union Guarantees of Improvements

Since the union's chief tactic will be the "big promise," the company must promptly negate the idea that employees will be assured improved wages, benefits, and other working conditions merely by the union's presence. The union will be quite adroit at implying that it will guarantee benefits and wage increases, or that it will automatically obtain a union salary scale. Employees must be told that an election victory means only that a union may ask the employer to change or improve conditions, and that the only way a change can come about is for the employer to *agree* to such a change in the contract.

A union victory means only recognition by the employer and bargaining in good faith for a period of at least twelve months. The basic element of the bargaining obligation is that the employer must meet with the union upon a reasonable request, display an open mind on union demands, make a reasonable effort to compromise those demands, and attempt to reach agreement. If the employer does not like the union proposals, it can reject them, and it may make counterproposals that may contain more restrictive benefits and lower wages than those that prevailed prior to the union's victory. In addition, negotiations, particularly for a first contract, are often lengthy. The fact that an employer is not legally required to sign a union con-

CAN THE UNION MAKE GOOD ON ITS PROMISES?

HERE'S THE LAW ACCORDING TO THE UNITED STATES COURT OF APPEALS:

"...the obligation to bargain collectively 'does not compel either party to agree to a proposal or require the making of a concession.'"

(NLRB v. Tomco Communications, Inc.)

DON'T SWALLOW THE UNION'S PHONEY PROMISES

VOTE ☒ NO!

---

tract at all, even after negotiating at great length and making every possible effort to reach an agreement, can be communicated, as long as the negotiating process is not depicted as futile.

It should also be made clear that the employer: (a) will not agree to demands that are unfair or unreasonable; and (b) will deal in good faith with the union, but any improvements will depend strictly on the outcome of negotiations.

The employer should make it known that unions do not pay wages or benefits—the *company* pays them. Once this is clearly stated, it becomes easier for employees to understand that a union cannot honestly promise or forecast what a third party, the employer, is going to do in the future.

In short, the employer may communicate that a union cannot obtain a single improvement that the employer is not ready, willing, and able to provide, and that the only means a union has at its disposal if an employer has to change benefits and wages is to strike.

To illustrate the extent to which the employer can go in explaining this concept, the following statement was approved by the Board:

> If the union wins, what happens? Many think that if the union wins the election it is an automatic contract. The law says that the company must negotiate with the union in good faith. Good faith bargaining does not include signing a contract. Good faith bargaining [includes rejecting] a demand we feel in any way would jeopardize this factory or in any way put this company in a noncompetitive position. That's what good faith means. We do not need to ever come to an agreement with this union. All we've got to do is sit at the table. For example, another thing, many people thought that bargaining starts at where you are today. This not true. Bargaining starts at what we call the bare table. That's the federal minimum and the necessary things that FICA and unemployment requires that we pay under the law. It starts at that level. We negotiate holidays. We negotiate vacations. We negotiate pension. We negotiate wages, base rates; you name it, and it's negotiable. The union knows this, but I doubt very much they told you this at their meetings or at your homes. It starts at the bare table. Many people think well, what's really so bad about being in the union? What can I lose? However, everything is up to negotiation. It's horse trading.

Employers should be cautioned not to make the statement that "good faith bargaining does not include signing a contract" *in isolation*. In order to validate the remark, the concept must be stated in the context of an employer's expression of his views about the nature of collective bargaining.

In another case, two questions were asked by an employee: If the union should not get in, will you really change the rates? If the union does get in, would they be taken away? The employer provided the following answer: "The answer to the first question is that I can guarantee you that if the union does not get in those rates will not be tampered with. If the union does get in, I would negotiate for the federal minimum. Then I would say yes, they can be taken away if the union gets in if the union agrees in negotiations that that is what we settled for, because it is negotiable. You negotiate for the bare minimum. We have no intentions of taking away; history proves that we never have." The statement was approved by the Board.

"Bargaining from scratch" statements must be handled with extreme care. Such messages have been held both to interfere with and not to interfere with elections, depending on the effect of the message. Where the employer's total campaign makes it clear that the employees' risk of loss stems not from any regressive bargaining posture predetermined by the employer but from the possibility that the union, in order to secure certain favorable provisions, might trade away some existing benefits, the statements will be upheld.

In one case, in response to a union representation that collective bargaining cannot result in loss of existing benefits, the employer asserted that all the employees' present and future benefits are negotiable, and that negotiation would start with a blank piece of paper. The Board found that the employer's statements were made in response to an exaggerated union claim and constituted nothing more than an accurate description of one of the possible consequences of lawful collective bargaining.

When campaigning in this area, it is advisable for the employer to make frequent assertions that it will bargain in good faith and state that the employer's views are intended to inform the employees of the realities of collective bargaining. To bring the point home further, some employers have developed posters or paycheck stuffers quoting, in large print, NLRB and/or federal court opinions that state that employees can lose wages and benefits in collective bargaining. One excellent statement is contained in *The Bendix Corporation v. NLRB*, 400 F.2d 141 (6th Cir. 1968), in which the court stated: "The United States Government and the NLRB do not guarantee employees that the collective bargaining process starts from where you presently are in wages, insurance, pensions, profit sharing and all other conditions of employment."

An example of an excerpt which may be used as a plant poster is shown on the following page.

"Bargaining from scratch" statements are popular during campaigns. Depending upon the surrounding circumstances, an employer who indicates that collective bargaining "begins from scratch" or "starts at zero" or "starts with a blank page" may or may not be engaging in objectionable conduct. Such statements are objectionable when, in context, they effectively threaten employees with the loss of existing benefits and leave them with the impression that what they may ultimately receive depends in large measure on what the union can induce the employer to *restore*. On the other hand, such statements are not objectionable when additional communications to the employees dispel any implication that wages and/or benefits *will* be reduced during the course of bargaining and establish that any reduction in wages

DO YOU KNOW
THIS IS THE LAW?
AT THE BARGAINING TABLE,

"...there is, of course, no obligation on the part of an employer to contract to continue all existing benefits, nor is it an unfair labor practice to offer reduced benefits..."

(Midwestern Instruments, Inc., 133 NLRB 1132)

VOTE FOR YOUR FUTURE

VOTE ⊠ NO UNION

or benefits will occur only as a result of the normal give and take of collective bargaining. *Campbell Soup Co.*, 225 NLRB 222 (1976); *Checker Motors Corp.*, 232 NLRB 1077 (1977). Here is an example of a statement found unlawful:

QUESTION: Local 250 has told us that we can't lose any wages or benefits we have now, and the only way we can go is up. What really happens?

ANSWER: *Under the law, negotiations would start from scratch. Wages, benefits, and working conditions you now have would be up for grabs.* In negotiations, you can lose, as has happened to other em-

ployees. In negotiations the union can only accept or reject what
the hospital offers: If they don't like it, they have two choices:

a. *Accept the offer*, and *all* employees are stuck with it for the full
contract period. *BUT*, you will still have to pay dues to the union
with a union shop to keep your job at Dominican.

b. *Call a strike*.

The Board reasoned that the answer was coercive on two fronts. It
not only threatened employees with loss of their present benefits by
telling them that such benefits "would be up for grabs" and that bargaining "would start from scratch," but it also clearly implied that the
employer will assume a take-it-or-leave-it posture during negotiations.
The predisposition not to bargain in good faith was demonstrated, in
the Board's view, when the company presented the union's only options to be to accept the employer's proposals or call a strike. *Dominican Santa Cruz Hospital*, 242 NLRB 153 (1979).

The concept that a union may "trade away" existing benefits in return for items that are important to the union, such as union security
clauses and a check-off provision, can be an eye-opener to employees.
The point should be brought home succinctly. The following statement has been approved by the Board:

> I'm sure you have been told your wages and benefits could only get
> better. But if you think I am going to start bargaining from where
> you are now you've got another think coming. I'm going to start
> from scratch, a minimum proposal. If the union wants something,
> like a checkoff of union dues or preferred seniority for stewards,
> they may have to change vacations, paid sick time or some other su-
> perior benefit you now have in order to get these things. Bargaining
> is just that, give and take.

In using this approach, avoid giving employees the impression that
a union victory will result in the employer's eliminating all existing
benefits, not all of which would necessarily be restored in the bargaining process. The impression should not be created that hard bargaining would be required by the union merely to get for employees
what they had already enjoyed before the union entered the scene.
Even statements such as "The company has the legal right to lower
wages to the minimum if the union came in" have been viewed by the
Board as a blatant threat of economic reprisal.

Exploding the Myth of Job Security

Unions are exceptionally facile in perpetrating the myth that they are
able to obtain job security for each individual who becomes a member

of a bargaining unit. This myth must be torpedoed as soon as it surfaces. The employer should state that unions are in no position to talk about achieving job security, since some of the most highly organized groups in the country (for example, the building trades) have the highest percentage of unemployment. The employer will also have no difficulty citing mass layoffs in the automobile industry, the steel industry, and other unionized industries. Copies of newspaper clippings reporting such layoffs should be used to support the argument and lend greater credibility to what the employer says.

In making this argument, it is best to cast the approach in terms of a response to what the union has said. Of course, care should be taken to avoid implying that the union presence will *cause* layoffs in the plant or office.

The employer should state that real job security can be provided only by the efficient manufacture of a quality product, sold at a competitive price and delivered on time. The company's *orders* and *contracts* provide job security, not unions. Unions can interfere with job security by hindering productivity, interfering with friendly cooperation between employees and supervisors, calling strikes, and invoking other restrictive practices that tend to destroy job security rather than enhance it. Bolster such arguments with facts, such as United States Department of Labor surveys that show a huge drop in new manufacturing jobs in the states that are most heavily unionized and a corresponding enormous increase in new manufacturing jobs in states that are the least unionized.

The employer should not make the mistake of stating that a union success in the election or in bargaining would *necessarily* mean that the employer would be pushed into a noncompetitive position. The safest course is to provide objective evidence and examples to support any statement.

In one case, the company stated that if the company were to accept the union's master contract it would undoubtedly have to raise prices, resulting in less volume, less business, and the possibility of employee layoffs. The NLRB validated this approach, but based on the fact that the employer was familiar with the union's master contract at the time it made the statement, that the union in its propaganda was maintaining that the employer would sign the master contract, and that stores that were parties to the master union contract did in fact charge higher prices than stores that were nonunion. The Board concluded that the employer had an objective and reasonable basis for the prediction of the possible effect of operating a store under the union contract. No *threat* of loss of jobs was involved; it was a *prediction* that was protected (under 8(c) of the Act).

One successful mechanism for explaining the adverse impact of unionism on job security is to relate the facts of cases decided by the NLRB. There are many cases in which firms that were recently unionized were forced to close, demonstrating the hardships that a union can create. There is no prohibition on relating, truthfully, the experiences of other companies as related in official reports of Board proceedings.

An excellent statement was made by a white-collar employer in the following manner:

> We have noticed that some staff members who are absolutely committed to the union seem to believe that in some mystical, unspecified way, coverage by a union contract would suddenly improve job security and automatically enhance career goals. This is an absolutely false and misleading view, and we would like to take this opportunity to outline why you should not be taken in by this deception.
>
> Certainly, unions are in no position to talk about job security. The building trades unions, unions in the arts, and other unions in the highly industrial sectors of our economy have some of the highest percentages of unemployment. That's not a very good example of the so-called security unions say they afford to their members. In short, unionized employers throughout the nation, when layoffs become necessary, have been forced to take layoff action. It is quite obvious that a collective bargaining agreement cannot guarantee against layoffs—nor, for that matter, does it protect against discharge for cause.
>
> However, let us bring the argument close to home. Many of you who have been with our company for a number of years have seen for yourself that we are progressive and that the ability to adapt characterizes our operations. We feel this has been a key to our success. Many of you have seen union members at our company experience unfortunate but necessary layoffs, discharges, and other reorganizational cutbacks. This experience has not differed at all from the experiences of other companies in our industry. The point is this: A collective bargaining agreement in no way prohibits any company from legally laying off or discharging employees. Anyone who knows us must agree that we do not enjoy staff reduction, but it must be recognized that they are an occasional but real fact of life in our industry.
>
> NOTHING COULD BE MORE OBVIOUS THAN THE PLAIN AND SIMPLE FACT THAT NO UNION CAN ACCOMPLISH JOB SECURITY FOR YOU.
>
> Frankly, isn't the union trying to seduce you into supporting them by claiming they can enhance job security, when in fact they are powerless to do so?

The employer attached a survey of reductions in staff with respect to its various bargaining units at the same location and contrasted that reduction with the nonunion group in which the election was to be held. There had been no layoffs in the voting group. Employers that do not have unions on the premises may develop a similar tactic, where applicable. Other local companies with unions or unionized competitors can be surveyed for layoffs and reductions in staff that have occurred.

When possible, the job security message should be reinforced by posters, handouts and flyers such as the ones shown on the following two pages.

The Prospects of a Strike

Every campaign must point out that a strike is the union's main economic lever, and that a strike might involve adverse consequences for the employee—loss of wages, inability to pay bills, violence, difficulties on the picket lines, unavailability of union strike funds, the employer's right to replace economic strikers, the fact that jobs may no longer be available once the strike is over, and other factors.

The "inevitability" of a strike may *not* be communicated. The employer is in this position: The more persuasive, effective, and competent its campaign theme is on this issue, the more likely the Board is to conclude that the employer never intended to bargain in any meaningful sense and that, accordingly, the election should be set aside. In order to minimize the possibility that the Board will find that the employer's communication laid out a choice between a strike or no union, it is wise for the employer to save the strike message for selected communications and to avoid minor references to strikes in its other campaign materials. *Frequency* of the strike theme is a factor that the Board considers among the primary considerations in its determination.

The employer need not pull any punches in communicating the strike theme, and a variety of techniques are permissible. Parading the union's strike record over a period of a year or five years or ten years is extremely persuasive. Newspaper clippings and stories about particularly long and costly strikes conducted by the union or its parent, or local strikes conducted by other unions, are influential. Employees should be told that if the union is voted in, the only way it can back up its demands if the company disagrees is to call a strike. Employees should be advised that a strike can be called by a majority of only those *employees who attend* a union meeting, and that these meetings are often called, purposefully, at times that are inconvenient for the general membership. The militants who appear at these meetings may

YOU HAVE SOMETHING TO LOSE BY VOTING FOR A UNION

YOU CAN LOSE JOB SECURITY

Which Comes Only From The Combined Efforts of All Employees To Keep Our Business Successful

Many Union Professionals Try To Mislead Employees Into Believing That Union Contracts Provide Job Security. They Do **NOT**! Only A Successful and Progressive Business with All of Us Working As A Team Can Give You Real Security

IT HAS HAPPENED ELSEWHERE ..DON'T LET IT HAPPEN TO US!

Stay Ahead Of Our Competition!

YOU HAVE SOMETHING TO LOSE BY VOTING FOR A UNION

YOU CAN LOSE ECONOMIC SECURITY IN THE FORM OF WAGE RATES AND EMPLOYEE BENEFIT PLANS

This Security Is Made Possible Only By Our Cooperative Efforts.

Have You Ever Heard of the Union Professionals Advocating Cooperation Between Employees and Management? Cooperation For Our Common Good Seems To Be The First Thing They Set Out To Destroy

IT HAS HAPPENED ELSEWHERE ..DON'T LET IT HAPPEN TO US!

Stay Ahead Of Our Competition!

determine the future of the entire bargaining unit.

Management should remind employees that wages stop immediately if a strike occurs. Surprisingly, many employees do not realize this aspect of the strike. Payments on the medical and hospital insurance premiums, as well as payments to any existing pension programs, will also cease if a strike takes place. Thus, if a strike occurs, employees will have to pay insurance premiums for medical coverage out of their own pockets, or risk having to pay medical bills out of their own pockets during the duration of the strike. Any notion that the union will pay for these premiums should be dispelled.

Employees should also be informed that unions don't guarantee strike benefits. The employer should investigate the policies of the union with respect to strike benefits, waiting periods connected with these benefits, and the amounts actually paid out at other locations. Often, the conditions attached to the receipt of strike benefits and the extremely low amount of benefits are enough to dissuade the employees from any thought of striking.

Many employees—and supervisors—do not understand that an employee risks *losing his job* if a strike is called and the employer exercises its right to permanently replace any economic striker. Employees should be told that new workers can be hired to permanently fill their jobs and that, at the conclusion of the strike, the *strikers are not entitled to bump the replacements.* The employer will often find that employees do not believe this. The union has told them that they may not be "discharged" for striking, but it did not point out the subtle distinction between being discharged for striking and being permanently replaced. A successful stratagem has been to issue a leaflet quoting United States Supreme Court cases on the right of an employer to permanently replace employees. Once the quotation is read, the employer will find that the employees are beginning to think seriously about the prospects of unionism and the disadvantages that the union may bring to the workplace. A graphic depiction of such a campaign statement appears on the opposite page.

An employer may state that no union can force it to sign a contract that is not acceptable to it after it has bargained in good faith and failed to reach an agreement. At the point of impasse, the only way a union can enforce its demands is by asking employees to go out on strike. Having laid that background, the employer may permissibly state the following:

> If you go out on strike for higher wages and benefits, you will get absolutely no benefits from the union while you are on strike. What is more, if there is a strike, we would not close down our operation

STRIKE: Is it worth the risk?

Suppose the union stages a strike at our Company. Do you risk losing your job? The answer is an emphatic, YES!

Undoubtedly the union organizer hasn't told you about that possibility, but it's true. Here's what the United States Supreme Court said about that in its decision:

> Nor was it an unfair labor practice to replace the striking employees with others in an effort to carry on the business.*** And the Employer is not bound to discharge those hired to fill the places of strikers, upon the election of (the strikers) to resume their employment in order to create places for them. The assurance by the Employer to those who accepted employment during the strike that if they so desired their places might be permanent was not an unfair labor practice nor was it such to reinstate only so many of the strikers as there were vacant places to be filled. (N.L.R.B. v. Mackay Radio & Telegraph Co., 304 U.S. 333)

All of which means if you choose to go on strike, you can be *permanently replaced* by another worker. This is the law. Your replacement can *keep your job* after the strike is over. **Is it worth the risk?**

---

even for one day. We would expect that most of our employees would continue working, but in any event we would hire employees permanently to replace our present employees who are on strike. This is our right under the law. We tell you this not as any threat, but to make sure you are well informed before you bring the union in and it is too late.

The Board ruled that the foregoing statement was merely a prediction of the possible consequences if a strike occurred. It is safest for the employer to outline the steps leading to a strike rather than to express the bare sentiment that a strike may occur. The Board often interprets a bare statement to that effect as implying that a strike and loss of jobs is inevitable if the union wins.

An employer may also tell employees that if a strike occurs, its customers could probably do business with other companies. It may state that customers are concerned not with the employees and the company, but with a steady and reliable source of supply. The company can conclude that with any stoppage or interruption of production its customers would not hesitate to take their business elsewhere and probably never come back. Such a communication reveals the risk of possible loss of jobs as one price of unionism. Yet, the Board has found that such a statement (within the context of the entire campaign) was not a threat, but a prediction of the possible unfavorable consequences that might follow from *union* action and a prediction of the risk of loss of customers that might be occasioned by a work stoppage.

However, even though the United States Supreme Court has held that an employer may legitimately protect itself against the effectiveness of an anticipated strike by transferring work from one plant to another, the Board has held an employer in violation of the Act when, during an organizing campaign, it states to employees that certain operations would be shifted to another plant if they selected the union in order to protect the company against the possibility of a strike by the organizing union.

Employees should be told that a strike can cause severe economic injury to them and their families. Begin with the truism that strikes rarely occur where there are no unions. Then, emphasize the frequency and incidence of strikes in our society. The Bureau of Labor Statistics publishes extensive information on strikes. In any given year, there will be between 5,000 and 6,000 strikes involving anywhere between two and three million workers. 35 to 40 million days are normally lost, with disputes most frequently lasting between 30 to 60 days. Most strikes occur over differences about wages, with the greatest concentration of labor disputes normally involving the smaller employer, who employs between 20 and 100 employees.

All of the aforementioned general figures, which are fairly typical in any given year, can be refined and marketed in the most persuasive form in order to accomplish the employer's prime goal in a campaign: one of the best reasons for employees to stay nonunion is to avoid the strife, tension and lost wages and benefits that occur under strike conditions.

Other information that can be communicated is found in Bureau of Labor Statistics material readily available to the general public. Union strike funds are one example. Department of Labor figures demonstrate that most unions which do pay a weekly benefit for strikers paid less than $50 a week. The most frequent benefit paid was $25. Also U.S. Department of Labor surveys show that most unions have a waiting period of two weeks or more before paying any benefits. The individual union's constitution and by-laws contains information concerning strike sanctioning by the parent body and disqualification for employees who decline to perform picket line duties or who have obtained employment elsewhere during the strike. Because employees know a great deal less about strikes and strike compensation than employers assume, it is imperative to communicate this information.

Because information about strikes may be the single most important theme that an employer may communicate, here is a summary of essential facts that *must* be articulated with clarity and force:

- Tell the number of strikes engaged in by the organizing union in the preceding year or two.
- Give Labor Department statistics on strikes, including an annual period's number of days lost (usually expressed in the millions) and the number of strikes by all unions in the particular year (usually expressed in the thousands).
- If a strike takes place, income stops immediately.
- Employees should be made aware that the company will no longer pay hospitalization premiums; the employees will have to pay the premiums, or will have to pay hospital and medical expenses incurred during a strike out of their own pockets. Life insurance premiums may also be cancelled.
- In the overwhelming majority of states, unemployment compensation will not be paid by the government.
- Employees can lose their jobs when they go out on strike because management has the right to hire a permanent replacement in order to run its business.
- When the strike is over not everyone will necessarily return to their jobs. *Replacements may remain on the job, and the strikers will have no right to bump the replacements.* This is always a shock to employees.
- The possibilities of violence. Examples should be used where possible. Stress the spectre of those employees who favor the strike turning upon those who do not, and the bitterness that strikes usually bring.
- Emphasize the fact that unions have the legal right to fine members who decide to cross the picket line and who want to come to work.
- Finally, impress upon employees the fact that their loss of income during a strike may take many years to make up. Make this point graphically. The leaflet reproduced on the next two pages is an example of this.

In summary, while the employer can outline the obligation of union members to picket during a work stoppage, the company's right to

HOW TO USE THE INSIDE TABLE

If your take-home pay is $120 a week and you strike for 10¢ an hour, the table shows it will take you 30 weeks to get back your loss—if the strike is settled in one week and you get the 10¢ an hour increase.

If the strike lasts longer than one week, simply multiply the number of weeks shown on the table by the number of weeks the strike lasts to find how long it will take to recover your loss.

Example: A four week strike under the above circumstances will take 30 weeks \ 4   2 years and 16 weeks to recover loss.

What would a strike cost YOU?

permanently replace economic strikers, the particular union's past strike history or the strike history of unions in general, as well as the drastic loss of income that can be sustained during strikes, the Board will set aside the election where the employer conveys the message that strikes are *inevitable*. It is permissible for management to merely state its opinion as to the possible consequences of a union victory; but where the employer leads employees to believe that they *must* strike in order to obtain a meaningful collective bargaining relationship, the election results will be set aside.

Comparison of Working Conditions at Other Locations

Companies faced with organizing attempts often can refer to their own nonunion locations that have wages and benefits that compare fa-

Everyone LOSES in a strike!

- **EMPLOYEES** lose pay checks and it takes a long time to recover the loss.
- The **COMMUNITY** and its merchants and stores lose the benefit of payroll dollars.
- The **COMPANY** loses production, sales and often customers. Money which might be available for more jobs and expansion is lost.

UNIONS claim a strike is their strongest economic weapon, but some **UNION LEADERS** use strike threats and strikes with complete disregard for how it will affect employees.

UNION LEADERS LOSE NO PAYCHECKS during a strike.

These same **UNION LEADERS** generally "call the shots" on when to strike and for how long.

Before YOU go on strike or vote to strike, think about WHAT IT WILL COST YOU!

For EVERY week you strike . . . in the hope of getting

an hourly increase of ——►
(and you eventually get the increase)

IT WILL TAKE YOU THIS LONG TO GET BACK WHAT YOU LOST

If your present take-home pay is:	You Will LOSE	0¢	10¢	20¢	30¢	35¢
$100-101	$100	Never	25 weeks	12 weeks	8 weeks	7 weeks
$110-111	$110	Never	27 weeks	13 weeks	9 weeks	7 weeks
$120-121	$120	Never	30 weeks	15 weeks	10 weeks	8 weeks
$130-131	$130	Never	32 weeks	16 weeks	10 weeks	9 weeks
$140-141	$140	Never	35 weeks	17 weeks	11 weeks	10 weeks
$150-151	$150	Never	37 weeks	18 weeks	12 weeks	10 weeks
$160-161	$160	Never	40 weeks	20 weeks	13 weeks	11 weeks
$170-171	$170	Never	42 weeks	21 weeks	14 weeks	12 weeks
$180-181	$180	Never	45 weeks	22 weeks	15 weeks	12 weeks

If a strike lasts several weeks, just multiply by number of weeks . . . *THINK HARD!!!*

vorably to the wages and benefits enjoyed at unionized locations. But exercise caution in this area!

In one case, the employer told its employees that benefit programs were the same at all its locations, whether they were union or non-union. It further stated that it did not give more benefits to employees who pay union dues. It concluded by saying that it had no intention of doing more for the employees in the voting unit until the company was prepared to improve the benefits at all of its other locations. The Board found this expression to be objectionable, since it tied bargaining at the voting location to what the company was willing to grant to all of its other plants, thus conveying a clear message that the company would refuse to bargain with the union about improving benefits.

This is an extremely delicate and still-developing area of the law. The best course is to present the employer's argument as *informational* and to outline in a leaflet or a letter the facts—for example, exactly what the better benefits at the nonunion location are. Present all data in a purely factual form and let employees draw their own conclusions.

Where an employer has a unionized location where all the rules and regulations are strictly enforced in accordance with the collective bargaining agreement, the employer may compare this with the more flexible working conditions at its nonunionized location. These statements are viewed as forseeable consequences of unionization.

A final caveat about communicating employee policies at other plants: Care should be taken when informing employees about improvements at other locations, take care to avoid creating the impression that employees will receive these benefits *only* through rejecting the union, or that employees will definitely not receive more if a union is selected as a bargaining agent.

In one case, the employer distributed individually tailored pension information sheets for each voter and compared pension benefits at union and nonunion locations. Benefits at nonunion locations, one of which was owned by the employer, were depicted as superior. Management officials specifically stated that they were merely giving an example of union versus nonunion benefits and that the company was not promising to implement the provisions of the nonunion pension plan if the union lost the election. Despite the care exercised in communicating its views, and the specific disclaimer of any promise, the Board found that the display charts containing the information would lead employees to readily assume that the greater pension benefits enjoyed by nonunion employees would be given to them if they remained nonunion. The NLRB decided that the employer's *repeated* emphasis on these *individualized* comparisons made it clear to employees that in order to obtain the superior pension benefits, they must vote to defeat the union. *Etna Equipment & Supply Co.*, 243 NLRB No. 101 (1979).

Injection of Racial Prejudice as an Issue

Where racial prejudice on the part of the union is made the dominant theme of a campaign by the employer, it is grounds for setting aside an election.

An employer may inject racial subjects into an election only where it limits the comments to truthful statements of the other party's position on racial matters. The employer must not overstress or exacerbate racial feelings by making irrelevant and inflammatory appeals. This rule applies to both employer and union communications. The party that brings racial statements into the campaign has the burden of establishing that they are both truthful and germane to the election issues.

But the employer should also be aware that the NLRB has sanctioned unions' recent strong appeals to the class consciousness of minority employees. In one case, a union organizer remarked to employees that if blacks did not stick together and the union lost the election, all the blacks would be fired. He also stated that the trend was that the blacks were going to be laid off if they didn't stick together and try to get the plant organized so they would have protection. The Board *refused* to set aside the election, reasoning that the statements did not appeal to racial prejudice on matters unrelated to the election issues but rather were germane to the larger issue of advantages and disadvantages of the union as a means of obtaining economic security and job rights. In that case, there had been three layoffs of black employees shortly before the election campaign.

Where the union makes such class-consciousness appeals (on the basis of race, religion, nationality, or sex), the employer should promptly set the record straight, indicating that job security and improvement in wages and benefits flow equally to all employees, regardless of race or minority status.

Whenever raising the issue of race, the employer should be watchful of independent civil rights risks and the possibility that either the union or an employee may file a charge with a state or federal discrimination agency. If an employer insinuates during a campaign that if the union were to win, white employees would be required to work alongside blacks, the Board will set aside the election unless the employer can prove the statements are factual and germane. However, where a supervisor told several black employees that a white employee who was antagonistic to blacks would probably be elected shop steward if the union won, and blacks would have no representative sympathetic to their problems, the Board viewed these statements as campaign propaganda which the employees were capable of fairly evaluating.

Quotations from Legal Decisions

A safe approach—and often an extremely effective one—is to offer quotations from court or NLRB decisions. People are impressed by the written word, particularly quotations from higher authorities or courts of law. When an employee reads a quotation from an authoritative opinion, the tendency is to believe it.

There are many opportunities for employers to use such quotations. Most frequently they occur in areas involving (1) the employer's right to permanently replace employees who engage in an economic strike; (2) the employer's bargaining obligations (and limitations thereon); (3) the Section 8(d) proviso that the employer need not make any concessions in bargaining; (4) Section 7 rights of employees to refrain from joining unions and engaging in any type of union activity; and (5) unfair labor practice provisions that prevent unions from coercing individuals.

Where appropriate, sections of the statute may be reproduced in full and quoted. Where appropriate, sections can be substantially paraphrased. Exact quotations from NLRB or federal court decisions may be given (see p. 240 for 2 sample quotations). Employer communications often contain a footnote stating that any individual wishing to see the statute or the decision itself is free to ask for a copy. Although few people ask for the original source material, the offer itself lends credibility to what is said.

When legal cases are too complicated, the facts may be broken down so that they are understandable. Care should be taken, however, to make certain that the representation of the law is accurate. For example, cases involving union fines for strike-breaking, failure to assume picket-line duty, or failure to observe union production quotas and other union rules may be summarized, and the conclusion of the case specifying the amount of the fines may be quoted exactly.

Involving the NLRB in Campaign Statements

An employer may involve the NLRB in its campaign in ways which are helpful to its efforts. However, care must be taken so as not to *improperly* involve the Board by implying that the NLRB favors the company or endorses a particular employer viewpoint. For example, management may refer to certain types of union campaign statements and advise employees to contact the Board agent or the Board's Officer-of-the-Day in order to obtain the truth. While the Board agent will not necessarily answer all questions, the mere willingness of the employer to refer employees to the Board lends credibility to the employer's position. Often, when the employer makes a legal representation, such as the fact that economic strikers may be permanently replaced by other workers, employees may be referred to the NLRB to verify the truth or falsity of that legal concept. The Board's publication "Layman's Guide" may also be used for this purpose.

Extreme care should be taken to avoid the issuance of written campaign material with any reference to the NLRB inscribed on the document (particularly in the same type face as used by the NLRB on its election notices). If the campaign material gives the appearance that the NLRB favors the employer, or even creates an ambiguity in the mind of the reader as to the document's originator, it may create the impression that the Board has allied itself with the employer. In such a case, the Board will view this as deceptive conduct and may set aside the election. Take the employer campaign piece shown on the following page.

Does this campaign literature suggest to the voters that a company choice is endorsed by the Board? The NLRB has always ruled that it would not permit its official ballot to be reproduced unless it is unaltered and clearly marked "sample" on its face. In cases where the information added to the ballot is clearly that of the company's management, and not part of the official ballot, the voters are not thereby misled by the information. Thus, where the added writing is in longhand and identifiable as a company comment, the campaign material will be approved. However, in the campaign piece shown on page 178, the company is not clearly revealed to the voter as the author of the added comments. Management remarks are in a type similar to the ballot itself and the hand is stamped rather than sketched. Moreover, the hand intrudes upon the actual dimensions of the official Board ballot. As there was no indication who was responsible for the altered ballot, and as the material added to the reproduction of the ballot by the employer was not readily distinguishable from the ballot itself, the impression was created that voting "no" had the Board's approval. The Board found this to be a misuse of the Board's processes and set the election aside. *Building Leasing Corp.*, 239 NLRB No. 3 (1978). However, where an employer showed three employees a reproduced portion of the NLRB's notice of election with notations and highlighting written on the notice by the employer, the election was not set aside. The Board reached this result because the marks were clearly discernible as additions made by employer representatives rather than by the Board. *Clark Equipment Co.*, 242 NLRB No. 194 (1979).

Campaign Misrepresentations

Because campaign misrepresentations may be the basis for setting aside an election, special care must be taken that the employer's campaign material does not contain deviations from the truth sufficient to

TO VOTE

UNITED STATES OF AMERICA

National Labor Relations Board

OFFICIAL SECRET BALLOT

SAMPLE

FOR CERTAIN EMPLOYEES OF

BUILDING LEASING CORPORATION, KANSAS CITY, MISSOURI

Do you wish to be represented for purposes of collective bargaining by -

SERVICE EMPLOYEES INTERNATIONAL
UNION LOCAL NO. 96, AFL-CIO ?

MARK AN "X" IN THE SQUARE OF YOUR CHOICE

YES	NO
☐	☐

DO NOT SIGN THIS BALLOT. Fold and drop in ballot box.
If you spoil this ballot return it to the Board Agent for a new one.

CAUTION

MARK YOUR BALLOT WITH AN "X"

DO NOT USE ANY OTHER SYMBOL

DO NOT SIGN

DO NOT WRITE ON THE BALLOT

ANY OTHER MARK MIGHT VOID YOUR BALLOT

YOUR X IN THIS

SQUARE WILL MEAN—

YOU DO NOT WANT

A UNION

cause the Board to nullify an election. The board will set aside an election where conduct creates an atmosphere that renders improbable a free choice even though the conduct may not constitute an unfair labor practice. *General Knit of California, Inc.*, 239 NLRB No. 101 (1978), reaffirmed the doctrine that where one party, at a time that prevents the other party from making an effective reply, makes a misrepresentation that may reasonably be expected to have a significant impact on employee free choice, the election will be set aside. While a misrepresentation may fall short of constituting a violation of the Act, the Board seeks to maintain, as much as possible, laboratory conditions for the exercise of employee voting rights. One factor, in the Board's view, that may so disturb these conditions as to interfere with this expression of free choice is a substantial misrepresentation about some material issue. Absolute precision of statement and complete honesty are not always attainable in an election campaign; complete accuracy is not expected by the employees or by the Board. Also, the Board recognizes the right of both the union and the employer to wage a free and vigorous campaign with all the normal tools of electioneering. Exaggeration, inaccuracies, half-truths, and name-calling, though not condoned by the Board, will not be grounds for setting aside elections.

On the other hand, misrepresentation that may be reasonably expected to have a significant impact on the election is grounds for overturning an election. Significant impact is measured by all of the circumstances in a particular case. Some of the more obvious ones are: (1) the subject being addressed—e.g., wages, benefits, and profits are obviously of great importance to the election and a misrepresentation with regard to them would be more likely to affect votes; (2) the timing of the statement; and (3) the degree to which the employees would be likely to rely on the accuracy of the statement. This is related to the extent to which the information is uniquely within the knowledge of either the employer or the union. The traditional tests for determining impact are:

1. The misrepresentation must be of a material fact and involve a substantial departure from the truth.
2. The other party must not have time to reply.
3. The misrepresentation comes from a party in an authoritative position to have special knowledge of the facts.
4. The employees lack independent knowledge with which to evaluate the statement.

The closer to the date of the election, the more the employer should temper its words and strive to avoid misrepresentation. Otherwise, the Board will scrutinize the "election bombshell" stringently.

The Board tolerates some degree of puffery in electioneering, and exaggerations regarding the value of fringe benefits, or predictions that a union dues increase is likely, have been held insufficient to invalidate the election.

While all of the tools of campaigning should be brought to bear during the critical pre-election period, care should be taken—particularly during the last week of the campaign—to insure that statements are accurate and truthful. The efforts of many a hard-fought campaign have been nullified when the employer has overlooked this.

Where the facts are not definitively known, the employer is safer expressing an "opinion" that a particular benefit given by the employer is better than a particular union benefit. For example, when referring to union dues structure, state that the employer "understands" that union dues are of a certain amount, or that they "may" be raised in the near future.

The Board engages in a delicate balancing act and tries to reconcile the right of employees to free choice versus the right of the parties to wage a free and vigorous campaign using all of the normal and legitimate tools of electioneering. The Board will not lightly set an election aside.

Since management has control over what it says, having an election set aside because of a misrepresentation of fact is normally inexcusable. In the following cases, statements were found to constitute a substantial misrepresentation leading to the nullification of the election:

Management Interference with Elections
Based upon Substantial Misrepresentations

- An employer told employees that if the union won the election and obtained a union security contract, expulsion from the union would result in discharge; the election was set aside since expulsion from the union does *not* affect job tenure unless the expulsion is for nonpayment of dues or initiation fees. *K-F Prods., Inc.*, 170 NLRB 366 (1968).

- A supervisor added to a union handbill a note that (a) the union had a scheme to circumvent its requirement that the local membership authorize a strike and that (b) another plant had closed after the union obtained the contract. No such scheme existed, and the other plant had closed solely for lack of business. *Eagle-Picher Industries, Inc.*, 171 NLRB 293 (1968).

- An employer linked an increase in wages to a wage survey and then attempted to withhold the results of the survey so as not to prejudice the election. The employer appeared to be trying to place responsibility on the union for withholding the survey results, and hence for any possible increases in benefits and wages. *General Dynamics Corp.*, 186 NLRB 978 (1970).

- A supervisor stated that since the union had filed the petition, the law was that management could not unilaterally grant bonuses or other benefits, and that the employees could blame the union for anything they did not get. *Wilkinson Mfg. Co. v. NLRB*, 456 F.2d 298 (8th Cir. 1972).

- An employer sent the unit employees a document containing a reproduction of the Board's seal and excerpts from an outdated Board publication. The election was set aside because the employer had used the Board publication for partisan purposes and the publication misled the employees by stating a false and misleading view as to the employees' reinstatement rights in the event of an economic strike. *Thiokol Chem. Corp.*, 202 NLRB 434 (1973).

- Employer's agent, a psychological testing firm, stated that the employer offered a 25-cent raise which the union rejected. Since there may have been valid reasons for such a rejection during the campaign, the employer's agent had unlawfully put the onus for the loss of the pay raise on the union, which is grounds for setting aside the election regardless of the truth or fallacy of the statement. *Sterling Faucet Co.*, 203 NLRB 1031 (1973).

Areas in which there is a high incidence of claims of *union* misrepresentation involve statements by unions that contracts they negotiated with other .employers provide exceptional benefits; representations about extremely generous pension programs; claims of certain benefits that in fact were not in any of the union's contracts; claims that benefits were won through union bargaining whereas in fact they existed before the union came on the scene; false representations about the wage rates or salaries unions have been able to obtain from other companies; misstatements as to classifications at other plants or offices; exaggerations regarding working conditions at other plants organized by the union; exaggerations about union strike benefits; misrepresentations about stockholders' dividends, company profits, managerial salaries, and how long it took employees to reach a certain wage or salary level; failure to explain that wages are based on a longer work week than the one prevailing at the company having the election; misstatements about premium pay enjoyed by members at other plants; failure to disclose onerous contract conditions when explaining benefits at other companies; and similar subjects. Appendix 6 contains specific examples (with citations) of rulings upholding employer objections to campaign fraud, misrepresentation, and other union tactics. The Appendix also includes a valuable listing of cases in which the federal courts have differed with the Board on whether an election should be set aside for misrepresentations and have denied enforcement of NLRB bargaining orders.

The Board also embraces the doctrine that inaccurate statements of employees' legal rights under the labor law *may*, standing alone, be insufficient to cause an election to be set aside. Yet, two or more such statements, occurring together, may be coercive. Consider what happened in the following case. The first statement involved the employer's characterization of the employees' right to oust the union once they had selected it as their collective bargaining representative:

> What the pushers have not told you, and hope you do not realize, is that once a union gets in, there is basically no turning back—you are stuck with it from then on.

While it is true that the number of decertifications is small when compared with the number of collective bargaining relationships, nevertheless, Section 9(c) of the Act provides employees with a clear and unmistakable right to oust the union as their collective bargaining representative. It was held that the employer's statement was misleading and that the failure to allude to the right to eliminate a union, when coupled with the admonition that "there is basically no turning back", is clearly an attempt to disguise that right and to convey the impression that employees have little or not recourse against the union when they become disaffected.

A second passage involved the rights of employees to communicate with their employer once they are represented by a union. The employer stated:

> A union is nothing more than an outsider. When this outsider comes on the scene, the employees lose all rights for direct communication with the company.

Since Section 9(a) of the Act emphatically reserves to employees the right to present grievances to their employer and to have such grievances adjusted without the intervention of the bargaining representative, the employer's statement flatly declaring that *all* rights for *direct* communication are lost under unionization, is inconsistent with the statue and involves a substantial departure from the truth.

It was held that a union election involves the decision of whether to sacrifice certain individual rights and interests in favor of representation by a union. Therefore, the extent to which the Act has preserved the rights of an individual employee even after the union has been selected is a matter of great concern to the employees in the process of voting. The employer's statement erroneously exaggerated the extent to which employees lose their individual rights to collective representation.

A final statement purported to describe the union security provision that the union would be likely to demand. It stated:

> If the union is elected, there are usually two things that they go after:
>
> 1. The first thing they go after is a closed shop. Closed shop means that the company agrees that no nonunion employees will be employed by the company—that everyone is union.

Likewise, the statement amounted to a misrepresentation that the union would seek an *unlawful* closed shop provision rather than a lawful union security provision. Basically, the statement warned that only union people will be employed by the company under the closed shop. This is substantially incorrect due to the fact that the closed shop is illegal in all states and secondly, because employees are only required to meet their financial obligations of unionization and need not become members of the union and swear allegiance to its institutional principles.

Although under different circumstances each of the misrepresentations made might not have warranted setting the election aside, the misrepresentations quoted above, occurring together, did form a proper basis for nullifying the vote. *Robbins & Myers*, 241 NLRB No. 11 (1979).

Information on Campaign Mechanics

In the heat of the organizational battle, many employers neglect to communicate certain fundamental principles concerning the election process. It is vital, for example, that employees be told that if they have signed an authorization card they are still free to change their minds and to vote "no" in the election. They should be told that attendance at any union meeting called by the union during the campaign is completely voluntary. The fact that the balloting is secret should be stressed. Many employees believe that since it is a union election, the union somehow handles the ballots and will know how each individual voted. Secrecy is the theme that should constantly be repeated. Employees should also be told that the union cannot discriminate against them if the union wins the election. The union has no way of retaliating against them if they express their disapproval of the union during the campaign. If the union wins, they can join the union at that time, and the union can not penalize them for not having joined earlier. Management should make it clear that the law prohibits the union from coercing or threatening employees.

The employer should also state that employees are not obliged to accept union organizers into their homes, to make appointments with organizers, or to accept telephone calls from them. A day or two before the *Excelsior* list is given to the NLRB for transmission to the union, the company may tell employees that they have given the names and addresses to the union pursuant to orders by the NLRB, and advise them that organizers may be telephoning or visiting them, but that they can refuse to deal with the organizers.

Explain the mechanics of the voting and show a sample ballot. In reproducing the ballot, make sure that it omits any reference to the United States Government, NLRB, or similar official designation.

A key issue is the number of people the union will need in order to win the election. A *majority of those voting* determines the outcome of the election, therefore the importance of *everyone* voting should be reiterated throughout the campaign. If management fears that many uncommitted voters will not vote in the election, a number of accepted practices involving raffles, contests, and other inducements may be used.

Contests and Prizes

In determining the legality of these vote-inducing mechanisms, the Board is concerned with whether or not the prize offered by that employer is dependent on the outcome of the election or the way in which the employee votes. If it is, the election will be set aside. If the prize or bonus is of a high enough value to create a feeling of obligation toward the employer, it will not be deemed a valid "inducing mechanism."

The Board is also concerned with whether the contest is conducted in such a way as to constitute an improper poll. The employer is safest in conditioning any gift *solely* on the condition that the recipient must vote in the election. In one case, where a *union* gave each employee who attended a meeting a $5 gift certificate, the Board found employee free choice was impaired. Presumably, the same reasoning would be applied to the employer's actions. In another case, the employer paid lunch money to employees who attended preelection meetings, and that practice was upheld.

Since getting out the vote is so important, there are a number of mechanisms that the employer may explore in generating employee interest in the election. TV sets, cameras, and "market baskets" full of goods and similar prizes to the winners of employer-sponsored raffles have all been approved.

In one case, a union promised to hold a raffle with a hundred-dollar prize if it won the election. The Board held that conditioning receipt of benefits on a favorable election result was impermissible even though the raffle was worth only $1.18 per employee in the unit. *Crestwood Manor*, 234 NLRB No. 160 (1978).

In one case, an employer adopted the novel approach of distributing a questionnaire containing a number of "true-or-false" questions. A gift worth $40 was to be given to the employee with the most correct answers. The questions tested employees on information that the employer had distributed during the campaign. No participant was identified, except for the winner, and a participation in the contest was voluntary. A sample question was:

> Can the company permanently replace employees who go out on strike in support of demands made by the union?

The Board ruled that the purpose of the contest was to make employees aware of the facts that the employer communicated during the campaign and to encourage their interest in voting in the election. The contest was viewed as a permissible campaign mechanism designed to help make sure that employees were aware of the issues and the employer's position with respect to those issues.

On election day the employer may use a wrap-up statement or flyer urging employees to vote, and containing a partisan message. Examples are shown on the following two pages.

The Libel Pitfall

The rules established by the NLRB are not the only legal restrictions the employer must worry about when communicating with employees during a campaign. Management should also be aware of the laws of

It's up to YOU!

In The Election Material Addressed To You, We Have Attempted To Describe As Accurately As Possible The Disadvantages Both To You and The Company If Any Union Should Inject Itself Into Our Plant.

In Presenting These Disadvantages, We Necessarily Used Direct and Clear Language. The Conditions We Have Been Talking About Cannot Be Properly Described In Any Other Way.

We Have Exercised Our American Right Of Free Speech, and You Now Have Your American Right of Voting Exactly As You Please.

WE THINK THE UNION SHOULD BE DEFEATED! WE HAVE PRESENTED ALL THE FACTS TO YOU! YOU KNOW THE ISSUES THE ELECTION IS NOW IN YOUR HANDS!

Vote and Vote With The Knowledge That Your Ballot Is Secret And You Are Perfectly Free To Vote As You See Fit.

It's up to YOU!

libel and slander. Although the laws vary from state to state, the fundamental principles are generally the same: To spell out a valid case against a company, the union must prove that the statements about the union were false and were circulated with malice and an intent to cause damage. The publication must be made with knowledge of its falsity or with a reckless disregard of whether or not the statements are true or false. If a union *official* claims to be slandered, he must also prove that he was injured by the false statement, i.e., that his reputation has suffered or that he sustained mental suffering or alienation of association or similar damages.

Nevertheless, the employer has a great deal of leeway when criticizing the union in campaign propaganda. Most statements arguably relevant to the organizing activity are entitled to protection. *Letter Carriers v. Austin*, 418 U.S. 264 (1974). Statements respecting arrests, indictments, and convictions of union officials should be scrutinized carefully before they are publicized. To avoid inviting lawsuits, campaign managers should follow these rules in issuing campaign statements:

- Venomous and insulting language should be avoided.
- The accuracy of any statement made about the union should be investigated thoroughly. The company should, if challenged, be able to prove the truth of any statement made.
- Statements should be characterized with words such as "we understand" or "the local newspaper has reported."

The NLRB has taken a traditionally liberal view toward insulting and potentially libelous statements made during campaigns. In one case, the employer stated that the union "took bribes" and was "corrupt."

The NLRB declined to find that the statement constituted libel and ruled in favor of the company on the grounds that the statements were expressions of opinion and were protected by the free-speech provision of the Act. *Montgomery Ward & Co.*, 234 NLRB No. 88 (1978).

The union is subject to the same rules. If management believes that a particularly vicious and false statement made by the union campaigners constitutes libel or slander, the possibility of instituting an action against the union in the state courts may be pursued with counsel.

The Totality-of-Conduct Doctrine

In asserting the free-speech rights allowed under the law, employers must understand that merely phrasing certain comments in accordance with the form approved by prior Board decisions does not insulate the employer from valid objections to the election and/or unfair labor practice findings. The Board is concerned with more than merely the statement that is questioned by the union in its objections; it takes into account the total campaign and *all the surrounding circumstances*. Thus, several individual statements, each of which is legal, may, when *taken together*, convey the total impression of the futility of employees' designating the union as bargaining agent.

It is therefore imperative that unnecessary emotionalism be avoided, and that the employer avoid *constant* reiteration of warnings about loss of job security, the inevitability of strikes, the possibility of loss of work, the uncertainty of the employees' future if the union is voted in, and similar concepts. Constantly repeated, statements like these amount to an attempt to influence employees not by reason, but by fear. The Board will look at the "total context" of a statement, including its timing, its background, and contemporaneous acts and utterances. An election may be set aside even though the statement objected to was not by itself an unlawful threat or promise.

As an example of the Board's approach, which considers the totality of the employer's conduct when evaluating written campaign communications or speeches, consider the following example. On three different occasions the employer made the following statements:

> If we ever get organized-we are required to bargain with that organization. Some people make the mistake that bargaining starts with what you have and goes from there. This is absolutely wrong—it is a give and take proposition. Everyone should understand early in the game that the law permits a company to bargain from scratch—from a blank piece of paper. When an A-T-O Company is organized, it is our policy to do just that.
>
> We doubt that the Union has told you that labor negotiations is a tough process and is a two-way street. . . The Company assesses its position on the basis of how much it can afford to pay and still remain competitive, and it takes a stand at this point. In other words, Interstate Engineering, if it loses the election, after bargaining in good faith, would be the sole judge of what type of labor contract was acceptable to it. Sometimes the Union fails or refuses to understand this "simple logic" and keeps promising its members what they can get for them. If this happens, it is likely a strike will follow with all the ensuing disorder, bitterness, lost wages, lost business, or sometimes permanent closing of the plant.
>
> We are positive that the Union will insist on a union shop if it wins. This requires that all employees be members of the Union and pay their monthly dues and initiation fees in order to be able to work. This would force your company to fire anyone who refuses to become a member of the Union. We are strongly opposed to this as

we would be required to force our people to join the Union to keep their jobs. If we were to lose the election, the union shop would be one of the key issues for negotiation, that you should know our feelings at this time.

We believe that the Union, if it wins, must try to fulfill its promises and insist on higher wages and benefits. We have the absolute right, under the law, to refuse to grant any union demands if we believe they are not in our company's best interest. As a matter of fact, we are not required by law to negotiate from existing wages and benefits; we can start from scratch, disregarding present benefits and wages.

We believe that the expected union demands for higher wages and benefits make a strike highly likely if we cannot reach agreement after bargaining in good faith. If there is a strike because we cannot agree on contract terms after bargaining in good faith, we will not close our plant for one single day. We will stay open. Each of you will be welcome to work if there is a strike-we will have jobs for you. But remember this, the law gives us the right to permanently replace any striking employees. We have the absolute right under the law to make the final decision of what is acceptable to the Company. No union can force us to sign any contract which is not acceptable to us.

Although each letter standing alone may have been protected by the employer's right of free speech, considered jointly and in the context of other unfair conduct they were found to violate the Act. *Interstate Engineering*, 230 NLRB 1 (1977), *enf'd, NLRB v. Interstate Engineering*, 583 F.2d 1087 (9th Cir. 1978).

One employer suggested to its employees that they wait to see what the organizing union accomplished at the plant of another employer. (Although this is a defensive approach, it may be appropriate where campaign conditions justify it.) Here is what the employer said:

If the union should win the election, all of you will be stuck with this organization even if you later want to get rid of the union. It is theoretically possible to decertify a union, but it is extremely difficult as a practical matter. Under the circumstances, you would be wise to wait and see what happens at [a nearby employer where the organizing union was recently certified] for one year. If you are unhappy with conditions one year from now, you can have an election then. Wait and see for the next year, and it will not cost you anything in union dues or hazards.

This type of statement is viewed as legitimate campaigning.

In view of the Board's strict approach to employer campaign conduct and the difficulties of predicting Board decisions, the legality of a campaign may hinge *on one word*. Any unfair labor practice during the

critical period may mean a new election will be directed by the Board.
The interrogation of only one or two employees, or the promise of a
wage increase to a single employee, will normally be sufficient to
cause the Board to invalidate an election. The employer and its counsel must carefully consider where permissible free speech ends and
impermissible appeals to fear begin. The penalties for committing unfair labor practices are severe and should be avoided. *Gissel* bargaining
orders are only one example. The Board has fashioned other remedies
and will not hesitate to invoke them. For example, the costs to the
union of an expensive six-month organizing drive, plus interest, were
assessed against an employer where the Board found a link between
extraordinary organizing expenses and the company's unlawful campaign. *J. P. Stevens & Co.*, 244 NLRB No. 82 (1979).

Sample employer campaign statements reflecting the Board's current thinking appear in Appendix 5. Union electioneering conduct
prohibited by the NLRB is synopsized in Appendix 6.

Chapter 9

Training Supervisors to Be a Campaign Force

Supervisors play a key role. They are the liaison between management and the employees. Ascertaining the attitude of employees through the supervisors and, in turn, using the supervisors as a means for the dissemination of information and the answering of questions are of prime importance. When supervisors remain neutral during a campaign, it is difficult for the employer to mount a successful effort. Thus, management should encourage supervisors to express to employees their procompany and antiunion opinions.

The Importance of Frontline Supervision

"Eyeball-to-eyeball" communications between supervisors and employees, if properly handled by supervisors trained in communicating during a campaign, can be a most effective method of influencing the way employees will vote. A properly balanced campaign contains not only well-written and well-timed communications to the home, leaflets, bulletin board postings, and speeches, but also a large measure of day-to-day discussion between the supervisors and those they supervise.

Employees' opinions will be most affected if the communicator has a high degree of credibility. Many companies have found that frontline supervisors have more credibility with employees than most members of top management. This is particularly true when top management does not communicate with employees during "peacetime," but engages in a flurry of communications when an organizing drive begins.

Management cannot afford to allow supervisors to engage in "business as usual" during the campaign. Supervisors must be impressed with a deep appreciation of their role in the campaign and must be told by management what is expected of them. The provisions of the

Taft-Hartley Act are extremely tricky; no employer should run a campaign without equipping frontline supervision with a working knowledge of labor law and the pitfalls inherent in the Act.

Frontline supervision is the company's first line of defense against union invasion of the workplace. Companies have often found that union activity arose as a result of poor relations between employees and supervisors.

Many supervisors do not understand the motivations that compel workers to search out unions; they are unaware of the basic conditions that lead to employee distontent and they do not recognize their own self-interest in having their employer remain nonunion. Management must be certain that it convinces supervisors that they have a personal stake in keeping the union out. The employer must let the supervisors know that management is ardently pro-employee and dead set against outside interference, and that the supervisor's role is to act as the liaison between employees and top-level plant management.

How Supervisors Bind the Company

The National Labor Relations Act includes any person acting as an agent of an employer, either directly or indirectly, within the definition of "employer." Since a supervisor is an agent of the employer, the company is held responsible for any statement or illegal conduct of a supervisor during an organizational attempt. In fact, the statements or actions of supervisors are the most common causes of unfair labor practices. Even when a supervisor engages in illegal conduct or speech in violation of the employer's express instructions, the employer is responsible.

When a supervisor has made an illegal statement that becomes known to the employer, repudiation of that specific statement and a declaration of neutrality in labor organization matters may exculpate the employer. Express instructions, preferably in writing, may also be sufficient to avoid liability, if the instructions are also communicated to the employees. Ordinarily, however, supervisory statements and conduct bind the employer, so the importance of proper training of supervisors at the beginning of any campaign is obvious.

The Supervisor's Role in Enforcing No-Solicitation Rules

Most supervisors are unaware of the employer's rights in the area of protecting working time and company premises against solicitation and distribution of literature. For that reason, they should be carefully counseled on the maximum permissible supervisory activities in preventing improper solicitation and in legally enforcing the employer's rules against solicitation. Sample guidelines incorporating basic principles which may be distributed and explained to supervisors are:

1. You can't discipline employees for breaking rules they haven't heard of. No-solicitation rules should be published in writing, preferably in the employee handbook as well as on plant bulletin boards. You can post a separate copy in your department.

2. No-solicitation rules should apply to *all forms* of employee solicitation, and not just to union solicitation, otherwise the NLRB will say you are "discriminating." You should not wait until a union organizing drive develops before publishing and enforcing these rules.

3. You must enforce the rule UNIFORMLY. If you expect to bar employees from soliciting for unions on company time, you can't openly tolerate betting pools, World Series pools, vending of items for sale, or other solicitations on company time by employees. This may seem an unreasonable hardship. But if you wish to enforce your no-solicitation rule, you must run a "tight ship" and not allow any employee solicitations for any purpose on company time.

4. No-solicitation rules must be enforced equally as to pro-union *and anti-union groups*. No favoritism can be shown. Check with your plant manager if anti-union groups are active during working time.

5. Your published rule can provide that solicitation for any purpose on company property by non-employees, including former employees—those on layoff and recently discharged employees—is prohibited.

6. Your rule can provide that solicitation by employees for any purpose is prohibited *during working time*.

7. This means that employees are free to discuss the merits and demerits of unionization before and after work, on their rest periods (coffee breaks) and at lunch time. This is true even if the company pays for this time.

8. You can prohibit the distribution of literature by employees (unrelated to their work) *in working areas at all times*. You can remove literature left around the plant, whether it is left in working or non-working areas. Your reason for doing so is to prevent litter. Don't take literature from an employee's possession. Do take a copy of

union propaganda if it is handed to you. Deliver it to your plant manager.

9. "Working areas" means those places where employees customarily perform their jobs. Non-working areas include such places as rest rooms, parking lots, cafeterias, and public sidewalks adjacent to the plant.

10. These rules must be applied with common sense. They are designed to prevent interference with a company's operations. If you customarily permit employees to carry on casual conversation while they are working together, you should not discipline them if they happen to mention the word "union."

11. You should, of course, impose the rules strictly on employees supporting the union who ignore their work, *leave their departments*, or otherwise engage in systematic union solicitation which tends to interfere with production.

12. If you must make an issue over an employee's breach of the solicitation rules, try where possible to have reliable witnesses present.

13. If you discipline employees for breaking plant rules, do not allow yourself to be drawn into an argument over their union views.

14. Write down conversations you have with employees over union matters, or disputes over enforcement of the no-solicitation rules. Naturally, don't write down conversations while the employee is present; do it later in your office. Note the time and place of the violation.

15. Report all union activity, or even *suspected* union activity, no matter how slight, to the plant manager. Never discount or underestimate any union activity or comment. "Simple" comments such as, "We could use a union around here," should be reported even where no union is presently organizing.

> YOUR COMPANY IS RELYING ON YOU.
> ENFORCE THE RULES. DON'T BE BASHFUL.
> USE YOUR LEGAL RIGHTS OR THE UNION
> WILL USE ITS LEGAL RIGHTS ON YOU.

Selection for Training

Care should be taken to insure that only employees who are truly supervisors are selected for training. Avoid borderline cases (such as working foremen) who may not be viewed by the Board as supervisors. If it turns out that the employees are not supervisors, the Board may view such employees' reporting on union activity or enforcing no-solicitation rules as "spying."

Dealing With Disloyal Supervisors

Avoid including in training sessions those who may not have undivided loyalty to the employer. When there is any suspicion that a pro-union sympathizer may be among the group to be trained, that person should not be invited to meetings.

When it is suspected that supervisors are disloyal or that they will not campaign on behalf of the employer, management must decide whether they will be retained on the staff or discharged. Employers are entitled to the undivided loyalty of their supervisors and have the full right under the law to discharge supervisors who are not loyal.

When one employer fired a supervisor for failing to comply with the employer's instructions to talk employees out of voting for the union, the Board found no violation. It reasoned that since an employer has the right to express its opposition to unionization, the instructions were lawful—and a supervisor can be discharged for failure to follow lawful instructions. He can also be required, at the price of his job, not to engage in union activities and not to be a union member.

Supervisors may not ordinarily invoke the unfair labor practice provisions of the Labor-Management Relations Act since they are not "employees" whose joining of unions or engaging in concerted activities is protected by the Act. In certain cases, however, the Board may find that discharge of a supervisor will interfere not only with the *supervisor's* union activities, but also with an *employee's* union activities, which are protected. It would be improper, for example, to discharge a supervisor for failure to spy on rank-and-file union supporters, for failure to carry out the employer's unlawful instructions to interrogate employees, for refusing to solicit the grievances that prompted employees to seek unionization, for giving testimony adverse to the employer's position, for refusing to look for pretexts upon which to discharge union adherents, or for not cooperating with the employer in giving false information to NLRB agents. On the other hand, discharging a supervisor on the basis of complaints by employees that the supervisor is unpopular is also a violation of the Act, since that constitutes a change in working conditions and is, in effect, a benefit or bribe—an attempt to resolve employee grievances and eliminate the cause of union activity.

Discharges of supervisory personnel during election campaigns for reasons connected with the pending election should be carefully reviewed with counsel prior to taking any action.

However, there is nothing improper in requiring supervisors to disclose information, even that pertaining to union activity, which they lawfully acquire in the normal course of their supervisory duties. Since supervisory knowledge is routinely imputed to employers by the Board, the prudent employer should institute such a requirement as a precautionary or protective measure. Its failure to do so could result in adverse legal consequences. Accordingly, the Board has upheld discharges of supervisors where they have failed to reveal to their superiors information which had come to their attention concerning the union and the union activities of the employees whom they supervised. Failure to assist the employer's lawful antiunion campaign is a grounds for discharge and does not violate the Act. As long as the instructions to supervisors are limited to reporting only information which might legally come by them in the performance of their duties and as long as the employer does not require the commission of unfair labor practices or unlawful interrogation and spying, both the instructions to report union activities and any discharge for failure to follow such instructions does not violate the Act. *See Belcher Towing Co.*, dissenting opinion, 238 NLRB No. 63 (1978).

It must not be assumed that supervisors are automatically loyal to the company. The discharge of disloyal supervisors may seem harsh, but the chances of winning an organizational election are weaker when the employer retains them on its staff. They may make statements disparaging the company, become friends with pro-union sympathizers, or yield to union organizers who tell them that if the union is successful, they will "make it easy" for them after the plant is unionized.

Management should realize that each supervisor has a different attitude about the union, and that many have no strong preference for a nonunion plant. Some may have come from the union ranks and may be actively in favor of unions. Some believe that if the union obtains a raise for the rank-and-file employees, they, too, will get the same amount of raise or more. The incentive to campaign against the union is obviously reduced where such attitudes prevail.

Motivating Supervisors

The employer must stress how unionism will affect the supervisors' ability to perform their own jobs. They can be motivated to become more involved in resisting the union effort by giving them an appreciation of the problems that a union can bring to the work group and the irritations that union officials, shop stewards, and pro-union employees may bring to supervisors' efforts to run their departments.

The fact that supervisors will be effectively eliminated from such decisions as promotions, transfers, merit increases, changing duties and responsibilities, leaves of absence, discipline, and other important areas of decision-making authority should be forcefully brought to their attention. Sample provisions from union contracts can be used to illustrate the ways in which the supervisor's ability to operate would be hampered by a union. The disadvantages should be spelled out: the problems of dealing with shop stewards and union business representatives, the loss of flexibility in dealing personally with employees, the excessive time consumed in the handling of grievances, the increasing rigidity of jobs, the inability to switch personnel to appropriate jobs because of seniority restrictions, the inability to perform emergency work because of restrictive contract clauses, the difficulties of assigning personnel to some types of equipment because of union prejudices, the role of shop steward in constantly bringing complaints to the attention of the supervisor, whether they be meritorious or not, the possibilities that the supervisor may violate unwritten rules that may become the basis for grievances, the undue pressures to conform to past practice when departures are necessary, the difficulties of administering discipline, the extreme burden of proof placed on the supervisor when his judgment is questioned, and, in general, the fact that supervisory decisions are constantly second-guessed, not only by the shop steward and the business representative of the union but by the employees themselves. These factors, once brought to the attention of the supervisors, will often result in a motivated front-line force ready to do battle with the union.

Effect on Employees

The employer should explain to supervisors why employees themselves do not need a union in the plant and why there can be an adverse impact on the employees if a union is voted in. For example, supervisors should be told that as long as they treat employees fairly, there is no need for a union. Without a union, problems can be adjusted individually, and there is more personal contact between employees and company management; supervisors and management can listen to employee complaints and adjust them without being restricted by union contracts or shop stewards who control whether or not an employee's grievance is filed.

But under union conditions, workers are less able to deal with their supervisors on a one-to-one basis regarding their problems, and they would not be assured that their problems would be kept private. In addition, grievance-handling is a slow process that is often not concluded for months.

Without a union, supervisors can assign work according to the individual needs of the employees; employees can develop their skills because a variety of job assignments is possible without union interference; supervisors may go to bat for employees and get them raises that would not be possible under rigid union contract conditions, which usually do not allow merit increases. The fact that a supervisor, under nonunion conditions, is able to render assistance and training to employees on job problems is an advantage that is less likely to occur under union conditions, which are governed by a collective bargaining agreement.

Effect on the Company

Supervisors should be informed about the impact of the union on the company. They should know about the restrictive effects of clauses granting immunity from discipline for employees who refuse to cross picket lines; "struck goods" clauses authorizing employees to refuse to handle goods or to perform services during strikes; no-subcontracting clauses and union "signatory" clauses; work-allocation clauses; product-boycotting clauses; so-called protection of conditions clauses, in which the company agrees that all conditions of employment, including production standards and a myriad of other customs and practices, be maintained at the highest standards in effect at the time the union agreement is signed; mutual-consent clauses, which prohibit certain conduct unless the union approves; clauses restricting transfer of operations and new plant locations; visitation rights of union officials during business hours; and various other clauses, many of which prevent the company and the supervisor from performing the duties necessary for a healthy, profitable company.

Developing Feedback

Don't overlook one of the best communication practices—*listening*. Supervisors should be encouraged to listen to employees during a campaign, since some of the best information about the union, its strategy and tactics, and the progress of the campaign will come voluntarily from loyal employees, and even from union sympathizers. By listening, supervisors will be able to isolate the issues in the campaign and report them to management so that they may be handled properly.

Supervisors are in the best position to listen to employees and find out what is happening during a campaign if they have built up a solid relationship with the people they supervise. For this reason, supervisors should be impressed with the importance of improving rapport and dealing fairly with their subordinates. Discipline must be reasonable, fair, and consistent, and company policy should be implemented in a manner that does not invite charges of favoritism. If charges of discrimination do arise, the supervisor should explain the reason for his action. Of extreme importance is informing supervisors, who often become hesitant during a campaign, that all complaints and problems should be treated as promptly as possible, and everyone expressing a complaint or asking questions about the campaign should be treated with respect.

The supervisor should also know the personalities and interests of those in his department, their job problems, and their motivations. Above all, supervision should act as a bridge between the voters and management. The following sums up what should be the attitude of supervisors:

> SUPERVISOR'S UNION-FREE CREED
>
> Because I (the supervisor) have the authority and the desire to make the changes I deem necessary in the daily operation of your life, I won't be here if I don't treat you fairly.
>
> Because I represent a direct line of communication to the people who establish the broad policies of the company, such as wages, salaries, job evaluation, benefit programs and working conditions, because I can persuade my own supervisors to review, consider, and modify any policy without third-party intervention, and
>
> Because management of this company is enlightened, (as proof of this, I point to the grievance procedures, fair treatment of employees, and generous benefit programs) I intend to be fair in all my dealings with you.
>
> Because we are a people-oriented company and we have a common interest in remaining union-free, I hope to preserve and foster this atmosphere by my conduct in relation to all the employees I supervise.

Using the Supervisors' Special Relationship

Supervisors differ in their ability to relate to the employees they supervise. Some supervisors are close to their employees and are highly regarded; others are not close to the employees but are nevertheless highly regarded and respected. Still other supervisors have no credibility whatsoever.

It is the responsibility of top management to analyze each supervisor's strength and weakness and to utilize (or not utilize) the supervisor accordingly. Management should not enlist the aid of supervisors who exert a negative rather than a positive influence on employee thinking. Management will find that some supervisors can be used extensively, even in areas beyond their immediate jurisdiction. Some supervisors may be actively trained to initiate discussions; others should be told not to speak directly with employees unless they are first asked questions.

The real value of a supervisor during a campaign is utilizing his knowledge of each of the employees who works under him—their predilections, personal characteristics, and attitudes. Supervisors can be told to make individualized arguments that will have the most impact on each individual, taking into account each employee's problems, job attitudes, and motivation.

Because the employer's campaign is general, directed to the employees as a whole, the selectivity supervisors bring to the campaign is invaluable. They may talk directly with small groups of employees or with individuals on any particular matter. For example, if the company has a better pension program than the union's, supervisors can counsel older employees that voting for the union may involve the loss of a valuable benefit. For employees who are extremely conscious of the need for maintaining take-home pay at a constant level, supervisors can emphasize the possibilities of interruption in work caused by unions and the heavy cumulative effect of dues payments over the years.

Supervisors can also play a key role by reporting to management on what they perceive to be the number and identity of uncommitted voters in their departments. In most elections, the "independent" vote determines the result, and it is extremely important for management to have some perspective on the size of this vote and the people who compose the group. The supervisors' daily contact with employees serves to fill in information gaps.

Management can also solicit the supervisors' opinions on prospective communications—what impact they think a particular statement, letter, or piece of campaign material might have on the employees. This can lead, in most cases, to more effective campaign materials. Many companies also poll supervisors to get their ideas and suggestions for future campaign tactics and strategies.

The Supervisor and Campaign Literature

Whenever company bulletins, leaflets, question-and-answer sheets, or letters are prepared, supervisors should be given advance copies. The communication should be thoroughly explained so they are prepared to answer questions.

Supervisors should be instructed on ways of using the employer campaign materials as an entree to discussing issues with employees. They should be cautioned against asking an employee, "What do you think about the company's letter?" Since this, in effect, is *interrogation* that forces the employee to declare himself or herself on the company's communication. But campaign materials can provide the basis for an *affirmative statement* by the supervisor. For example, a supervisor may say, "I read the president's letter that you received yesterday, and I agree with him that the pension program we now have is an excellent one." The supervisor can then point out the value of the pension system and other company benefits. Using this kind of introduction will avoid charges of illegal interrogation and interference with employee rights.

Pro-Union Insignia

Supervisors should be told that employees are free to wear union badges and any other type of union clothing, such as tee-shirts, pins, or other campaign materials on the premises and during work hours (with certain unusual exceptions in customer service and retail types of industries. Supervisors cannot order employees to remove the union insignia or make remarks that deprecate those who are wearing these items.

What Supervisors May Say

Crucial to the success of any training program is informing supervisors what they may say during a campaign. The most common mistake is to frighten them with horror stories about what is not permissible, focusing on all the rules prohibiting supervisory speech during election campaigns. The end result of this improper training is that supervisors are discouraged from communicating and adopt a silent attitude during the campaign for fear of committing an unfair labor practice.

The proper method is to first spend several hours on what may be said and done by supervisors during a campaign. Once they are introduced into the wide world of permissible activity, the employer may then inculcate a healthy respect for the law and provide constructive advice on what may not be said during the campaign, reviewing the information in Chapter 3. After two or three such sessions, most supervisors learn what is permissible and what is taboo. As long as the permissible overshadows the improper, the company will find that most of its supervisors look forward to communicating with employees and will become effective communicators on behalf of the company.

Employers should not rely solely on transmitting canned "do's" and "don'ts" or assume that a reading of these lists will result in knowledgeable supervisors. Written materials must be reinforced with a great deal of verbal support and explanation. Role-playing and mock employee-supervisor discussions should be used, with the company trainer playing devil's advocate. Questions that employees have actually asked should be discussed and analyzed, and answers expressing management's position should be carefully prepared and explained. Supervisors should be instructed not to handle questions or issues on the basis of intuition, but to follow the guidance of top management. They should then be given practice in expressing these positions so that they become familiar in stating them. They should be encouraged after each session to talk on union topics that they know best, and to analyze and approach each employee with the issue that is most effective for him.

Encourage questions from the supervisors during training sessions. Management should emphasize that it is anxious to answer questions and that the asking of any questions, no matter how simple, will not be viewed as a sign of weakness or ignorance.

Despite the restrictions on campaign statements, there is a great deal that supervisors can say during a campaign. Here are some things they should be told to do:

(1) Tell employees what the company's negotiating position will be if it is unionized.

(2) Inform employees of the benefits they presently enjoy.

(3) Inform employees that signing a union authorization card does not mean they must vote for the union if there is an election. Emphasize that the ballot is secret.

(4) Inform employees of the disadvantages of belonging to the union—the possibility of strikes, serving in a picket line, dues, fines, and assessments.

(5) Inform employees that it is better to deal with management directly rather than have the union or any other outsider involved with employee grievances.

(6) Tell employees what the supervisor thinks about unions and

union policies, and about any prior experiences with unions, and about the union officials trying to organize them.

(7) Inform employees that no union can obtain more than the employer is able to give.

(8) Inform employees how their wages and benefits compare with unionized and nonunionized shops where wages are lower and benefits are less desirable.

(9) Inform employees that the local union will probably be dominated by the international union, and that the members will have little to say in its operation.

(10) Inform employees of any untrue or misleading statements made by the organizer and give them the correct facts.

(11) Reply to union attacks on company policies or practices.

(12) Insist that any solicitation of membership or discussion of the union not be conducted during times when employees should be working.

The Supervisor and/or Authorization Cards

Even after a petition has been filed, unions often attempt to consolidate their strength by continuing to solicit employee's signatures on authorization cards. Because cards have already been submitted to the NLRB to support the union's request for an election does not mean the company should ignore card signing activity during the campaign. Training sessions with supervisors should continue to explore how these authorization cards are used, why organizers continue to solicit them, and how obtaining more than 50 percent of the cards of employees in the voting unit might ultimately prejudice the company in the event the union seeks a card-based bargaining order. The following fundamental points should be impressed upon supervisors:

Urge the employees not to sign union authorization cards.

Remind the employees that because they have signed union authorization cards doesn't mean they have to vote for the union in the election—the election will be secret and no one will know how they marked the ballot.

Tell the employees that they do not have to sign any union authorization cards.

Tell the employees that a union authorization card can bind the employees to rules (in the union's constitution and by-laws) that they have never read.

Tell the employees that union authorization cards are *not* strictly confidential because very frequently: (a) the employees who sign are called upon to testify at government proceedings about circumstances surrounding their signing of the authorization card, and (b) the union simply turns over the cards to the employer for inspection and demands recognition based upon the number of people who have signed cards.

Tell employees that the union will make wild promises and misrepresentations in order to get employees to sign cards. Stress that the union organizers will say *anything* in order to get these cards signed.

Advise employees on how they may withdraw their union authorization cards—but you may not solicit these withdrawals, question employees on whether or not they wish to withdraw their cards, pressure them into requesting their cards back, or keep track of which employees withdraw and which do not.

General statements should be supported by a specific factual background; supervisors must be armed with facts and figures wherever possible. For example, if the union has called numerous strikes, supervisors should be provided with a list of the strikes it has engaged in during the preceding few years.

When the company campaigns on the theme that strikers may be permanently replaced, supervisors should be provided with statements of the law and newspaper clippings or other examples of local companies that have permanently replaced strikers.

Supervisors should be familiar with the company's prior experience with unions, either at their location or at other facilities operated by the company. They should have all the legal or factual information they need to understand the issues and communicate effectively with their subordinates.

There is one concept to which supervisors should be especially attuned. Many employees assume that wage and benefit increases result automatically once the union wins—they do not understand the meaning of a union victory and the events that follow a union victory on election day. Supervisors are likewise naive about the impact of a union victory. Accordingly, they must be instructed so that they, too, understand a union victory does not mean automatic improvements in working conditions. The collective bargaining process must be outlined for supervisors, step by step, so they can accurately relay this concept back to the people they supervise.

Statements such as "wages and benefits will start from scratch" are best left to management to give under the strict advice and control of counsel. However, supervisors can make the point without the threatening tone that "bargaining from scratch" implies. For example:

> I understand some people are under the impression that the benefits that we have now can "no way" be in jeopardy if a union was to get in. That's not true; let me tell you how it works.

In negotiations, certain existing benefits may be traded away for other items the union wants. For example, if the union wanted a union security clause, which would force everyone to join the union and pay dues even if they didn't want to, the company could agree, in return for reducing or eliminating a present benefit. This has happened many, many times. The union has nothing to trade away except your benefits. Many companies start negotiations with a blank piece of paper and negotiate each benefit. Some companies have a policy of "bargaining from scratch." It is important for you to know that if the union were voted in here, ALL BENEFITS WOULD BE NEGOTIABLE. Of course, we will negotiate in good faith, but that doesn't necessarily mean we will agree with the union on a particular demand. One possible result of our bargaining with the union would be that you would have less than you now enjoy. Just imagine what it is worth for the union to have a check-off clause under which they deduct money from your paycheck automatically via company payroll. The union would normally have to pay for such a system at the bargaining table—and the only thing they have to pay for it with is *your* benefits.

We could trade any existing benefit in return for giving the union something very important to them. As you all know, forcing everybody to join is important to any union—and having the company deduct your dues and send them one big check at the end of each month, rather than collect dues from each employee individually, is *very* important to this union.

Auditing Supervisory Performance

Management should monitor the activities of supervisors during the campaign to insure that they are, in fact, campaigning for management. If a supervisor has not been effective in developing feedback, he has probably done nothing during the campaign. Supervisors should be told that they are not expected to run a mistake-free campaign. This will encourage them to bring management's viewpoint to the employees without the fear that they will be criticized for natural mistakes.

An effective device is to assign supervisors to make certain communications to *specified* employees and ask them to report back on when and where the conversation took place and what was said. Knowing that they will be audited by management, most supervisors will carry out the assignment. Without such follow-up, supervisors will often attend management training sessions but then will remain silent in the workplace because of fear that they will commit unfair labor practices.

Individual campaign assignment sheets such as the following may be used during the campaign.

INDIVIDUAL CAMPAIGN ASSIGNMENT SHEET

Supervisor's Name _____ Department _____

Employee Assigned	Date/Possible Vote (Y, N, ?)									
1.	3/15	Y	3/25	Y	4/1	?	4/10	?	4/15	Y
2.										
3.										
4.										
5.										

In making such assignments, the employer should not hesitate to cross departmental lines. Each of the voters should be analyzed with a view toward which supervisor or other middle manager, or non-voting employee, might have more "suasion" with the voter than the employee's immediate supervisor. Determine which supervisor or person has the respect of the particular voter. Then, instruct those individuals to communicate with the voter and perform the communications assignment in place of the regular supervisor. All supervisors should keep a running daily commentary, in writing, of what is happening and what is being said. These communications should be routed up the line to the campaign manager on a routine basis.

Debating

Supervisors should be cautioned against arguing with employees, particularly with union sympathizers. The supervisor's job is to *listen* for information of value to management and to *impart* information to employees. Argument rarely helps, since pro-union employees will not be argued out of voting for the union by front-line supervision. Moreover, they ask unanswerable types of questions designed to make the supervisor look foolish.

Supervisors should take notes on conversations with employees that relate to the campaign, particularly when the discussions take place with union sympathizers. The supervisors' notes may be admissible as evidence at any subsequent NLRB hearing and bolster the supervisor's credibility. Many employers supply supervisors with notebooks for making such notes.

Looseleaf Notebooks

Lengthy training presentations to supervisors should be followed up with written outlines summarizing the material. All supervisors should be issued looseleaf "campaign handbooks" that are built up as the campaign progresses. They should be instructed to leave the notebooks at home rather than in the plant to avoid pilferage or other leakage of information. As new information is issued, it can be added to the notebook so that all campaign materials will be in one binder.

Early Warning Signs of Union Activity

Union organizing activities can be difficult to detect in the early stages of an organizing campaign. In what we can call the undercover phase, union organizers are busily stirring up dissatisfaction and trying to obtain employees' signatures on authorization cards so they can claim to have the support of a majority (or at least a substantial portion) of the members of the work unit. At this point, the organizers are keeping a low profile, but since most of these activities are carried out in or near the workplace, supervisors are in the best position to spot them.

The longer organizers work without your knowing it, the better your organization's chance of losing a representation election. However, knowledge of employees and constant supervisory presence in the department will enable supervisors to detect the key changes in behavior or in routine which may indicate that a union is trying to organize.

Here are some typical early warning signs of union organizing activities. Teach supervisors what they are, and teach them to report them immediately.

• Small gatherings of employees, perhaps in unusual parts of the plant or office. You know the way your employees ordinarily behave. When you see them getting together in an atypical fashion, it could be a sign that something out of the ordinary is being discussed or done—and that something could very well be an organizing campaign.

• The grapevine suddenly goes dead. When people are signing cards, they don't tend to talk about it; if your sources of information are drying up, it's a bad sign.

• A former employee—one who has quit or has been fired—periodically shows up after work and buttonholes people in the parking lot or in local employee hangouts. He could well be a union organizer; perhaps he was organizing the plant before he left, or perhaps he is disgruntled because he was fired and is trying to get back at the company by organizing his former co-workers.

• A great deal of "busyness" during breaks, before work, after work, and during lunch. Instead of people relaxing and sitting around, you see them going from here to there getting together in small groups, moving from place to place, lots of activity. These nonwork periods are when authorization cards are signed, so all this activity can mean that an organizing campaign is in progress.

• New groups form and new informal leaders suddenly emerge. The common bond in the new groups might be their desire for a union in the plant or office.

• Groups of people who are deep in conversation suddenly clam up when supervisors approach. Obviously, they don't want you to know what they are talking about. There are various things they could be discussing, and union organization is one strong possibility.

• A sudden increase in questions about company policies and benefits. For no apparent reason, people are asking questions about long standing company policies and practices: What's our policy about this? Why do we do that? How many sick days do we get? Why don't we have a dental program? What happens if I want a leave of absence? This sudden interest may well be the result of a union organizer's encouraging people to find out what company policies are in certain areas.

• Groups of employees raise complaints in a militant manner. They are extremely assertive of their "rights"—not asking, but demanding satisfaction of their complaints. The tone they adopt may well indicate that they are being influenced by a union organizer who is prodding employees to demand more from their company.

• People who are ordinarily amiable become sullen and uncommunicative. This is the way some people handle the situation when they find out that a union is signing up employees and trying to organize the department and they are opposed to the union. They don't want to sign authorization cards, but, at the same time, they don't want to stick their necks out and tell the boss what's going on, just in case the union does eventually get in. Consequently, they retreat into silence and keep to themselves. There could, of course, be other reasons for mood changes of this kind, but you should be aware that some people react to union organizing activities in this way.

• A previously popular employee suddenly becomes unpopular and is needled by his or her co-workers. This can happen if the employee has refused to sign an authorization card and is being shunned or harassed by co-workers who support the union.

• A new employee, usually someone in the probationary period, goes overboard in asserting enthusiasm for the job and loyalty to the company. Again, there can be other reasons for this kind of behavior, but it can be an indication of union organizing activity. The new employee comes in and sees the organizing activities going on, and he thinks to himself, "I'm new here. As soon as the boss finds out that a union is trying to organize the department, he's going to think that I'm one of the organizers, and he's going to find an excuse to get rid of me." So he reacts the other way, and he takes every opportunity to express his loyalty to the company and thereby disassociate himself from the organizing efforts he sees going on.

• Similarly, a formerly poor worker who has always had sloppy work habits may suddenly and inexplicably become a model employee—doing his work well, getting it done on schedule, increasing his productivity, and so forth. A possible explanation for this change in attitude and working habits could be that the employee is aware of the organizing activities going on in the department and wants to establish himself as a loyal and competent worker who has nothing to do with the union outsiders who are trying to force their way into the department.

• Anti-company graffiti appears on the walls of restrooms, locker rooms, and other places. This is no indication of the *extent* of anti-company feeling, since one or two people could be responsible for all the scribblings, but it is an indication that there may be some union organization efforts in the department.

• Restrooms suddenly become very popular. Unless you know that some kidney disease is going around, you can guess that people are getting together in the restrooms to discuss *something*—and that something is likely to be the union, since restrooms are one of the places where authorization cards are often signed by employees who are reluctant to sign them in plain sight at their workplaces.

• You may experience an unexplained slippage in workmanship in conjunction with a union organizing campaign. For example, a higher number of rejects, more scrap, or an increasing amount of work that has to be done over before it is acceptable. This might be attributable to a number of causes—changed working conditions or problems with a particular process or with new equipment, for example. But if the deterioration can't be explained by any ordinary factors, it may well be the result of union activity. Some employees may feel that their jobs are soon going to be protected by the union and that therefore they don't really have to perform very well any more.

Of course, none of these warning signs, by itself, is a sure indication that union organizers are at work. But, it would be a mistake to ignore any of them, no matter how insignificant it might seem. If you detect any of these changes in behavior or routine, they may form a pattern that indicates that a union organizing campaign is under way. This is important, because the earlier a company is aware of union organizing activities, the better it can plan to counteract them and the greater are its chances of winning a representation election.

The Timing of Training

Supervisory training programs should be instituted long before the advent of any union activity. Nevertheless, there is a great deal that still may be done by the employer once union organizing activity becomes known. Intensive training programs are crucial. The effort spent in motivating supervisors and making them effective soldiers in the employer's campaign can make the difference between maintaining or losing the company's nonunion status.

Chapter 10

The Fine Art of Rebuttal

Although the employer's campaign must be primarily affirmative and should take the initiative on most issues, there will be a need, from time to time, to rebut what the union has said and written to employees. There is also a need to reply to legitimate (or planted) questions by the employees. Because the type of response the employer makes can be critical, careful attention should be paid to the manner and style in which responses are made.

Union Promises and Allegations

Union literature should be studied carefully: it will provide a clue as to the union's issues. The union's campaign material should be preliminarily evaluated on the basis of defensive and offensive union arguments. When the employer's campaign is effective and persuasive, management will find that much of the union's argument is defensive.

This is the preferred position for the employer in a campaign. As long as the union is busy defending against arguments put forth by the employer, it has less time for persuading employees of the need to join the union and the benefits it believes a union could obtain.

Another clue as to where the employer stands can be gained from determining whether the union's campaign material is using standard union arguments or arguments directed to the individual company. In the former case, management may conclude (without becoming too sure of itself) that the union is doing a less than effective job and is not fully familiar with the company and the issues. But where the union makes telling points against the company, its practices, specific policies and programs, or promises certain benefits, the employer should respond to these allegations along the points outlined in this chapter.

The Union Will Obtain Automatic Benefits

Management should reply that a union cannot guarantee any increase in benefits and that it is the practice of the company to provide benefits in accordance with its ability to pay. It may further state that all union proposals for higher benefits are subject to negotiation and that, in fact, all present benefits are also negotiable. The point should be stressed that there are no automatic increases in benefits simply because a union wins the election.

The Union Will Obtain Higher Wages

Management may state that the union can make promises but cannot guarantee that they will be fulfilled. The company should remind employees of wage progress during the past year or longer. It may state that it has watched competitors' rates carefully, that its wage scales compare favorably with local companies, both union and nonunion, and that its policy of wage administration is a fair one.

The Union Will Obtain the "Standard Union Rates"

Management should respond that the "standard union rate" is a myth. There is no union rate in the overwhelming number of cases. Rates vary from company to company and from job to job. The rates quoted by the organizers and represented as "standard" are often the rates for jobs requiring a great deal of skill. It may also be pointed out that wages are negotiable, and that the mere presence of a union does not guarantee that some arbitrary union rate will be achieved. Where the union has several different rates for the same job in different categories, these rates may be referred to and the myth exploded.

The Company Will Be Forced to Sign a Contract if the Union Wins

The company's only obligation is the duty to bargain in good faith. Management should state that it is not required by law to sign any contract that it believes is unreasonable. Management must inform employees that the company can say "no" to any union proposal that it cannot afford to meet or that it feels would not be in the best interest of the company.

The Union Will Provide a Formal Grievance and Arbitration Procedure

Management should point to its existing grievance procedures (where applicable) and ask why dues should be paid for the union's type of procedure. The adverse side of the union's grievance procedure should be emphasized: A union can require the employee to agree to the union's method of handling the grievance, or to agree with the union's decision not to process the grievance because it might be too costly for the union to pursue. Employees can be shown illustrations from reported decisions of cases in which employees have had to sue unions in order to force them to process grievances. Also, the employee's grievance may fall into the hands of a shop steward who does not approve of the grievance, who may not wish to push the grievance for political reasons, or who may dislike the employee filing the grievance.

Under typical *company* grievance procedures, *any* complaint may be taken to management; under most *union* contracts, only certain grievances (those arising because of a difference of opinion as to what the language may mean) may be arbitrated. The company should stress that it has always listened to and adjusted any problem, citing specific examples of complaint adjustment.

The employee can also be advised that unions often settle grievances on terms unfavorable to the employee, or may "trade" one employee's grievance in order to resolve a different grievance for a favored employee. The prolonged steps and lengthy time spent processing grievances to a conclusion under union contract procedures may also be referred to.

The Union Will Guarantee Present Benefits

The union cannot guarantee *any* benefit. Benefits are provided by the company if financial conditions justify them. Most employers can truthfully say that never in the history of the company has a benefit been taken away or reduced. After relating the company's list of benefits, the employer can state that no one needs to pay dues to outside organizations in order to protect what they already have. Cite examples found in newspaper clippings and other sources to show that unions have traded away existing benefits in order to get other concessions, or have agreed to benefit reductions as a concession to management.

The Union Will Force the Company to Eliminate Unpopular Supervisors

Management may tell the employees that unions cannot force the company to fire anyone—employee or supervisor—except in non-right-to-work states for failure to pay dues. Management may say that a union cannot tell the company how to run its business, whom to hire, or whom to fire. The management rights clause of union contracts may be cited or paraphrased in support of the company's position; such clauses often specifically enunciate the employer's right to "fire and hire".

The Union Will End the Company's Practice of Subcontracting

Management may state that if union restrictions result in operational inflexibility, thus making it more expensive to produce the product, management will have to consider *more* subcontracting, not less. Management should state that the company does not have to agree to any union contract proposal forbidding subcontracting. Management may show, where applicable, how subcontracting is crucial to its business and how it *must* continue to subcontract. Employees should be advised that subcontracting is a means of *protecting* employees' jobs.

The Union Will Provide Job Security

Management should stress that a union contract is not a contract of employment and does not guarantee permanency of employment. When management refers to layoffs at other unionized companies and points out that every employee—whether in the union or not—is subject to layoff, employees will begin to perceive the union argument as a misrepresentation. Union contract provisions, particularly provisions negotiated by the organizing union, can be quoted, enlarged, and distributed by means of handouts or posters. These provisions will clearly indicate that even with the union in the plant, *management* has the right to lay off.

Management should stress that job security is obtained when the business makes a profit and as long as business conditions remain good; unions cannot insure good business conditions and therefore cannot insure jobs. The best job security is working for a growing company with foreseeable profits. The recent difficulties of many large unions, such as the auto workers, the steelworkers, and the unions in the building and construction trades industries, are examples.

Where applicable, the company should boast of its record of job security and lack of layoffs over recent years. It should compare its layoff record (where favorable) with the record of other companies under contract with the organizing union. If the company follows seniority in layoffs, and particularly if a provision in the employer's policy handbook can be cited to that effect, rebuttal of the union's argument is complete.

The Union Will Protect Jobs

When the company has a good discharge record, it should be spelled out for the employees; the discharge procedures in employee handbooks may be quoted. If the company feels that it must explain why certain discharges were made in the recent past, it may point out that the discharges were justified and that even under a union contract they would have been upheld. Union contract provisions abound that specifically reserve to the employer the right to discharge; these provisions may be quoted and liberally displayed. Employees should be told that outsiders should not be paid dues for job protection.

Such company policies as avoiding layoffs by performing plant maintenance during slack periods should be stressed. The company should refer to the great number of high-seniority employees in the plant and point out that as long as an employee performs a fair day's work, his job is secure. It should be explained that in non-right-to-work states the union can cause a worker to be discharged for failure to pay dues.

The Union Can Obtain More Business for the Company

Management should expose this ridiculous concept and challenge the union to show how it can provide such business. Certainly, the union cannot obtain business from nonunion shops, and if it obtains work from other unionized shops, it would hurt the employees it represents at that plant. For example, employees may be asked: "If the union wins, in some subsequent campaign with another employer, will it make the promise that work will be taken from us and given to the employees who are voting?"

Join the Bandwagon

Management should warn employees not to fall for the "bandwagon" appeal. It may say that many employees who have signed cards have done so simply to avoid being harassed by the union. Advise employees to consider their own interests and to evaluate management's arguments first before jumping on the bandwagon. To show that not everyone favors unions, management may cite election losses in local areas or NLRB summary statistics or U.S. Department of Labor figures showing that the percentage of the unionized work force is decreasing and revealing that tens of millions of employees in the country—indeed, an overwhelming majority, approximately 75 percent of the work force—are presently nonunion.

Try the Union for a Year; If You Don't Like It, Vote It Out

This is an appealing argument that must be combatted vigorously and effectively. Point out the difficulties inherent in getting a union out, including the Certification Year Rule, the Contract Bar Rule, and the rules relating to the timely filing of petitions. Stress the union's rights to fine or expel members who favor decertification. Emphasize the fact that if a first contract is signed for a period of three years, it will bar any change for three years. Explain that the union will not surrender the bargaining unit without a fight (cite, as the reason, the income that the union would receive over a three- or four-year period).

Employees should be told that, in most cases, once a union is in, it is there forever; their decision on election day therefore will probably govern their lives forever, and it is not the type of decision that can be easily reversed.

The Federal Government Favors the Union

Employees should be told that federal law and the NLRB neither encourage nor discourage employees from joining unions. The NLRB and the federal government are theoretically completely neutral on this issue; the government protects the right of employees to be against the union and allows employers to campaign against unions. Relevant provisions of the law may be cited, and excerpts from the NLRB's own document, "A Layman's Guide to the National Labor Relations Act," may be reproduced and distributed. Employees may be told that the only reason for having a secret ballot supervised by the federal government is to enable the employees to exercise their own free choice.

The Company Will Eliminate Benefits if the Union Loses

This defensive argument on the part of the union relies solely on a fear appeal. The employer should point to its record of never having lowered benefits (or explain the justification for reductions if they have occurred). Point out that if the company reduced benefits after the union lost, it would certainly encourage employees to turn around and seek out a union after the election. The logic of this appeal is undeniable.

The Union Will Protect Seniority

This can be a difficult argument for the employer to rebut, depending on its own practices. Where the employer *has* followed seniority in all or most decisions, this should be stressed. Company policy statements in handbooks and specific actions taken by the company respecting seniority should be cited.

When the company has not always followed seniority, the reasons should be carefully explained. If no real explanation is available, a company's best defense may be to ignore this union argument.

Answering Union or Employee Questions

Careful analysis of rhetorical questions posed by the union in its literature or of voluntary questions posed by employees often provides the employer with a clearer view of the campaign; the nature of the questions may provide a clue to the union's strengths and weaknesses, and the tenor of the questions is indicative of the depth of union penetration. When there are questions about the protections a union can offer or weaknesses in company policies and programs, it may be a sign of the weakness of the company's campaign. Conversely, if the questions concern what may happen to employees if the union wins on election day—i.e., the adverse effects of the union in the plant or office—this may be considered a sign of strength. Employer answers may follow the guidelines contained in this chapter.

Since the Employer Belongs to an Industry Association, Why Can't the Employees Also Form Their Own Association?

The purpose of joining employer associations is to learn information that will make the company more profitable and provide more work for employees. No employer association penalizes the company for *not* joining, and the company's association with these employer associations is completely voluntarily. Specific examples of how membership in an employers' association has benefited the company and the employees should be cited. The employer may also point out that joining employer associations voluntarily does not lead to strikes, operational restrictions, and all the other disadvantages of unionization.

What Will the Company Do for Us if the Union Loses?

The employer must emphasize that under NLRB rules a union can make all the promises in the world, but an employer may make no promises whatsoever. The employer can add that this is an unfair rule, but that it nevertheless intends to comply with the law because if it does not, the election will be set aside even though the employees vote for the company.

How Much Does It Cost to Belong to a Union?

The employer may state that unions are expensive organizations to belong to. The amount of dues charged is usually available from the Disclosure Bureau in Washington, D.C., from employees who may volunteer such information, or from local companies that have a collective bargaining relationship with the union. Employees may be told not only about the dues obligation, but also about the fees, assessments, and fines that may be levied. Reference to union fines may be supported by newspaper articles or court cases in which heavy penalties have been assessed by unions against members for various infractions.

The use to which the money is put by union officials may also be stated; reference can be made to the union officials' expensive automobiles, office buildings, and the amount of money that is contributed to political causes or is diverted to a parent or international union. The amount of money spent on organizing and other "expenses" can be contrasted with the amount of money indicated on the union's financial report in the column headed "Money Spent on Members." Most financial reports will reveal the word "zero" in that column.

If the Union Calls a Strike, Would We Be Able to Continue to Work?

Management may say to employees: You have the legal right to cross a picket line, but unions frequently become "nasty" during strikes and refuse to let employees who wish to work come into the factory or office. Even if you wish to work, you may expect a great deal of pressure from militant and aggressive employees who favor the union. Threatening phone calls and damage to personal property and automobiles have been experienced by employees who cross picket lines; employees will often cross a picket line for one day and decide not to return to work because of the insults and threat of physical harm made by co-workers.

This rebuttal argument can be supported by newspaper material reporting violence on the picket lines and litigation against unions for such violence and by references to the union's legal ability to fine members large amounts of money for working during the strike.

What Can We Do to Keep the Union From Winning?

Tell the employees that the best way is to vote "no" on election day. The balloting is secret, and co-workers who are in favor of the union and the union organizers will never know how anyone voted. Be sure they know that even if they have signed an authorization card and have promised co-workers and union organizers that they will vote for the union, they may still vote "no". The employer may tell employees that they have the right to try to persuade their fellow employees to vote "no."

How Can I Get My Signed Card Back From the Union?

The employer may inform the employee that he or she has the right to request, orally or in writing, the union (or the person asking the employee to sign the card) to return the card. The name and address of the union may be given to the employee to facilitate the request. However, the employee should be warned that the union will probably not give the card back. But he can vote no as a means of rescinding the card. Reassure the employee that even though the union has his card, it has no way of checking how he voted.

Must We Join the Union if the Company Loses the Election?

In non-right-to-work states, most unions successfully negotiate a union-shop clause; the employer can predict that if the union gets in, it will seek to obtain such a clause. Under the union-shop provision, every employee would be forced to join the union as a condition of employment. Employees should be told that if any employee, even one with serious scruples against union membership, refuses to pay the initiation fee or dues, the union can cause the employee to be fired. Cite and explain federal laws so that the employees will understand that the company can be forced to fire an employee for nonpayment of dues, regardless of how long the employee has worked for the company or how good his work record is. The explanation should end with an appeal to the employees to think long and hard about this loss of freedom.

I Can't Make Up My Mind About the Union; Do I Have to Vote?

This is one of the most important questions; you must answer it. Explain to employees that if they do not vote, their future will be determined by those who do, for a majority of *those who vote* will decide the outcome of the election. If the union wins, the union will represent all employees, whether some want it or not, and they may be *forced* to join and to pay dues, other fees and assessments, and possibly fines. Stress the importance of voting and the fact that the militant prounionist will certainly vote so failure by a number of employees to exercise their right to vote will mean that pro-union employees will gain an automatic victory. Some employers have referred to elections that were decided by one vote.

Will We Be Paid by the Company or the Union During a Strike?

This question may appear naive, but it is surprising how many employees believe that wages are returned to them after a strike. Management should explain that wages are lost during a strike, and that they may *never be recouped.* Employees should be advised that, in the event of a strike, the company will *discontinue payments for insurance premiums for health coverage.* This would mean that the costs of any doctor or hospital bills would have to be borne by the employee. The employee should also be told that union strike benefits amount to very little and often are not paid until after a waiting period—and then only on the condition that certain picket-line duty be performed. Employees should also be advised that in most states strikers cannot collect unemployment compensation. The company should also contrast the potential suffering of employees with the lack of injury to union officials, whose pay is maintained during a strike.

Why Is the Company Campaigning So Strongly Against the Union?

The employer should state frankly that it does not believe that the best interests of either the employees or the company are served by outsiders coming into the plant or office. Strikes that hurt business do not help anyone, and if the union wins unreasonable demands, the company could become unable to compete, the price of its product might be driven up, and a lack of business resulting in layoffs could occur. The fact that the company must provide reliable service to its customers without the constant threat of a strike should be stressed as a strong factor leading the company to campaign against the union. The company's record of providing fringe benefits, fair wages, and steady work should be emphasized as proof that a union is not needed.

If the Union Wins, Will There Be a Strike?

The union's strike record should be spelled out in detail, including dates, companies, locations, and length of strike. Management may state that it does not know whether a strike would occur, but that if the union did press for unreasonable demands, or if it sought to obtain the excessive wages and benefits it was promising to employees, the only way the union could obtain those demands would be through strike action.

Aren't the Monthly Dues Worth the Protection Obtained From Joining a Union?

Arguments concerning the fact that unions offer no real protection should be reiterated, and the amount of dues paid over long periods of time (two to five years) should be graphically displayed so that the true cost of unionization is dramatized. These figures can be enlarged by compounding the interest on the dues money as if it had been deposited in a savings account. The fact the union can increase its dues should be emphasized. Assessments and contributions to various political campaigns, building funds, strike funds, and other projects that do the local member no good may also be advertised. Workers should be asked if they would enjoy contributing their hard-earned money to support a strike by the same union at a distant location.

What Do I Have to Lose by Joining the Union?

Many of the arguments related in Chapter 8 can be condensed and reiterated in answer to the question. The loss of individuality, the possibility of strikes, dues, fees, and assessments, union fines, the tendency to destroy a preexisting friendly atmosphere, the subjecting of existing benefits to the negotiating process—all combine to form a cogent answer to this question. Where applicable, the possibility of shutdowns of operations and relocation may also be lawfully communicated, provided that such statements are made within the leeway provided by the NLRB under Section 8(c) of the Act.

If a Strike Took Place, Would the Company Continue to Operate Its Business?

Management should stress the company's legal right to operate during a strike. To bolster its credibility, it should explain *specifically* how it would maintain operations, either by hiring permanent replacements for the strikers, by using supervisors and managers, or by using nonstriking personnel from inside or outside the bargaining unit. Various methods for reducing the impact of a work stoppage, such as arrangements with subcontractors for the production of goods at other facilities, may also, in the company's discretion, be publicized. The company can indicate that *it will not* capitulate to unfair union demands.

Will the Union Cause Me to Be Fired If I Vote Against It?

Management should point out that the ballot is secret and that the union will never know how anyone voted. Moreover, it should state that the union has no power to fire anyone or cause anyone to be fired for any reason. (Exception: where there is a union security clause and an employee is expelled from the union for not paying dues or initiation fees.) The company's absolute right to hire and to discharge should be restated as reassurance.

How Did the Union Organizer Obtain My Phone Number and Home Address?

The company should state that, under the law, it is required to deliver the names and addresses of all voters to the NLRB for transmission to the union. The company should apologize for this intrusion into the employees' privacy and take the opportunity to inform them that they do not have to allow the union organizers into their homes or speak to them if telephone calls are made to the household.

If There Is a Strike, Isn't It True That We Cannot Be Discharged?

There is a distinction between telling an employee that he is fired for engaging in a work stoppage (without replacing that striker), which is illegal, and actually having that worker's job performed by a permanent replacement, which is lawful. Management should inform employees that it has the right to protect the company by continuing in business, and that it is permitted by law to permanently replace economic strikers. The union can be ridiculed for informing employees that they may not be "discharged," when in fact the difference between discharge and permanent replacement is, as far as the employee is concerned a distinction without a difference. It should be specifically indicated that the permanent replacement is entitled to the job *even after the strike is over*, and that the striking employee has no right to bump the replacement.

When explaining the right to permanently replace strikers, the company should avoid causing any misunderstanding that would indicate that the company would not bargain in good faith and would not attempt to avoid a strike.

Why Is the Company Afraid of the Union Coming In?

Management should explain that it is *concerned*, not afraid. It should reiterate the reasons unionization would not be good for the employees or for the employer and indicate that it is taking a strong stand against the union because it strongly believes that a union would be harmful.

If the Union Loses, Can We Expect to Get a Raise as a Reward for Voting the Union Out?

Management should indicate that this question cannot be answered because the law prohibits it from making any kind of implied promise. Upon advice of counsel and after an evaluation of the background facts, management may also state that it does not intend to bribe employees to vote against the union by taking a position on possible wage increases.

Could We Have a Union of Our Own, Rather Than the Union That Is Presently Organizing Us?

Management should handle this response with care. It may tell the employees that they are free under the law to organize their own independent union if *they* want to. However, management should advise the employees that it can have no connection with initiating the union, helping it to organize, or allowing it to use company facilities.

Why Does the Company Allow Pro-Union Supporters to Solicit Other Employees and Distribute Literature During Breaks and Lunchtime?

Management should explain that if the company prohibited such solicitation or distribution, it would be breaking the law. Management can state that employees are not required to listen to any solicitations, nor are they required or obliged to accept any leaflet.

Why Doesn't the Company Let the Union Come
Into the Plant
to Debate Management?

Management should state that if the company allowed this, it really would not be a "debate." The union representative could simply promise anything he wished. Such promises are legal under NLRB rules, yet the company is strictly forbidden from promising *anything*. Under such conditions it would be an unfair debate.

Management should also point out that having meetings on company time is costly because production would have to be suspended. Employees who want to hear the union's side of the argument can visit the union office and listen to the union organizer on their own time. Management should state frankly they do not want the union in the plant at any time and under any conditions.

Can We Pro-Company Employees Hold a Rally in the Plant
After Work?

Management should express gratification that many employees are so vigorously opposed to the union. However, it should relate the NLRB rule that if a company allows an antiunion group any privileges, it would also be required to allow the pro-union group the same privileges, and it would prefer not to do that. Management can suggest that the rally can be held off the company premises.

Are There Any Advantages at All to Having a Union?
Don't They Help a Little?

Management can say that unions can represent you and do your talking for you; that is one advantage. However, most employees are capable of speaking up for themselves, and under company grievance and complaint procedures, there are existing channels for employees to speak out. When compared with all the disadvantages of the union, the possibility of strikes, and the price of unionization in terms of dues and assessments, management believes the disadvantages of a union outweigh the advantage of having someone else speak up for you.

If the Union Loses the Election Will the Company
Retaliate Against Those Employees Who Are in
Favor of the Union?

Often, pro-union supporters will attempt to evoke co-employees' sympathy by stating that co-employees must vote in favor of the union or else union supporters will be dismissed. The company's answer should assure the voters that if the union wins, all employees will be treated equally, that it will be business as usual and that no one will be mistreated simply because they had previously been in favor of the union. Such an answer will usually serve to reduce or eliminate this emotional appeal by union solicitors. Where there have been prior campaigns, and no pro-union supporters have been laid off or discharged, the employer may also point to this historical fact in order to bolster the credibility of the employer's answer.

Effective Utilization of Question-and-Answer Techniques

Although the question-and-answer technique is useful and effective, there may be some pitfalls in connection with its use. In structuring the answers to questions, care must be taken to avoid promises that improved benefits will follow if the union is defeated. For example, wherever question-and-answer methods are used, they may not be utilized as a vehicle for the solicitation of grievances and implied promises of their resolution. Even where employees initiate a request for a suggestion box, it does not constitute a defense to what otherwise may be viewed by the NLRB as solicitation. The most recent Board pronouncement on this issue however, leaves enough room for the employer to be able to continue the use of the question-box method. In another case, an employer announced that a question-box system was being put into effect to apprise employees of all the facts; employees were asked to place their questions, unsigned, in a box set up for that purpose. The employer promised to check the box each morning and to post the company's answer on the bulletin board within forty-eight hours. The Board approved the use of this technique on the ground that the system was used to answer factual questions raised by the employees, not to solicit grievances for the purposes of resolving them.

In such decisions in this area, the Board is more concerned with the use of the system to identify problem areas than with its use to express the company's position on election issues. Thus, the employer should take care to use the question-box system solely as a means of communicating its position on election issues and as a mechanism for answering questions with facts. Any implication that the procedure is being implemented to identify problem areas should be avoided.

A skilled use of the question-and-answer technique can produce excellent results covering a great deal of ground. Moreover, management does not have to wait for a question to be asked; it may assume that certain questions are in the minds of its employees, phrase the question on behalf of the employees, and answer it.

The answers should be short and to the point, and no more than two or three answers should be posted at any one time. To convey management's views in the most effective way possible, the answers should be factual rather than argumentative. Antiunion tirades should be avoided in this form of campaign material; the answers have the most impact if they are presented in a temperate and factual manner.

The use of the question-and-answer form gives management a unique opportunity to utilize supervisors in the direct communications campaign. Supervisors can be equipped with copies of the questions and answers when they are posted and discuss them with employees who are on the fence. This will prompt greater communication between supervisors and employees while avoiding the danger of questioning employees and exposing the company to possible violations of the Act.

Management should not assume that any question is unimportant. Skilled campaigners are aware that some of the most elementary questions reflect issues that are on the minds of a number of employees—issues that may determine the way they will vote.

It's also a mistake to assume too much knowledge on the part of employees. The employer should take pains to explain even the simplest facts and concepts.

The suggested answers in this chapter are provided as a basis for communicating. The answers management actually provides should be tailored to the particular situation and geared to the level of education and understanding of the employees, the progress of the campaign to date, the amount of literature already issued on the topic, and other factors.

Simply posting questions and answers in mechanical, routine fashion, is of little value. The technique is effective only when the questions and answers are truly responsive to issues that have developed in that particular campaign. Then it becomes a powerful method of erasing doubts and replacing ignorance with procompany information. Sample questions and answers demonstrating the recommended style and tone are contained in the Appendix materials.

Conclusion

If the principles outlined in this book are followed and careful legal advice is obtained, the employer may expect to win the election.* The feeling of exhilaration after witnessing the ballot count and having the

---

*Employers who have lost should read Appendix 6, which explains the grounds on which a lost election may be invalidated.

NLRB agent declare the employer a winner is virtually unparalleled. However, as much as the employer deserves to celebrate this tremendous victory and the employees' vote of confidence, the period of celebration should not be an extended one. Rather, the employer should view the election victory as a year of grace.

While NLRB rules do not permit an election to be held within a year in the same unit, or a subdivision of the election unit, nevertheless the NLRB will permit a union to organize, obtain signed authorization cards, and otherwise attempt to reconvince your employees of the values of unionism, within the year's period. Only an *election* is prohibited within the one-year period. The Board has permitted a union to demand recognition on the basis of newly signed authorization cards obtained during the one-year period.

The first postelection move the employer should take is to promptly express his appreciation to the employees. A letter, sent after the five-day period of objections has passed without objections being filed, should thank employees for their support, express trust in their judgment, and indicate that both employees and management can continue to work as a team on a mutually beneficial basis.

The next step is to draw up a chronological history of the election containing all union and employer materials published during the campaign and a transcript of any speeches which have been made. These may prove invaluable if other campaigns follow; they will also enable successors to the management team and outside legal advisers to obtain a firm and quick grasp of the previous issues as background for laying out and planning any subsequent defense to union organization. The election results should be checked against supervisory predictions on the outcome of the election so that the company will have a fair idea in the future as to whether or not supervisory opinion may be relied upon as a valid indicator of preelection employee sentiment.

The job at hand now becomes one of putting the employer's house in order. Election issues should be studied to determine company weaknesses and strengths, to determine what aspects of company policies and programs need to be improved, and to attempt to improve the image of the company in the eyes of those who voted for the union. The initial reaction by most employers is to want to immediately improve wages and benefits. This may or may not be the best approach. Granting immediate wage increases, apparently because of the election results, may have the effect of conditioning your employees to use threats of unionization as a mechanism for inducing you to make improvements.

While the employer is generally free after an election to grant increased wages and to make any other improvements in terms and condition of employment, the employer does not necessarily have carte blanche in this respect. A sudden increase in wages, coming close on the heels of a union loss at the polls, and combined with any preelection implication that the increases were conditioned upon a union loss, may involve the employer with an unfair labor practice charge and further dealings with the National Labor Relations Board in postelection proceedings. Even where the increases are planned to take effect shortly after the period for filing objections has passed, the manner and amount of any improvements should be carefully planned to avoid any possibility that the Board will view the beneficial changes as a reward to employees for having rejected the union and as an inducement to employees to vote against the union should the opportunity arise again.

That impatience may lead to charges of improper postelection increases may be seen from the following set of circumstances:

Two days after the election, which the employer won, management notified employees that a detailed salary evaluation would be made. Two weeks later, the company announced specific wage increases and adjusted its pay scales according to seniority, which was a change from the existing practice. The increases were larger than previous increases. The employer defended on the grounds that the raises were justified by normal business considerations. Under NLRB rules, the question of whether a postelection grant of benefits violates the Act is a question of fact; the question to be decided is whether the purpose of the grant was to interfere with the employees' rights or was for some legitimate business consideration. Where a postelection wage adjustment is intended as a reward to employees for having voted against union representation, the employer violates the Act. Employers also interfere with employee rights by granting postelection benefits in situations where it is clear that the employer seeks to obtain an advantage in the event a second election is ordered.

Under the circumstances just noted, the Board found that the employer's preelection conduct of soliciting grievances, combined with its postelection increases, served both to reward employees for rejecting the union and to eliminate the source of employee unrest over inequity in wage rates. *Raley's, Inc.*, 236 NLRB No. 97 (1978).

Since it comes as a surprise to most employers that postelection increases may be viewed as an unfair labor practice, the following ground rules should be carefully observed: During the five-working-days period following the election, no changes in wages, benefits, or conditions should be made, even if no objections have yet been filed by the union. The reason is that an election under Board auspices does not consist solely of the physical balloting of the employees.

Necessarily, the vote and the validity of the election itself must await the Board's postelection investigation of objections. Therefore, if the employer announces or grants benefits during the five-day period following the election, this may be viewed as having been accomplished with precipitous haste and as an attempt to assure a continued majority against a union organizational attempt in the event a second election is directed. The election proceedings are not final until the period for filing objections has passed. The same rationale applies to changed conditions implemented after the five-day period has expired but while objections to the election are pending before the Board. However, if the employer can support improvements in working conditions with cogent and persuasive business justification—for example, cost of living increases, employee turnover, failure to meet area standards, an unusually long period since the last increase, or other substantial reasons supported by valid evidence—improvements will be viewed as lawful. The burden of proof in such cases, however, is a heavy one.

The difficulty an employer encounters in persuading the Board to validate wage increases during the pendency of objections to the election may be illustrated by the following case: While the NLRB was investigating objections to the election, the employer, a hospital, became aware that because of its low wages problems had arisen in recruiting personnel and many employees had left the company. A survey of wages in the area disclosed that the employer's wages were indeed lower than its counterparts in the locale. An increase was granted. Notwithstanding an apparently sufficient and documentable business reason for the increases, the NLRB found that the hospital had known for a period of time that its wages were low; therefore, while the employer did have compensation problems, a wage increase was not imperative and there was no justification for the increases at the critical time when objections were pending and the possibility of a rerun election existed. The increases were viewed both as a reward to employees for having rejected the union and as an inducement for them to reject the union again in the event of a new election. See *Westminster Community Hospital*, 221 NLRB 185 (1975), *enf'd*, 97 LRRM 1522 (9th Cir. 1977); *N.L.R.B. v. Eagle Material Handling, Inc.*, 224 NLRB 1529 (1976), *enf'd*, 558 F.2d 160 (3rd Cir. 1977). Improper postelection conduct may even prompt the Board to issue a card-based bargaining order on the grounds that the interference makes a fair rerun election impossible.

Even after objections to the election have been disposed of by the Board, and even if the five-day period passes and no election objections have been filed, the employer should make certain that the letter containing the announcement as to improved working conditions does not refer to the election results or in any manner intimate that the announced benefit is a reward for having rejected the union.

After a victory at the polls, the employer must become concerned with the causes that enabled the union to gain support. Unions make periodic attempts to organize a particular employer, and a company which has had an election and has won it may, paradoxically, be more vulnerable to repeated unionization attempts than a company that has never experienced an election. Employees do not easily forget statements made by company officials during a campaign, and they will be dissatisfied if in the year subsequent to the rebuff of the union they believe that conditions indicate that management is more concerned with its own problems than with the working conditions of its employees. In a second election campaign, management's credibility could be fatally vulnerable under such conditions. The union stands ready to redouble its efforts in most cases; and having been stung by defeat, it will be a smarter and more capable adversary the second time around. Former prime movers will still harbor resentment at having lost. Both they and the union will be primed to exaggerate management mistakes, publicize them, and attempt to exploit miscues to their benefit during a subsequent election.

Management's postelection program should provide for a regular review of benefits and working conditions. Personnel policies and practices should be reorganized and republished. Supervisors should continue to be trained. Regular readjustment of wages and benefits, together with adequate communications explaining the basis for these changes, should be made. In hiring new employees, look for conscientious workers who do not readily lean toward unionization. Institute workable grievance procedures, and guarantee employees' access to supervisors and other managers. Experience shows that nonunion grievance programs do not run by themselves; it takes specific reinforcement and continuing attention by top management to establish a procedure, publish it, acquaint employees with its use, implement it, and publicize the results of grievance proceedings.

In summary, maintaining union-free status takes as much energy and continuing attention as defeating the union in the first place. Yet, it is being accomplished by hundreds of thousands of union-free employers who conduct their organizations in a manner that makes unions unnecessary. *The employer's vigilance against unionization continues forever.* The employer who has won a campaign must be thankful that the issues have been brought to his attention. While it is beyond the scope of this book to examine union prevention techniques, the best systems are those that provide employees with many of the advantages promised by union organizers: fair wages and comprehensive benefits; grievance procedures which are used and do dispose of and adjust employee problems; relative protection against job loss; systems to insure that promotions, discharges, and discipline are fair; avoidance of favoritism by supervisors; and other trademarks of well-run companies. Attitude surveys provide a diagnostic tool for determining management's reputation among its employees.

If these systems are followed, employees will have no inducement to join a union and pay dues to it, for they already enjoy a congenial work atmosphere and an employer which demonstrates that it cares about its employees. Retain and utilize all of the communications systems established during the campaign. The periodic letters to the home, group meetings, plant-wide speeches, bulletin board postings, and other systems should not deteriorate and disappear to be put into use again only if the union appears on the scene. The two-way communications and dialogue that won the election can also keep the employer union-free forever.

As an incentive to continuing the communications which have developed during the campaign, the employer need only be reminded that a union can afford to lose many, many elections, but a good union organizer needs to win only one election at your plant.

The final chapter of this book describes an actual campaign which may serve as a model and as a useful day–to–day guide on the strategy and tactics of conducting an election campaign.

Chapter 11

Anatomy of
an Election Reversal

A classic example of effective campaigning occurred in the following case, which resulted in reversal of a union victory in an election conducted one year earlier.

When the union, an exceptionally successful and well-established one, began campaigning, the company, unaware of its rights under the law, and believing that a majority of its "loyal" employees would never vote for a union, did little campaigning. The employer concluded, based upon discussions with its supervisors, that there was very little sentiment in favor of a union, and thus no need for a comprehensive communications program or affirmative campaign.

During the preelection period, union activity involved only the distribution of a few leaflets. The company was led into a false sense of security by a combination of what it perceived to be lack of employee sentiment for union representation and a low level of union activity. It approached election day with confidence.

The results of the election were a shock to management: The union won by a vote of better than three to one. Objections to the election were filed on the basis of a misleading campaign statement made by the union in one of its leaflets (to which the company had not responded). The NLRB agreed that the statement constituted a misrepresentation sufficient to cause the election to be set aside, and a second election was ordered.

Granted a reprieve, the company campaigned vigorously. The result was a victory for the employer by a small margin.

The employer's campaign, together with samples of the literature and materials it published during the preelection period, is described in this chapter together with comments on the strategy and tactics involved and the purpose behind each campaign move. This sample campaign draws upon all of the principles and concepts the reader has learned in all of the preceding chapters and serves to assist the campaigner to implement the earlier materials.

Choosing the Campaign Theme

Fundamental to planning any campaign is establishing whether or not the employer's story will be legally geared to play upon employee fear—the fear that entry of a union into the plant or office would not be beneficial to employees. On the other hand, the employer might choose an appeal to the employees' loyalty to the company and the employer's previous record on wages, fringe benefits, and fair treatment of employees. In the campaign under study, the first election was lost by a wide margin; therefore, it was decided that the loyalty theme could not have enough persuasive effect. Accordingly, the campaign was directed strongly *against* the union and involved a presentation of the adverse consequences that could result from the introduction of a union into the plant.

The Campaign Calendar

Professional campaigning calls for the establishment of a preliminary game plan. Developing such a program at the beginning of the campaign for the entire period of electioneering is essential to orderly planning and will insure that communications will be properly spaced and timed for maximum impact on the voters. The campaign calendar will also serve to give adequate notice to various representatives of management as to how much time is alloted for such work as fact collection, poster printing, obtaining campaign materials, typing, mailing, reproduction, and a multitude of other details that must be coordinated.

Of course, no campaign strategy can be predicted entirely in advance. Thus, the calendar is really an estimate of intended time targets and deadlines which may vary in accordance with the ebb and flow of campaign issues. Some dates should be left open to allow for unanticipated events, rebuttals of union propaganda, substitute communications, and new information. The only thing certain about a campaign calendar is that it will change as the campaign progresses. The calendar developed for the case discussed in this chapter is reproduced on the following page.

CAMPAIGN CALENDAR

SUN.	MON.	TUES.	WEDS.	THURS.	FRI.	SAT.
Establish New Bulletin Boards / Supervisory Training Session #1	Pease Poster / Valley Kitchens Poster	First Letter: Official Announcement of Campaign	Union Dues Poster / Poll of Supervisors		Distribute Brochure "What Union Is and Is Not" / Exhibit Film	
Question & Answer Box Established*	Distribute "Guarantee" / Post Job Security Posters	Supervisory Training Session #2 / Developing Feedback	Cartoon: "Look Before You Leap"	Job Security: Newspaper Clippings	Poll of Supervisors	Mail Second Letter: Impact of Union Wage Demands
	Distribute Brochure: "You Can't Trust Union Organizers"		Plant Manager Speech to Departments Day #1	Plant Manager Speeches Day #2	Poll of Supervisors	Supervisory Training Session #3
	Post Strike Poster		Announce Raffle to Induce Voting	Payroll Stuffer: "Some Questions to Ask the Union"	Deadline for Printing Company Handbook / Mail Strike Theme Letter, Attach Montage	
Supervisory Training & Feedback Development Session #4		Final Straw Vote	24-hour Speech to All Employees / Distribute List of Strikes / Election Eve Dinner	Election Day / Dues Deduction from Payroll / Election Instruction to Supervisors		

* Answers to be posted as questions are received.

Establishing Credibility

The company began the campaign in an extremely poor financial condition. As a framework within which to credibly establish its poor finances, several posters were placed around the plant indicating that the company had lost a substantial amount of business from customers who had been regular buyers of the company's product. Rather than simply assert that the company faced difficult times, posters were designed to reinforce what each employee knew from his or her own experience, namely, that business was slow. An example of such a poster—shown below—involved the Pease company.

MISSING !

PEASE IS MISSING—AND WE MISS PEASE'S SINK TOP BUSINESS — ALL 300,000 DOLLARS OF IT.

WE DON'T LIKE TIGHTENING OUR BELTS— BUT WHEN A GOOD CUSTOMER LIKE PEASE DISAPPEARS...

WHAT ELSE CAN WE DO ???

Suggesting Union Weaknesses

Another poster (reproduced on the following page) noncoercively imparted the clear message: A union company in the area went out of business. The union didn't obtain job security for its members at that plant. Did the union *cause* the company to go out of business? Employees could reach their own conclusion. It was not implied in the communication that the employer would close down operations as a result of a union victory at the polls.

As soon as the date of the second election was set, the company commenced its attack. It decided upon a letter to the home as the first communication. The concept behind the letter was to shock the employees into recognizing that voting for the union could have serious adverse consequences for them. The communication was also designed to avoid creating the feeling that the new election would automatically have the same results as the first. It put employees on notice that the company had not adequately explained the reasons why employees should have rejected the union during the first election, and that the employer was "dead serious" about keeping the union out. The letter has ominous (but lawful) overtones concerning the possible adverse impact upon employees and puts them on notice for the first time that selecting the union might not be in their best interest.*

TO ALL EMPLOYEES
Dear _____
 You have heard by now that a new election has been scheduled by the federal government (NLRB) for December 22 in our plant.
 During the last election we did very little to tell you about the many disadvantages of bringing a union into our small company.
 This time we will be telling you a lot about how bringing a union in:
WOULD NOT BE IN YOUR BEST INTEREST AND COULD

---

* Care should be exercised when making ambiguous statements about the adverse effect that a union would have on employees. General statements indicating that the introduction of a union would lead to "serious harm" or "undesirable consequences" have been held by the Board to be illegal when accompanied by other unfair labor practices. *Holly Farms Poultry Industries, Inc.*, 194 NLRB 952 (1972); *Ajax Magnethermic Corp.*, 227 NLRB 477 (1976). However, the statement that "A union will only make things more difficult for all of us" has been ruled to be legal. *Howard Johnson Co.*, 242 NLRB No. 59 (1979). The campaigner should be warned that even though the Board has authorized a particular phrase in a given decision, the Board will consider the employer's overall conduct and the context of the individual campaign in deciding whether or not a violation has occurred. The same or similar language in a subsequent case could be found to be coercive where the facts differ somewhat.

VALLEY KITCHENS
WAS...

- **A UNION SINK TOP COMPANY**

- **UNION SENIORITY CLAUSES DIDN'T HELP THERE**

- **THE COMPANY WENT OUT OF BUSINESS BECAUSE THEY COULDN'T COMPETE**

*HARM YOUR PERSONAL RELATIONSHIP WITH YOUR COM-
PANY.*

*Yes, affect you and injure us. Injure us badly. We'll tell you much
more about this in the next two weeks.*

*For now, though, let me say this. The federal government found as a
FACT that the union lied to you before the last election. Think that one
over. They also promised you that they could do things for you like get
more money and better benefits. This, too, is a lie! Your company is in
bad financial condition now, due to a loss of business. (The attached sheet
tells about losing one of our best customers.)*

*How can the union get you the improvements they are promising, if we
can't afford to pay them??? There are no automatic increases in pay or
benefits, not even a guarantee that any existing benefit will stay the
same, if the union wins.*

*The LIE is that the union can get you something just because it is
voted in.* Don't believe it!

THE TRUTH IS THAT GETTING A UNION IN HERE CAN
GUARANTEE YOU NOTHING! *We're dead serious about keeping
the union out. We'll do everything legal to see that they never get in.*

*December 22 will be one of the most important days you will have as
an employee here at our company. If you voted for the union last time,
without having all the* facts, WAIT! *Before you vote again, listen to
what your company has to say—give the election some careful consideration—it's one of the most serious decisions you'll ever make.*

DON'T vote without thinking first about how it is your job *that
may be affected by having a union in this plant. I'm writing this letter to
your home, because after all is said and done, it's your family that depends on your paycheck.*

*I'll be in touch with you many times between now and election day on
this union issue.*

Sincerely,

Bulletin Boards as a Campaign Medium

Extensive use was made of the bulletin boards.* Three new bulletin
boards were set up (under glass) at strategic locations around the plant
and were used only for communications on the union election. The
first poster—reproduced on the following page—depicted the union
as solely interested in dues.

---

* Proper and effective use should be made of bulletin boards throughout the campaign. Materials posted on boards should not be allowed to become stale. Care should
be taken to substitute fresh campaign material for older information. The principles
involved in maintaining effective control over bulletin boards and in determining the
employer's legal rights where pro-union sympathizers also seek to use company bulletin boards for pro-union information are discussed in Chapter 7.

THIS IS WHAT THE UNION WANTS FROM YOU

VOTE 'NO'

SAVE

YOUR

DOUGH

I LOVE $$$

$$$

$$

$

We Need Your —

- INITIATION FEES
- MONTHLY DUES
- FINES
- ASSESSMENTS
- STRIKE CONTRIBUTIONS

UNION BOSS

$

$

"UNION BOSS"
He Wants Your Money!

VOTE NO ☒

The Use of Payroll Stuffers

Shortly thereafter, a payroll stuffer was distributed asking some pointed questions about the union. The questions are all leading and are designed to pique employees' interest in the answers, which are largely self-evident. The groundwork is laid for employees to begin to suspect that a union in the plant might not be a complete bed of roses.

Some Questions
To Think About
And To Ask The
Union People

1. You say that a union means a raise. Can a union guarantee this? What if the Company does not agree to give us a wage increase?

2. Will we have to go on strike to get a raise? If we do strike, how long will the strike last? Even if we strike, are we guaranteed a wage increase?

3. Does the union pay our wages while we are on strike? If the union does not pay our wages, what will it pay us? Will it put in writing whatever sum it guarantees it will pay us while we are on strike?

4. If I am receiving nothing from the union during the strike or only fifteen or twenty dollars a week, who will provide grocery money for me and my family? How will I make house and automobile payments? Will anyone give me credit when I tell them I am on strike?

5. What about union dues? Suppose we get a contract through the union that does not increase our wages? Will we have to pay union dues anyway?

6. What if I do not want to go out on strike, but some of the men and women do? Will I have to go on strike with them? Will the union give me permission to work while other employees are on strike or will I be subjected to pressure by the union and even THREATS to keep me from my work even though I need my wages to take care of my family and meet my obligations?

7. How much will my union dues be? Can the union guarantee me that they will not *ever* be more than $10.00 each month? Suppose I want to get out of the union, can I stop my obligation to pay dues?

8. Can the union guarantee me work all year? Can the union guarantee that some employees will not be laid off?

9. Can the union protect me from discharge if I violate a company rule?

10. What CAN the union guarantee that it will do for me?

11. Can the union stop the company from hiring new workers to replace me permanently if we decide to go out on
strike?

THINK LONG AND HARD ABOUT THESE
QUESTIONS. IF YOU DON'T KNOW THE ANSWER,
ASK YOUR SUPERVISOR. THE <u>TRUE</u> ANSWER TO
EACH QUESTION TELLS YOU TO VOTE <u>NO</u> IN OUR
ELECTION.

BE SURE AND VOTE BY SECRET BALLOT

Involving Supervision in the Campaign

In order to establish greater communications between the employees
and front-line supervisors, the next communication was physically distributed to each employee by his or her immediate supervisor. The intention was to involve supervisors actively in the campaign to show
that top management was not alone in being opposed to the union.
Distribution of information on the "Inside Story" of a union made it
absolutely clear that the supervisors were aligned with management in
opposing the union. The pamphlet—reproduced on the following
pages—makes a number of hard-hitting negative assertions about
unionism.

Depicting the Adverse Consequences of a Union

A second communication to the home reinforced the company argument that it was in a financially bad position and that the union could
not correct the basic problem of a lack of business. The message indicated that if the union won the election its excessive wage demands
might add to existing losses and *force* the company to close. In order
to remain within the scope of NLRB rulings permitting such expressions of position, the communication assured employees that the company would not close simply because the union was voted in, but

★★★★★★★★★★★★

The Inside Story
What a Union

IS
&
IS NOT!

It's important that everyone understands exactly what a Union can and cannot do--by law.

★★★★★★★★★★★★

WHAT A UNION IS -----

A Union is an organization that makes a lot of <u>phony promises</u>.

A Union is something that <u>you pay</u> a lot of money to.

A Union is run by people who live off <u>your earnings</u>.

A Union is more interested in their own union bosses <u>than you</u>.

A Union is run by shop stewards that have control over <u>you</u>.

A Union is able to <u>call you</u> out on strike and to make you walk a picket line.

A Union is capable of <u>fining you</u> if you refuse to strike.

A Union is liable to turn your friends against you.

A Union is big business for Union <u>Bosses</u>.

A Union is a group that <u>needs you</u> to replace its lost members.

A Union is often guilty of <u>breaking promises</u> and mistreating members.

A Union is something that involves everyone -- once in, it's hard to get out and a picket line affects everyone.

Don't let anyone USE YOU or YOUR NAME and SIGNATURE for their own self-interest.

> (1)   A Union might do something "to" you-- instead of "for" you.

> (2)   A Union may involve you in something which might not work to your advantage but instead could be something <u>you might wish you had stayed out of</u>.

----- AND IS NOT

A Union IS NOT *going to give you anything.*

A Union IS NOT *going to get you anything by itself.*

A Union IS NOT *going to pay for any of your benefits.*

A Union IS NOT *automatically going to do anything for you.*

A Union IS NOT *going to pay your paycheck.*

A Union IS NOT *going to provide you with a job.*

A Union IS NOT *going to keep our facility open.*

A Union IS NOT *going to sell our products or service our customers.*

A Union IS NOT *going to run this company.*

A Union IS NOT *interested in you--only in collecting from you.*

A Union IS NOT *responsible for lies and false promises made to you.*

A Union IS NOT *interested in you or your personal problems.*

----- *BUT YOUR COMPANY is and that's why we can and will furnish you factual proof of everything we have said above.*

You see, there's a lot more to this Union thing than what the Union would have you believe. Simply by voting a Union into a plant means absolutely nothing--a Union cannot do one single thing about your job or pay--the only thing the Union can do is talk it over with the Company--and if it is not reasonable to the Company and the Company says "NO" then there is nothing left for the Union to do but to give up--go away-- or call a strike. REMEMBER, a strike is a work stoppage by some pro-union employees, who, with the Union, combine to prevent those who want to work or need to work from working.

R E M E M B E R -

<u>N</u> O <u>U</u> N I O <u>N</u> <u>M</u> E A <u>N</u> S

/X/   NO WAGES LOST

/X/   NO DUES

/X/   NO STRIKES

/X/   NO FINES

/X/   NO TURMOIL

/X/   NO PICKETS

/X/   NO ASSESSMENTS

/X/   NO UNION BOSSES

/X/   NO STRIFE AND BITTERNESS

/X/   NO POSSIBLE VIOLENCE

DON'T AGREE TO GIVING AWAY A PART OF
YOUR PAYCHECK FOR THE REST OF YOUR LIFE!

might be forced to close due to financial circumstances beyond its control if union demands were excessive.*

Dear

Please read this letter carefully, it has important information for the vote coming up this Thursday.

The union people have been saying that voting the union in will get you job security and a contract with many benefits in it.

LET ME SET THE RECORD STRAIGHT!

It's no secret that the company has been losing money during the last year. We're in hot water because of the loss of big customers and everyone knows it. So, how can the union improve things around here?—THEY CAN'T HELP OUR FINANCIAL SITUATION.

The union has made a lot of promises—suppose you vote them *in* and they make good on their promises and get a contract which causes much higher increases in the company's operating costs and causes us to lose even more money than we have recently lost. If costs rise, as good businessmen, we would be forced to seriously consider moving the plant. If excessive wage demands add a lot to our already existing losses—it could force us to close. Would *you* continue to operate your own business if you continued to lose money? We doubt it!

Please remember: We won't close just because a union is voted in.

We would only close due to financial circumstances absolutely beyond our control.

Only if union demands are excessive and cause substantial additional losses would we be forced to consider the business as unprofitable.

You're free to vote as you please—but vote *smart*. Don't be taken in by the union promises—and let's hope that the coming year will see an improvement in our business. *That's* the best security for us all.

Sincerely,

———————

———————

* It is worth repeating the Supreme Court's admonition in *NLRB v. Gissell Packing Co.*, 395 U.S. 575 (1969), to the effect that any prediction as to the precise effect a union may or will have on the company's future continuation of its business must be *carefully phrased on the basis of objective facts*. The actual language of Board cases approving such statements should be used where possible. An old case, containing approved language frequently used by veteran campaigners, is *Lord Baltimore Press*, 145 NLRB 888 (1964).

Encouraging Employee Questions

Despite the surge of communications from management, feedback from the voters was insufficient. Little was being said by employees about the upcoming election, and therefore it was deemed advisable for management to become more active in ferreting out questions from the voters. Accordingly, the company established a question box for purposes of fielding employee questions about the election. The notice announcing the question box was carefully phrased to avoid any implication that employee *grievances* were being solicited (a violation sufficient to invalidate the election). Instead, questions *about the election only* are solicited. If employees nevertheless make their complaints and gripes known, or ask questions about company policies, benefits and wages, those questions could be answered even though they deal with working conditions. Under such a system, it is imperative to answer questions promptly and accurately. Also, promises, whether direct or implied, that conditions will be changed in response to complaints should be carefully avoided. The principles involved in avoiding unfair labor practices based upon unlawful solicitation and remedying of employee complaints are discussed in Chapter 6, "Ascertaining the Causes of Union Interest."

Let's Have Your Questions!

DO YOU HAVE ANY QUESTIONS ABOUT THE UNION ELECTION?

IF SO, HERE'S WHAT YOU CAN DO:

TO KEEP YOU INFORMED SO YOU CAN HAVE ALL THE FACTS BEFORE YOU VOTE, WE ARE ESTABLISHING AN ANSWERING SERVICE FOR ANY QUESTION YOU MAY HAVE.

IF YOU WANT TO ASK ANY QUESTION ABOUT WHAT IS GOING ON DURING THE UNION CAMPAIGN, WRITE IT OUT ON A SLIP OF PAPER AND DROP THE QUESTION IN THE BOX WE HAVE SET UP FOR THIS PURPOSE NEAR THE TIMECLOCK.

BETWEEN NOW AND ELECTION DAY WE WILL ANSWER PUBLICLY AND IN WRITING ALL BONA FIDE QUESTIONS ASKED BY ANYONE VOTING IN THE ELECTION.

DON'T SIGN IT BECAUSE WE ARE NOT INTER-
ESTED IN YOUR IDENTITY. WE ONLY WANT TO
MAKE ALL THE FACTS ON THIS VERY IMPORTANT
VOTE KNOWN TO ALL. WE'LL CHECK THE BOXES
FOR QUESTIONS EACH MORNING AND GIVE YOU
OUR ANSWERS IN WRITING, ON THE BULLETIN
BOARD, WITHIN 48 HOURS.

DON'T BE BASHFUL! IF YOU HAVE A QUESTION—
ASK IT!

Answers should be posted periodically so that voters have time to
absorb them and to discuss management's response with co-workers.
Moreover, the employer must use its judgment with regard to answering non-genuine, highly argumentative, snide, or obscene questions placed in the box by pro-union supporters in order to goad management or to trick the company into committing an unfair labor
practice. Normally, such questions should not be answered.

Some of the questions received and the actual answers given during
the two weeks following the establishment of the question and answer
box are reproduced below.

1) *Who picks the Shop Steward?*
   The *Union* picks the Shop Stewards. Here is what the
   By-Laws of the Union state:
   Section XII(p. 5)
   "Business Agents and Stewards are APPOINTED and
   may be REMOVED at any time by the Executive Board."

2) *Will there be a Shop Steward in every Department or 3 or 4
   for the whole plant?*
   In most cases there would be 2 to 4 Shop Stewards in
   each plant. The Union's contract with ICI calls for 4
   stewards. This is a negotiable item. We would definitely
   not want more than two Shop Stewards, or at most 3. If
   the Union wanted more we could say NO.

3) *What can the Union take away from us?*
   The Union can take many things away from employees.
   To begin with, the Union will collect dues from your
   paycheck every month. In addition, the Union can
   impose periodic assessments and taxes on its members;
   but most importantly, the Union takes away your right
   to be treated as an individual. When you are a union

member, you are just another face in the crowd, another invisible dues payer.

4) *Who will answer questions that are in favor of the Union? For instance, what good can they do for us?*
We honestly believe that the Union will not do any good here. As a matter of fact, we believe that this Union's reputation is so bad that all it will do here is cause trouble and bring regret to our employees.

5) *Why is the Company so afraid of the Union coming in?*
Our Company is opposed to any Union coming between the Company and its employees. We feel that in the last year wages, benefits and working conditions have been greatly improved. The Company did not need a Union to make these improvements. Our policy is to constantly review our wages, benefits and working conditions so as to make sure that our employees are receiving fair compensation. You don't need to pay dues to the Union to insure this kind of fair treatment.

6) *I feel the wrong approach was taken asking if anyone had a question about the Union. I feel the question should be asked why do people want the Union. Could be the key point. Maybe call a meeting.*
We intend to have a number of employee meetings prior to the election. However, the law tells us that we may not ask questions as to why certain employees would want a union. Basically, we plan to talk about our problems here and how we expect to be dealing with them next year. For a number of years, we have had a number of ways by which employees can communicate with management. We have the President's Meeting as well as the Direct Line for our employees to voice their opinions. In addition, we have a Problem Solving Procedure for all employees to use. If any employee has a problem, he or she should utilize any one of these methods to express it. We want our employees to voice their opinions to us so that we may continuously evaluate our programs and policies.

7) *If the Union called us out on strike over wages and other conditions of employment, would we get paid while the strike is going on?*
No. If you don't work, you won't get paid. The Com-

pany won't pay your wages, and neither will the Union. Sometimes unions pay a few dollars to strikers who carry a picket sign in all kinds of weather. Very few people are allowed to picket, however, so most of the strikers get nothing. But the Union continues to pay the big salaries of the professional Union organizers from *your* union dues while *you* are out of work on strike!

8) *Can we collect unemployment compensation while we are out on strike?*
No. Under our state laws you *cannot* collect unemployment compensation while you are out of work on strike.

9) *If the Union decided to call a strike over wages and other conditions of employment, could I lose my job?*
Yes. Under the federal law, if the Union made you strike to try to force the Company to agree to the Union's wage and other economic demands, the Company is free to *permanently replace all strikers* with new workers. This means that after the strike is over you may no longer have a job, and the law does *not* force the Company to rehire you if you are an economic striker and have been permanently replaced by someone willing to work in your job.

10) *If the Union came in here, could we be cut down to a shorter work week, with loss of wages and overtime?*
We can't predict that. We do know that unions are continually trying to get a very short work week. This is because when shorter hours are worked, more employees are needed, and that means *more union members* and more dues money for the Union treasury.

11) *I'm not that interested in the Union; do I have to vote?*
Yes, it is very important that everyone vote. If you don't, the pro-Union employees will vote for the Union and we will have a Union whether you like it or not. The Union does not have to get a majority of the employees eligible to vote but only a majority of those *actually voting*. For example, if 50 employees vote then all the Union needs is 26 votes to win. *DON'T LET OTHERS DO THE VOTING FOR YOU. IT IS YOUR FUTURE—VOTE.*

12) *Can the Company give an increase to employees now?*

Under the law, the federal government has rules prohibiting a company from making any promises or giving unscheduled increases to certain employees or to everyone in general while a campaign is going on. (The Union, however, is legally allowed to make all the promises they want.) So we can't give an unscheduled increase to anyone now as it would appear as a bribe and would be an unfair labor practice.

Rebutting Union Promises

Further reinforcing the idea that the union could not necessarily produce on the promises it was making to employees, the employer challenged the union to sign a "guarantee." The employer's leaflet is reproduced on the following page. When the union representative refused to sign it, the supervisors then conducted individual discussions with employees explaining why the union could not sign *any* guarantee and that employees were taking a risk by relying on union promises made in order to solicit votes.

Lawfully Assisting Employee Defection From the Union

The first active sign that employee sentiment might be switching away from the union was some information received by management that certain employees wished to know whether or not they could withdraw the authorization card which they had previously signed in favor of the union. While the union has no obligation to return the authorization cards upon request by the employee who originally signed the card, the demoralizing effect of a "withdrawal movement" on prounion supporters and campaigners within the plant is great.

The following communication was both posted on the bulletin board and distributed to employees by supervisors.*

---

* An employer may not improperly encourage or solicit revocations of signed authorization cards. The reader is referred to the discussion in Chapter 5, "Withdrawing Authorization Cards," for an analysis of the legal principles and cases applicable to employer attempts to advise employees of their rights regarding withdrawal of signed union authorizations. Additional NLRB decisions that will be useful to the campaigner are: *Fortex Mfg. Co.*, 184 NLRB 22 (1970) (The employer furnished voters with forms); *C. W. F. Corp.*, 188 NLRB 554 (1971), *enforced*, 458 F.2d 794 (D.C. Cir. 1972) (the employer furnished postage, prepared forms for mailing and mailed withdrawal letters); *Aircraft Hydro-Forming, Inc.*, 221 NLRB 581 (1975) (the employer

UNION PROMISES ARE BUNK!

TAKE THIS TO THE UNION AND ASK THEM TO SIGN IT

THEN YOU WILL KNOW HOW PHONY THEIR PROMISES ARE!

GUARANTEE

The union guarantees employees that if you vote us in at the union election we will pay you:

1. $50.00 a week in strike benefits, if there is a strike, from the first week and thereafter, as long as the strike continues.
2. Full premium costs for health coverage insurance, for the life of the strike.

We also guarantee:

3. Your monthly dues will never be increased.
4. No union member will ever be laid off.

I personally guarantee that the union will live up to all their promises, or I will personally pay the difference to each employee for any of their promises not kept.

_____

gave unrequested advice regarding the mechanics of revocation); *NLRB v. Monroe Tube Co.*, 545 F.2d 1320 (2d Cir. 1976) *denying enforcement* of 220 NLRB 302 (1975) (the employer suggested to employees the possibility of withdrawing their authorizations); and *Jimmy-Richard Co.*, 210 NLRB 802 (1974), *enforced*, 527 F.2d 803 (D.C. Cir. 1975), *cert. denied*, 426 U.S. 907 (1976) (employees initiated requests to withdraw and the employer gave employees a form letter for mailing to the union); *Lebanon Apparel Corp.*, 243 NLRB No. 136 (1979) (the employer sent employees a letter setting out two methods of revocation solely in response to employee questions or requests).

Dear Employee:

    It has come to my attention that certain employees would like to know if they can stay out of the union if it gets in here.

    As far as the Company is concerned, all employees are welcome to work here and their ability to do their job is the only requirement. The union, however, has a different opinion. In every union contract that I have read there is a provision called a "union shop." This provision forces all employees to join the union after 30 days or be fired. Therefore, if the union wins, you must join the union and pay union dues whether or not you want to. If the union loses the election, there will be no threat of anyone here being forced to join. So it is all up to you.

    Some employees have asked: "If I signed a union card can I now withdraw it?" The Company does not wish to influence you in any way; however, in order to answer the questions, our attorneys have informed us that you can withdraw any card you may have signed by sending a letter to the union telling it that you are resigning your membership. Your resignation as far as we understand would become effective immediately. This is a voluntary matter and the Company takes no position on your right to withdraw. If you have changed your mind and want to leave the union, you have every right in this democratic society of ours to withdraw your card right now.

    The best way is for you to vote NO in the election to keep our plant going without the problems that can be brought by outsiders coming in.

                                     Sincerely,

The Film as a Campaign Tool

The first of three separate meetings between the plant manager and groups of employees by department included the showing of a film designed to influence employees to vote against the union. Following the film, the plant manager reinforced the antiunion message with commentaries of his own relating the experiences depicted on film to possible consequences of unionization at the plant.

    A number of films on the market are readily available and suitable for viewing by potential voters. These films are discussed in Chapter 7. Additional information concerning the use of films during election campaigns may be found in "Representation Elections, Films and Free Speech," *Labor Law Journal*, April 1974.

    The meeting concluded with the distribution of a brochure, "Our Employees Want to Know," reproduced on the following three pages.

Our Employees Want To Know

Many of you have some questions about the second election which has been scheduled for December 22. Here are the best answers we can give.

1.   QUESTION.
Since the union won the first election,
they will certainly win the second one,
won't they?

ANSWER: NO! There are a great many facts
about having a union in this plant which you
never knew about before you voted last time.
Once you have all the facts, we believe you'll
agree that unions might be good for some big
companies, but they won't be right for us.
By the time you vote you'll know everything
you need to know to find out that a union won't
help you one bit.

2.   QUESTION.
Do we have to pay the union if they win?

ANSWER. You Bet! They haven't said much
about their dues, assessments, initiation
charges and other fees, but, you will pay
$8.00 to $10.00 a month just in dues. What's
more, the union's constitution allows them
to double your dues. Also, the dues can be
increased each year.

3.   QUESTION.
If the union is voted in, when do we get an
increase?

ANSWER. You don't get an increase just because
a union is voted in. The union has no way of
forcing the company to agree to anything it
does not want to agree to. If we can't afford
to pay an increase we have the right to tell
the union: "No, we won't pay what you demand,"

4.   QUESTION.
What happens if the company and the union don't
agree on wages?

ANSWER. Ask your co-employees who are in favor
of the union what they think. If you get the
answer, let us know.

5.   QUESTION.
      If we vote to keep the union out, what will
      the company do for us?

      ANSWER. We can't answer that one now, because
      under the law a company can't make any promises
      to employees during a campaign. That's considered
      to be unfair and we would be in trouble with the
      Federal Government if we did so. However, we
      will always try to do the best we can and we
      hope business will improve.

6.   QUESTION.
      How come the union can make us promises?

      ANSWER. They're allowed! Under the law, a union
      can make you all the promises in the world to get
      you to vote for them. BEWARE OF PHONY PROMISES.
      Ask the union people how they will make good on
      their fancy promises.

IF YOU HAVE ANY ADDITIONAL QUESTIONS ASK THEM! WE'LL
GIVE YOU THE BEST ANSWER WE CAN--FAST.

                                        MANAGEMENT

Developing Feedback

The first series of department-wide meetings produced a number of
questions by employees. The two main themes were:
      What do we have to lose by voting the union in?
      Won't the union improve job security for all of us?
   In order to credibly answer this question, and to impress employees
with the facts that employees may lose even with a union in the plant
and that unions do not necessarily bring job security, the company
briefed supervisors thoroughly on the answers to the questions,
including a great deal of role playing on the part of campaign managers and individual supervisors. Once supervisors were made knowledgeable as to the company position on these two issues, a fact sheet
was distributed by the front-line supervisors to each employee under
their jurisdiction.
   Job security posters—two are reproduced on the pages follow-

ing—were also placed around the plant and in nonwork areas so as to provide a constant visual reminder that employees have job security without a union.

THE FACTS

---

1. OUR COMPANY HAS FOUND ITSELF IN GREAT FINANCIAL DIFFICULTY OVER THE PAST YEAR.
2. YOUR FUTURE AND OURS RESTS ON HOW WELL WE ARE ABLE TO REGAIN THE CUSTOMERS WE HAVE LOST AND KEEP THE ONES WE HAVE.
3. IF WE CAN MAINTAIN A LOW PRICE FOR OUR CUSTOMERS, THEN WE WILL BE ABLE TO MEET COMPETITION AND SURVIVE.
4. IF WE DO NOT DO BETTER THAN OUR COMPETITORS, THEN JOB SECURITY WILL NOT EXIST FOR ANY OF US.
5. THE ONLY WAY TO KEEP OUR PLANT OPERATING IS BY GETTING NEW CUSTOMERS AND KEEPING OUR PRICES REASONABLE. NO UNION OR UNION CONTRACT CAN PROVIDE WORK FOR THIS PLANT.
6. SOME UNION PLANTS HAVE BEEN FORCED OUT OF BUSINESS BECAUSE THEY COULD NOT SURVIVE THE COMPETITION BY OTHER COMPANIES WHO CHARGED LOWER PRICES. WE HAVE TOLD YOU ABOUT THESE SHOPS AND MANY OF YOU HAVE FRIENDS AND RELATIVES WHO NO LONGER HAVE JOBS AT THESE COMPANIES.
7. A UNION DOES NOT NECESSARILY MEAN AUTOMATIC IMPROVEMENTS FOR ANYONE. JOB SECURITY COMES ONLY FROM THE COMPANY'S ABILITY TO MEET COMPETITION, NOT FROM ANY UNION CONTRACT.

JOB SECURITY IS:

Having a good place to work,
Having a clean plant, with good
equipment,
Never having to lose work,
Getting a regular paycheck every payday,

Enjoying many excellent fringe benefits, at Pepsi

THE UNION CAN'T GET THIS FOR YOU BECAUSE...

YOU ALREADY HAVE IT!

VOTE NO

Mid-Campaign Speeches

A second departmental discussion was conducted about halfway into the campaign. The speech by the plant manager covered issues that supervisors had indicated were important to employees. A supervisory poll of how employees would vote (polling techniques are discussed in Chapter 7, "Estimating the Extent of Union Organization"), taken immediately before the speech, demonstrated that the company could expect 45 percent of the vote. Another poll taken two days after all departmental group speeches were concluded revealed that the company was slightly ahead of the union. The plant manager's speech follows.

PLANT MANAGER SPEECH
TO INDIVIDUAL DEPARTMENTS

Soon you will be voting in one of the most important elections you'll ever vote in. The result of the election will affect you—your family—and your future.

Therefore, I will be speaking to you about the election during the next 15 minutes because it is so important to all of us.

Let me start from the beginning.

Several months ago, a majority of you voted in favor of the union. Fortunately for all of us, the union lied to you and the federal government gave you a second chance to decide whether a union should come in here or not. We didn't speak to you like this during the last campaign because we were misled into believing there was no way a union could get in. Now, we are taking no chances and are letting you know why a union here would not benefit any of us.

Why don't we need a union here? Because we are a company which cares. How do I know this? How do *you* know this? Don't just believe me—but look at the record—here it is in black and white. 21 changes in the last eighteen months! (waving sheet containing policy and benefit changes). I defy any of the strongest union supporters to show me any union contract that has had more than just a few changes in benefits every three years—yet, we, by ourselves, without being forced, have constantly changed our programs—voluntarily—for everyone's benefit. We'll be passing out copies of this list containing these improvements at the conclusion of this talk.

That's why our parent company has never had a successful organizing attempt at any of the many plants that it owns and operates. And there have been dozens of these attempts to organize other locations over the years. They have all failed. Why have all these union attempts failed to organize a single plant? Because all the employees who voted against the unions in their attempt to snatch dues from employee's pockets were members of a company which cares about *you*. We have proved it. That's why it makes me fighting mad to hear that a few of you, just a handful, have talked a majority into believing that we need a union in this plant.

Let me make some things very clear.

1. A union cannot force us to pay more than we can afford.

2. There is no law that can force a company to agree to the demands of any union. The union doesn't tell you this, however—they just make promises which they may never be able to fulfill.

3. We will always pay fair wages and benefits.

4. Our company is never required to say "yes" to any of the union demands. We will bargain in good faith with the union. But what happens if the company says "no" to union demands? The only way a union has of enforcing its demands is to call a strike. Some of you may be eager to strike—some of you may feel you want to force the company to do better. The union, and the union favorites—those of you who support the union—can then throw a picket line around the plant—we've all seen that before. Those of you who want to work may not have a choice—you may be threatened by violence to stay away and not cross a picket line out of fear. The union has made a big issue out of this strike possibility. They say they wouldn't call a strike. They say that even if a strike did occur you would have the right to go to work if you chose. Let's look at the truth—how this would happen in real life.

Suppose you want to work and cross a picket line to come into the plant so that you can continue to earn money and pay your bills?

Suppose you get a call at night by an unknown person asking you if you know where your kids are during the day. Will you risk going to work the next day?

So, this is what can happen—most of you want to work, but you can't because the *plant* is on strike even though *you* want to work. *That* is what a strike is all about.

If that happens, the company can hire permanent replacements—they can take your jobs and *keep them* even after the strike is over.

Who gets hurt?

The *union* people don't. They go back to where they came from and they still earn their money. When the strike is over, they still collect dues. They collect them from the replacements anyway, so they don't care where they get the money from as long as they get it from someone.

Now let's look at this union.

1. The union did not give you your job.

2. The union has never paid your wages.

3. The union has no real interest in you.

Why are they here?

They are after your money—that's why.

Are they really interested in your jobs? Do they travel over 60 miles to see you because they care about your holidays, or your vacations, or your medical policies? No!

In my opinion, all they want is to come out here, get a fast contract, and get out. The quicker the better!

Do you really want a union contract? If you do, I have one here for you; as a matter of fact, I have three of them signed by this union that is asking you to vote for them.

You can ask the people who support the union to take their pick. Our conditions are better than any one of them. [Comparisons made between specific contract provisions and existing company fringe benefit programs.] Suppose we offer one of these contracts to the union and they accept? What guarantee do you have that they won't do that? You would lose, but they would collect their dues.

Suppose we offered them just the benefits and wages we have now and they accept it? What guarantee do you have that they would not do that? You would lose, but they collect their dues.

Suppose we offered them *less* than you have now and they accept? What guarantee do you have that they won't do that? You would lose, but they collect their dues.

Can you trust them not to do that? What union are we talking about? The people who are giving you a party next week. They started out offering you drinks, and now they feel they have to do something more in order to induce you to pay over your dues, so, as I understand it, now it's up to a buffet. I suppose the next thing they might offer you is full-scale dinner.

On the other hand, can you trust us? Can you trust me? Of course you can. You can trust *us* better than any bunch of strangers who are not really interested in you. You can trust us because we have a good record.

Our record deserves your support and your vote.

In closing, I believe you should save your money. We can continue our excellent record ourselves without their help.

I know we have made some mistakes—we are not perfect and we hope to improve. Our communications with you and your communications with us have not always been the best. We have tried to establish many different systems, president's meetings, departmental meetings, question boxes, and other avenues. Whenever mistakes have been made known to us, we have tried our best to correct them. It seems to me that we can do better by facing our problems honestly and discussing our problems directly and resolving our problems peacefully.

We are not so big here that we can't work things out without the problems that have been experienced in plants where unions take over.

I believe our record over the past two years, even though we have been experiencing financial difficulties, deserves your faith and your trust. Even if you voted for the union last time without thinking about the consequences, you can *change* your vote at the second election. I believe that our record and my record with you as plant manager deserves a "no" vote on election day.

Cartoons as Campaign Tools

Intermingled with the serious campaign communications was an occasional "cartoon" type of approach, such as "Look Before You Leap," "Stand Pat," and "Examine Your Freedom."

STAND PAT

YOU'VE GOT A
GOOD DEAL NOW
WITHOUT PAYING
UNION DUES

Examine Your
FREEDOM

UNCLE SAM SAYS
YOU HAVE THE **RIGHT** NOT TO JOIN THE UNION AND

To Vote Against the Union

These Rights are Legally and Morally Yours as a Free American Citizen

You Are
Free From
Strikes......

you are free to work in the job of your choice without interference from any union or outside group....

You Are
Free From
Union Assessments......

you are free to reject union membership without fear of losing your job....

You Are
Free From
Union Dues......

REMEMBER you are free to hold your job without paying any kind of fee to a union.

The U. S. Government will punish any union that tries to restrain or coerce employees in their right not to join a union.

* * * * * * * * * *
EXERCISE AND PRESERVE YOUR FREEDOM

Vote Against The Union

Be Alert   **Be Aware**   **Be on Guard**

Combatting the Union's Security Argument*

In order to further combat the union argument that voting for the union would lead to job security, a montage of newspaper headlines depicting layoffs in the steel and automobile industries was distributed by supervisors. Intermingled with the layoff headlines were references to the limited amount of strike benefits made available to employees by unions and a paraphrase of a newspaper article reporting on a union plant that went out of business.

Campaign Flyers

Campaign flyers fulfill the need for information and constitute simple, readable, and interesting ways to impart information.

The flyer "You Can't Trust Union Organizers"—reproduced on pages 268–70—was distributed by supervisors, posted on bulletin boards, and left in employee lounges, cafeterias, and nonwork areas for voters to read. It was geared to rebut union statements and promises made by the organizers.

Utilizing the Strike Theme

The last day or two before the election was when the employer attacked with its major argument: the fact that the introduction of a union in the plant might result in a strike with resulting loss in income. The oversized campaign leaflet (poster size)—reproduced on pages 271–74—was made available for employees to read and was posted throughout the plant. The communication firmly brings home the potential loss of income that might be caused by a union. By listing the number of strikes engaged in by the organizing union, the idea that a strike does not always happen to somebody else is reinforced.

---

* Communicating the theme that the presence of a union may lead to job losses and/or plant closings presents a difficult communications objective, even for the skilled labor law practitioner. The principles and pitfalls involved in such communications are discussed more thoroughly in Chapter 8, "Predicting the Adverse Consequences of Unionization." Additional sample statements and case citations are also referred to in Appendix 5.

Ohio Works Stays, Officials Reaffirm

Long Layoff Embitters Linden G. M. Workers

No profits, so Armco laying off

Auto Layoffs Keep On

Union Strike Funds

Curtiss-Wright Plant Hit by UAW Walkout 12/13/77

Company officials met with U.A.W. in June advising them of labor costs much higher.

Decision to terminate all manufacturing operations.

1. Out of 91 employees, 64 have never been laid off.
2. Most employees with us 5 years or more have NEVER been laid off.
3. Most layoffs go by seniority (unless an employee has a bad record).
4. Volunteers are asked first.

On the other hand . . . Look at the UNION'S record of LAYOFFS at General Motors, Ford and other plants.

These newspaper articles are proof of job security *union style!*

Reinforcing the Strike Theme

The last letter to the home will normally contain a plea to avoid the union on the basis that a strike can be damaging to the employees, not only through loss of income, but also because they may lose their jobs by permanent replacement. The following letter makes all of the

WHAT YOU NEED TO KNOW
ABOUT UNION PROMISES

You Can't Trust Union Organizers !

THERE ARE TWO SIDES TO EVERY QUESTION-
THE UNION'S SIDE
THE ACTUAL TRUTH

UNIONS PROMISE:

1. That it can get you a raise and other benefits. Can a union . . . . . .
   guarantee this?

2. That it is only interested in your welfare and your family's . . . . . .
   welfare.

3. That the company can well afford to increase your pay, ...
   shorten your working hours, give you more benefits, etc.,
   etc., etc.

4. That if it calls a strike your pay will continue during the . . . . . .
   strike period.

5. That if you don't join the union they will get you fired if . . . . . .
   they win an election.

6. That if they win an election you will be required to join . . . . . .
   the union.

7. That they will guarantee you job security.   . . . . . .

8. That if an employee goes out on strike for higher wages, ...
   they will guarantee him his job back.

BUT THE ACTUAL TRUTH IS:

. . . . . . 1. No, it cannot. No union can get more than your company is willing to give. The
   union will never guarantee you anything in writing.

. . . . . . 2. The union couldn't care less about the welfare of you and your family. It is
   interested only in getting your money through dues, fines, and costly fees.

· · · · · · 3. The union is wrong again. If we could afford to do this we would have done it already. A union hasn't the slightest idea of basic economics. It means nothing to them if they bankrupt a company with their unreasonable demands.

· · · · · · 4. Your pay will not continue during a strike. In fact, you are not eligible for unemployment compensation while on strike. But the pay of the union officials will go on during a strike regardless of how long it lasts.

· · · · · · 5. The union will never have anything to say about who works for our company. Management determines who works for this company on the basis of merit and qualifications.

· · · · · · 6. The Federal Law gives an employee the right to belong or **not belong** to a union. It's the employee's choice, not the union's.

· · · · · · 7. There's no way they can guarantee you anything except strikes. Where a union is involved you can almost be sure of strikes, work stoppages, disputes between employees and employer, etc.

· · · · · · 8. They can't guarantee this either. Such an employee can be permanently replaced.

Remember this — the union has never paid your wages or done anything else for you. All they want is your money through costly UNION INITIATION FEES, UNION FINES, MONTHLY UNION DUES AND UNION ASSESSMENTS.

Union dues, we demand.
We collect them anyway we can!
Fines, assessments, special fees.
We get them all — if you please!

Dues pay for our salaries, drinks, big cars — oh, yes!
After we get ours, you can have what's left??

We will promise you anything to get in,
And after that, you can sink or swim.
We don't love you, but we love your dues —
That is why union bosses cannot lose.

DID YOU GET YOUR STRIKE CARD PUNCHED TODAY?

Look at this card carefully — The Union has a card like this waiting for the employees when it calls a strike.

The Union can call a strike even if you as an individual do not want to strike!

If you don't strike and do picket line duty when the Union calls, you don't get your "Strike Registration Card" punched. If your card isn't punched you get fined.

DOES THIS UNION CALL STRIKES?

YOU HAD BETTER BELIEVE IT— IT'S YOUR FUTURE !

Look At The Recent Strikes This Union Has Called !

STRIKES! **STRIKES!** **STRIKES!**

IS THIS THE UNION IDEA OF JOB SECURITY?

147 STRIKES IN ONLY ONE YEAR!

COMPANY NAME CITY STATE	DATE
Eagle Electric Mfg. Co. Long Island City, New York	Began: 9/1/76 Ended: 1/29/77
Utility Trailer Sales Co. Los Angeles, California	Began: 12/2/76 Ended: 2/3/77
Chrysler Center Line Detroit, Michigan	Began: 1/20/77 Ended: 2/13/77
Certified Metals Co. Nutley, New Jersey	Began: 2/1/77 Ended: 2/11/77
Fountain Plating Co. West Springfield, Mass.	Began: 10/1/76 Ended: 2/10/77
Mark Controls Corp. Lake Zurich, Illinois	Began: 2/1/77 Ended: 2/9/77
Pierce Governor Co. location unknown	Began: 9/1/76 Ended: 1/19/77
Applied Arts Corp. Grand Rapids, Michigan	Began: 2/1/77 Eended: 2/16/77
Fleetguard, Inc. Cookeville, Tennessee	Began: 4/15/77 Ended: 2/18/77
Mead Pipe Co.—Water Pipe Unit Anniston, Alabama	Began: 1/3/77 Ended: 2/22/77
General Motors Corp.—Hyatt Bearing Rahway, N.J. and other locations	Began: 2/17/77 Ended: 2/25/77
Federal Drop Forge Lansing, Michigan	Began: 2/4/77 Ended: 2/23/77
SGL Batteries Inc. Detroit, Michigan	Began: 1/7/77 Ended: 2/18/77
Percival Refrigeration Boone, Iowa	Began: 2/1/77 Ended: 2/23/77
Rockwell International Troy, Mich. and other locations	Began: 2/5/77 Ended: 2/28/77
AMF Alcort, Inc. Waterbury, Connecticut	Began: 1/13/77 Ended: 3/4/77
Norplex Div.—Universal Oil Products, Franklin, Indiana	Began: 2/1/77 Ended: 3/12/77
Jeep Corp. Toledo, Ohio	Began: 3/8/77 Ended: 3/12/77
Hayes-Albion Corp. Jackson, Michigan	Began: 3/2/77 Ended: 3/15/77
Kewaunee Scientific Equipment Corp., Adrian, Michigan	Began: 3/1/77 Ended: 3/11/77
Lansing Drop Forge Co. Lansing, Michigan	Began: 2/1/77 Ended: 2/23/77
Ross Operating Valve Co. Detroit, Michigan	Began: 12/1/76 Ended: 3/14/77
Mid-State Die Casting Co. Grand Rapids, Michigan	Began: 11/4/76 Ended: 3/14/77
Acme Manufacturing Co. Ferndale, Michigan	Began: 3/14/77 Ended: 3/18/77
De-Sta-Company Highland Park, Michigan	Began: 3/4/77 Ended: 3/18/77
General Motors—Allison Engine Div. Indianapolis, Indiana	Began: 3/4/77 Ended: 3/21/77
Benrman—Marsdale Service Lansing, Michigan	Began: 3/2/77 Ended: 3/16/77
Metal Forge Company Deshler, Ohio	Began: 3/1/77 Ended: 3/16/77
H. O. Trerice Co. Oak Park, Michigan	Began: 3/1/77 Ended: 3/15/77
Keebler Company Toledo, Ohio	Began: 1/24/77 Ended: 3/18/77
DME Corp. Madison Heights, Michigan	Began: 12/11/76 Ended: 3/23/77
Angell Nail & Chaplet Co. Cleveland, Ohio	Began: 2/14/77 Ended: 3/29/77
Means Stamping Co. Saginaw, Michigan	Began: 3/1/77 Ended: 3/25/77
Pall Trinity Micro Corp. Cortland, New York	Began: 3/7/77 Ended: 3/31/77
Kagen-Dixon Wire Corp. Rahway, New Jersey	Began: 3/30/77 Ended: 4/12/77
ITT Thompson Industries Selmer, Tennessee	Began: 4/1/77 Ended: 4/10/77
Kewaunee Scientific Equipment Co. Adrian, Michigan	Began: 3/1/77 Ended: 4/5/77
Burrougs Corp. Detroit, Michigan	Began: 3/1/77 Ended: 4/5/77
Reef Industries Mt. Clemens, Michigan	Began: 3/21/77 Ended: 4/11/77
White Motor Corp. Cleveland, Ohio	Began: 4/1/77 Ended: 4/7/77
Almco Steel Products Bluffton, Indiana	Began: 3/7/77 Ended: 3/30/77
Ward School Bus Mfg. Co. Conway, Arkansas	Began: 3/10/77 Ended: 4/7/77
General Motors Corp. Freemont, California	Began: 3/28/77 Ended: 4/1/77
American Sun Roof Corp. Southgate, Michigan	Began: 3/2/77 Ended: 4/17/77
Hillsboro Mfg. Corp. Hillsboro, Ohio	Began: 3/10/77 Ended: 4/19/77
Stowe-Woodward Co. Sandusky, Ohio	Began: 3/21/77 Ended: 4/20/77
Ford Motor Co. Hazelwood, Missouri	Began: 3/21/77 Ended: 4/4/77
G & W Metals Forming Mancelona, Michigan	Began: 4/1/77 Ended: 4/15/77
General Motors Corp.—Delco Moraine, Dayton, Ohio	Began: 4/11/77 Ended: 4/17/77

COMPANY NAME CITY STATE	DATE
Standish Products Inc. Standish, Michigan	Began: 4/1/76 Ended: 4/8/76
Standard Products Co. Lexington, Kentucky	Began: 4/1/76 Ended: 5/12/76
Woodall Industries Detroit, Michigan	Began: 3/1/76 Ended: 5/17/76
Chamberlain Manufacturing Albie, Iowa	Began: 5/4/76 Ended: 5/21/76
Atlas Chain Co. West Pittston, Penna.	Began: 3/1/76 Ended: 5/28/76
Allied Products Corp. South Bend, Indiana	Began: 6/1/76 Ended: 6/14/76
Kawneer Co. Carrolton, Kentucky	Began: 5/28/76 Ended: 6/16/76
Auto Specialties Mfg. Barberton, Ohio	Began: 5/13/76 Ended: 6/17/76
Commercial Steel Treating Corp. Madison Heights, Mich.	Began: 4/5/76 Ended: 6/17/76
Lundberg Screw Products Lansing, Michigan	Began: 3/1/76 Ended: 6/17/76
Peterbuilt Motors Inc. Madison, Tennessee	Began: 6/1/76 Ended: 6/21/76
Pyco Corp. Penndel, Penna.	Began: 3/1/76 Ended: 5/11/76
Sheffer Collett Co. Traverse City, Mich.	Began: 6/2/76 Ended: 6/23/76
Cowles Tool Co. Cleveland, Ohio	Began: 4/1/76 Ended: 6/29/76
Otis Material Handling Cleveland, Ohio	Began: 6/1/76 Ended: 7/9/76
Ferro Mfg. Co. Detroit, Michigan	Began: 5/5/76 Ended: 7/6/76
Hoover Ball & Bearing Co. Fowlerville, Mich.	Began: 5/28/76 Ended: 7/16/76
Fedders Corp. Greenville, Mich.	Began: 5/3/76 Ended: 7/16/76
Con-Tex Industries Sparta, Tennessee	Began: 6/2/76 Ended: 7/2/76
SSP Products, Inc. Burbank, California	Began: 5/3/76 Ended: 8/2/76
Scott Mfg. Co. Scottsburg, Indiana	Began: 6/25/76 Ended: 8/9/76
Lake Center Switch Co. Winona, Michigan	Began: 6/15/76 Ended: 8/11/76
Central Aluminum Co. Columbus, Ohio	Began: 8/2/76 Ended: 8/15/76
Jo-Han Models Detroit, Michigan	Began: 7/15/76 Ended: 8/16/76
Globe Union Inc. Louisville, Kentucky	Began: 7/2/76 Ended: 8/13/76
Michigan Seat Co. Jackson, Michigan	Began: 6/17/76 Ended: 8/16/76
Royal Industries—Hinson Div. Waterloo, Iowa	Began: 8/2/76 Ended: 8/17/76
Michigan Precision Industries Detroit, Michigan	Began: 8/2/76 Ended: 8/23/76
Simplex Paper Corp. Adrian, Michigan	Began: 7/15/76 Ended: 8/19/76
Jackson Vibrators, Inc. Ludington, Michigan	Began: 6/3/76 Ended: 8/20/76
Brooks and Perkins, Inc. Cadillac, Michigan	Began: 5/21/76 Ended: 8/20/76
Atlas Tack Corp. Fairhaven, Mass.	Began: 8/11/76 Ended: 8/19/76
Alloy Mfg. Co. Chicago, Illinois	Began: 8/3/76 Ended: 8/30/76
Federal Mogul Corp. Mendon, Michigan	Began: 7/21/76 Ended: 8/27/76
Ainsworth Mfg. Co. Marysville, Michigan	Began: 8/1/76 Ended: 8/31/76
Joy Mfg. Co.—Bedford Gear & Machine, Bedford, Ohio	Began: 7/20/76 Ended: 9/4/76
General Electric Co. Cleveland, Ohio	Began: 8/9/76 Ended: 9/9/76
Union Carbide—Linde Wire Div. Ashtabula, Ohio	Began: 7/16/76 Ended: 9/13/76
Jered Industries Troy, Michigan	Began: 7/13/76 Ended: 9/9/76
ITT Higbie Mfg. Co. New Lexington, Ohio	Began: 4/22/76 Ended: 9/10/76
Quinco Tool Products Southfield, Michigan	Began: 6/21/76 Ended: 9/17/76
V. E. Anderson Co. Rome, Georgia	Began: 7/12/76 Ended: 9/16/76
Four Star Corp. Cadillac, Illinois	Began: 9/16/76 Ended: 9/22/76
Miller Industrial Products Jackson, Michigan	Began: 9/1/76 Ended: 9/17/76
Mallory Mfg. Co. Fraser, Michigan	Began: 8/2/76 Ended: 10/4/76
Lucas Steel Co. Toledo, Ohio	Began: 6/30/76 Ended: 9/24/76
The Richardson Co. Indianapolis, Indiana	Began: 8/2/76 Ended: 10/11/76
Harlow Products Corp. Grandville, Michigan	Began: 5/1/76 Ended: 10/7/76
Stolper Industries DeWitt, Iowa	Began: 12/8/75 Ended: 10/27/76

COMPANY NAME CITY STATE	DATE
Donaldson Co. Minneapolis, Minn.	Began: 6/17/76 Ended: 10/13/76
Gatke Corp. Warsaw, Indiana	Began: 4/28/76 Ended: 10/25/76
Ford Motor Company Dearborn, Michigan	Began: 9/15/76 Ended: 10/12/76
Genova Products Davison, Michigan	Began: 7/10/76 Ended: 10/18/76
Hamilton Tool Co. Hamilton, Ohio	Began: 6/6/76 Ended: 10/20/76
Hall Steel Co. Flint, Michigan	Began: 6/1/76 Ended: 10/21/76
Monotone Mfg. Co. Hazelton, Penna.	Began: 9/18/76 Ended: 10/22/76
Franklin Electric Subs. Levittown, Penna.	Began: 8/16/76 Ended: 10/21/76
U.S.M. Corp. Medway, Maine	Began: 8/30/76 Ended: 10/22/76
Plastic Products Inc. Inkster, Michigan	Began: 10/4/76 Ended: 10/20/76
Chemtron Corp.—Wilding Products Div., Hanover, Penna.	Began: 10/4/76 Ended: 10/25/76
Penna. Wire & Rope Co. Williamsport, Penna.	Began: 8/16/76 Ended: 10/27/76
Martin Steel, Inc. Huntington, West Virginia	Began: 8/16/76 Ended: 8/26/76
American Bumper Co. Los Angeles, Calif.	Began: 9/27/76 Ended: 11/3/76
John Deere & Co. Moline, Illinois	Began: 10/1/76 Ended: 11/9/76
Standard Products Gaylord, Michigan	Began: 11/5/76 Ended: 11/7/76
Moeller Mfg. Co. Belleville, Michigan	Began: 10/12/76 Ended: 11/3/76
Heat Controller, Inc. Jackson, Michigan	Began: 10/1/76 Ended: 11/5/76
Basic Aluminum Castings Co. Cleveland, Ohio	Began: 3/31/76 Ended: 11/3/76
K. B. Axel Co. Los Angeles, California	Began: 11/1/76 Ended: 11/16/76
Mack Motor Truck Co. Dearborn, Michigan	Began: 11/1/76 Ended: 11/4/76
Empire Plow Co. Cleveland, Ohio	Began: 9/1/76 Ended: 11/15/76
International Harvester Co. various locations	Began: 11/18/76 Ended: 11/22/76
Randall Bearings, Inc. Lima, Ohio	Began: 10/1/76 Ended: 11/24/76
Gould, Inc. Shreveport, Louisiana	Began: 9/22/76 Ended: 11/29/76
Unarco-Rohm Co. Inc. Peoria, Illinois	Began: 11/1/76 Ended: 12/9/76
General Motors Corp. Detroit, Michigan	Began: 11/19/76 Ended: 12/8/76
Harry W. Dietert Co. Detroit, Michigan	Began: 11/8/76 Ended: 12/7/76
Mid-State Die Casting Co. Grand Rapids, Michigan	Began: 11/4/76 Ended: 12/6/76
Hart Carter Corp. Mendota, Illinois	Began: 11/1/76 Ended: 12/20/76
Coastal Trailer Corp. White Marsh, Maryland	Began: 11/22/76 Ended: 12/16/76
NAPA, New England Warehouse Wilmington, Mass.	Began: 11/18/76 Ended: 12/17/76
LaCrosse Cooler Co. LaCrosse, Wisconsin	Began: 10/1/76 Ended: 1/12/77
Tappan Co.—Murray Division Murray, Kentucky	Began: 6/23/75 Ended: 1/5/77
Brown Pintube Co. Elyria, Ohio	Began: 1/12/77 Ended: 1/14/77
Prestole Everlock Co. Toledo, Ohio	Began: 1/3/77 Ended: 1/17/77
Johnson Mfg. Co. Atlanta, Georgia	Began: 12/2/76 Ended: 1/19/77
Berger Industries Metuchen, New Jersey	Began: 12/16/76 Ended: 1/16/77
Purex Pools Inc. City of Industry, Calif.	Began: 12/2/76 Ended: 12/23/76
General Motors—Saginaw Steering Gear, Saginaw, Michigan	Began: 1/20/77 Ended: 1/23/77
Federal Screw Works Detroit, Michigan	Began: 1/12/77 Ended: 1/26/77
Cripper Mfg. Co. Alma, Michigan	Began: 1/6/77 Ended: 1/14/77
Lear-Siegler—Metal Products Div. Detroit, Michigan	Began: 11/1/76 Ended: 1/24/77
CTS of Paducah, Inc. Paducah, Kentucky	Began: 8/17/75 Ended: 1/20/77
Johnson Bronze Co. New Castle, Penna.	Began: 10/1/76 Ended: 1/24/77
Allen Mfg. Co. Bloomfield, Connecticut	Began: 10/9/76 Ended: 1/20/77
Budd Company Inc. Gary, Indiana	Began: 1/26/77 Ended: 2/7/77
RB&W Powdered Metals Products Coldwater, Michigan	Began: 1/18/77 Ended: 2/3/77
Ex-Cello Corp. Howell, Michigan	Began: 12/14/76 Ended: 2/4/77

Millions of dollars in lost wages due to Union strikes!

DON'T RISK ANY LOSS OF INCOME

VOTE NO!

272 WINNING ORGANIZING CAMPAIGNS

IF YOU ARE CALLED ON STRIKE

Who

would buy

the

Groceries . . .

While you walk the Picket Line?

STRIKES BRING
UNION VIOLENCE
LOST WAGES
HARDSHIP

BEFORE YOU VOTE — REMEMBER —

DURING A STRIKE YOU GET <u>NO WAGES</u> AND HAVE NO INCOME. NOW—
CHECK THIS LIST OF NORMAL MONTHLY BILLS TO SEE IF YOU WILL
BE ABLE TO SUPPORT YOURSELF AND YOUR FAMILY WHEN THE UNION
HAS YOU OUT ON STRIKE.

1.	INSTALLMENT PAYMENTS	NO
2.	MONTHLY FOOD BILL	NO
3.	PAYMENTS ON LOANS	NO
4.	CLOTHES FOR YOU AND YOUR FAMILY	NO
5.	ELECTRIC AND GAS BILLS	NO
6.	LIFE INSURANCE PREMIUMS	NO
7.	DENTIST & DOCTOR BILLS	NO
8.	SCHOOL SUPPLIES FOR YOUR CHILDREN	NO
9.	ETC., ETC., ETC., ———————————————————	

NOW TURN THE PAGE AND SEE WHAT A "NO" VOTE MEANS TO YOU!

A "NO" VOTE MEANS

"NO" UNION

"NO" WAGES LOST DUE TO STRIKES

"NO" DUES

"NO" STRIKE VIOLENCE

"NO" FINES

"NO" ASSESSMENTS

"NO" UNION BOSSES

points necessary to acquaint employees with the possible loss of income. A montage containing newspaper clippings of recent strikes was attached to the letter which further brought the point of a possible strike closer to home.*

Dear Employee:

This vote on Friday will be perhaps the most serious vote you will ever participate in. That is why I am sending you this last communication so that you will be fully informed.

In some of my discussions with you, a few of our more militant and aggressive employees have indicated that they wanted the union so it could "force" us to do things we have not already done. Let me assure you, we are not the type of company that has to be forced to do things. We have proven it by our record of making improvements more frequently than in any union contract I have ever seen.

Have you ever stopped to think what would happen if some of the militant employees, the ones who would be put on the union committee to deal with management, might do if they persuaded the union to try to force us to agree to do something we believed was unreasonable? The only answer is that those few militants among you might force the union to call a strike. If there is a strike—and I certainly hope there never will be one here—here are some very important facts you should remember.

1. If a strike occurs, you stop earning any wages immediately.
2. Also, the company would be entitled to stop making payments on your medical, hospital and life insurance premiums. If you had a medical bill or a death while on strike, there would be no insurance coverage. (The Union officials, however, still earn their salaries).
3. You would not be eligible for unemployment insurance. Our state does not pay for employees on strike. That's the law.
4. The union cannot guarantee you that it will pay you any strike benefits whatsoever.
5. You can *lose your job* when you go out on strike. Yes, that's right, we have the right to run our business and hire many, many replacements (that is, people who are willing to work here and learn the jobs) for anyone who is out on an economic strike.

---

* Since the strike is the union's chief economic lever, a factual discussion of strikes as involving certain adverse consequences is lawful. However, care must be taken to avoid creating the impression that a strike is inevitable. (This issue is discussed in Chapter 8, "The Prospects of a Strike.") Although each communication about strikes may by itself be lawful, unions often claim that by constantly repeating the strike theme the employer created an atmosphere of fear of loss of jobs because of a strike, which is portrayed as an inevitable consequence of unionization. Excellent cases for the campaigner to study are: *R & R Processors, Inc.*, 217 NLRB 562 (1975); *Amerace Corp.*, 217 NLRB 850 (1975); *Morristown Foam & Fiber Corp.*, 211 NLRB 52 (1974).

6. When the strike ends, you would not have the immediate right to come back to work if you have been permanently replaced by someone else. Your replacement can stay on and do your work. You would be out of a job under those circumstances. That's the law.

7. There is always the possibility that violence can occur during a strike. Emotions run high and there is no telling what may happen during a time like this when many of you may want to go to work but have to face union pickets and co-employees who are on strike.

8. For many of you who may feel you want to work and not risk losing your job, the union would have a right to fine members who decided to cross the picket line and work in our plant. The fines can run as high as the pay you earn. That's how unions can work.

9. It usually takes many years for you to make up the loss of income which you can suffer during a period of a strike.

10. When you do come back from a strike, you must ask yourself these questions—was I better off without the loss of pay, without the union, without the strike that a union can bring to the workplace?

This will probably be the last word you'll hear from me on this issue. I do not want a strike here and I will do my best to avoid one. We would negotiate in good faith with a union and hope to reach an agreement. That agreement might contain better benefits, the same benefits, or it might contain fewer benefits, such as the ones that are already contained in the union's contracts, and which we have shown to you. However, the *one thing* we do know is that where there are no unions there are no strikes. Where there *are* unions there *are* strikes. As we have previously shown you, unions conduct strikes as a way of life. The union had 147 of them recently!! The proof is in writing!!

To sum it up, we are just not the kind of company that needs a union—I hope you'll recognize this and will give our company a vote of confidence for the excellent workplace we have tried, in good faith, to provide for you. Vote *NO* on Thursday.

Sincerely

_____

Rebutting Union Campaign Statements

As the campaign progressed, the strike issue became the biggest single item in dispute. The company was now fighting the campaign battle on its own ground with its own issues. Attention was diverted away from what the union could get for the employees to what harm the union might accomplish.

In an attempt to rebut the employer's argument, the union made a

crucial misrepresentation to employees: It erroneously indicated that two-thirds of the plant would have to vote for a strike in order for one to be called. The company quoted a section of the union's constitution in order to expose the misrepresentation, and a hypothetical example was posted outlining how just a few employees could force a strike. The information exposing the union's misstatement was posted on bulletin boards throughout the plant and is shown on the following page.

THE FACTS

HERE'S WHAT THE UNION SAYS

"If there is a strike, ⅔rds of the entire membership must vote to approve a strike." They are trying to lead you to believe that out of 90 members, 60 have to vote for it.

THAT'S A LIE!

HERE'S THE PROOF

The union's constitution says:

All members must be given due notice of the vote to be taken and it shall require a two-thirds (⅔) majority vote, by secret ballot, *of those voting* to request strike authorization from the International Executive Board.

THE TRUTH

If 15 employees show up at a union meeting to vote, only *10* have to approve it and *you* are on strike even if you are not there. 10 voters can put you out on strike! This is true, because it's ⅔rds of those who show up at a meeting and vote, not ⅔rds of the whole factory.

The Union "forgot" to tell you that.

DON'T TRUST UNION PROMISES

Encouraging Employees to Vote

When supervisors reported that a number of employees had expressed uncertainty about whether or not they would vote on election day, the company decided to motivate the work force by means of holding a raffle for a TV set open to all employees who voted in the election. The raffle was successful since every employee present in the plant on election day voted. Encouragement to vote was considered advisable since it is a valid assumption that all employees desiring to change the status quo by introducing a union into the plant will certainly vote. A full turnout will normally offset the 100 percent vote by pro-union supporters.*

The Captive Audience Speech

The final communication effort was a major speech given by the employer's president 24½ hours before the commencement of balloting and ending exactly 24** hours before the polls opened. The speech recapitulated most of the major arguments made by the employer during the campaign and concluded with a plea to reject the union on the grounds that the employees should give the company a chance without the presence of a union. Employer policies, customs and practices were also reduced to writing in the form of an employee handbook for the first time, and, as promised in the speech, distributed to employees on the day of the election as a counterpart to the "union con-

---

* Further discussion concerning voter encouragement is found in Chapter 8, "Contests and Prizes." Raffles and other voter inducement mechanisms have been approved by the Board as long as the anonymity of the voters is preserved and the value of the prize is not too great. *American Induction Heating Corp.*, 221 NLRB 180 (1975). A trip to Hawaii as a first prize would inherently induce those eligible to vote in the election to support the employer and would result in a second election being ordered. In no event should the employer keep a list of voters or in any other way use a system that can identify those who voted. *Marathon LeTourneau Co.*, 208 NLRB 213 (1974). Other issues for the employer to be aware of are: (1) the announcement that a raffle will take place should explain that the purpose of the raffle is to encourage all eligible employees to vote; (2) the notice should state that eligibility is not conditioned upon how an employee votes; (3) all business pertaining to the raffle (distribution and collection of tickets) should be conducted away from the polling area; (4) employees should be told that they may vote in accordance with their own free choice; and (5) to avoid misinterpretations of what is said concerning the raffle, supervisors should be told not to discuss the raffle with voters. See, *Drilco, a Div. of Smith International, Inc.*, 242 NLRB No. 9 (1979).

** Principles applicable to the "24-hour speech" and distribution of last minute campaign material are discussed in Chapter 7, "The 24-Hour Speech."

tract." The handbook tended to make employees feel that their existing benefits were guaranteed in writing. The fact that benefits and policies were put in writing for the first time meant to employees that the company would live by its "contract" and would not reduce benefits or change practices without notice. Care was taken to insure that the booklet did not change or improve existing benefits or privileges. The speech given by the employer's president was the company's final mass appeal. Because of the adverse experience in the first election, management officials also discussed campaign issues with approximately half of the voting staff in individual discussions, at work stations, during the last 24 hours preceding the election. Officials concentrated on those employees believed to be slightly in favor of the union, or undecided.

SPEECH GIVEN BY COMPANY PRESIDENT 24½ HOURS BEFORE VOTING BEGINS

I have called all of you together today so that we can take this last opportunity to discuss this Union threat to your company. I have been in fairly close touch with many of you during the last several weeks and have had many opportunities to speak with you in smaller groups.

The last time we had a vote here, last spring, it was a mistake to vote the union in. When you voted last time, I don't believe any of you had all the facts in front of you so that you could make a good decision on whether or not a union in our plant would be the best thing. I believe it was a mistake, and I also feel that once you have been given the facts you will definitely vote against the union. Therefore I am giving this last talk to you to review much of what has been said as to why we should keep the union out of here and to explain to you some last-minute facts about the union which would surely make any employee conclude that a union is not needed here.

Let's see where we are today. The union has been out there for over a year. Why are they out there? They do not tell you this, but the sole reason they are trying to organize this shop is to obtain money from you in the form of dues and initiation fees. The union will very rarely tell you that this is why they are here. Instead, they will try to promise you the moon and get you to believe that they can achieve all the promises they have made and that they are really interested in your welfare and nothing else. That is a lot of bunk. Here's why. If this plant were organized, the union would stand to gain over $200,000 in dues and initiation fees over the years. *That* is why this plant means so much to them. *That* is why they would like to see you vote for them next Thursday. It would cost you over $100 a year just in dues, not counting initiation fees, assessments and strike fund monies which you may be required to contribute for strikes at other locations.

I have been in touch with you over the last several weeks, and from what I have heard I feel that many of you who unknowingly voted for the union last time have changed your minds. I am confident that on Thursday, we are going to win. Let us take a look at some of the facts.

We don't need a union here. Unions may have a place at big companies, which employ thousands of people. Those big companies make millions of dollars a year and may be able to afford unions; we are a small company—we don't need a union in here as a partner with us.

You know that we are losing money. There is no doubt about this. Each of you can see for yourself that the company is in a poor financial position.

Don't let those people who support the union fool you into thinking that we are making all kinds of money here. The plain truth is that we are not and you know it. You know that we lost many big customers, such as Montgomery Ward, Pease, and Sears, Roebuck, as well as others. Many of you worked on their orders and shipped the finished product out to these companies. They are gone now and we are hurting because of it. Also, we are one of the last companies of our type left in business in this area. It is really tough to make it in our business today. We used to have several other companies like ours in this area, but they are all gone—all stopped producing. Valley Products was one of our competitors. They couldn't make a profit and went out of business. The same is true of Building Supply, National Top, and A & G, to name just a few. They couldn't make it because the profit just wasn't there. They were forced to go out of business. No union could help those employees. No union could supply customers to those companies. When they went out of business, everyone lost their jobs and a union was not in a position to do a thing. Nothing! No protection at all. Yet, somehow this union out here seems to want you to believe that somehow job security can be achieved through voting for a Union. It is not true.

Now, we are in financial trouble and you all know it. It is not your fault. You have been working hard and have been doing an excellent job to get our products out of the door. I can't pinpoint the exact reason why we are not doing well, but I can say to you that we—I, as well as every other company official—all are doing our best to keep this company alive. We all want to stay in business.

What can the union do here to improve our position? The answer is: nothing. Some of the union supporters may believe that the union can help, but it just can't. The union put out a flyer yesterday about the wages and benefits they have obtained for employees at BRG Co. But they didn't tell you *all* of the facts. Here is what they did not tell you. BRG has recently built three plants outside the state. The BRG plant the union is so proud of has not done any hiring in the factory area for the last four years. In the last five years, the BRG work force has shrunk from 800 employees to 450. Ask the union this: where did those 350 jobs go?

Suppose the union were voted in? What could they do? The answer is that they would have the right to negotiate with management. Discussions would then take place concerning Union demands. After the last election, the Union thought they were in and they submitted to us a list of demands. Here is what they asked for:

Page 1 of the contract demands that we recognize the union as exclusive collective bargaining representative. That doesn't help you at all—that just helps *them*.

Page 2 contains a union shop clause. This forces you to join the union whether you want to or not, even if you voted against the Union. Under this clause you can be *forced* to join and pay dues and initiation fees. This helps the Union—*it does nothing for you*. Therefore, everyone of you who does not want the union in here should absolutely get out there and vote against it. If you don't vote, then the union people will vote the union in and you will be losing your right to vote. All it takes is the majority of those who show up and vote. Suppose only 100 employees show up to vote. That would mean that all the union needs to win is 51 votes. Therefore, you see how important it is for everyone to get out there tomorrow and cast their ballot against the union. Even if you are undecided, and in doubt about what to do, my suggestion to you is that you vote NO. Don't let the small number of union people control the way the election will go. Remember too, even if you signed a card for the union or voted for them in the last election, the ballot is *secret*: neither the union nor the company will know how you voted in that election.

On the third page, they have a demand that we check off your dues before you even get the money in your pocket—in other words, take the dues out of your pay check and send it to the Union automatically. That helps *them*, it doesn't help you.

The next demand is having a shop committee and a chairman. That is four union jobs. They would be the union representatives here. Who do you think they will be. I am sure they will be the people who helped bring the union in here if they win. They have to be paid off politically somehow and that is the way the union does it. They get them off from the job in order to meet with business officials of the union, and they will have the right to work overtime whenever other employees are working. This is how the union will compensate them for persuading you to vote in their favor. It is all politics. So far, none of these demands really helps *you*.

The union has a demand for seniority rights. They want layoffs to be by seniority. Basically, that is the way we do it here anyway. Every once in a while, we might lay off someone out of seniority but only if that employee has been a poor employee and has a bad record. We would rather keep the good employee and lay off the one with the bad record. I don't see how that particular provision would help most of us. Why pay union dues to get seniority protection in layoffs, when basically, except for a couple of exceptions, which I mentioned, you already have that protection? Anyway, we often call the layoffs by volunteers, which helps those of you who want to work. The union has no provision like that in their contract, and no request for voluntary layoffs in the proposals they submitted to us.

Also, the union demands, they want the Shop Stewards, and Shop Committee people—in other words, all of their favorites, all of their people that are now telling you, "Bring the Union In"—to have "super seniority." That means that even if all of these people have only one year's seniority, they would be the last people in the shop ever to be laid off. That is union politics, and that is why they are asking you to vote the union in. There are many other demands the union has made, which I won't get into. Also, they are asking for many things you already have—for example, leaves of absence, forty-hour work week, overtime after forty hours.

Here is one demand which is a beauty: They want twelve company-paid holidays. Right now we have nine holidays. This would add a tremendous cost to our existing operations. The union can *ask* for these holidays, but, we have every right to say "no" to that particular demand as being too costly. Just because they promise it to you, and just because they demand it, doesn't mean, for a minute, that we have to agree to twelve holidays, or, for that matter, even one additional holiday. We will tell them the reasons why additional producing time is costly, we will tell them about our financial difficulties and will deal with the union in good faith. However, the bottom line is that we just have no obligation under the law to agree to their demands.

I am sure that many of you never even knew that these demands were submitted to the company by the union. But let us take a better look at them. They want you to have job specifications for each job. I don't think this is good for the company or for you. It sounds fine but let us look at it. Once you have job classifications in a contract, working conditions become very rigid. Under many union contracts, it becomes difficult to transfer people from one classification to another. Also, this has happened under union contracts—when there is no work in a particular category, the employee in that category is laid off. I don't think you would want that system to work here. I think the system we now have—where an employee can be transferred to various other jobs—is good for the company and is good for you.

I don't even know what wage rates the union has been demanding but I hear they are asking for a lot. How in God's name can the company meet a demand for a great deal of extra money in wages given the present poor financial situation we are in? *If we don't have it, we can't give it.* What could the union do then? I just don't know.

They also want a lot of other costly items, such as vacation pay and improved hospitalization, insurance and life insurance. You know the story on hospitalization insurance. Things are so tight here, that we had to try to save those premium costs. Fortunately, we reinstated the best part of the insurance program. Suppose the union wants to get the old program back or suppose they want a better program. We are finding it difficult to finance the existing insurance system at its present level of cost. We would have the right to say to the union, "Sorry, Union professional dues collectors, we can't afford the additional cost of reinstating the insurance benefits." What could they do then? I don't know.

This one is a joke. They want a pension program financed by the company. We are having a difficult time making ends meet now. How on earth could we afford to finance a pension program when we are not making enough money now to sustain ourselves? You know we have just had a series of layoffs. The fact that we are laying off shows that we are in tough financial shape, yet the union has these extreme financial demands. They also want a cost-of-living increase in addition to wages. How much could we stand?

I don't know what would happen in bargaining. We would do our best to come to an agreement. But if the union would not agree with us, and if they believe they have to make good on their promises to their supporters, the people who got them in here, they would have the right to strike if we would not agree to these demands. Now I will be completely honest with you. We don't want a strike. We will do our best to avoid one. But it has been a hard fight to keep this plant open. So far we have been successful and have managed to keep it going and still alive even though our competitors have gone down and under. We have been able to do this because we haven't had to worry about a lot of other problems here at the plant. Also, we haven't had to worry about spending hundreds of hours bargaining with the union.

We haven't had to worry about union strikes or other Union troubles and grievances. We have been able to spend all our time keeping this plant open.

I will also tell you something else: I believe that as long as things stay the way they are we can continue to keep this plant open. However, if the union gets in here and causes a lot of trouble or causes a strike which cripples our operation, I do not know what will happen. I can only solve one major problem at a time. We will do our best to keep our plant open. As a matter of fact, you may already know that we are so concerned with keeping the plant open that we will operate during a strike by using supervisors and by hiring outside replacements. We have to do this to protect ourselves in case the union strikes over unreasonable demands and in case we simply can't meet what the union feels they must have to show their supporters they were able to do something here.

Now there are a lot of things the union hasn't told you about a strike, and a lot of things they lied to you about.

For example, they will tell you that we won't have a strike here, but that they will agree with the company. That may very well happen. However, they didn't tell you about 147 strikes they called at other locations. I will tell you another thing, since that list of 147 strikes was compiled we have dug up a list of 55 other strikes this same union has called—*since* we compiled the list!

Who is going to pay your bills while you are on strike? Not the union—but the salary of the union officials will continue while you are on strike. Who will pay hospitalization premiums for health insurance coverage if the strike goes on? Certainly the company will not pay these costs, and neither will the union.

If they have told you that you will collect strike benefits, you have no guarantee that this will happen. When it comes to shelling out money during a strike the union can be very stingy. They probably haven't told you that often you have to wait for a period of time, maybe a week or two before you are even eligible for strike benefits; that they have to get approval from the parent union in Washington. The union people in Washington don't like to give out strike benefits to new members thousands of miles away from the home office. What makes you think they will pay strike benefits out here? Also, even if they pay you, how much do you think it will be? In most cases it is about $35 a week—can you live on that? Ask the union officials to *guarantee* you that they will pay your benefits, and ask them to guarantee you that they will pay you $55, $65 or $75 a week. I know they won't do it. They can be mighty stingy. Also, they may not help you if you do go on strike. If the company decides to operate, we can hire permanent replacements for your jobs. If the company does hire permanent replacements while you are out on strike for improved wages and benefits that the union is demanding, the replacements would have the right to fill your jobs. Even after the strike is over, the permanent replacements would have the right to keep your job and you would have no legal right to come back to the plant as long as the replacement hired during the strike was there. The union hasn't told you this. But they know it is the law, they couldn't deny it. You can't be fired for striking, but under the law you certainly can be permanently replaced. This is true. But the union never tells you these unfortunate facts of life. If you want proof of this, we are handing out Xerox copies of some pages from a book published by the National Labor Relations Board, which shows you this is the law.* So, you see, when you voted last time there was a lot you didn't know about the union. It is not a bed of roses. There are severe disadvantages to becoming a union member.

Let us get into another lie they have told you. They said that it takes two-thirds of the *membership*, voting at a secret ballot, to call a strike. This is bunk. It is an outright lie. They say this to make you feel you have a real choice on whether you go out on strike or not. The true facts are that you may not have any choice at all. They lied to you. I have the union's constitution right here in my hand. Any of you can come up and see it at any time. We have already posted copies on the bulletin board for you. What it says is that a majority of those members who appear at a meeting can cast their ballots in favor of a strike. What that means is that they could call a meeting at midnight, and if 12 of its supporters show up, all the Union needs is 8 votes out of 12 in order to call a strike. So you could be home watching TV, or asleep, while the small minority of people, the militant ones around here, will be voting for a strike and you may not have a chance at all. This is a fact, it could happen and that is the way unions operate. They *lied* to you on this issue and on that basis alone they deserve to be voted out.

Who is telling the truth? How should you vote tomorrow?

Let us face it: If the union comes in and increases the cost of our doing business substantially, we are going to lose even more money. If we do lose much more, then as good businessmen we will seriously

---

* Excerpts from the "Layman's Guide" were distributed to all employees at the conclusion of this speech. The guide, more formally titled "A Guide to Basic Law and Procedures Under the National Labor Relations Act," is available from NLRB Regional Offices.

consider moving our operation, closing it down for lack of profit, or running the business with replacements if the union strikes. Now, I am not saying there will be a strike, I do not know what will happen. If the union scales down its demands to keep our costs at present levels, it may very well be that we can agree with them and negotiate a no-increase contract.

Right now you do have a decent job with fair pay. We have made many improvements through our parent company, even though we have lost money. Folks, we have done our best. You have pretty decent job security. I would like to see this company turn around. You do have benefits and policies here that we follow which are beneficial to you. As a matter of fact, I put together a little booklet outlining all of our policies and I think you will be pleasantly surprised to see that we have some nice working conditions here. They are not the best, but they are not the worst either. They are about average and you should enjoy them. The booklet is still at the printer's, we are getting it tonight, and tomorrow morning the supervisors will be passing out a copy of our Employee Handbook. I would like you to read it before you vote. The Handbook is our guarantee to you. As I was saying to you, you do have security here; you do have a decent job. We are not the best, we make mistakes, but we are asking for your support. I will be working closely with you over the next year or two in order to help make our future here successful. Security for you in *your* position can be accomplished in only one way—by being able to continue selling quality products to our customers and being able to continue giving our customers good, competitive, prompt, and efficient service. Anything less than that and the future of our company would be imperiled.

Let us all work together toward this goal.

Please, we don't need a union in this plant. Give us a chance; once the union is in you may *never* be in a position to get it out. It very rarely happens that unions are voted out once they are in. They may be in here forever and you may not have another chance to vote them out if you don't like them.

I have reached my time limits and under the law I can't speak to you beyond 2:00 P.M. Therefore, although I would like to, I can't answer any questions you may have right now. However, between now and voting time tomorrow you can ask any individual question you want. Ask me, ask any manager, or ask your supervisor. We'll do our best to give you an honest answer.

So, my last word to you is, I urge you to vote tomorrow, and when you do vote, VOTE NO!

Election Eve Dinner Party

Partially to offset the effects of a party given by the union for employees the week before the election, it was decided that a company-sponsored election eve dinner would prove uplifting to employee morale and create a pro-company attitude. The company provided free food and drink after working hours at a local establishment often frequented by employees. It was decided, because of the intensity of the campaign and the fact that the 24-hour captive audience speech had been given just a few hours before, that the party would be a purely social affair and that no speeches or other campaigning would take place.*

Dramatizing the Cost of Union Dues

The date agreed upon by the company and the union for the election was intentionally selected by the company to coincide with a payday. The intention was to dramatize the cost of unionization by distributing, on the day of the election, a separate paycheck in the amount of the monthly dues charged by the union. The amount of the dues was placed in a separate envelope and distributed with the paycheck with the following inscription:

> This $12.00 is yours now—but the union will want to take this much—or more—out of your pay envelope each month.
> To keep the union from getting over $120.00 a year from you, vote against the union on election day.
> The $120.00 a year, or more, is only a starter.
> DUES go UP. Assessments can be charged.
> VOTE "NO" on election day.

The separate paycheck in the amount of monthly dues was a vivid and graphic illustration that unionization may be costly. This tactic re-

---

* Giving an election eve party raises several technical issues which must be assessed by management. The principles involved in deciding whether or not to undertake such an event, together with a sample notice telling all employees about the dinner party, are contained in the text. See Chapter 7, "Election Eve Parties." The meeting must not be compulsory, nor may it take place during working hours. Neither may second shift employees, or those regularly scheduled to work during the time the party is given, be allowed off from work in order to attend the party, which may be conducted on company premises if appropriate. The Board has allowed the employer to provide refreshments. *Hasa Chemical, Inc.*, 235 NLRB No. 112 (1978).

minds employees that their payroll deductions are sufficiently large without adding to them the cost of dues.*

Election Day Checklist
for Supervisors

In order to prevent unfair labor practices from arising during the actual conduct of the election, this checklist was distributed to all supervisors on the morning of the election:

1. *BEFORE THE ELECTION POLLS OPEN.* You may talk to employees individually in normal work areas at their work stations (not in an office) with respect to the election up to 15 minutes before the time the polls open at 9:00 o'clock. Do not talk to employees *in a group* on company time and property at any time within the 24-hour period immediately preceding the time the election actually begins. In other words, since the election starts at 9:00 A.M. on Thursday, you should not talk to any assembled group of employees on company time and property after 9:00 A.M. on Wednesday.

   You may, however, talk with individual employees at their work stations or in other nonisolated areas where they are customarily found in the course of their work, at any time right up until about 15 minutes before the polls are officially opened.

2. *WHILE THE ELECTION IS GOING ON.* Supervisors should avoid the voting area, which will be the lunchroom. *Do not talk to employees lined up to vote for any reason.* It is recommended that all supervisors stay out of the voting area at least 15 minutes before polls open and at least 15 minutes after polls close.

3. *NO SUPERVISOR SHOULD KEEP A WRITTEN TALLY OF EMPLOYEES WHO HAVE VOTED OR NOT VOTED.* Do not give employees the impression that you are keeping a list of voters.

4. *VOTING HOURS.* Arrangements have been made to give everyone plenty of time to vote. Voting will take

---

* Further discussion on the dues theme occurs in Chapters 7 and 8. The Board has approved the payroll deduction stratagem in a number of cases. See, for example, *Island Holidays Ltd.*, 208 NLRB 966 (1974); *The William Carter Co.*, 208 NLRB 1 (1973).

place between 9:00 A.M. and 10:00 A.M. and 3:30 P.M. and 5:30 P.M.

5. *EMERGENCIES.* In case of any confusion as to where or when employees should vote, please notify the Plant Manager. Everybody should know that they are free to vote at the appointed time. Do not get caught in a situation in which you may be accused of directing or insisting that an employee vote against his or her will.

6. *WORK DISRUPTIONS.* Normal work orders and instructions should be given employees on election day. Aside from the inevitable interruption to work caused by the election, employees and supervisors are expected to treat this day as a normal work day. However, supervisors are expected to make allowances for the necessary disruption caused by the election. If any problem arises, please contact the Plant Manager for instructions.

7. *THE VOTING AREA.* Please remember that during the time the polls are open, supervisors should not enter the area where the voting is taking place. You should not put yourself in any position where you can be seen from that area, except where absolutely required by your work. If it is required that a message be sent to someone in the voting place, the message should be carried by a nonsupervisory employee, preferably an ineligible office clerical employee.

8. *CAMPAIGN MATERIALS.* Be sure that all signs and posters on company bulletin boards with respect to the campaign or election, including stickers and other campaign materials placed on walls by anyone on the morning of the election, *except* the official Labor Board election notice, are removed no later than 1 hour before the polls open.

On election day, here are the guidelines you are instructed to follow:

WHAT YOU CAN DO

1. We can and should encourage every employee to vote.
2. We can visit each employee at his or her work station and ask for their support by voting "NO."
3. We can say to each employee at work stations, "We're counting on you to vote in the election for your Company. I know I can count on you."

4. We can say, "By voting "NO" you will be voting for yourself, for me, and for your family."
5. We can say, "Even if you have signed a union card, you can now vote "NO." The ballot is completely secret."
6. We can answer any question of employees as to where to vote and when to vote.

But remember—*you cannot* force, insist, or demand that a person vote.

The Election Results

Election day produced a victory for the company by a margin of 10%. Thus, this campaign is a textbook example of how strong, vigorous campaigning can reverse the attitude of a staff that was virtually the same one that voted in the first election.

Since no objections were filed by the union, none of the letters, communications, or speeches were litigated before the NLRB. Since the campaign did not receive Board approval, the legality of the communications cannot be guaranteed. However, the statements, letters, and speeches were carefully phrased in order to comply with existing Board decisions and with the language used in other campaigns which did receive Board approval. It is therefore believed that the campaign was an entirely permissible one. The vigorous campaigning, and the high level of communications needed to overcome the existing employee predisposition illustrated by the union's victory in the first vote, demonstrates that silence is not golden in a union representation election.

The last campaign communication was a short but sincere letter from the Plant Manager to all employees:

> I want to give you my heartiest thanks and express my appreciation for your support of us in the election.
> We feel the election result is a victory for everyone in the company.
> Both local management and our parent company have tried hard to show you that we are seriously interested in you, and you may rest assured that we will work hard to justify the vote of confidence you have given us.
>
> Sincerely,
> ———————

Appendix 1

A Representative Sampling of NLRB Decisions Involving Card-Based Bargaining Orders Under The Principles Established By The Supreme Court in *NLRB v. Gissel Packing Co.*, 395 U.S. 585 (1969).

It is difficult to predict exactly when the Board will issue a card-based bargaining order rather than its traditional remedy of ordering a second election. The facts of the cases vary, and apparently conflicting or inconsistent *Gissel* orders may be explained by minute differences in the factual setting of each case. The Board will, however, order a *Gissel* remedy where the employer unfair labor practices have the tendency to undermine the union's majority strength and impede the election process, and where the union has secured authorization cards signed by a majority. On the other hand, the Board will not issue a card-based bargaining order where (a) the employer's independent unfair labor practices are not so coercive, pervasive, or extensive as to require a bargaining order to remedy their unlawful effects, or (b) the application of the Board's traditional remedy would insure a fair election. Cases in which the Board has applied or declined to apply this drastic approach to the remedying of unfair labor practices are contained in this Appendix.

One court has even permitted the NLRB to take the *Gisell* remedy one step further and order a company to bargain with a union *before the Board had decided unfair-labor-practice charges pending before it.* Such interim relief was ordered where the company's threats, changes in wages and working conditions, and discharge of union supporters was found to have been designed to crush a unionization drive and defeat the union at the polls. *Gottfried v. Mayco Plastics, Inc.*, —— F. Supp. ——, 101 LRRM 2815 (E.D. Mich. 1979).

Part A
Cases in which the NLRB ordered employees to bargain because of unfair labor practices following union's obtaining authorization-card majority.
(*Gisell* bargaining orders)

● Change in operation resulting in the transfer of an employee in retaliation for union activity; harassing that employee until she quit (constructive discharge); discharging a union supporter; reducing the hours of two union supporters and threatening to freeze the wages of union supporters. *Dodson's Market, Inc.*, 194 NLRB 192, (1971).

● Questioning employees as to union support; threat of loss of jobs of employees who didn't sign sham contract; supporting and assisting in the foundation of a company union; suggesting that employees form an inside union;

suggesting and signing a ten-year contract with a fictitious local; assembling employees to discuss contract terms; paying employees for time in consultation with management; refusal to bargain with a legitimate union that had obtained a majority of cards. *Overland Distribution Centers, Inc.*, 194 **NLRB** 727 (1971).

• Threats to fire anyone who signed a union card; soliciting one employee to withdraw from the union and encouraging him to do so through an increase in salary; threats by president and co-owner of the company that if the union was chosen as the bargaining agent, the company could not afford to pay union scale and would, therefore, have to go out of business; refusal to reinstate a union supporter when foreman wanted that employee back; threatening physical harm against a union adherent. *Oahu Refuse Collection Co.*, 212 **NLRB** 224 (1974).

• Discharge of five drivers (the entire employee complement) for allowing unauthorized personnel on company premises. Employer failed to show that rule was universally applied. Unauthorized personnel were union organizers. *Fotomat Corporation*, 202 **NLRB** 59 (1973).

• The granting of wage increases at around thirty-five cents per hour for all employees; raising wages an additional thirty-five cents per hour to one employee who complained of not receiving a raise in eighteen months; wage increases accelerated. *Montgomery Ward & Co.*, 220 **NLRB** 373 (1975).

• Solicitation of grievances with a promise to remedy them; granting additional benefits in the form of wage increases to two employees; an announcement as to a change in health benefit plan, increasing the benefits thereunder. *Dallas Ceramic Co.*, 219 **NLRB** 582 (1975).

• Interrogation without adequate safeguards or assurances against reprisal; promises of wage increases; unlawful discharges for union activity. *Hennepin Broadcasting Associates, Inc.*, 215 **NLRB** 326 (1974).

• Soliciting grievances (with the express promise of benefit) from three of fifty-four employees; introduction of new work regulations; threat to one employee of reduction of hours; unlawful surveillance by the employer and his son; awarding a general wage increase. *Schwab Foods, Inc.*, 223 **NLRB** 394 (1976).

• Threats of plant closure and discharge by supervisor and manager; hiring of new employees to defeat union majority status; unlawful interrogation of employees as to union adherence; firing shots to intimidate pickets; denying reinstatement to strikers who made unconditional offers to return to work. *Hargis Mine Supply, Inc.*, 225 **NLRB** 660 (1976).

• Coercive interrogation of employees as to union activities; threatening discharges; promulgating invalid no-solicitation rule; discriminatory discharge. *Pilot Freight Carriers*, 223 **NLRB** 286 (1976).

• Offering medical, pension, and other benefits in return for withdrawal of employees' support from the union. *Zim Textile Corp.*, 218 **NLRB** 269 (1975).

• Changes in work rules as to break periods and smoking time; threatening at a meeting of the employees to close a store if a union came in; threatening to one employee that all pro-union employees would be eliminated; telling employee not to talk to anyone about the union at any time; closing of one of the employer's stores to chill unionism; discriminatory discharge of one employee for failing to call in every day that that employee was sick, contrary to prior practice. *Serv-U-Stores*, 225 NLRB 37 (1976).

• At a meeting attended by most of the employees of the unit, solicitation of grievances with a promise to remedy them; discharge of a supervisor in order to remove an unpopular condition of employment voiced by the employees; promising guarantee of a year's employment after scheduled election; impliedly threatening to transfer operations if union won; fulfillment of preelection promises after the election by granting employees further benefits of additional sick pay, vacations, holidays, and paid hospitalization, and replacing the 3 percent commission plan with a program more beneficial to the employees. *Eagle Material Handling*, 224 NLRB 1529 (1976).

• Questioning fourteen of the unit's twenty-three employees to learn who was behind the union campaign and what the employees expected to gain by having a union; subjecting two employees to detailed and patently coercive interrogation upon learning of their union adherence; granting a new benefit in the form of health and life insurance during the campaign: refusing to hire an employee who quit after unlawful interrogation, and conditioning rehire upon the union's loss of election; statement at employee meeting that selection of a bargaining representative would be a futile act. *Red Barn System, Inc.*, 224 NLRB 1586 (1976).

• Interrogation of employees; threat of plant closing; discharges for union activity. *Ultrasonic, DeBurning*, 233 NLRB No. 165 (1977).

• Bargaining ordered even where union engaged in strike misconduct since employer misconduct caused strike; promising wage increases; allowing supervisor to begin a decertification campaign; refusal to bargain after decertification petition was filed. *Grede Foundries*, 235 NLRB No. 40 (1978).

• Discharges due to union activity; interrogation and polling of employees; after strike, ending regular bonus of ten dollars per week; refusal to bargain. *726 Seventeenth, Inc.*, 235 NLRB No. 89 (1978).

• Threats of more stringent application of work rules; liberalization of pension eligibility requirements; withholding of raises because of union activity; withholding raises while election is pending after employer told employee that raises would be forthcoming. *Chatfield Anderson Co*, 236 NLRB No. 9 (1978).

• Discriminatory discharges of union adherents after employer learned of their union activity; no reason given for discharge and supervisor admitted union activity was a reason; state unemployment board found discharges not for misconduct; maintenance of a rule preventing solicitation on employee break time; discharge for violation of the rule; interrogation and impression of surveillance. *Flavo-Rich*, 234 NLRB 1011 (1978).

• Interrogating employee concerning union activities; informing employees that employer would not permit them to be represented by a union; employer stating he would go out of business if union was selected; employees were told that some were laid off so the company would have enough money to fight the union; laying off employees two days after union demanded recognition. *Unimedia Corp.*, 235 NLRB No. 215 (1978).

• Interrogation of employees concerning union activity; threatening reprisals because of union activity; threatening discharges of employees and plant shut-down; telling employees not to discuss union matters; discriminatory discharges due to union activity. *East Side Sanitation Service*, 234 NLRB 1099 (1978).

• During captive-audience speech, asking employees to wear "Vote No" buttons; making such buttons available only in plant manager's office; altering hiring dates of two employees to make them eligible to vote; telling employees that employer would not sign an agreement with union; telling two employees they were hired to vote against union; telling an employee she would be fired if she didn't vote for union; coercive interrogation of employees; threatened plant closure; solicitation of grievances and promise of remedy; postelection grants of benefits after "discussion" with a company-created and -dominated "labor organization." *Kurz-Kasch, Inc.*, 239 NLRB No. 107 (1978).

• Big hike (about 35 percent) in the basic wage schedule after union demanded recognition. *Honolulu Sporting Goods Co.*, 239 NLRB No. 173 (1979).

• Posting unlawful no-solicitation rules; interrogating employees; soliciting grievances and promising remedy; granting increased wages and benefits; threatening to close its store; creating an impression of surveillance; discharging union adherent; asking employee, who was applying for a leave of absence, if she was for the union. *Naum Bros., Inc*, 240 NLRB No. 50 (1979).

• Interrogating employees about their own and other employees' union activities; discharging a union adherent; giving an employee the impression of surveillance by correctly identifying the union adherent who brought the union to the company. *Baker Trucking Co.*, 241 NLRB No. 14 (1979).

Part B
Cases in Which the NLRB Decided that Employer's Conduct Did Not Warrant Card-Based Bargaining Order.

• Initiation, support, and domination of an employee committee; contrary to past practice, allowing contact with employer's president and personnel director. *Rennselaer Polytech. Inst.*, 219 NLRB 712 (1975).

• Threats to an employee fifteen months before an election; interrogation of an employee two weeks before the election; an ambiguous statement to top union adherents. *New Alaska Development Corp.*, 194 NLRB 830 (1972).

• Solicitation by management of grievances from two employees; further solicitation of grievances at two employee meetings where about ten of sixteen were addressed; promising shift differential to all of the potential members of the unit. *Flight Safety, Inc.*, 197 NLRB 223 (1972).

• Threatening reprisal (to one employee) and bankruptcy of the company if the union won. *Claremont Polychemical Corp.*, 196 NLRB 613 (1972).

• Threats by supervisor of stricter control as to whom each waitress would be permitted to serve, thereby lessening the amount of tips; coercive questioning of three employees as to their union adherence. *Treadway Inn*, 217 NLRB 51 (1975).

• Discriminatory termination of union adherent; violation of the Act by a single threat before the demand for recognition. *Munro Enterprises*, 210 NLRB 403 (1974).

• Unlawful interrogation of employees at a meeting; unlawful solicitation of employee grievances and promise of benefit; subsequent withholding of promised benefits. *Ring Metals Co.*, 198 NLRB 1020 (1972).

• Offer by supervisor to striking employees to arrange a meeting with employer for the purpose of obtaining increased pay and benefits; preparation and sponsorship of an employee petition to assist those employees in withdrawing from the union. *Dakota Sand & Gravel Co.*, 211 NLRB 1026 (1974).

• In a unit of 1,360 nonsupervisory employees: (1) telling one employee on one occasion that if the union won the election the store would probably close and, on another, that packing machines might be brought in to replace certain employees; (2) urging 10 to 15 employees to form a company union; (3) telling one employee that a union contract would require an examination; (4) telling a total of 10 to 13 employees that certain benefits would be lost if the union won; (5) interrogating approximately 20 employees as to their union sympathies. *May Department Stores Co.*, 211 NLRB 150 (1974).

• Promulgating and enforcing a discriminatory no-access and no-distribution rule against an employee; interrogating employees; threatening employees with loss of overtime; encouraging the formation of a grievance committee instead of a union. *Litho Press of San Antonio*, 211 NLRB 1014 (1974), *enf'd*, 512 F.2d 73 (5th Cir. 1975).

• Maintaining a rule prohibiting employees from distributing union literature on company premises even during their nonworking time in the nonworking areas; interrogating an employee as to whether he had signed a union card; soliciting signatures to the petition by which employees who had signed the union card had repudiated their further support of the union; discriminatorily discharging eight employees out of a group of eighty-five. *Grismac Corp.*, 205 NLRB 1108 (1973).

• Recognition of a rival union and assisting it by coercing employees to sign authorization cards for favored union; entering into a contract with favored union and enforcing a union security clause against nonunion employees. *Colony Knitwear Co.*, 217 NLRB 245 (1975).

• Interrogating three employees to force them to reveal their knowledge about the union and its activities; promulgation and enforcement of an unlawful no-solicitation rule; asking an employee to attend a union meeting for the purpose of providing the employer with the names of the employees present. *C&E Stores, Inc.*, 221 NLRB 1321 (1976).

• Interrogation of employees by a low-level supervisor whose exclusion from the unit was in doubt; single unlawful reprimand concerning supposed violation of a valid no-solicitation rule; wage increase not specifically tied to the organization campaign. *Walgreen Co.*, 221 NLRB 1096 (1975).

• Statements in the form of preelection letters containing a veiled threat from the employer that voting in the union would inevitably result in ultimate job loss for the union supporters. *NLRB v. Four Winds Industries*, 530 F.2d 75 (9th Cir. 1976).

• Warning employee against supporting the union and threatening loss of job; warning two other employees not to do anything to jeopardize their jobs and indicating their union support would do so; interrogation of six employees concerning their or other employees' union activities; threat by supervisor that unionization would bring the closing of the plant. *Sturges-Newport Business Forms, Inc.*, 227 **NLRB** 1426 (1977).

• Employer assaulting employee and threatening to harm employee's family if employee became or remained a member of the union; threatening to close office if employees chose to be represented by union. *Bruce Duncan Co.*, 233 **NLRB** 176 (1977).

• Supervisor stated to leading union adherent, in the presence of other employees, "You have just crucified yourself," after adherent had asked for equal time to reply to an employer's speech; issuing an unprecedented written reprimand to same union adherent allegedly for his tardiness; interrogating an employee about union activities of other employees notwithstanding a good faith belief that the employee was a supervisor. *Dependable Lists, Inc.*, 239 **NLRB** No. 195 (1979).

• Threatening employees with closing of bakery department of supermarket and threatening a cut in part-time employees' hours. *Shulte's Foodliner*, 241 **NLRB** No. 142 (1979).

Appendix 2

Board Rules on Invalidation of
Union Authorization Cards

Union authorization cards have been invalidated by the Board for the following reasons:

- Signature on the card was either forged or not authenticated by the General Counsel.
- Signatures on the cards were obtained by threats and coercion. (Coercion invalidates the cards only of those employees who were actually coerced or threatened. To invalidate *all* of the cards, there must be a showing of a pervasive pattern of threats, coercion, or intimidation.) See, *Wylie Mfg. Co.*, 170 NLRB 991 (1968).
- Signatures on cards were obtained by way of material misrepresentations that the employees relied upon. In *Marie Phillips, Inc.*, 178 NLRB 340 (1969), the Board stated the rule in the following manner:

> Where the objective facts, as evidenced by events contemporaneous with the signing, clearly demonstrate that the misrepresentation was the decisive factor in causing an employee to sign a card, we shall not count such card in determining a Union's majority. However, . . . where the only indication of reliance is a signer's subsequent testimony as to his subjective state of mind when signing the card, such showing is insufficient to invalidate the card . . . [F]or cards to be invalidated on the basis of such misrepresentations, it is necessary that the asserted reliance on the misrepresentations be established by objective evidence corroborating or supporting the subjective assertion.

- Signatures on cards were obtained through promises of benefits, e.g., improper waiver of initiation fees.
- The cards are ambiguous on their face, i.e., it is not clear from a reading of the card that the employee intended to designate the union as his bargaining representative.
- Cards were *unambiguous* on their face, but the union representatives soliciting the employees' signatures said that the cards would be used "only," "merely," or "exclusively" to obtain an election. *Serv-U-Stores, Inc.*, 234 NLRB 1143 (1978). Notwithstanding the union solicitor's statement, however, the cards may be valid if the employees read them before signing them, or knew their purpose. See *Hedstrom Co.*, 223 NLRB 1409 (1976); *Mutual Industries*, 159 NLRB 885 (1966); *Walgreen Co.*, 221 NLRB 1096 (1975); *W&W Tool & Die Mfg. Co.*, 225 NLRB 1000 (1976).
- The cards were revoked prior to a demand for recognition (unless such

revocation was provoked by the employer's coercion). *S.E. Nichols Co.*, 156 NLRB 1201 (1966).

• Signatures on the cards were solicited by supervisors. However, if cards were merely passed along by supervisors, or if the person soliciting was not represented to be a supervisor, or the supervisor did nothing more than voice his approval for the union, or attend a meeting when other employees signed their cards, or merely signed a card himself, the cards would not be invalidated.

• The cards are stale, i.e., there is too long a delay between the signing of the cards and the union's current representational campaign. A card signed one year prior to the union's demand for recognition was deemed to be too long a delay. See *Red & White Supermarket*, 172 NLRB 1841 (1968). However, a two-year delay was not deemed too long a period of time when there was no hiatus in proceeding upon an election petition.

• Signed cards were obtained from employees who were lawfully terminated, or left their employment, prior to a demand for recognition. See *General Stencils, Inc.*, 178 NLRB 108 (1969).

• An employee executed similar cards for rival unions; the Board's practice is to disallow both cards. See *Raymond Buick, Inc.*, 173 NLRB 1292 (1968).

• The card was altered by the employee before he signed it by lining through the word *membership*. See *NLRB v. Boyer Bros., Inc.*, 448 F.2d 555 (3rd Cir. 1971).

• The card was signed by an employee who later professed complete lack of understanding of the function of the union. See *Breaker Confections, Inc.*, 163 NLRB 882 (1967).

• If the employees who signed the card did not speak English and the purpose of the cards they were signing was not explained to them by union solicitors, and the employees had no independent understanding of what they were signing, the cards may be deemed invalid. See *Broncato Iron Works, Inc.*, 170 NLRB 75 (1968). Similarly, if the signer was illiterate and did not know what he was signing, the card may be invalidated. See *NLRB v. Texas Elec. Cooperatives, Inc.*, 398 F.2d 722 (5th Cir. 1968). On the other hand, if the non-English-speaking employees knew what they were signing, or the purpose of the cards they were signing was explained to them, the cards may be deemed valid. *726 Seventeenth, Inc.*, 235 NLRB No. 89 (1978).

• The card was signed by an employee who did not belong to the unit. See *Red & White Supermarket*, 172 NLRB 1841 (1968).

The following were not deemed sufficient grounds for invalidating union authorization cards:

• The union breached its representation to the employees that their cards would remain confidential. See *Steele Apparel Co.*, 172 NLRB 903 (1968); *Donna Lee Sportswear*, 174 NLRB 318 (1969).

• The employee who signed the card had impaired vision.

• The employee who signed the card was intoxicated at the time of signing. See *Mid-State Beverages, Inc.*, 153 NLRB 135 (1965).

• The employee later declares that when he signed the card he had no intention of joining the union. It is the Board's position that an employee's subjective state of mind cannot negate his overt conduct. See *J.M. Machinery Corp.*, 155 NLRB 860 (1965).

• Union solicitors induced signatures by making "no obligation" statements to the employees. *Fort Smith Outerwear, Inc.*, 205 NLRB 592 (1973). However, if a "no obligation" clause actually appears on the card, this might invalidate it if it was accompanied by oral assurances that the card would be used to obtain an election. See *Silver Fleet, Inc.*, 174 NLRB 873 (1969).

• Union solicitors made statements that only employees signing cards could attend union meetings. See *Sheet Metal Works*, 65 LRRM 2916 (1st Cir. 1967).

• The union distributed severance paychecks during a meeting in which union cards were signed. See *Liz of Rutland*, 156 NLRB 121 (1965).

• An authorization card was signed by an employee who was a minor at the time. See *U-Tote-M of Oklahoma, Inc.*, 172 NLRB 228 (1968).

• The card solicitor made certain insertions on the authorization card. See *S.E. Nichols Co.*, 156 NLRB 1201 (1966).

• The authorization card was signed by an employee before he commenced employment with the employer. See *General Steel Products, Inc.*, 157 NLRB 636 (1966).

• The cards did not name the union local or its international, but merely referred to "AFL-CIO." *Southbridge Sheet Metal Works, Inc.*, 158 NLRB 819 (1966).

• The card was completely filled out by a union organizer, except for the date and the signature of the employee, but it was ultimately signed by the employee himself. See *Mid-Western Manufacturing Co.*, 158 NLRB 1698 (1966). Similarly, cards have been deemed valid where they were not signed by the employees themselves but were signed by others on their behalf and with their express approval. See *Duboise Fence and Garden Co.*, 156 NLRB 1003 (1966). On the other hand, cards have been disallowed where it was shown that the employees could not write and there was insufficient evidence establishing the fact that the employees had authorized someone to sign the cards on their behalf. See *Shapiro Packing Co*, 155 NLRB 777 (1965).

• If the cards were properly signed they will be deemed valid even if the employees (1) claim they cannot remember signing the cards, (2) assert that the signatures are not theirs, or (3) refuse to identify their signatures. See *Yazoo Valley Elec. Power*, 163 NLRB 777 (1967); *Don the Beachcomber*, 163 NLRB 275 (1967). However, cards have been disallowed when employees testified that they had never signed such cards. See *Trend Mills, Inc.*, 154 NLRB 143 (1965).

• The employees printed their names rather than signed them; this is acceptable as long as the employees intended their printed names to be their signatures. See *Hercules Packing Corp.*, 163 NLRB 264 (1967). This practice has also been deemed to be acceptable if the employee only printed his first name. See *Foedge, Delivery & Trucking Service*, 172 NLRB 46 (1968).

• The card was signed by an employee who, prior to signing, announced his intention to quit at a future date. See *Blade-Tribune Publishing Co.*, 161 NLRB 1512 (1966).

- The cards contained a statement that authorization was irrevocable for one year; this does not make the authorization ineffective unless the employee testifies that the wording on the card caused him to believe that he could not withdraw his authorization. See *Southbridge Sheet Metal Works, Inc.*, 158 NLRB 819 (1966).
- The employee affixed his signature on the line marked "name" rather than on the line marked "signature." See *Shapiro Packing Co.*, 155 NLRB 777 (1965).

Appendix 3

Employee's Solicitation Rights and Corresponding Rights of Employers

Part A

A number of United States Supreme Court decisions and National Labor Relations Board cases have clarified employees' rights to discuss union organization among themselves and the corresponding right of an employer to protect itself against undue solicitation. The NLRB has developed and currently observes the following guidelines for dealing with the issues of union solicitation and distribution of union literature to employees by other employees (see Chapter 5 for a discussion of these rules):

- A rule that prohibits employees from distributing union literature in nonwork areas on the employees' own time is illegal, in the absence of special circumstances making the rule necessary to maintain discipline or production.

- A rule prohibiting the **distribution** of union literature in working areas, even on the employees' free time, is presumed valid. But **solicitation** during the employees' free time can't be forbidden, not even in work areas.

- Both distribution and solicitation anywhere in the plant or office on *working time* can be prohibited. However, rules prohibiting solicitation or distribution "during working *hours*" (e.g., blanketing the period 9:00 to 5:00 without excepting lunch periods and break times) are presumed invalid.

- Handing out union authorization or membership cards, with or without conversation, is *solicitation*, not distribution, and cannot be prohibited anywhere in the company during nonworking time, absent unusual circumstances.

Employers wishing to post a no-solicitation/no-distribution rule combined with a no-access rule may consider using either of the two following examples:

> In order to avoid interruption of your work and to protect you from unnecessary annoyance, employees are not permitted to solicit other employees on working time for any purpose.

> Distribution of literature during working time is not permitted. Distribution of literature in working areas is prohibited at all times.

> No employee should remain or enter upon company-owned premises unless the employee is on duty or scheduled for work.

Our employees are encouraged to take an active part in civic affairs and worthy charitable activities. However, in order to avoid interference with work and to protect *you* from unnecessary annoyance—soliciting of any kind, or distribution of literature on the premises during an employee's working time, is not permitted. Distribution of literature in working areas is not permitted at any time.

Due to the security requirement of our business, employees should not remain or enter upon company premises unless the employee is on duty or scheduled for work.

Another example, but without the no-access rule, is:

Our record of good citizenship is important to us. Therefore employees are encouraged to take an active part in civic affairs and worthy charitable and educational activities. However, to avoid interference with work and to protect you from unnecessary annoyance, soliciting of any kind, or distribution of literature on the premises during an employee's working time is not permitted.

Where it becomes necessary to implement a no-solicitation/no-distribution rule during a campaign, and where no prior rule has been established, the following may be posted:

As we all know, a drive to organize the plant is being conducted by the _____ union. While this activity is in progress, it is necessary for us to maintain normal production. Therefore, we ask that all employees refrain from union activities in the plant during working hours. This applies both to employees who favor the _____ union and those opposed to it. If necessary, employees violating this rule will be disciplined. We ask you to cooperate so that this will not be necessary.

The validity of a no-solicitation rule sometimes depends upon the particular industry. **Retail establishments** (i.e., companies that tend to have customers on the premises at most times) may post the following type of rule and apply it to stairways, corridors, escalators, customer elevators, and the selling floors.

Solicitations and distributions by persons who are not employees of this store are not permitted during store hours.

See *Montgomery Ward & Co.*, 202 NLRB 978 (1973); *Marshall Field & Co.*, 200 F.2d 375 (7th Cir. 1953). A restaurant is considered to be a retail establishment and may prohibit solicitation, even during break and lunch periods, in areas where customers are likely to be present. *Marriott Corp.*, 223 NLRB 978 (1976).

A retail employer—who may permissibly establish and enforce a broad no-solicitation rule that prohibits solicitation in customer areas during both working and nonworking time—must be aware of the disadvantage of such a broad rule. Because of the character of such businesses, they are permitted to significantly restrict employees' self-organizational rights by foreclosing union discussion among employees at their place of work. However, in the Board's view, where such an employer utilizes not only company premises but company time to bring its antiunion message to employees, it creates a glaring imbalance in organizational communication. Therefore, the Board has ruled that although a retail employer was not obliged to forego utilizing its working time and premises for its own antiunion campaign, it was under an obligation, in order to allow a proper balance to be maintained, to accede to the union's request to address the employees on company time and property. Refusal to do so is a violation of the Act. To avoid being required to grant a union's request to reply to management talks about the union, the retailer may, as a matter of strategy, decide to apply the less broad rule generally used in other industries.

A permissible rule in **hospital and health care industries** is:

> In the interest of maintaining a proper hospital environment for our patients, solicitations and distributions by employees are forbidden in patient care areas at all times. Patient care areas include: patients' bedrooms, x-ray areas, therapy areas, operating rooms, and preoperation and postoperation preparation and recovery areas.
>
> Furthermore, solicitations and distributions of any kind by nonemployees are forbidden at any time on hospital property.
>
> Off-duty employees shall not return to the interior of any hospital building for any purpose.

Due to the complex and often conflicting Board decisions, no-solicitation/no-distribution or no-access rules should be cleared by counsel prior to being published in employer handbooks or on bulletin boards. This is especially true of rules or practices that seek to exempt certain company-sponsored solicitations from the operation of the rule. Since the *timing* of any such rule is often questioned by the NLRB, special care must be taken in such a case to obtain approval of counsel.

Part B
Legal Principles Applicable to No-Solicitation/
No-Distribution and No-Access Rules

• Under the law, there is a presumption that the enforcement and promulgation of a rule prohibiting union solicitation by employees outside working time, even though conducted on company property, is an unreasonable impediment to self-organization. Such a rule is discriminatory in the absence of evidence that special circumstances make the rule necessary for maintaining production and discipline. *Republic Aviation Corp. v. NLRB*, 324 U.S. 793 (1945).

• A no-solicitation rule for working time is presumed valid in the absence of evidence that it was adopted for a discriminatory purpose. Working time is for work; but time outside working hours is an employee's time to use as he or she wishes without unreasonable restraint even though the employee is on company property. *Peyton Packing Co.*, 49 NLRB 828, 142 F.2d 1009 (5th Cir. 1944), *cert. den.* 323 U.S. 730 (1944).

• An employer may prohibit the distribution of union literature by *non-employee* union organizers if reasonable efforts through other available channels of communication will enable the union to reach employees and if the employer does not discriminate against the union by allowing distribution by other non-employees. *NLRB v. Babcock & Wilcox Co.*, 351 U.S. 105 (1956); *G.C. Murphy Co.*, 171 NLRB 370 (1968).

• If access to employees is not otherwise available (for example, in company towns and lumber camps), the employer's property must be made available to the union organizers. *NLRB v. Babcock & Wilcox Co.*, 351 U.S. 105 (1956); *NLRB v. Lake Superior Lumber Corp.*, 167 F.2d 147 (6th Cir. 1948); *NLRB v. Stowe Spinning Co.*, 336 U.S. 226 (1949).

• While oral solicitation by employees may be prohibited only during working time, distribution of literature and other written campaign material by employees may be prohibited during working time *and* in working areas. *Stoddard-Quirk Mfg. Co.*, 138 NLRB 615 (1962).

• The solicitation of co-employees' signatures on union authorization cards is treated by the Board as oral solicitation. *Stoddard-Quirk Mfg. Co., supra,* and *Rose Co.*, 154 NLRB 228 (1965).

• When a no-solicitation rule is drawn so broadly as to cover nonworking time it will be considered presumptively unlawful by the Board. Where there is an ambiguity in the rule, making it difficult for an employee to determine whether or not the rule applies to working time, the risk of ambiguity will be held against the employer rather than the employees. *NLRB v. Miller Charles & Co.*, 341 F.2d 870 (2d Cir. 1965); *Fashion Fair, Inc.*, 163 NLRB 97 (1967).

• An exception to the presumption that no-solicitation rules may not encompass nonworking time exists in retail department stores, which may prohibit employee solicitations on the selling floor even during nonworking time because of the nature of the retail business. *Marshall Field & Co.*, 34 NLRB 1 (1941).

• If the employer's rule prohibits solicitation for any cause during working time and the distribution of literature during working hours or in working areas without permission, the Board will consider such a rule invalid unless the employer can show that its practice in enforcing the rule did not prohibit distribution of literature during nonworking periods. This is so because the phrase "working hours" could mean the entire time the employee is on the clock; "working hours" is broader than the term "working time." *Essex International, Inc.*, 211 NLRB 749 (1974).

• A no-solicitation rule prohibiting solicitation during "working time" is presumptively valid because "working time" means the time the employees actually spend performing employee functions. *Lebanon Apparel Corp.*, 243 NLRB No. 136 (1979).

• A presumptively valid rule will also be presumed by the Board to be validly promulgated and enforced. However, these presumptions can be rebutted if an antiunion discriminatory purpose was involved in either the adoption or the application of the rule. *Walton Mfg. Co.*, 126 NLRB 697, 289 F.2d 177 (5th Cir. 1961).

• The Board will scrutinize the extent to which the promulgation of a no-solicitation rule coincides with the advent of a union on the employer's premises. *William H. Block Co.*, 150 NLRB 341 (1964); *Ward Mfg. Inc.*, 152 NLRB 1270 (1965). If the union is able to demonstrate that a rule was posted during a time of intense union activity, that its first application was with respect to a union sympathizer, that permission for solicitation of other kinds has been given during working time, and that there was hostility toward union organizational efforts, the presumption of validity will normally be rebutted. *State Chemical Co.*, 166 NLRB 455 (1967).

• However, if an employer promulgates a no-solicitation rule in order to stop a provable decline in productivity, the rule will not be deemed in violation notwithstanding its promulgation shortly after the advent of union campaign activity. *Bankers Club, Inc.*, 218 NLRB 22 (1975); *North American Rockwell Corp.*, 195 NLRB 1046 (1972).

• An employer which has not adopted a no-solicitation rule may not, even prior to working hours, seize union literature placed by employees on the unattended desks of co-workers. *F.W. Woolworth Co. v. NLRB*, 530 F.2d 1245 (5th Cir. 1976), *enforcing* 216 NLRB 945 (1975).

• A nondiscriminatory rule prohibiting off-duty employees from entering or remaining on the plant premises for any purpose is valid. *GTE Lenkurt, Inc.*, 204 NLRB 921 (1973). However, a no-access rule directed solely at employee solicitation is presumptively invalid and unlawful. *M. Restaurants, Inc.*, 221 NLRB 264 (1975).

• A rule denying off-duty employees access to the employer's premises is valid only if it applies solely to the interior of the plant and other working areas, is clearly disseminated to all employees, and applies to off-duty employees seeking access to the plant for any purpose. *Tri-County Medical Center*, 222 NLRB 1089 (1976).

• It is unlawful to prohibit solicitation by employees on company premises when they have completed their shift but are still lawfully on company property pursuant to the work relationship. *M Restaurants, Inc.*, 221 NLRB 264 (1975); *East Bay Newspapers, Inc.*, 225 NLRB 1148 (1976).

• A no-access rule prohibiting all loitering "on the premises" by off-duty employees is ambiguous, potentially unlimited in its application, and therefore illegal. *Continental Bus System, Inc.*, 229 NLRB No. 180 (1977).

• Where an employer allows non-employees, such as food vendors and news salesmen, to enter and utilize a parking lot, the employer will lose the right to enforce its valid no-access rule against an employee. *Chrysler Corp.*, 232 NLRB 466 (1977).

• A no-access rule that attempts to restrict solicitation by employees after their shifts have ended will be invalidated where employees would otherwise be permitted to remain after work. Such rules are also invalid if they specifically prohibit solicitation. *Sparks Nugget, Inc.*, 230 NLRB 275 (1977); *Carda Hotels, Inc.*, 228 NLRB 926 (1977).

• Parking lots and other areas within a shopping center complex present their own particular problems. In determining whether prohibition of access to such areas is reasonable, the standards enunciated by the Supreme Court in *Babcock & Wilcox*, 351 U.S. 105 (1956), apply. *Hudgens v. NLRB*, 424 U.S. 507, 91 LRRM 2489 (1976).

• An employer violates the Act when it causes or induces the arrest of pickets for picketing on shopping mall premises. *Scott Hudgens*, 230 NLRB 414 (1977); *Eastex Inc. v. NLRB*, 556 F.2d 1280 (5th Cir. 1977), *cert. granted,* ____U.S.____ (1978); *Hutzler Bros. Co.*, 241 NLRB No. 141 (1979) (where the Board held a department store violated the Act by barring union organizers from distributing literature outside two entrances opening onto parking lots owned by the store).

• The rules in the health care industry are governed by different considerations. A hospital may prohibit solicitation *even on nonworking time* in strictly patient care areas. Any ambiguity will be resolved against the employer. *St. John's Hospital*, 222 NLRB 1150 (1976); *Lutheran Hospital of Milwaukee*, 224 NLRB 176 (1976). However, health care facilities must permit employee solicitation of union support and distribution of union literature during nonworking time in nonworking areas unless such activity is necessary to avoid disrupting health care operations or disturbing patients. *Beth Israel Hospital v. NLRB*, 434 U.S. 1033 (1978).

The United States Supreme Court has upheld the right of a hospital to bar employees from soliciting union support or distributing union literature in corridors and small public rooms or sitting areas adjoining or accessible to patients' care floors or rooms. However, a hospital may not enforce its no-solicitation rule in a hospital cafeteria, gift shop, or first-floor lobbies. *NLRB v. Baptist Hospital, Inc.*, ____ U.S. ____, 101 LRRM 2556 (1979).

Appendix 4

Attitude Surveys

Chapter 7 contains a discussion of the legal ways of developing employee feedback during a campaign. Attitude surveys are one of the methods of determining employee opinion, but they must be handled with care. Sample questionnaires appear in this Appendix as a useful guide to the campaigner. Prior to undertaking the use of any particular survey or individual question, the principles and pitfalls discussed in Chapter 7 should be studied carefully and advice of counsel obtained.

TO: ALL EMPLOYEES
FROM: PERSONNEL DIRECTOR
SUBJ: EMPLOYEE ATTITUDE SURVEY

The purpose of the attitude survey is to improve motivation, efficiency, productivity.

Please answer the questions frankly. We want your opinions. The questionnaire cannot possibly be identified with you in any way.

Check the *one answer* to each question that best describes what *you* think. If you care to comment or add to your answer, write on the back of the questionnaire. Please number such comments to correspond to the question number.

Thank you for your cooperation.

<u>DO NOT SIGN YOUR NAME!</u>

1. My workplace is
   (a)_____swell
   (b)_____okay
   (c)_____not too good
   (d)_____pretty bad

*2. The toilets and dressing rooms are
   (a)_____fine
   (b)_____okay
   (c)_____not too good
   (d)_____pretty bad

*3. I think our lunch break should be
   (a)_____one hour

   (b)_____45 min.
   (c)_____30 min.

4. The training I got was
   (a)_____all I needed
   (b)_____nearly all I needed
   (c)_____not enough
   (d)_____I didn't get any training

*5. The hours I work are
   (a)_____fine
   (b)_____okay
   (c)_____not too good
   (d)_____pretty bad

*6. The amount of work I have
to do is
(a)_____fine
(b)_____okay
(c)_____a little too much
(d)_____too much

7. The way my supervisor treats
me is
(a)_____fine
(b)_____okay
(c)_____not too good
(d)_____pretty bad

8. My supervisor plays favorites
(a)_____never
(b)_____seldom
(c)_____usually
(d)_____always

*9. The way my complaints are
handled is
(a)_____fine
(b)_____okay
(c)_____not too good
(d)_____pretty bad

10. My supervisor lets me know
where I stand
(a)_____always
(b)_____usually
(c)_____seldom
(d)_____never

11. My supervisor gives me credit
for a good job when I do one
(a)_____always
(b)_____usually
(c)_____seldom
(d)_____never

12. I get orders from too many
people
(a)_____never
(b)_____seldom
(c)_____frequently
(d)_____always

*13. The pay here is
(a)_____good
(b)_____okay
(c)_____somewhat low
(d)_____very low

*14. My pay here, compared with
that for the same work at
other companies, is
(a)_____higher
(b)_____about the same
(c)_____somewhat lower
(d)_____much lower

15. My opportunity to advance
here is
(a)_____very good
(b)_____all right
(c)_____fair
(d)_____poor

16. Company policies are made
clear to me
(a)_____always
(b)_____usually
(c)_____seldom
(d)_____never

17. I think that conditions here,
compared with other companies
in this area, are
(a)_____very good
(b)_____okay
(c)_____not too good
(d)_____pretty bad

*18. If I were offered my same job
at another company at the same
rate of pay, I would
(a)_____not be interested
(b)_____check into it
(c)_____probably change
(d)_____take it right away

19. The people in this community
and area think the company is
(a)_____a very good place to
work
(b)_____a good place to work
(c)_____not too good a place
to work
(d)_____a pretty bad place to
work
(e)_____I don't know how they
feel about it

*20. The life insurance plan
(a)_____is okay

(b)_____is not needed
(c)_____should be replaced
    with something else

21. I think the Profit-Sharing
Program
    (a)_____is a good idea
    (b)_____has not been
        explained to my
        satisfaction
    (c)_____is not too good
    (d)_____should be replaced
        with something else

22. The Blue Cross-Blue Shield
Plan
    (a)_____is okay
    (b)_____is too expensive
    (c)_____should provide more
        coverage

23. A suggestion plan to help make
the company more profitable and
a better place to work is
    (a)_____needed
    (b)_____not needed

24. The people I work with
    (a)_____are okay
    (b)_____spread too many
        rumors
    (c)_____gripe too much
    (d)_____do not work as a
        team

25. I think chances like this to
say what I think
    (a)_____have been needed before
    (b)_____are a good idea
    (c)_____are worth a trial
    (d)_____are a waste of time

	AGREE	DISAGREE
1. I always feel free to speak to anyone in top management.	☐	☐
2. Top management here tries to make this a good company in which to work.	☐	☐
*3. The hours of work (starting and ending) are satisfactory.	☐	☐
4. The company tries to make this a safe place to work.	☐	☐
5. Pay for this type of work is not as good here as in other companies in this area.	☐	☐
6. My boss gives praise where praise is due.	☐	☐
7. Good cooperation exists between departments.	☐	☐
*8. Our insurance plan provides good coverage.	☐	☐
9. My efforts and cooperation are not recognized by this company.	☐	☐
10. This company keeps us informed about new plans and developments.	☐	☐
11. As long as I do good work, I feel sure of my job.	☐	☐
12. I would not recommend this company to my friends for employment.	☐	☐
13. My pay rate is fair and equitable.	☐	☐
14. If layoffs should occur, the company would be fair in its layoff system.	☐	☐
*15. I am not supplied with proper safety equipment.	☐	☐
16. My boss often doesn't keep his promises.	☐	☐

17. People here get promotions when they are deserved.   ☐   ☐
*18. My pay provides me with a comfortable living.   ☐   ☐
19. My co-workers are cooperative and work well together.   ☐   ☐
*20. Our benefit plans, including holidays, vacations, etc., are good.   ☐   ☐
21. I am well trained on new and old jobs.   ☐   ☐
22. Many times, top management here does not have my interest in mind.   ☐   ☐
23. My abilities and skills are not used by this company.   ☐   ☐
24. Frequently I am sorry that I applied here for a job.   ☐   ☐
25. My boss is not capable of doing his job.   ☐   ☐
26. This company pays little attention to its employees.   ☐   ☐
27. Frequently I become bored with my job.   ☐   ☐
*28. Rest rooms are adequate—neat and clean.   ☐   ☐
*29. In my opinion we do not have benefits equal to other companies in this area.   ☐   ☐
30. The longer I work here, the better I enjoy it.   ☐   ☐
31. Communications are poor; we are given little or no information about the company.   ☐   ☐
32. There is not much chance for promotion.   ☐   ☐
33. My boss generally gives me clear-cut instructions.   ☐   ☐
34. We are encouraged to make suggestions for improvements in our work.   ☐   ☐
35. I am pleased to tell others where I work.   ☐   ☐
36. Top management here is fair and honest with me.   ☐   ☐
37. My work is pleasant—I am not pushed for more than I can do.   ☐   ☐
38. My boss is very fair with me.   ☐   ☐
*39. I feel I have very little job security.   ☐   ☐
40. I do not think our top management here will make any improvements for our benefits as the result of my completing this form.   ☐   ☐
41. Top management here is efficient in running the company.   ☐   ☐
42. My boss is always pushing me for more work than I can do.   ☐   ☐
43. This company never informs us about changes, even those affecting our welfare.   ☐   ☐
*44. I feel that I am underpaid.   ☐   ☐
45. Some of my co-workers think they run the company.   ☐   ☐

46. My boss is a poor organizer and does not manage his job well. ☐ ☐

47. Consideration and attention are shown to me when I use good judgment and initiative. ☐ ☐

48. Top management here is not friendly toward the employees. ☐ ☐

49. You can be fired here for petty things. ☐ ☐

50. In my opinion, top management here could operate the company more efficiently. ☐ ☐

*51. I could do better work if safety conditions were improved. ☐ ☐

*52. The company's benefits for its employees are inadequate. ☐ ☐

53. I think filling out this form is a good thing. ☐ ☐

54. I am always expected to do more than I am able to do. ☐ ☐

55. There is a future here for those who wish to advance. ☐ ☐

56. This company generally gives recognition for my cooperation and loyalty. ☐ ☐

57. Too much friction exists between co-workers. ☐ ☐

58. Top management here does not supply me with the necessary equipment to do a good job. ☐ ☐

59. I can see no good in filling out this form. ☐ ☐

60. I think top management here will use the results of this survey to our best interest. ☐ ☐

The asterisked questions deal with terms and conditions of employment. The employer may wish to omit these questions in order to avoid a charge alleging solicitation of grievances with an implied promise to correct them. (See Chapter 7, Development of Feedback.)

Appendix 5

Lawful or Unlawful—Employer Campaign Statements the NLRB Has Ruled on

Part A
Campaign Statements Ruled Lawful

The Disadvantages of Unionization

I am sure that it is not any news to you that some union organizers have been busy in town for several weeks now making an effort to get you involved by signing their cards. I have heard reports about their promises . . . high wages . . . funeral pay . . . free insurance, and so forth . . . However they have never told anyone exactly how they expect to accomplish these things. . . . For almost thirty years we have never lost a day's work or a single paycheck because of being involved in a strike or because you were forced to stand on a picket line . . . Yet there are thousands of union members across the country who are out of work and are looking for jobs . . . You have never had to experience plant closings or work cutbacks like many union plants in this area. . . . So if the union salespeople come around our best advice is simply to tell them that you do not wish to become involved unless they can give you a written guarantee they will never cause you any trouble or cause you to lose your job or your paycheck. . . . If they don't have enough respect for you to give you that written guarantee . . . I surely wouldn't trust them with my signature . . . Because when you sign a union card you give them a blank check to use your name for any reason they see fit . . .

One thing disturbs me and that is the reports that I have heard saying the union salespeople have threatened some of you by saying if you don't sign their card if they get in you would lose your job . . . I would like to make this perfectly clear: No one now or in the future will lose their jobs here because they refused to sign the union card . . . The union has no power to hire or fire anyone . . . This threat evidently is a last-ditch try to get our people involved. . . . They really don't give us credit for having any sense . . . They must think we are stupid enough to swallow anything they say . . .

Let me tell them this . . . We are not stupid; we know what we have now . . . We know from our past experiences that our factory is run better . . . works steadier . . . and gives us more privileges than any other plant like ours . . . We keep building up our benefits—which were all given to us voluntarily . . . No one has ever had to threaten me to get any of these benefits . . . and no one will ever have to threaten me for future benefits.

But more than any benefit is the fact that we work in a friendly atmosphere . . . We do not enjoy having outsiders coming in to cause friction amongst us in order for them to collect around $35,000 each year out of your pockets in union dues alone. Why don't they put their efforts in helping people who are unfortunate enough to have been involved in their unions and are practically starving because they are out on strikes and are not drawing any paychecks?

Should any of you find that you are being threatened or coerced by these people, feel free to discuss it with me . . . Also, if you have any questions as to what a union can or cannot do, meet with me and I will try to get you an answer which would be true and accurate.

One more thing . . . one of the main points these union people are making is that for your dues and assessments you will get free insurance . . . these people carry their own policy and they control it accordingly . . . and it is my understanding that it is not as good as the policy we have. Our insurance happens to be the best for the money and it gives you full protection. Free insurance . . . with no strings attached.

Wilker Bros. Co., 236 NLRB No. 178 (1978).

The Disadvantages of Unionization Combined with Appeal to Company Loyalty

We have been a struggling company that has tried to make a success. Now, with Dart Industries behind us there should be a wonderful future.

You have an absolute right to know what your part in this future will be as we see it.

First, the future of the job security of each of you that does his or her job is good. We are not going to discharge a person because they backed a union.

You have a right to ask what kind of financial future you are going to have if you stay non-union. We are restricted by law as to what we can tell you during a union organizing campaign. We can lawfully tell you the things that are in existence. You may choose to share in our Profit Sharing Plan which is known as one of the finest programs for working people. If you stay with the company and develop, as we are sure that you will, you should have much more money in this plan compared with any Teamster plan. You get to take all or part of this money with you after the very first year that you are in the plan. Under Teamster plans you would, in most cases, forfeit all that had been put into it for you if you leave while you are young.

The Teamsters are not very important in the chemical industry. If you wish to progress, then in my judgment, you are better to leave them alone and stay in the chemical industry, whether with us or with other companies. This is a highly specialized and skilled industry. This is an industry which pays well when plants are running, producing and profitable.

* * *

Our policy is to pay fairly. By fairly we mean in accordance with the standards of the community and similarly situated plants in the community. I have been planning a review of our wage structure. We should re-examine the relationship between the wages of our various groups of employees. We should re-examine the fairness of our classifications to see if there need to be more or fewer classifications. We should take another look at the time it takes to reach the top rates. We should look at those top rates.

You have a right to ask whether we would give a raise if the Teamsters get in. No one can say. I would expect that you will get just as much nonunion as you would union.

There are many reasons why with a good, modern, soundly managed company the *non-union* life is better. A few reasons are:

1. You don't have to pay dues.
2. You don't have to attend union meetings.
3. You don't get pulled into strikes over other peoples' problems.
4. You don't have to pay initiation fees.
5. Most important, you can often more easily be a partner with your company if you are non-union.

You have a right to ask, "Would the company take a strike with a union as powerful as the Teamsters." The Chemical Division over its lifetime has had four negotiations.* All these unions are gone from our plants now. There have been three strikes out of the four negotiations. One of these was the Teamsters. We did have a seven week strike with them. Do not take this to say that the company would cause a strike. We would try not to. A strike would come (if it came) if the union tried to push us into an area which we regard as being unsound for our company.

We are beginning to put together the kind of team that can accomplish great things here. Each and everyone of you is an important, even an essential, part of the team. I think that you should give this team a chance to function without any interference from the outside. I think that you will find that what we have here with a little bit of success is something that you can be very proud of. We still have a long way to go. We still have a lot of work. We still expect to make major mistakes. We do hope to manage better than we have ever managed before.

I personally pledge that I will take a deep and continuing interest in what is happening in the plant and in the laboratory. By doing this, if I do my job and you do yours, I am sure it will be better than if we have the Teamsters.

You have an absolute right to vote your own wishes. Be sure to vote. Be sure to regard this vote as one of the most important in your life because you spend a lot of time in this plant. Your future and the plant life here will be affected by this vote. It can't possibly be the same here if there is a union. The union would say that the change would be for the better. I don't think so.

Pure Chem. Corp., 192 NLRB 681 (1971)

Expressing the Possible Futility of Selecting
the Union in Light of Company's Past Record

"If you want to be treated like number or machine—several plants in the area work that way. . . ."

*   *   *

"Better communications will solve most of our problems here and we've made a good start on improving them. Let me just add two of our basic company policies in case you need reminding: One is that any member of management is available to any member of the work force to discuss problems of any nature. The other is that we will always be willing to give as much without outside interference as we would be willing to give because of union pressure." He concluded by stating, "I've been quoted as saying that I would close this plant if it went union, but I have not said that, nor could I say it, because I believe we are here and we are here to stay, because we want to be here."

*   *   *

"Any member of management is available to any member of the work force to discuss problems of any nature. We will always be willing to give as much without outside interference as we would be willing because of union pressure."

Munro Company, Inc., 217 **NLRB** 1011 (1975).

Appeal to Company Loyalty

Despite our size, we have *always* done all we could to make you happy, and to make this a place where you would be proud to work. We, in turn, are very proud of the many outstanding benefits we have been able to provide our employees, and we are equally proud of providing these benefits *without* the intervention of an outside union. Remember, the benefits and working conditions you have received here have all been *free*. By "free" I mean that you have *never* paid a union initiation fee to receive them, nor have you *ever* been forced to pay union dues, fees or assessments. Most importantly, you have never had to *miss work* because of *strikes, picketing or boycotting* to achieve what you now have at Woods.

*   *   *

The benefits described in this letter have been provided to all of us, *without any pressure whatsoever* from any outside union. There has been no union standing between us, nor have you been required *to pay* union dues, fines, assessments, or *be subject to* any union discipline to receive these benefits. Most importantly, *you did not* have to strike or picket *or lose paychecks* to get these benefits. They have been provided voluntarily *because they were the best we could provide at the time, and that is exactly what this Company always intends to do*. No union on earth can ever get us to provide more benefits than we can afford to pay.

I know that things are not perfect here at Woods. In the past, improvement has come about largely because of *your* suggestions. *Let's keep it that way*.

Because of this election, Federal law prohibits me from telling you about any of our future plans regarding your wages, hours and working conditions. In this regard, our hands are thus temporarily tied.

All I can say for now is that this election means a lot to all of us. When you hear the union make its typical *promises* (and that's all they are—*mere* promises), I hope you will keep in mind the things this Company *has done* voluntarily for you, and the fact that these things have been done *without* your paying union dues, fees, fines or assessments whatsoever. It has *always* been our policy to provide you with the *best benefits we can*, and no union on earth can make us do more than that.

J. R. Wood, Inc., 228 NLRB 593 (1977).

Characterizing the Consequences of Bargaining

The election that we've all been talking and thinking so much about will be held right here in our plant on Friday, September 26, from 10:00 a.m. to 12:00 noon, and again from 5:00 p.m. to 7:00 p.m. I urge everyone to vote. The election will truly be a *secret ballot* election conducted by the United States Government. The Union will not conduct the election. *The Union will not know how you vote. Other employees will not know how you vote.*

It doesn't matter whether or not you signed any kind of Union cards or other Union papers because Federal Law protects your right to vote against the Union no matter what you may have said, signed, or done before. It is illegal for the Union or anybody else to interfere with your right to vote against this Union.

If you make the mistake of letting this outside Union win the election, as I explained before, there will be no automatic increases in wages or in overtime or in anything else, *regardless* of what the Union may have told you. Instead, the Teamsters will have to sit down and bargain with us about everything. So everything you now have can be put on the bargaining table and you could end up with more benefits, the same benefits, or fewer benefits than you now have. We may be able to reach agreement or we may come to a deadlock and have no contract, depending upon what happens in negotiations. We have no duty to agree on a contract and neither does the Union. If we do not reach agreement, and if there is a deadlock in negotiations, there is one way that the Teamsters could try to force us to agree to its demands, even if we consider those demands unreasonable or which we otherwise cannot see our way clear to accept. What this Union can do is pull *you* out on strike! How many of you have ever been out of work on strike?

I think most of you know me well enough to know that I mean it when I say that we have no intention of yielding to pressure tactics of that kind —ever! I think you also know that we've always voluntarily tried to provide you with the best wages and benefits we can afford.

J. R. Wood, Inc., 228 NLRB 593 (1977).

Predicting the Consequences of a Lockout

YOU COULD BE LOCKED OUT*

Did you know that if this Union is unable to reach agreement with us, we are entitled by law to lock out employees. Have the Teamsters been honest enough to tell you about this? Did you know that such a lock-out could *permanently* cost you your job? We would sure hate to ever have to make that decision, but anything is possible when a union is fighting an employer. I hope, of course, that you will vote against the Union so that it will never be necessary for you or your families ever to consider the possibility of a strike or lock-out. But in deciding whether or not you want to support this Union, you should realize that strikes, picketing and trouble are facts of life whenever a union is involved. Where unions are, that's when strikes occur.

Some union strikes have, of course, been longer and rougher than others. During Teamster Union strikes in Northern California, it has often been necessary to get temporary restraining orders or court injunctions against Teamsters' interference with employees, customers and suppliers, threats of violence, actual violence, and illegal picketing, in order to maintain law and order. I hope we never have anything like it here. I don't say for sure that the Teamsters would definitely strike at Wood's, or that picketing and violence necessarily are going to happen here, but I do know that it has happened before with many unions and I do know that it *could* happen here. In recent months the newspapers have been full of news about various strikes, picketing and Teamster violence and trouble. You may have read the article about Local 748's strike against Carnation Company in Modesto earlier this year, and the violence, vandalism, jailed pickets, and court orders issued against Local 748 because of that strike. I would hate to see anything like that happen to you and me. Don't let it happen at Wood's—vote "NO."

If the Teamsters win, and in order to try to deliver on its promises you are

---

* In its decision in this case, the lawfulness of the *lockout* communication was not considered on its merits by the Board majority. One member was of the opinion that the communication was coercive and outside of the free speech protection of the Act.

called out on strike, I want you to understand what it really can mean to you and your family:

J. R. Wood, Inc., 228 NLRB 593 (1977).

Depicting the Realities of Bargaining

Our wages are reviewed on a continuing basis, and we have made every possible adjustment within the reimbursement formula which is imposed on us by the . . . State Department of Health. The union would be powerless to change your wages at this time, and they know it.

Nevertheless, the organizers will undoubtedly make many promises during this election campaign, and you should know:
- The union cannot guarantee a wage increase;
- The union cannot guarantee job security;
- The union cannot guarantee better working conditions;
- The union cannot guarantee that you will keep the benefits you already have.

Only we can make these commitments.

*   *   *

From what I hear, the union organizers are continuing to make vague promises without any indication of what, if anything, they intend to get for you. You don't have to look far to see an example of a union's failure to obtain any significant benefits for its members. We have had the Operating Engineers' Union at BEECHWOOD for over four years. Its members have not received any more fringe benefits than any other BEECHWOOD employee, nor have they received any more wage adjustments than anyone else at BEECHWOOD. In fact, because they pay union dues each and every month, they take home less than other nonunion BEECHWOOD employees earning the same amount.

Although the union will tell you that they can be easily removed if you should change your mind, don't believe it for a minute. Once a union is in, it is extremely difficult to get them out. Decertification elections are rare and normally do not occur unless there has been a strike or serious labor unrest. You can be sure that once they enroll you on their dues list, they will fight any attempt by you to get out of the union. It would be a tragedy for you and your family if you did not vote and a small group of disgruntled employees seized control of your working life.

I am still not aware of any concrete benefit that the union intends to seek if it should win the election. We believe the working conditions at BEECHWOOD are at least equal to any in the industry. Our benefits and wages are constantly being reviewed, and we have upgraded them as frequently as possible within the reimbursement rates imposed on BEECHWOOD by New York State. In order to obtain these wages, benefits, and working conditions, no employee has been required to pay dues or otherwise contribute any part of his pay to a labor union. As you know, paying union dues could actually result in less take home pay for you and would be a severe hardship for our many part-time employees.

*   *   *

The first important issue seems to be what the union intends to do for you. I have not heard of one instance where they told you in plain English what they propose to do for the employees at Beechwood. As I have said before, our wages are at least as good as any in the industry, and you are fooling yourself if you think getting the union in here is going to result in any immediate increase in your wages. Those wage rates are fixed by the reimbursement plan of the state, and we are doing everything we can to get more for our employees. Employees at other health care facilities did not receive any more due to the fact that they were in a union. Each and every month they have to take out a significant amount of money from their pay and give it to the union in the form of dues. You should feel free to ask people working in other nursing homes in the area whether they think they are getting their money's worth from the union. I think you'll find they wish they had never gotten involved.

*   *   *

I have mentioned wages, but I think it is also important to talk about your benefits. Once again, Beechwood pays benefits that are comparable to any in the industry. You should know that you may be jeopardizing those benefits by letting the union in here. When the union negotiates a contract, they can negotiate away existing benefits in order to get something they want, such as a union shop clause. A union shop clause would require every Beechwood employee to join the union or else Beechwood would be forced to terminate their employment. That is not the way we have run this facility, and I hope that it never comes to that. We think we have an open and honest relationship with our employees, and I would hate to see it jeopardized by the intrusion of outsiders into a small facility like Beechwood. The best way to guarantee that our existing benefits are not jeopardized and that you and your fellow employees are not forced to pay dues to a big union like the nursing home council is to vote "no" in the election on Thursday.

Niagara Frontier Methodist Home, Inc., 232 NLRB No. 59 (1977).

Predicting the Possible Closedown of Operations

Against a background of a very substantial business decline with no foreseeable relief from the bleak economic climate existing within the industry at the time of the election, the employer, after assuring employees that the plant would *not* shut down just because of unionization, and in response to aggressive union statements and promises, sent a letter to his employees saying:

*　　*　　*

Right now *you* have it *better* than unionized employees represented by the union.

*　　*　　*

While you are free to vote as you please, if we were faced with added costs such as the union had indicated in the event of unionization, we might be pushed to the wall—it might be the straw that broke the camel's back—vote as if your job depended upon it.

> The Board held that prediction by an employer of possible adverse consequences of unionization, when pyramided on demonstrated existing business stringencies through reasonably foreseeable piling on of added cost factors, is not equivalent to a threat to close down operations in the event of unionization—particularly where the employer takes pains in writing to assure his employees explicitly that the plant will *not* be shut down just because of unionization.

Chrysler Airtemp, Inc., 224 **NLRB** 427 (1976). See also, *Mission Tire and Rubber Co.*, 208 **NLRB** 84 (1974); *Birdsall Construction Co.*, 198 **NLRB** 163 (1972).

Describing the Possible Consequences of Lawful Collective Bargaining

If the union tells you that what you now have is guaranteed, it is not telling you the truth! As the United States courts have said, the truth is that you can lose wages and benefits in collective bargaining. An excerpt from a federal case was printed in bold typeface reading:

THE UNITED STATES GOVERNMENT AND THE NLRB DO NOT GUARANTEE EMPLOYEES THAT THE COLLECTIVE BARGAINING PROCESS STARTS FROM WHERE YOU PRESENTLY ARE IN WAGES, INSURANCE, PENSIONS, PROFIT SHARING AND ALL OTHER CONDITIONS OF EMPLOYMENT.

*　　*　　*

The employer also stated: All your present and/or future benefits are ne-gotiable . . . the negotiation is going to start with a blank piece of paper and each present wage or each present benefit will be negotiated. . . . There is nothing automatic. . . ." and "negotiations is nothing else but very simple horse trading, it gets down to: I want this, what will you give me instead? And since the Union themselves have nothing to trade away, obviously the present and/or future benefits may be discussed and may be traded in order to get a union shop or check-off clause." President Bohn testified that throughout the speech he stressed his intention that, "if negotiations should start, that Ludwig Motors obviously would bargain in good faith, would bar-gain within the frame of the law."

Ludwig Motor Corp., 222 NLRB 635 (1976).

Predicting the Adverse Consequences of Unionism

Job Quotas and Layoffs

The employer stated that the union was the worst union, that it wanted only to organize the people for their money, and that he would be a hard bargainer if the union won; quotas would have to be raised if the union were successful because the union would cost him a lot of money and employees would have to go home if they ran out of department work rather than transferring to another department as they were accustomed to. The em-ployer also referred to the fact that in some cases union contracts are based on productivity rather than just granting raises without raising quotas.

Wesco Electrical Co., 232 NLRB No. 75 (1977).

Merit Systems and Sick Pay

There have been claims of unfair treatment in administering our merit sys-tem and our policy of pay continuation. The alternative, as I see it, should the union be involved, is to negotiate regulated pay increases for all employ-ees and to pay no one for absences. This is contrary to our philosophy of trust and recognition of better work performance. Accepting the possibility for errors in all systems, we feel that the opportunity to reward an individual is far superior to the inequities of a forced system of uniform rules.

Federal-Mogul Corp., 232 NLRB 1200 (1977).

Part B
Campaign Statements Ruled Unlawful

Depicting the Futility of Negotiations

The following written communications came from the employer:

1. *Why is the Company opposed to the Union?* The Company feels that the Union has nothing to offer the employees. At present, the Company offers you a secure job, good benefits, and a rate of pay which compares favorably with pay rates in other similar operations. We do not feel that the Union can honestly offer any improvements on these items, and, in fact, might destroy what we now have, by strikes, picketing, or harassment. If the Union is voted in, you will be handing over your job to a group of men who earn their living by stirring up trouble between employees and management. None of us need a lot of dissention, nor can any of us afford strikes or labor disputes.

2. *If the Union wins the election, will there be a raise in pay?* All hourly paid employees in the Auto Service Center will be receiving higher wages, whether or not the Union wins the election. Our present wage plan calls for automatic increases in pay, based on length of service, and we will continue this policy. In addition, we will continue to conduct wage surveys to make sure that our rates of pay stay competitive with other businesses in the same line of work. Of course, tire and battery men can earn promotions and higher wages by qualifying for mechanic helpers. Although the Union is promising higher wages if they are voted in, they are not telling you that whatever raise they might negotiate could well be *less* than you would receive by voting the Union down.

3. *Do Unionized employees earn more than non-union employees?* The Company does not believe in discriminating against any employee based upon whether he is or is not a member of a Union. In either case, the Company will pay a fair wage, based upon the type of work performed, the geographical area, and the length of service with the Company. These factors are not affected by Unionism, and it has not been our experience that Union employees at Wards earn more than non-union employees. In fact, there have been instances in which the Company has voluntarily granted wage increases over those called for by Collective Bargaining agreements, in order to remain competitive with other businesses and other Wards units.

4. *Do you Unionized employees have better benefits than non-union employees?* No. Retail, mail order, and service personnel who are subject to Teamster Union contracts at Wards have identically the same benefits that you now enjoy, with the same rate of employee contribution. In terms of benefits, the dues paid by the Union members are simply a waste, since they receive no better benefits than if they worked in a non-union location. Improvements in the Company's Benefit Plans (and there have been many), have been placed in effect at the same time, and on the same terms, in Union and non-union locations.

5. *Can the Union guarantee any improvements whatsoever?* No. The employer must agree to any changes, and the changes that are agreed upon may not benefit the employees at all. The Union can promise you "pie in the sky", but the Union knows very well that it cannot guarantee any particular change or benefit. When the Union does not make good on its promises, there is absolutely nothing the employees can do about it. Union promises and inducements are nothing more than "smoke" designed to get you to join the ranks of dues paying members. The only guaranteed benefits that will result are the benefits the Union will get from your dues money.

> The Board concluded that the employer in effect told the employees that a union victory would be a futility, and that in no event would union representation result in improvements of working conditions. *Montgomery Ward & Co.*, 234 NLRB 13 (1978).

Implied Promises

The employer told voters that they were idiots for petitioning for the Union because they weren't acting as individuals. He also said all that unions did was take employees' money and offer nothing more than a mouthpiece, that they drove Cadillacs and came around once a year to get their money and negotiate a contract. The employee should have come to him for a raise before petitioning for a union. He said, "You should see what raises and benefits I could give you without a union" and "You should have given me a chance. You should have come in and sat down and discussed it."

The employer took a piece of blank paper, held it up and said, "You see there is nothing on here? . . . this is how all union negotiations start; with a blank piece of paper. And no matter what the Union puts on here, if I don't put anything back on it you can't get a raise unless I am willing to give." The employer added that he would show a $130,000 loss for the year and whether or not there was a union, an employee would not get a raise because Brown could not afford to give one.

> The Board concluded that the foregoing statements, read as a whole, were, in effect, a message that a vote against the Union would result in wage increases and that there would be no increases if employees voted for the Union. *Freedom Dodge, Inc.*, 236 NLRB No. 145 (1978).

Implied Threats

Of course I told them if you vote for the Union that is certainly up to you, it is your decision and you got to make the decision yourself. If you make the decision to vote for the Union, Dana [the parent company] and Ludwig, then we will have to make [a] decision and will have to decide what to do depending on the developments, and Dana is a big company and has various operations and warehouses in the U.S.

> The Board held that the reference to the Company's having to "decide what to do" would have conveyed to the employees the idea of a move or a closing. This "prediction" was not made with reference to union demands, but rather to its victory in the election.

Ludwig Motor Corp., 222 NLRB 635 (1976). For other cases involving implied threats of plant closing, see *Ann Lee Sportswear, Inc.*, 220 NLRB 982 (1975); *Mohawk Bedding Co.*, 204 NLRB 277 (1973); *Marathon Mfg. Co.*, 208 NLRB 213 (1974); *Stride-Right Corp.*, 228 NLRB 224 (1977).

Scheduled Increases

A wage increase was scheduled to take place during the course of the organizational campaign, and the employer told employees:

> Negotiations start with a blank piece of paper. If the union were to be voted in, every item [would be] a negotiable item and you would start out with a blank sheet of paper, and if the wages were a negotiable item, then it would affect the increase. The scheduled raise would probably be an item to negotiate if the union gets in and the previously scheduled raises . . . no longer automatic.

> The Board ruled that during an organizational campaign an employer must continue on whatever course it had set prior to the union's appearance. Making the raise negotiable if the union were selected, when the raise had previously been scheduled unconditionally, was considered a threat of reprisal. *General Tel. Directory Co.*, 233 NLRB 422 (1977); *North Elec. Co.*, 225 NLRB 1114 (1976).

The excerpts in this appendix are intended as examples of permissible and impermissible usages of an employer's freedom of speech under § 8(c) of the Act. Caution must be exercised not to rely entirely upon the quotations reproduced herein since the Board will analyze the legality of an employer's campaign statement from the standpoint of the *entire context* of the speech, the factual background, the timing of the employer's statements, the extent of union campaigning, and other nuances. A quotation from a previously Board-approved expression may in another case constitute the basis for setting aside the election, or for a card-based bargaining order, depending upon the setting in which the statement is made.

Appendix 6

Union Electioneering Conduct Prohibited by the National Labor Relations Act

A management checklist of improper union campaign conduct that may lead to setting aside the election

Just as there are restrictions against *management* campaigning, the NLRB has also established certain rules that may invalidate an election if the *union* wins. Where the employer's objections are upheld, a second election will be ordered. Unfortunately for the employer, the rules of prohibited conduct which apply to unions are far less severe than the rules applied to management. However, where improper union conduct is suspected, an employer may file objections within five working days after the date the election was conducted. Valid objections may also be based upon grounds such as the conduct of the NLRB agent on election day and other factors. This Appendix deals only with union conduct. The grounds for challenging election results on the basis of improper union conduct fall into the following general categories:

- Threats;
- Monetary gifts and waiver of fees;
- Conduct of union agents at the polls;
- Misrepresentation;
- Lack of laboratory conditions.

All of the union conduct described in the following pages of this Appendix was found improper by the NLRB.

Threats

- Telling employees that if the union lost the election it would cause its members who work for the employer's customers to refuse to handle the employer's goods, and other threats of reprisal. *Superior Wood Products, Inc.*, 145 NLRB 782 (1964); *M/G Transport Services, Inc.*, 204 NLRB 324 (1973).

- Intimidating or threatening to use force or physically harming any employee (for example, threatening that employees who try to cross a picket line won't make it because the union has ways of taking care of people who do). *Provincial House, Inc.*, 209 NLRB 215 (1974).

- Telling employees that if the union lost they would face union charges or would be blackballed, or other threats to discriminate against company supporters. *Hurwitz Elec. Co.*, 146 NLRB 1265 (1964); *Knapp-Sherrill Co.*, 171 NLRB 1547 (1968).

- Pushing and other physical contact; tampering with plant machinery in a manner that creates unsafe conditions to others; and other acts of low-level violence. *Stern Bros.*, 87 NLRB 16 (1949); *Gabriel Co.*, 137 NLRB 1252 (1962); *Ciervo Blanco, Inc.*, 211 NLRB 578 (1974).

● Threatening to prejudice employees by implying disadvantageous economic consequences, loss of jobs, threats of violence, bomb threats, and similar conduct. *Vickers, Inc.*, 152 NLRB 793 (1965); *National Gypsum Co.*, 133 NLRB 1492 (1961).

● Threatening alien employees with deportation unless employee signed union authorization card. *West Side Hospital*, 218 NLRB 96 (1975); cf. *Yourosek, Mike & Son*, 225 NLRB 148 (1976).

● Stating that an employee could lose his union book if he voted against the union where loss of union book might result in losing access to union jobs. *A. Rebello Excavating Contractors*, 219 NLRB 329 (1975).

● Telling employee that if union lost election the names of employees who had signed authorization cards would be revealed to employer. *Brown Steel Co.*, 230 NLRB 990 (1977).

● Any aggravated conduct creating an atmosphere of fear of reprisal rendering a free expression of choice impossible. *Steak House Meat Co.*, 206 NLRB 28 (1973).

● Union threats of possible violence in the event of a future strike were held *not* objectionable where the statements did not relate to a possible strike before the election, but were made wholly in reference to some unspecified time in the future after the union became the employees' bargaining representative and a strike was called. *Prince Mfg. Co.*, 240 NLRB No. 48 (1979).

● Belligerent and abusive behavior toward management and employees by union officials in the employer's hotel bar and lobby, including challenging the hotel's authority to prevent the official's disruptive conduct, informing an employee that official was prepared to be arrested while participating in these activities, and telling a management representative, "I am going to get you . . . you and I is going to be in a fight." *Exeter I-A Ltd. Partnership v. NLRB*, _____ F.2d _____, 101 LRRM 2649 (1979).

Monetary gifts and waiver of fees

● Inducing employees to sign authorization cards by representing that if they sign before the election the union will waive payment of initiation fees. *NLRB v. Savair Mfg. Co.*, 414 U.S. 270 (1973).

● Promising free life insurance coverage to all voters who applied for union membership prior to the election date, or misstating extent of pension workers could expect under union conditions. *Wagner Elec. Corp.*, 167 NLRB 532 (1967); *NLRB v. Snokist Growers, Inc.*, 532 F.2d 1239 (9th Cir. 1976).

● Paying bonuses or other dollar amounts to employees for voting, attending campaign meetings, and similar conduct. *Teletype Corp.*, 122 NLRB 1594 (1959); *General Cable Corp.*, 170 NLRB 1682 (1968).

● Improper or excessive reimbursement of employees by union for various duties, such as testifying at trials or representation hearings, where compensation may amount to bribe. See *Commercial Letter, Inc.*, 200 **NLRB** 534 (1972) (excessive pay for serving as election observers); *GTE Lenkurt, Inc.*, 209 **NLRB** 473 (1974) (election not set aside where observers received substantially less than twice their normal pay).

• Excessive payments of strike benefits or hardship relief to strikers. *Servomation of Columbus, Inc.*, 219 **NLRB** 504 (1975).

• Paying employee's traffic ticket received on way to union meeting. *NLRB v. Madisonville Concrete Co.*, 552 F.2d 168 (6th Cir. 1977).

Conduct of union agents at the Polls

• Electioneering at the polls is forbidden. *Star Expansion Industries Corp.*, 170 **NLRB** 364 (1968).

• Placing "Vote Union" signs near the NLRB's directional sign pointing way to polls on election day. *Electro Cube, Inc.*, 199 **NLRB** 504 (1972).

• Union observer improperly turning away employee in presence of others. *NLRB v. Carlton McLendon Furniture Co.*, 488 F.2d 58 (5th Cir. 1974).

• Conversations between the union representative and prospective voters near voting booth during time polls are open. *Lincoln Land Moving & Storage, Inc.*, 197 **NLRB** 1238 (1972); *Pastoor Bros. Co.*, 223 **NLRB** 451 (1976); *Southeastern Mills, Inc.*, 227 **NLRB** 57 (1976).

Misrepresentation

• Union organizer telephoned a significant number of unit employees the night before election and misrepresented to them that a previous unsuccessful attempt to organize the employees in another office resulted in the involuntary termination of over half of those who voted. *NLRB v. A. G. Pollard*, 393 F.2d 239 (1st Cir. 1968).

• The union misstated in a leaflet that all union contracts in the area contained superior health, pension, and wage benefits and that the company had contracts with the union affording workers greater benefits than the non-organized workers were receiving. *NLRB v. Bata Shoe Co.*, 377 F.2d 821 (4th Cir. 1967).

• The union issued two circulars within the twenty-four-hour period before an election which misrepresented apprentice wage rates by $600 per year and implied that the higher wage scales of a different geographical area were the scales of the local area of the plant. *Graphic Arts Finishing Co. v. NLRB*, 380 F.2d 893 (4th Cir. 1967).

• The union sent a letter to the employees misstating an unidentified competitor's wage rates to employees represented by the union. In fact, the quoted wage rates were the highest rates paid to special highly skilled workers at that plant. The quotes exaggerated the differential between the union and nonunion plants by 42 cents per hour. *NLRB v. Millard Metal Services Center, Inc.*, 472 F.2d 647 (1st Cir. 1973).

• The union stated that employees in another unionized plant "had received" 75 cents more an hour; in fact, the 75 cents increase was over a three-year period and the employees had received only about 40 cents per hour. *Cross Baking Co. v. NLRB*, 453 F.2d 1346 (1st Cir. 1971).

• Union letter stated that employees could obtain the wage scale stated therein. The wage scale was for the New York City area; however, the employer in this case was based in New Orleans. *Bill's Int'l Commissary Corp.*, 200 NLRB 1148 (1972).

• The union misinformed employees concerning extent of pension coverage they could expect under union conditions. *NLRB v. Snokist Growers, Inc.*, 532 F.2d 1239 (9th Cir. 1976).

• The union misrepresented average skilled worker wages by two to three thousand dollars, what the employees would receive in the event of layoff, and what the union had won in cost-of-living increases. *J. I. Case Co. v. NLRB*, 555 F.2d 202 (8th Cir. 1977).

• Union misrepresented that employer made it appear that company was losing money by the manipulation of funds and the making of intercorporate loans. *Cormier Hosiery Mill, Inc.*, 243 NLRB No. 5 (1979).

• The union told employees the wage rates of other companies in the area. While the wage rates were correct, the amount of time an employee had to work for the employer in order to receive that wage was changed by the union to indicate large wage increases over a shorter period of time. *Western Health Facilities, Inc.*, 208 NLRB 56 (1974).

• Union agents erroneously informed unit employees that they were covered by the state minimum wage law and that this law required the employer to pay them $1.60 per hour (a wage increase). Only a small part of the work force was covered by the state minimum wage law. *ABC North Central Theaters, Inc.*, 215 NLRB 742 (1974).

• A rival union involved in an election campaign erroneously stated, in a handbill, that the employees represented by the other union in other plants were not receiving overtime. *Western Elec. Co.*, 172 NLRB 563 (1968).

• The union circulated a leaflet containing false and misleading statements regarding voluntary transfers (the leaflet omitted the fact the company had the right to make involuntary transfers), holiday pay, and the number of years it would take an employee to reach the top wage rate in a union plant as compared with a nonunion plant. *National Cash Register Co. v. NLRB* 415 F.2d 1012 (5th Cir. 1969).

• In a union handbill, the union falsely attributed to the company president a degree of inhumanity which would have led the employees to believe that the union was their only source of protection. In addition, in a union radio broadcast which repeated and expanded the material contained in a previous handbill regarding benefits derived by a union as a result of an economic strike, the union made false and misleading statements regarding these benefits. *Schneider Mills, Inc. v. NLRB*, 390 F.2d 375 (4th Cir. 1968).

Misleading Statements Regarding Board Processes

• The union distributed a document which contained in part an altered reproduction of a complaint issued by the Board against the employer. The complaint was altered in such a manner as to give the impression that the employer had been found to have violated the Act. The caption at the top of the document read: "Uncle Sam Says 'Mallory Bosses Guilty.' " *Mallory Capacitor Co.*, 161 NLRB 1510 (1966).

• The union distributed a handbill containing false statements attributed to the Board concerning a previous election lost by the union but set aside because of employer misconduct. The union circulated a second handbill which falsely represented that an employee was discharged when he in fact had quit of his own volition. *Lake Odessa Machine Products v. NLRB*, 512 F.2d 762 (6th Cir. 1973).

• The union distributed a leaflet stating that the NLRB had found the company violated the employees' rights. Such a statement was misleading since the Board had not adjudicated the merits of the union's complaint. *Dubie-Clark Co.*, 209 NLRB 217 (1974).

• Less than thirty-six hours before the balloting, a union representative showed employees the complaint and answer in an unfair labor practice proceeding, "proof" of his assertion that the company president had not told the truth when he said that he was innocent of unfair labor practices. The case had been informally settled. *Jobbers Warehouse Service, Inc.*, 210 NLRB 1038 (1974); *Formco, Inc.*, 233 NLRB 61 (1977); *ONA Corp.*, 235 NLRB No. 85 (1978).

• In a letter to the employees, the union included a copy of an official telegram sent by the NLRB Regional Director to the union in another representation case at another employer's plant. Beneath the name of the Regional Director was a statement urging the employees to vote "yes". *J. Ray McDermott & Co.*, 215 NLRB 570 (1974).

• Mailing employees a leaflet duplicating the NLRB's letterhead in the same typeface used in Board election notices and containing the words "It's the Law" together with the union's name, address, and logo created the impression that the NLRB endorsed the union in the election campaign and that the government urged voters to select the union as their collective bargaining representative. *GAF Corp.*, 234 NLRB 1209 (1978). See also, *Mercury Industries, Inc.*, 238 NLRB No. 124 (1978) (NLRB ballot altered by union); *Huntsville Mfg. Co.*, 240 NLRB No. 172 (1979) (election not set aside where union issued leaflet depicting Uncle Sam with a statement "Uncle Sam Stands Behind You.")

• Sending voters documents claiming that they were published by the NLRB (a pro-union article and a "win-loss" record of the union in prior elections) when in fact the documents were taken from a union publication. *Donner Packing Co.*, 236 NLRB No. 220 (1978).

• Distribution of 5-page propaganda leaflet stapled to a duplication of part of the Board's Notice of Election, creating the impression that the federal government supported union, ruled insufficient to show abuse of Board processes. *Alyeska Pipeline Service Co.*, 236 NLRB No. 128 (1978); distribution of campaign document berating employer and followed by "secret ballot" designation with an "X" marked in the "yes" box did not constitute document which might be interpreted as NLRB approval of union. *Pillowtex Corp.*, 237 NLRB No. 108 (1978).

Misleading Statements Concerning Bargaining

• In a letter to employees, a union that represented the employer's drivers and was seeking to represent the production and maintenance employees misrepresented a wage offer made by the employer to the union during collective bargaining. The union stated that the employer had offered a wage increase of 47 cents per hour. In fact, the amount was only thirteen cents per hour. *Ore-Ida Foods, Inc.*, 160 **NLRB** 1396 (1966).

• In a reply to a company letter advising employees of the benefits they currently enjoyed, the union erroneously stated that it had won those benefits for the salaried employees while at the collective bargaining table for the production and maintenance employees. In fact, the salaried employees enjoyed five of the nine benefits listed prior to the union's appearance. *Allis-Chalmers Mfg. Co.*, 176 **NLRB** 588 (1969).

• The union falsely told employees that the union and another association of employers had agreed to a wage increase of 30 cents per hour. *NLRB v. Producer's Cooperative Ass'n*, 457 F.2d 1121, (10th Cir. 1972).

• A hearing was ordered by the court where the union misrepresented to employees that it had negotiated provisions permitting security guards to transfer to production positions and to return to their previous position if they didn't like the new job. *Firestone Tire and Rubber Co.*, 533 F.2d 336 (6th Cir. 1976).

Misrepresentation of Adverse Consequences of a Union Loss

• At a meeting of 19 of 21 unit employees, a union representative stated that he had spoken to one of the employer's customers who advised the representative that he would discontinue doing business with the employer if the union lost the election. *The Aire-Flo Corp.*, 167 **NLRB** 679 (1967).

• In a letter to employees, the union's business manager stated that other oil contractors would take back raises already granted if the union lost the election. *NLRB v. Cactus Drilling Corp.*, 455 F.2d 871 (5th Cir. 1972).

Misrepresenting Employer Conduct or Attitudes

• Union misrepresented that management personnel, while publicly denouncing union, conveyed privately that they were sympathetic to it. *Cranbar Corp.*, 173 **NLRB** 1287 (1968).

• Union said a company official stated, "the Puerto Rican is bought cheap," where almost all of the unit employees were Puerto Rican. *Caribe General Elec., Inc.*, 175 **NLRB** 773 (1969).

• Union misrepresented that employee, who had a mild form of emphysema prior to his employment, had contracted a serious illness (black lung) while on the job and that management had told the employee he would not be transferred to a less "dusty" job but instead would be given the dustiest job in the plant. *Ipsen Industries Division of Alco Standard Corp.*, 180 **NLRB** 412 (1969).

• Union erroneously stated that employee had been hurt while operating a new piece of equipment and terminated him for getting hurt on the job. *Wesloch, Division of Tool Research and Engineering Corp.*, 199 NLRB 549 (1972).

• Union intentionally led employees to believe that an employee was terminated for union activities when in fact he was given a medical leave of absence. *NLRB v. Samtee River Wool Combing Co.*, 537 F.2d 1208 (4th Cir. 1976).

• Union official stated that employer had been cheating the employees on overtime and that the Wage and Hour Division of the Department of Labor would require the employer to pay the employee back pay. *Bor-ko Industries, Inc.*, 181 NLRB 292 (1970).

• Union representative misrepresented employer's attitude and conduct toward employees by saying that employees were told that if they didn't vote they would be replaced, and employees were not being paid for overtime. *Medical Ancillary Services, Inc.*, 212 NLRB 582 (1974).

• Union campaign literature attributed parent company's profit figures to subsidiary it sought to organize when subsidiary had net losses for the previous two years. *Aircraft Radio Corp. v. NLRB*, 519 F.2d 590 (3rd Cir. 1975). See *General Knit of Calif.*, 239 NLRB No. 101, (1978). (Union literature ambiguous as to whether profit figures were of subsidiary's operation or of parent's operation.)

• False statements were made that U.S. Government was behind the union and desired unionization, that church leaders urged employees to organize, and that owners and officers were getting wealthy by exploiting wage earners; union supported its claim with false figures. *Tyler Pipe Industries, Inc.*, 447 F.2d 1136 (5th Cir. 1971).

• First union leaflet omitted relevant wage/cost of living comparison in statement of wage increases won by union over thirty-year period; exaggerated the improvement in work week; stated a speculative figure for cost of fringe benefits; and misrepresented vacation schedule, number of holidays, and sick leave provision in master contract. The second union leaflet misrepresented that unions could determine the bargaining unit; that only a secret-ballot vote by the employees could start a work stoppage; and that the employer had taken away an allowance. *NLRB v. Winchell Processing Corp.*, 451 F.2d 306 (9th Cir. 1971).

Lack of Laboratory Conditions

Any union conduct that might prejudice voters so as to deprive them of a free choice may constitute grounds for setting aside the election. Here are some examples of forbidden behavior.

• Inflammatory appeals to racial prejudice or bigotry. *Sewell Mfg. Co.*, 138 NLRB 66 (1962).

• Major participation by a supervisor in the campaign in favor of the union. *Sheraton Motor Inn*, 194 NLRB 733 (1971); See, also, *NLRB v. Ethan Allen, Inc.*, ____ F.2d ____ (10th Cir. 1979), 100 LRRM 3208.

• Distribution of materials accusing employer of foul tactics and implying that NLRB favored employer. *Lake Odessa Machine Products, Inc.*, 210 NLRB 90 (1974), denying enforcement of 86 LRRM 1464, 88 LRRM 3164.

• Statements creating impression that NLRB looks with favor upon selection of the union as a bargaining representative. *NLRB v. Clarytona Manor, Inc.*, 479 F.2d 976 (7th Cir. 1973).

• Union letter urging employees to vote for it and enclosing a copy of NLRB's official sample ballot with "X" inserted in the box under union's name. *Arlen House*, 187 NLRB 1030 (1971).

• Any sufficiently disruptive occurrences at the polls. *Alper's Jobbing Co. v. NLRB*, 547 F.2d 402 (8th Cir. 1976).

All union campaign literature should be scrutinized carefully for any possible basis for alleging objectionable conduct. Normally, conduct alleged by the employer to be objectionable must be traced to union officials or its agents. Nevertheless, where threats or promises create an atmosphere of confusion and fear of reprisal for failing to support the campaigning union, an election may be set aside even though the employer cannot prove that the union or its agents were responsible for the objectionable conduct. However, the burden of proof as to confusion or fear is a heavy one in such cases.

The concepts in this Appendix are by no means all-inclusive but are set forth to give a basic idea as to the types of conduct that may be a basis for setting aside an election. The theory of the objections in such cases may or may not be upheld in a different case where the facts vary or the composition of the Board panel deciding the case differs. The law relating to objections is complex; Board precedents must be studied in depth and the proper allegations made and factual support provided in order to induce the Board to set aside an election. Often, however, time and effort expended in filing objections are rewarded by a second chance for the employer to maintain nonunion status.

Cases in Which the Courts Have Denied Enforcement of Board Bargaining Orders After Employer Claims of Union Misrepresentations

When an employer is unsuccessful in filing objections to union conduct during an election, the fight to avoid a bargaining obligation is by no means over. Many Board decisions rejecting employer claims of union misrepresentation have been reversed or unfavorably received by the federal courts. In misrepresentation cases, the Board has lost before the courts approximately 50 percent of the time. Under the *Hollywood Ceramics* and *General Knit* approach, courts have denied enforcement of Board bargaining orders in the following cases:

NLRB v. The Lord Baltimore Press, Inc., 370 F.2d 397 (8th Cir. 1966); *United States Rubber Co., v. NLRB*, 373 F.2d 602 (5th Cir. 1967); *NLRB v. Bata Shoe Co.*, 377 F.2d 821 (4th Cir. 1967), *cert. denied* 389 U.S. 917; *Graphics Arts Finishing Co. v. NLRB*, 380 F.2d 893 (4th Cir. 1967); *Collins & Aikman Corp. v. NLRB*, 383 F.2d 722 (4th Cir. 1967); *Schneider Mills, Inc. and Jimmy and Josh, Inc. v. NLRB*, 390 F.2d 375 (4th Cir. 1968); *United States*

Fidelity and Guaranty Co. v. NLRB, 393 F.2d 239 (1st Cir. 1968); *Gallenkamp Stores Co. v. NLRB*, 402 F.2d 525 (9th Cir. 1968); *NLRB v. Smith Industries, Inc.*, 403 F.2d 889 (5th Cir. 1968); *Tyler Pipe and Foundry Co. v. NLRB*, 406 F.2d 1272 (5th Cir. 1969); *Electra Mfg. Co. v. NLRB*, 408 F.2d 570 (5th Cir. 1969); *National Cash Register Co. v. NLRB*, 415 F.2d 1012 (5th Cir. 1969); *NLRB v. Bill's Institutional Commissary Corp.*, 418 F.2d 405 (5th Cir. 1969); *NLRB v. Maine Sugar Industries, Inc.*, 425 F.2d 942 (1st Cir. 1970); *S.H. Kress & Co. v. NLRB*, 430 F.2d 1234 (5th Cir. 1970); *NLRB v. Southern Foods, Inc.*, 434 F.2d 717 (5th Cir. 1970); *NLRB v. W.R. Ames Co.*, 450 F.2d 1209 (9th Cir. 1971); *NLRB v. Winchell Processing Corp. and Winchell Donut House, Inc.*, 451 F.2d 306 (9th Cir. 1971); *Cross Baking Co. v. NLRB*, 453 F.2d 1346 (1st Cir. 1971); *NLRB v. Janler Plastic Mold Corp.*, 82 LRRM 2174 (7th Cir. 1972); *NLRB v. Cactus Drilling Corp.*, 455 F.2d 871 (5th Cir. 1972); *NLRB v. G.K. Turner Associates*, 457 F.2d 484 (9th Cir. 1972); *NLRB v. Producers Cooperative Ass'n*, 457 F.2d 1121 (10th Cir. 1972); *Cascade Corp. v. NLRB*, 466 F.2d 748 (6th Cir. 1972); *Luminator Division of Gulton Industries, Inc. v. NLRB*, 469 F.2d 1371 (5th Cir. 1972); *NLRB v. Millard Metal Service Center, Inc.*, 472 F.2d 647 (1st Cir. 1973); *Walled Lake Door Co. v. NLRB*, 472 F.2d 1010 (5th Cir. 1973); *NLRB v. Southern Paper Box Co.*, 473 F.2d 208 (8th Cir. 1973); *NLRB v. Skelly Oil Co. (Kansas City, Missouri, Skelgas Direct Marketing Branch)*, 473 F.2d 1079 (8th Cir. 1973); *NLRB v. Medical Ancillary Services, Inc.*, 478 F.2d 96 (6th Cir. 1973); *Thiem Industries, Inc. v. NLRB*, 489 F.2d 788 (9th Cir. 1973); *NLRB v. Carlton McLendon Furniture Co.*, 488 F.2d 58 (5th Cir. 1974); *Henderson Trumbull Supply Corp. v. NLRB*, 501 F.2d 1224 (2d Cir. 1974); *LaCrescent Constant Care Center, Inc. v. NLRB*, 510 F.2d 1319 (8th Cir. 1975); *Lake Odessa Machine Prods., Inc. v. NLRB*, 512 F.2d 762 (6th Cir. 1975); *Argus Optics, v. NLRB*, 515 F.2d 939 (6th Cir. 1975); *NLRB v. Mr. Fine, Inc.*, 516 F.2d 60 (5th Cir. 1975); *Aircraft Radio Corp. (Division of the Cessna Aircraft Co.) v. NLRB*, 519 F.2d 590 (3d Cir. 1975); *Alson Mfg. Aerospace Div. v. NLRB*, 523 F.2d 470 (9th Cir. 1975); *NLRB v. Snokist Growers, Inc.*, 532 F.2d 1239 (9th Cir. 1976); *The Firestone Tire and Rubber Co. v. NLRB*, 533 F.2d 336 (6th Cir. 1976); *NLRB v. Santee River Wool Combing Co.*, 537 F.2d 1208 (4th Cir. 1976); *J. I. Case Co. v. NLRB, supra; Blackman-Uhler Chem. Division v. NLRB, supra; Diamond Electronics Division v. NLRB*, 570 F.2d 156 (6th Cir. 1978); *Beaird-Poulan Division v. NLRB*, 571 F.2d 432 (8th Cir. 1978); *Peerless of America, Inc. v. NLRB*, 576 F.2d 119 (7th Cir. 1978); *NLRB v. Gulf States Canners, Inc.*, 585 F.2d 757 (5th Cir. 1978); *Monmouth Medical Center v. NLRB*, _____ F.2d _____ (3rd Cir. 1979).

Appendix 7

The Question-and-Answer Technique

The question-and-answer technique—posing questions to employees about the election and providing answers that benefit the employer's campaign—is an important mechanism. The strategy and tactics of raising and answering such questions is fully discussed in Chapter 10.

Virtually all veteran campaigners utilize the question and answer system in almost all campaigns. The thirst for knowledge on the part of the employees during an election period is great, and properly phrased answers to standard questions are a valuable weapon in the campaigner's arsenal. This appendix provides numerous illustrations of the form, tone, and length that questions and answers may take. Some of the samples in this appendix can be reproduced verbatim and transmitted to the employees. However, the standard caveat is in order: All communications, including the forms contained in this appendix, should be scrutinized carefully for suitability for the particular employee group voting in the election; when necessary, the language in the sample questions and answers should be tailored to the intellectual level of the work force and the employees' exposure to unions in general.

QUESTIONS AND ANSWERS

Starting with this bulletin, we will try to answer questions which have come up about the union. Questions you have been asking, together with the facts and answers, will be posted on the bulletin board from time to time between now and election day.

1. Q. WHY CAN'T WE TRY OUT THE UNION FOR A YEAR AND THEN DROP IT IF WE DON'T LIKE IT?

   A. It is almost impossible to get a union out once it is voted in!

   THE CHANCES ARE YOU WILL NEVER GET THE UNION OUT NO MATTER HOW DISAPPOINTED YOU ARE, EVEN IF THE UNION DOES NOT NEGOTIATE A RAISE. There is no such thing as trying a union out for a year. Once a union is in, you will never get it out! You can even be *fined* for trying. Remember, the union expects to collect substantial sums of money at our company—they won't let that kind of money go without a big fight.

2. Q. IF THE UNION IS VOTED IN, WILL THAT MEAN AN AUTOMATIC RAISE?

A. Some people have the mistaken belief that all they have to do is vote for a union and they will automatically receive higher pay and benefits.

SUCH AN IDEA IS ABSOLUTELY IN ERROR!

The union cannot force us to do anything or pay more than we feel we should in order to keep our plant profitable. We can say "NO!" to any union demand which is unreasonable. *Everything is negotiable.* Benefits can even be reduced or eliminated as a result of bargaining. The union cannot force the company to pay more than we are now paying.

The plain fact is—A UNION CAN'T FORCE US TO DO MORE THAN WE FEEL WE OUGHT TO DO.

Question: Is the company allowed to hire people to replace us if we go on strike?

Answer: Yes! If the union pulled you out on a strike, we would continue to operate the plant and would hire new employees. That is a right any company has. Under the law, a company can hire permanent replacements and tell them that after the strike is over they can keep their jobs. After the strike is over, STRIKERS ARE NOT ENTITLED TO COME BACK IF A PERMANENT REPLACEMENT HAS BEEN HIRED. The union won't tell you this because they know it has happened. Monsanto operated its plant with replacements and so have many other companies. GOING ON STRIKE RISKS LOSING YOUR JOB FOREVER to a permanent replacement. If anyone has any doubts about it, we urge you to call the NLRB [phone number]. They will tell you what can happen if the union tries to force us to pay what we feel is unreasonable.

DID YOU KNOW?

... More Questions—More Answers ...

Q. 1. THE "UNION RATE" FOR JOBS IS HIGHER THAN I AM PAID NOW. DON'T I GET MORE MONEY BY

GETTING THE PROPER RATE FOR MY <u>CLASSIFICA-TION</u>?

A.   There is no such thing as an established "union rate" in our industry. EACH COMPANY IS DIFFERENT. Union organizers often show you a so-called union rate which may or may not be the same job in another company. You may find that you do not perform all of the tasks required by another company in its classification. In fact, you may find that the rate you would be receiving under a union contract for a certain type of job in another company may be <u>lower</u> than you are presently getting.

Q. 2.   I HAVE BEEN TOLD EVERYONE ELSE IS JOINING THE UNION. WHY SHOULDN'T I JOIN?

A.   It is a common organizing device of the union to say that nearly everyone has signed up and they want only a few more signatures to make it 51%, 75%, 100%, etc. The only thing we do know is that the union submitted a number of cards. Each card had the name of an employee on it. However, the NLRB has a policy of not checking the signature on the card with a signature from company records. We have no assurance that all the cards submitted by the union were really signed by our employees.

Also, even if unions have a very few people signed up, they may tell others who have not signed, "don't be last." Many employees may even have signed to keep from being annoyed by union representatives.

<u>"VOTE NO"</u>

QUESTION:

If I am not interested in a union, do I need to bother to vote?

ANSWER:

It is very important that everyone votes. The union does not have to get a majority of employees eligible to vote, but only has to get a majority of those actually voting. Therefore, when you do not vote, you may be helping the union. I'm sure you don't want to stand back and let others decide the future of you and your family.

QUESTION:

If I signed a union card, can I still vote against the union in the election.

ANSWER:

Yes, you can vote against the union. It doesn't make any difference if you signed a union card or went to union meetings. You can still vote against the union. I certainly hope you do. The vote is by secret ballot. No one will ever know how you voted, unless you tell them.

Appendix 8

An Outline of
NLRB Procedures*
from Petition Filing to Election

Upon filing of the Petition with the Regional Director, the case is immediately assigned to a Board Agent.

Immediately upon the docketing of a Petition, acknowledgment of the filing together with a copy of the Petition is sent to the employer.

If the union has not submitted authorization cards at the time it files the Petition, the Board will give it 48 hours to do so.

If the showing of interest is insufficient, the Board will give the union a reasonable time to furnish additional cards. The amount of time given is in the discretion of the Regional Director.

The authorization cards are checked in privacy by the Board Agent against the list of employees submitted by the employer. Signatures are not verified.

The authorization card must be made out in favor of the labor organization submitting it. However, authorizations to a parent federation are accepted on behalf of an international. Authorizations running to the international are accepted on behalf of the local and vice versa. Designations in blank will be rejected by the Board. Also, where the employee has changed his affiliation from one union to the other after having once signed a card for the original union, the card will be rejected.

The employer will be requested to submit interstate commerce information concerning the volume of business it performs. The Board will require a list of employees in the employer's alleged appropriate unit, by job classification, for the payroll period ending immediately preceding the date of the Board's initial letter to the employer. Payroll lists should be submitted to the NLRB with the specific condition that the list be returned or destroyed after the proceeding is over. Counsel should supervise preparation and submission of these materials.

The Regional Director will mail form NLRB 666, "Notice to Employees," along with the initial communication and will request that the employer post the notice. Displaying the notice is voluntary and the employer should not post the form.

The Board will transmit a "Notice of Appearance" form, NLRB 4701, so

---

* When dealing with the National Labor Relations Board in connection with any union election matter, this general outline, designed to acquaint the layman with the rudiments of Board procedure, must be supplemented by recourse to the actual rules of the Board in representation proceedings and should be undertaken with assistance of counsel.

that the employer may designate the representative who will appear on its behalf.

Within two or three days from the date the petition is filed, the Board Agent will call the employer requesting the aforementioned information and inquiring whether an election by consent is possible. Where a consent election is a reasonable prospect, a meeting will normally be arranged between union representatives, the Board Agent, and the employer, in the Regional Office, in order to work out the details.

If the Board Agent believes that a consent election is not a reasonable possibility, or if the consent election conference breaks down, a date for a notice of hearing on the case will be scheduled. The Board Agent will check with the employer as to the acceptability of specific hearing date.

[Normally the employer will receive notice of any hearing at least five days before the date scheduled for the hearing to commence.]

Where the employer does not readily agree to a date, a Notice of Hearing will issue establishing a fixed date for evidence to be taken and for the parties to make their position known.

In the normal case, the Notice of Hearing will issue no later than eight days after the filing of the Petition.

An employer does not have a right to litigate the showing of interest (i.e., the number of authorization cards) given by the union to support its Petition.

Where other unions intervene in the case in an attempt to acquire bargaining rights, a showing of interest by at least 10 percent of the employees in the unit it claims to be appropriate is required. An intervening union may participate fully in the hearing and may block any consent election.

A union which seeks to intervene on a showing of less than 10 percent of the authorization cards may not block a consent election. However, it is entitled to a place on the ballot and to participate fully in any hearing.

If the employer furnishes evidence to the Regional Director that there are forgeries involved in the showing of interest, the Regional Director will undertake a suitable investigation. [The employer, in a case where there is an indication of forgery, should request the Board Agent to check signatures on the authorization cards with the employee's signatures on record with the employer.]

Evidence of fraud will not be accepted at any hearing. Proof of fraud will only be considered during a separate administrative investigation conducted by the Regional Director, usually within five days from the request by the employer. The hearing will continue notwithstanding any allegation or investigation into the fraudulent signing of pledge cards.

Undated cards will not be accepted as valid if they are returned by the Board to the union, and subsequently dated and resubmitted to the Board.

In determining whether employees have a right to participate in Board proceedings during working hours, the Board has considered several factors, including: (1) whether the employees' presence is necessary or helpful to the proceedings; (2) whether the employer will encounter substantial production problems because of the employees' absence; (3) whether the employees were subpoenaed by the Board (not crucial), and the nature of the Board proceeding; and (4) the employer's attitude toward its employees' collective activity. For a brief discussion of applicable principles see discussion in the text, Chapter 3, Discrimination Against Employees Who Testify or Participate in Board Proceedings. Cases of assistance to the campaigner are: *Standard Packaging Corp.*, 140 NLRB 628 (1963), *NLRB v. Scrivener*, 405 U.S. 117 (1972); *Neptune Meter Co.*, 212 NLRB 295 (1974); *Walt Disney World Co.*, 216 **NLRB** 836 (1975); *Western Clinical Laboratory*, 225 **NLRB** 725 (1976); *Supreme Optical Co., Inc.*, 235 NLRB No. 193 (1978); *Service Employees Local 250 v. NLRB*, _____ F.2d _____, 101 LRRM 2004 (D.C. Cir. 1979) *denying enforcement* of *E.H. Limited*, 227 NLRB 1107 (1977).

Even after a Notice of Hearing has been issued, it is still possible to consent to an election at any time.

A.   An "Agreement For Consent Election" leaves any questions that arise in connection with the election to be determined by the Regional Director only.

B.   A "Stipulation for Certification Upon Consent Election" leaves such questions to be resolved by the NLRB in Washington.

C.   The consent agreement will specify the appropriate unit in detail; the places on the ballot where there is more than one union; the payroll eligibility date for employees; and the time, date, and place where the election will be held. The voter eligibility date established will be the payroll period ending immediately before the: (a) signing of the consent election agreement; or (b) issuance of the Regional Director's Decision and Direction of Election. [The employer may often postdate the signing of a consent which has already been worked out in order to obtain a later, more favorable, eligibility date which would include newly hired employees.]

Once a consent election agreement has been executed, the Notice of Hearing will be automatically rescinded. No notification of the withdrawal of the Notice will be transmitted by the Board.

Until a consent election agreement has been approved by the Regional Director, a union may withdraw from the agreement or insist upon changes in it. However, once the election agreement has been approved by the Regional Director, a party may withdraw from it or change it only under a showing of unusual circumstances.

A withdrawal of the petition for an election by the union will normally be accepted by the Regional Director, unless the withdrawal request is accompanied by union action inconsistent with the withdrawal, such as striking or picketing.

Where the request for withdrawal of the petition is received by the Regional Director prior to the close of any hearing, or before the approval of any election agreement, the request will be granted without prejudice to the union in case there is any subsequent filing of a new petition several days or several weeks later.

However, if the union seeks to withdraw the petition *after* the approval of a consent election or after the close of a hearing, but before the election is held, the union's request will be granted with six months' prejudice to the filing of a new petition and the election will be cancelled. Employer opposition to the withdrawal will not be considered by the NLRB. However, if there is inconsistent union action, such as striking or picketing, the election will be conducted.

Where the union files another petition after the six-month prejudice period, a new 30 percent showing of interest is required to support the petition.

If the union continues to organize within the six-month period and makes a demand for recognition within the six months, the Board will entertain a motion by the employer to reinstate the petition and to conduct the election as previously intended.

A union is allowed to amend its petition and to make a different claim regarding the composition of the unit after the issuance of a Notice of Hearing.

The Board will not readily allow an employer to postpone hearing dates. Any request for postponement of a hearing date should be in writing, with an original and two copies served on the Regional Director and a copy served on the union. The request should contain a detailed statement of the reasons for the postponement, stating with specificity the reason for the inability to attend the hearing on the date scheduled and suggesting dates for a new hearing. Any request should be filed at least three days before the date set for the hearing is sought to be postponed. Moreover, the positions of all of the other parties to the proceedings should be ascertained and set forth in the request.

At the hearing, the hearing officer has the duty to see that a full record containing all of the facts is developed. Accordingly, he may cross-examine witnesses and elicit information that may be adverse to the employer's interest, and he may call or question any other witness he deems appropriate, including witnesses who are not in attendance in the hearing room.

If a payroll list has not previously been submitted by the employer, the Hearing Officer will ask that such a list be submitted at the hearing.

During the course of the hearing, the union will be allowed to amend its petition. Where this occurs, the employer may be, but is not necessarily, entitled to additional time to prepare its case. An adjournment will depend upon the substantiality of the changes requested in the amendment.

The Board will allow, but not encourage, oral argument at the end of the hearing. [The employer should argue orally on the record and should state case citations where appropriate. Such oral argument is necessary because of the Regional Director's frequent practice of promptly issuing decisions without necessarily having read the employer's briefs].

An employer automatically has seven days within which to file its brief and may request up to fourteen additional days. Normally, the hearing officer will only grant seven additional days. [In most cases, briefs should be filed]. In the average case, the employer may expect fourteen days to elapse from the close of the hearing to the time when its brief will be filed.

In the average case, the employer can expect a median* of: (a) thirteen days to elapse from the Notice of Hearing to the close of hearing; (b) twenty-two days to elapse between the close of the hearing and the Regional Director's decision; (c) forty-seven days to elapse between the filing of the petition to the Regional Director's decision.

---

* Tactical reliance upon median time periods elapsed is misleading since many situations vary from the median. Thus, the employer may encounter considerably shortened time periods in any given case.

While elections may be expedited if the employer agrees, the employer who needs campaigning time can expect between twenty-one and twenty-five days from the date of the Regional Director's decision to the date of the election.

Under present Board practice more than 80 percent of all NLRB elections occur sooner than forty-five days after a petition has been filed. More complicated cases involving serious issues constitute the remaining 20 percent. Where the employer deals with the Board in good faith, most Regional Directors will allow the company to set an election date as much as six weeks after the date the consent election conference is held.

Appendix 9

Checklist of Management Strategy and Tactics*

I. *Basic Approaches*
   A. *Loyalty*—Appeal to company's record of fair dealing.
      1. The best approach in most cases. Wage/salary and benefit policies, personal touches, instances of fair treatment, job security offered by employer, existing complaint-handling systems, lack of need for third party intervention, etc.
   B. *Fear*—Legal appeal to adverse consequences of unionism. Financial obligations, loss of individuality, strikes, possibility of rigid job classifications, permanent replacement of economic strikers, impact of increased costs on employer's ability to compete, etc.
   C. *Promises*—Basically illegal
      1. Optimistic tone (falling short of illegal promises) on company progress and future working conditions.
II. *Methods of Communicating in Crisis*
   A. *Verbal*
      1. Supervisors
      2. Area managers
      3. Plant manager
      4. Top local management
      5. Corporate officials
      6. Friends and acquaintances of employees
      7. Co-employees
      8. Other individuals employed by company but not in bargaining unit who know voters.
      9. Local personalities
      10. *24-Hour Speech*
         The 24-hour speech serves a crucial function. It must be carefully drafted, a day or two before the time it is to be given so that it can be completely up-to-date and can both provide an overview of the entire campaign and relate last-minute developments. The speech should be given by someone the employees believe. No questions allowed; taping of speech is necessary.
      11. *Departmental Speeches*
         Conducted at beginning and middle of campaign. Speaker: prime spokesman, supervisors or others. Contents: usually

---

* This checklist is a basic reminder only and does not purport to be a comprehensive guide to all of management's tactical options and obligations during a campaign.

company record of benefits, but any topic is permissible if relevant. Mechanics: liberal use of exhibits, handouts, films/slides, etc.

Do allow questions at end of meeting.

B. *Written*

1. Letters to home: tie in company theme with graphic displays illustrating main point made in letter.

   Send letters to employee's spouse with personalized signatures where practical.

   Deride union, spell out strike history, unsavory involvements, financial obligations and antimember conduct.

   Avoid long letters.
   - Ascertain number of employees who must be communicated with in foreign language.
   - Line up translator for immediate and crisis translation for written materials.
   - Send two copies, one in English and one in foreign language.

2. Leaflets and payroll stuffers.
3. Bulletin board notices.
4. Question-and-answer systems.
5. Posters
6. Films and slides
7. Campaign insignia: buttons; T-shirts and clothing emblems; Bumper stickers.

III. *Collecting Information*

A. *What Information to Collect*

1. *Union Constitution and By-Laws*

   Review union's constitution and local by-laws; select sections that are harmful to members, such as fines, fees, assessments, initiation fees, loss of membership, picket-line duty requirements, fines for missing meetings, trial procedures, etc.

2. Obtain financial reports from appropriate government agencies, including salaries of officers and staff, strike fund information, strike vote procedures and strike pay practices and obligations.

3. Collect history of strikes.

4. Use all available local source materials to develop information about union, area plant closings and other relevant data.

5. Determine union officers' and organizers' past criminal involvements, arrests for civil disturbances, and other conflicts with the law.

6. Acquire decertification information, lost elections and unfair labor practice records, including citations for improper coercion of employees, strike violence, secondary benefits, etc.

B. *Sources of Information*
1. Newspaper clipping bureaus
2. Local newspapers' libraries
3. Trade publications
4. The union's newspaper or journal
5. NLRB election reports
6. Industry trade publications
7. NLRB unfair labor practice decisions
8. Employer associations
9. U.S. Department of Labor, Bureau of Labor Statistics, state labor departments.
10. Contracts between local employers and organizing unions.
11. Bureau of National Affairs, National Association of Manufacturers, statewide employer associations, chamber of commerce, and similar agencies.

IV. *Housecleaning.*
A. Gripes and grievances must be obtained through supervisors and employees who volunteer such information. These issues must then be evaluated and dealt with within framework of the law.
B. If supervision is at fault, supervisors must be instructed to avoid conduct leading to excessive complaints.
C. Basic housecleaning, such as adequate ventilation: keeping areas neat; windows clean; blowers working; providing relief men, etc., should be attended to.

V. *Monitoring the Vote.*
A. Prepare plant-wide and departmental lists of all employees who will vote in election.
B. Prepare list of foremen, supervisors, and/or clerical people and others who may be in contact with voters.
C. Classify employees in 3 columns: "Yes," "No," and "Undecided." This analysis should be done by those most familiar with the voter.
D. Resolve all doubts in favor of union.

VI. *Keep Close Track of Employee Sentiment.*
A. Do not question employees about their voting intentions.
B. Seek out procompany workers who are liked or well-respected by coemployees.
C. Seek out the most influential members of ethnic groups. If they are available, explain to them their right to help convince dissidents or undecided employees to vote for the company.
D. Determine natural leaders. Do not pressure them into proselytizing other employees.
E. Assign specified persons to the undecided workers. Monitor the results of these discussions.
F. Help campaigners to discuss issues that are most important to undecided voters.
G. Look for signs of union strengths and weaknesses.

1. *Signs of union weakness.*
   a. Picketing for recognition.
   b. Delay after demanding recognition.
   c. Extreme promises.
   d. Overreaction to small issues.
   e. Poor attendance at meetings.
   f. Many employee questions at company meetings.
2. *Signs of union strength.*
   a. Easy agreement to company contentions as to questions of eligibility, appropriate unit, election dates, and similar issues.
   b. Dues collections (a rare occurrence before there is a union—but a sure sign the employer is in trouble).
   c. Pervasive appearance of buttons and other union insignia.
   d. Election of mock shop stewards or temporary in-plant union representatives.
   e. No questions asked by employees at company meetings.
3. *Ambiguous signs.*
   a. Continued card-signing activity by unions.
   b. Home interviews.
   c. Filing charges with NLRB.

VII. *Dealings With NLRB.*
   A. Notify Regional Director of any proof of forgery, fraud, or supervisory taint in connection with authorization cards.
   B. Obtain Board agent agreement to keep voting list secret.
   C. Do not post NLRB "Triple Six" Notice to Employees (a form saying that petition has been filed and a vote may take place in the future).
   D. Ensure that new hires will be on payroll before eligibility cut-off date.
   E. Consent to an election only if optimum bargaining unit can be obtained.
   F. Scrutinize eligibility of all peripheral status employees such as:
      1. Part-timers.
      2. Seasonal employees.
      3. Casual employees (employees whose employment is irregular and uncertain).
      4. Dual-function employees (those who work partly out of unit and partly elsewhere in company).
      5. Special status employees (relatives of management).
      6. Leadpersons & part-time supervisors.
      7. Economic strikers and replacements.
      8. Laid-off employees.
      9. Those on personal, maternity, or military leave.
      10. Temporarily transferred employees.
      11. Students and management trainees.
   G. Set election day taking into consideration:
      1. Payday—have election then when possible.

2. Vacations—avoid losing favorable votes.

3. Time of day—in afternoon to counteract possible union misrepresentation or propaganda.

H.   Submit Excelsior list to Regional Director within 7 days after approval of consent election or direction of election.

I.   Explain to employees why company gave list of employee names and addresses to NLRB.

J.   Do not retaliate against prounion employees or threaten them.

K.   Do maintain order and discipline during campaign.

L.   Check all disciplinary action with counsel.

M.   File unfair labor practice charges against union for coercion of employees or improper harassment of neutral or procompany employees.

VIII.   *Electioneering.*

Explain how union victory does not mean automatic wage/salary increases or improvements in benefits.

Prepare visual aids, select films and slide presentations and prepare posters, enclosures and printed materials well in advance of date needed. Line up graphic artists, cartoonists, printers, research assistants, and fringe benefit specialists well in advance.

Use graphic displays, charts, graphs, newspaper clippings, montages liberally.

Make comparisons between organizing union's contracts with other employers and existing company wages and benefits.

Do not change conditions of employment, even minor ones, except with advice of counsel.

Check all communications, even seemingly simple ones, with counsel.

Give merit increases if motivated by reasons unrelated to union activity and if approved by counsel.

Implement general wage increases only if clearly supported by past practice, if previously—and provably—promised to employees, and only upon consent of counsel.

Avoid speaking to employees in supervisory and management offices.

Utilize paycheck deduction technique on day of election.

Hold election eve party for voters where indicated, observing all NLRB rules and other tactical considerations.

Urge all employees to vote and explain secrecy of ballot and significance of everyone voting. Use proper voter inducement methods where necessary.

Hype up campaign tempo if employees are silent at company meetings.

Answer the union's demand for recognition and notify employees as to why the company has rejected the demand and/or request for independent card check.

Counter all significant union electioneering propaganda.

Stress the arithmetic of union dues and assessments in terms of yearly or multi-year cumulative costs.

Use sample ballots where necessary.

Do not visit employees' homes, but do make last minute phone calls (where suitable) to undecided voters.

Be the first to notify employees of significant campaign developments.

Avoid "peaking" too early. Save the biggest arguments and most persuasive points for the last week.

Prevent undue pressure on employees by prounion sympathizers by notifying employees to report badgering, harassment, and improper pressure or coercion to management officials.

Select the most credible and well-liked management official to give the "24-hour" speech.

Avoid dealing with procompany employee committees, except upon advice of counsel.

Anticipate the union's reaction to management campaign material.

Emphasize the following critical points:
- A union victory does not mean automatic wage/salary increases or improvements in benefits.
- The duty to bargain does not compel agreement.
- Employees may lose their jobs to permanent replacements in the event of an economic strike.
- Present benefits can be bargained away or traded off.

Avoid specifying or implying the loss of privileges such as time off on request, freedom from time clocks, special favors, and other personal privileges.

Insure that the message delivery system is well-oiled. Night-time typists, stenographers, reproduction employees, and other support personnel should be notified of possible emergency service. The postmaster should be consulted on anticipated mail delivery dates for timing the home receipt of employer communications. Addressograph systems should be prepared and updated, envelopes and/or labels addressed in advance and held in readiness for crisis communications.

IX.   *Supervisory Training.*
Distribute do's and don'ts to supervisors.

Conduct frequent training sessions.

Prepare packets of materials for information and distribute to supervisors.

Explain why company is opposed to the union.

Explain why a union victory would have adverse impact on supervisors.

Audit supervisory discussions.

Give supervisors a feeling that they are an integral part of the employer's campaign and highly involved in the outcome.

Advise supervisors to pass on to the campaign spokesman known items of employee discontent and all union literature discovered by them.

Instruct supervisors how to handle employee questions on how they may request the return of union authorization cards. Do not solicit the return of such cards.

Conduct frequent polls on departmental and plantwide basis.

Explain significance of union card-signing activities and provide information to be given to employees.

Instruct supervisors on how properly to enforce all no-solicitation/no-distribution/no-access rules.

Give supervisors advance copies of all campaign materials.

Solicit supervisory opinion on election matters.

Warn supervisors not to be provoked into arguments by prounion enthusiasts or to waste time proselytizing them.

Advise supervisors to concentrate on the undecided voters.

Advise supervisors to determine each undecided voter's attitude and emphasize and tailor their approach to the individual.

Command supervisors not to repeat to employees what they have heard in confidential management meetings. Supervisors should reveal only what they have been instructed to state to employees.

Distribute copies of union's literature to supervisors with instructions on how to rebut union claims and propaganda.

Require that all threats of physical harm and harassment of employees by pro-union sympathizers be reported to management.

Remind supervisors to conduct election discussions at or near employee work stations and other places away from the "locus" of management authority.

Appendix 10

Employer Action Regarding the Conduct of the Election

A Checklist for Management Action on Election Day

Distribute last-minute handouts, leaflets, brochures, rebuttals of union last-minute statements, and other electioneering material where appropriate, but not during the time polls are open.

Do not conduct speeches with groups of three or more employees. *Remind supervisors of this rule.*

Make last-minute efforts to speak to undecided employees on a one-on-one basis, but not in any supervisor's office or other area of management authority.

Do not electioneer when the polls are open.

Remove all campaign material from plant walls, cafeterias, rest rooms, and other locations.

Instruct supervisors not to campaign while the polls are open. To be safe, supervisors should be instructed to cease campaigning one-half hour before the polls open.

Warn supervisors and other management officials not to discuss election issues during the time polls are open.

Check all voters on leave of absence and others absent for the day, and remind those believed to be favorable voters of the time of the election. Where possible arrange to have them brought in to vote. But do not provide transportation for absent voters.

Do not pressure absentee voters into voting.

Inspect the voting area and take appropriate steps to insure that the election will be conducted in secret (pasting over windows, blocking unnecessary entrances and exits in the voting area, etc.).

Provide the necessary number of tables and chairs for the polling place.

Instruct supervisors to remain away from the polling area during the time the election is conducted and to avoid meeting or talking with employees while on their way to vote. If supervisors' duties involve passing through or near the polling area, they should find an alternate route or delay the trip until after the polls are closed.

Recommend that all supervisors and managers remain away from the voting area from at least 15 minutes before polls open until ballots are counted.

Advise supervisors not to direct or insist that employees vote and not to otherwise pressure anyone into voting.

Inform supervisors to make allowances for the necessary disruption to work caused by the election. If a message must be sent to someone in the voting place, the message should be carried by a nonsupervisory employee.

Select competent, trustworthy observers and outline voting procedure with them prior to appearance of Board Agent on the premises.

Review with observers what challenges the employer intends to make and the challenge procedure.

Ensure that no question could possibly be raised as to the supervisory or managerial status of the observer. When in doubt, select another observer.

Resolve eligibility questions, if this can be done on a favorable basis, prior to the election to reduce the number of potential challenges.

Make last minute deletions, additions, changes or corrections on eligibility list. (Discharges, layoffs, quits, retired, permanently ill, etc.)

Prohibit union representatives from appearing on the scene more than one-half hour prior to the election; ensure that representatives do not tour the plant or office and that they leave the premises a few minutes prior to the scheduled commencement of the election.

Instruct observers to record and report to management any electioneering by union agents or prounion employees that takes place during the hours of voting at or about the polling place, within the no-electioneering zone.

Warn observers not to electioneer during their hours of duty whether at or away from the polling place.

Remember, voters need not remove electioneering insignia from their clothing while voting.

Determine the manner in which voters will be released in order to vote: alphabetically, or by department or work unit, or via public address system and other methods.

Caution supervisors not to keep a written tally of employees who have voted and not to give the impression that a list of those who vote is being kept.

Define carefully the no-electioneering zone (including all possible entrances and exits from the polling place) with the Board Agent.

Instruct observers to closely watch and check the counting of the ballots.

Advise observers not to sign any form called "Certification of Conduct of Election" whether or not they have observed any unusual or unfair conduct by union representatives, observers or prounion employees.

Instruct observers to report any unusual activity or possibly improper conduct by union agents or representatives to management officials after the election.

Do not sign the Tally of Ballots if observers report unusual or possibly improper conduct on the part of union agents.

Resolve challenges after the polls have been closed, but before the votes are counted, if there is a possibility of "tradeoffs" favorable to the employer.

Resolve challenges after the ballots have been counted where it is possible to concede on weak employer challenges in return for acceptable concessions on the challenges by the union.

Warn observers that they have no authority to resolve challenged ballots and so advise the Board Agent.

Do not pay union observer for work time spent acting as union observer during Board Election; do pay company observer regular wages for time spent during election. See, *Golden Arrow Dairy*, 194 NLRB 474 (1971).

Do not speak to voters on line, shake hands with them, or pat them on the back.

Do not stand near line of employees waiting to vote and say "Vote No."

Prepare a last-day campaign piece for possible use on election day if needed.

Be on the lookout for last-minute union campaign misrepresentations or rumors. Be prepared to rebut on day of election if necessary.

Avoid having union representatives on the premises and engaging in last-minute campaigning by planning in advance (including the route) for the escort of union representatives to the preelection conference.

What Supervisors Can Do on Election Day Prior to Opening of Polls

- Can and should encourage every employee to vote.
- Can say to each employee at his work station, "We're counting on you to vote in the election for your Company. I know I can count on you to vote "No."
- Can say, "By voting 'No' you will be voting for yourself, for me, and for your wife and children."
- Can say, "If you have signed a union card, you can now vote 'No.' "
- Can answer any question of employees as to where and when to vote.

Remember, you
- cannot force, insist or demand that a person vote.